ARTHUR GODMAN

# METHUEN THESAURUS OF COMPUTER SCIENCE



METHUEN
Toronto New York London Sydney Auckland

Published in Canada by Methuen Publications,
2330 Midland Avenue, Agincourt, Ontario M1S 1P7



ISBN 0-458-97300-9

This book was designed and produced by
BLA Publishing Limited, Swan Court,
London Road, East Grinstead, Sussex, England.

A member of the **Ling Kee Group**
LONDON·HONG KONG·TAIPEI·SINGAPORE·NEW YORK

Illustrations by Hayward & Martin, BLA Publishing Limited.
Phototypeset in Britain by Composing Operations Limited
Color origination by Planway Limited
Printed in Spain

# Contents

# How to use this book

This book combines the functions of a dictionary and a thesaurus: it will not only define a word for you, but it will also indicate other words related to the same topic, thus giving the reader easy access to one particular branch of the science. The emphasis of this work is on interconnections.

On pages 3 and 4 the contents pages list a number of broad groupings, sometimes with sub-groups, which may be used where reference to a particular theme is required. If, on the other hand, the reader wishes to refer to one particular word there is, at the back of the book, an alphabetical index in which 2600 words are listed.

## Looking up one particular word or phrase

Refer to the alphabetical index at the back of the book, then turn to the appropriate page. At the top of that page you will find the name of the general subject printed in bold type, and the specialised area in lighter type. For example, if you look up **compiler**, you will find it listed on p. 54, at the top of which page is **LANGUAGE**/TRANSLATION. If you were unsure of the meaning of the phrase, you may now not only read its definition, but also place it in context. Immediately after the word or phrase you will see in brackets (parentheses) the abbreviation indicating which part of speech it is: *(n)* indicates a noun, *(v)* a verb and *(adj)* an adjective. Then follows a definition of the word, expressed as far as is possible in language which is in common use. Where a related word is listed nearby, a simple system using arrows has been devised.

(↑) means that the related term may be found above or on the opposite page.

(↓) means that the related term may be found below or on the opposite page.

A page reference in brackets is given for any word which is linked to the topic but is to be found elsewhere in the book. You will soon appreciate the advantages of this scheme of cross-referencing. Let us take an example. On p.51 the entry **dictionary** is:

**dictionary** *(n)* a list of directives (↑), produced by a compiler (p.54) from a high-level language (↓). *See also data dictionary* (p.252).

To gain a broader understanding, the reader will look at the entry **directives** on the opposite page, at the entry **high-level language** below on the same page, and will also refer to the entry **compiler** on p. 54.

Occasionally, in the index, you will find the page reference for a word has been printed in brackets, for example **quicksort** (254). This means that the word is referred to on that page, but does not have a separate entry. When we turn to p.254 we discover that **quicksort** is a common **file-sorting** technique; **file-sorting** is, of course, defined.

## Searching for associated words

As the reader will have observed, the particular organisation of this book greatly facilitates research into related words and ideas, and the extensive number of illustrations and diagrams assists in general comprehension.

## Retrieving forgotten or unknown information

It would appear impossible to look up something one has forgotten or does not know, but this book makes it perfectly feasible. All that is required is a knowledge of the general area in which the word is likely to occur and the entries in that area will direct you to the appropriate word. If, for example, one wished to know more about **microfiche**, but had forgotten the term, it would be sufficient to know it was connected with **microfilm**: the reader looking up **microfilm** on p.211 would be referred to **microfiche** on the same page. This in turn would refer the reader to two methods of recording on microfiche. Below the entry the reader would find more relevant information on microfiche, e.g. **fiche** and **microfiche reader** .

## Studying or reviewing a subject

Two methods of using this book will be helpful to the reader who wishes to know more about a topic, or who wishes to review knowledge of a topic.

*(i)* For a broader understanding of **memory**, for example, you would turn to the section dealing with this area and read through the different entries, following up the references which are given to guide you to related words.

*(ii)* If you have studied one particular branch of the science and you wish to review your knowledge, looking through a section on **semiconductors**, by way of example, might refresh your memory or introduce an element which you had not previously realised was connected.

# THE THESAURUS

**computer** (*n*) an electrical machine which can both process and store information; the information may consist of numbers, or words, or both. A computer accepts information using an input unit. The information is processed by a central processing unit (p.146) or stored in a storage unit and then processed. The result is supplied by an output unit. If the input and output units are connected to a manufacturing process, the computer can control the process. Instructions are usually given by means of a program (p.64) to the computer to control the input, processing and output of information.

**word processor** a specialised type of computer concerned only with words. It accepts text (p.19), can check spelling, stores the text and can rearrange the text for printing, including the use of different styles of print. The output may consist of many copies.

**calculator** (*n*) a simple type of computer concerned only with numbers; it may vary in size from a hand-held model to a number cruncher (↓). It is suitable for mathematical and arithmetical calculations that need the supervision of an operator as well as for those which operate on a program (p.64).

**number cruncher** a type of computer which makes complex calculations with numbers fast and with high accuracy, or solves complicated mathematical problems. It may process a large quantity of small calculations.

**mainframe computer** the largest type of computer capable of storing large quantities of information and serving over one hundred terminals (p.10). It can operate a network (p.23) and a multiplexing unit (p.150). Such computers operate in banks and government departments, etc.

**minicomputer** (*n*) a smaller computer than a mainframe (↑), capable of serving a few terminals (p.10). It has a rich set of instructions, and can use more than one program language (p.48). It performs many of the processes of a mainframe, but on a reduced scale.

**microcomputer** (*n*) the smallest type of computer, usually designed for a single user. The commonest program language is BASIC (p.52). A microcomputer consists of four basic units: central processing unit (p.146), input/output unit, control unit (p.160) and memory store. Original input is by means of

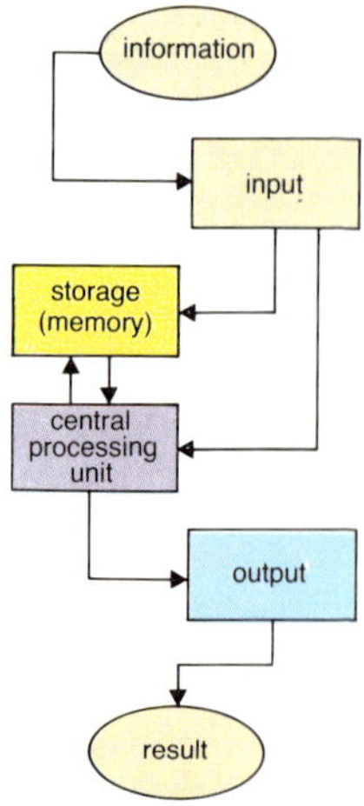


**basic principle of a computer**

**minicomputer**

**microcomputer and display unit**

a keyboard (p.191). Output may be by a visual display unit (p.203) tape cassette (p.217) or floppy disk (p.213). A peripheral interface (p.219) connects the cassette and floppy disk to the central processing unit, and allows both input and output of information. This forms a complete computing system, less powerful in speed and computing power than a minicomputer (↑).

**PC**[1] (*abbr*) personal computer; designed for a single user.

**analog** (*adj*) an analog measurement shows a *continuous* relationship between two quantities. A physical quantity, such as voltage or electric current, is used as an analogy of the magnitude of a measurement. The circular motion of the hands of a clock form an analog measurement of time. **analogy** (*n*).

**analog computer** a computer which accepts an analog input and provides an analog (↑) output of information; e.g. the magnitude of a changing pressure can be represented by a changing voltage. Varying quantities are processed by means of amplifying circuits producing an analog result.

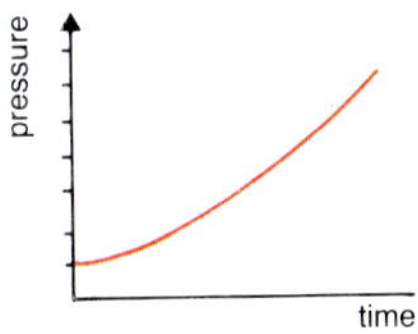


**analogue relationship**

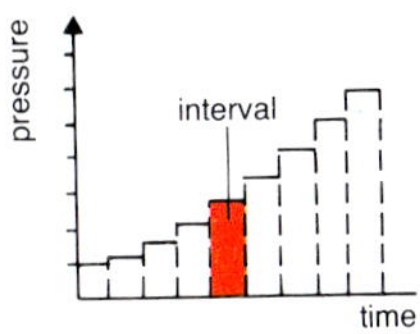


**digital relationship**

**digital** (*adj*) a digital measurement shows a *discontinuous* relationship between two quantities; the measurement changes by steps. The number of people working in a factory is a digital measurement; it changes by steps of one person.

**interval** (*n*) the smallest digital change in a measurement; e.g. the interval of a digital watch is generally one second.

**digital computer** a computer which provides a digital (↑) output from an input of information represented in digital form.

**hybrid computer** has both analog (↑) and digital (↑) methods of processing information; it combines the precision of analog measurement and the greater degree of control of digital methods.

**host computer** a computer in control of a computer system which contains terminals (↓). It is able to operate with more than one terminal at a time.
**terminal**[1] (*n*) a device which has access to a computer. It can be an input device such as a keyboard or an output device such as a television display screen or both together. The device can be **local**, connected by wire, or **remote**, connected by a communication device, such as a telephone system.
**inquiry display terminal** a terminal (↑) with input and output facilities for requesting and displaying information.
**video** (*n*) the display on a television screen. The conversion of electric impulses to a visual signal.
**VDU** (*abbr*) video display unit; visual display unit. A terminal (↑).
**VDT** (*abbr*) video display terminal (↑); visual display terminal.
**dumb terminal** a terminal which is an input/output device only; it is not capable of processing information. Examples: airline reservation terminal, hotel reception display terminal.
**intelligent terminal** a terminal which has storage facilities, both internal and external, is able to take decisions on information received, and can operate a host computer and its peripheral devices (p.13). It can calculate, be programmed (p.64) for various operations and control other terminals. It has a stand-alone (↓) capability.
**smart terminal** a terminal intermediate in characteristics between a dumb terminal and an intelligent terminal. It is capable of some processing of information, but cannot use the full facilities of its host computer (↑). It is programmable (p.64) for certain simple tasks. Basically it consists of a keyboard (p.191), a CRT (p.130), an input/output interface (p.222), a printer, and microcomputer storage (p.165).
**front-end processor** a subsidiary computer placed between a terminal and its host computer. It processes information for the host computer reducing the demand, and thus freeing the host computer for other work. Minicomputers (p.8) can be used as front-end processors to mainframe computers (p.8).
**slave terminal** a terminal (↑) under the control of signals from a master computer or master terminal (↓).

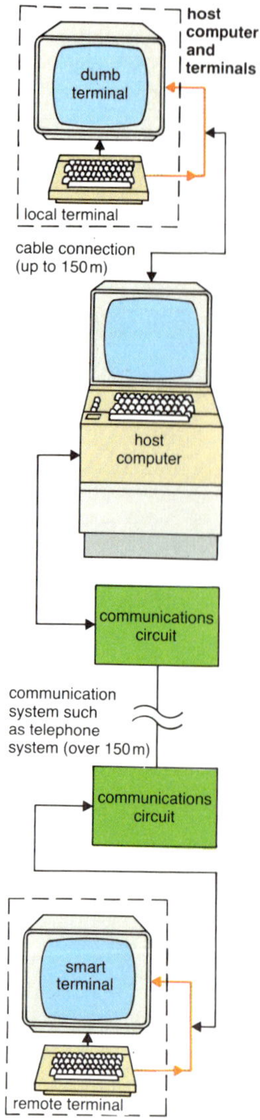

**master computer** the computer, in a system with more than one processor and/or subsidiary computers, which controls and coordinates the whole system.

**central terminal** a terminal (↑) which organizes communications between a host computer (↑) and remote terminals (↑).

**master terminal** an intelligent terminal (↑) which takes control of other terminals in a computer system. Only one terminal can be the master at any one time; it can control all other terminals in the system.

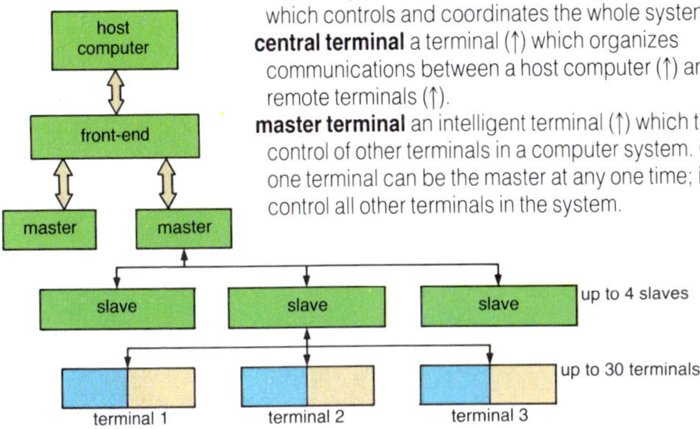


**host, master and slave computers**

**slave microcomputer** a general-purpose microcomputer with its own storage and input/output. It operates in parallel (p.104) with its master or host computer with access to the host or master's storage. It can operate peripheral devices (p.13) on the host or master without affecting the working of the host or master. A slave microcomputer can be dedicated (p.12) to particular tasks and perform them 10 to 100 times faster than the master or host computer, putting the result into the master computer.

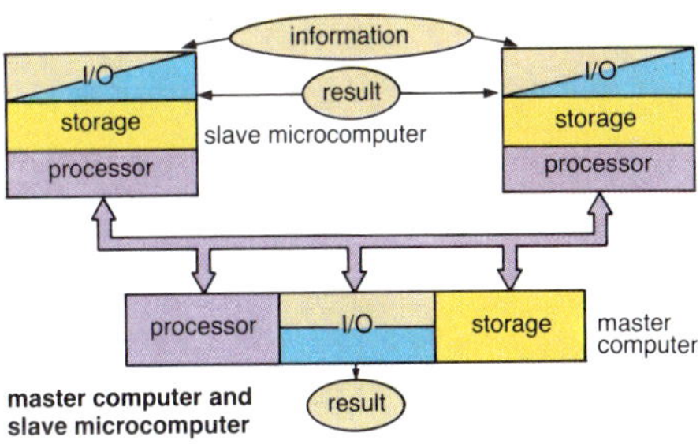


**master computer and slave microcomputer**

**stand-alone** a device, or system, that does not need help or does not depend on any other device or system for its operation.

**dedicated**[1] (*adj*) describes a computer, terminal (p.10), program (p.64), or communications line, which is used or reserved for a specific purpose, e.g. an airline booking terminal. **dedication** (*n*) **dedicate** (*v*).

**general-purpose computer** a computer able to process a wide variety of applications; the opposite of a dedicated computer.

**compatible** (*adj*) describes computers which can use the same program without any alteration; also describes various computer units which can replace one another and still function correctly. **compatibility** (*n*).

**conversational** (*adj*) describes a method of working between a computer and a terminal (p.10), in which an input from the terminal immediately receives a response from the computer, that is, as in question and answer in conversation.

**interactive mode** conversational (↑) method of working.

**user-friendly** describes a terminal (p.10) or computer which has input facilities specially designed for an uninformed user so that supplying instructions is simplified for specific tasks, e.g. a point-of-sale terminal (p.248).

**user-transparent** describes operations carried out by a computer which are not obvious to, or observable by, the user, for example refreshing dynamic memory (p.165).

**automatic sequencing** the action of a microcomputer in following instructions to perform successive operations without any other form of assistance.

**autonomous working** of computers, a method of working in which different sets of instructions are obeyed simultaneously, that is, performing multiple operations (p.57).

**ambient** (*adj*) of, or to do with, the surroundings of a device or object; e.g. the ambient temperature of a computer is the temperature of the air immediately surrounding it.

**device** (*n*) an object used for a special purpose; e.g. a thermometer is a device for measuring temperature, a clock is a device for measuring time.

**hardware** (*n*) the physical objects, metallic and plastic, that make a computer or any device working with the computer. The hardware is operated by software (p.65), and firmware (p.173).

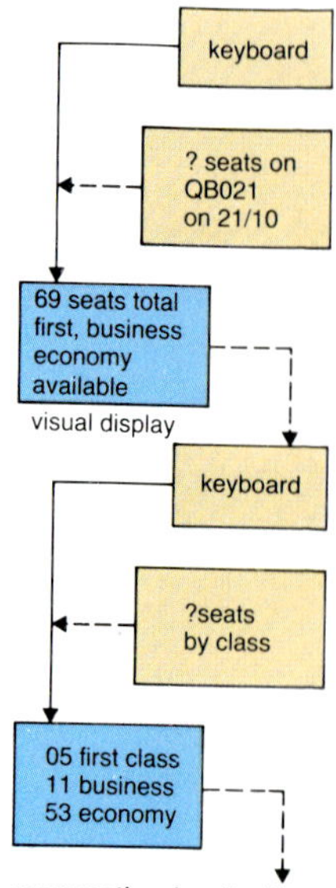


**conversational method/ interactive mode**

**peripheral device** a device which can be controlled by a microcomputer or a central processor (p.147), but is not part of it, e.g. a cassette tape recorder controlled by a microcomputer.

**architecture** (*n*) the arrangement and interrelation of the various parts of a computer or a device (↑) connected to a computer; e.g. microcomputer architecture describes the arrangement and interrelation of the various units comprising the microcomputer.

**module** (*n*) a hardware device (↑) that is self-contained and identifiable. Modules frequently are interchangeable and can be combined to form a complete unit. A module takes part in the function of the whole unit. A program section is also known as a module; it must be self-contained to complete a particular small operation, e.g. a program module for multiplying two numbers together.

**black box** any device (↑) or module (↑), the operation of which is not known to the user, but which produces a specific result from a given input. A black box approach is the acceptance of computer results without knowledge of the computer method of working.

**power supply** most microcomputers use a 5-volt d.c. supply. The power supply unit has a transformer (p.93), a rectifier (p.123), a ripple filter (p.123), and a voltage regulator (p.124). Most power supplies use solid-state circuits (p.105).

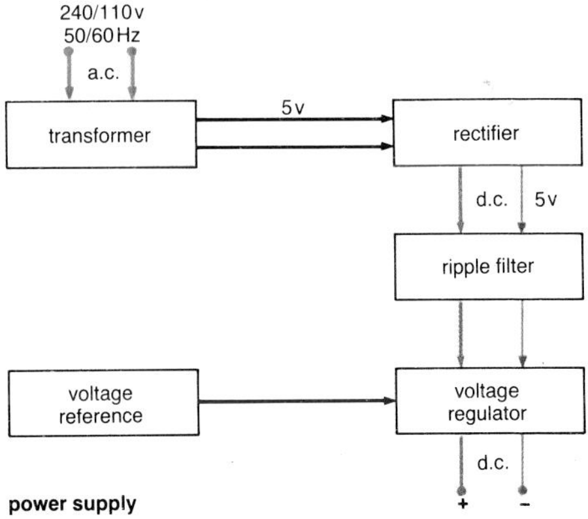


**power supply**

**card**[1] (*n*) a thin piece of resinous, insulating material, of standard size 215.9mm × 279.4mm. It provides a base for a printed circuit (p.104), and has pins (edge connectors) for electrical contact with other components of a device.

**circuit card** a card (↑) on which is a printed circuit (p.104) connecting printed components (p.104).

**PC card** a card (↑) on which is a printed circuit. Components have to be added to the card. *See PC board* (↓).

**card module** a circuit card with sufficient additional components (p.104) to form a module (p.13) for a computer. Examples are: CPU (p.146) module, memory (p.165) module, interface (p.219) module.

**card cage** a box-like device made of steel into which card modules (↑) can be positioned. The back of the cage has sets of edge connectors (↓).

**edge connector** a socket on a card cage (↑) or a motherboard (↓) into which a pin, on a card module or circuit card, fits. The connectors and the pins are arranged in rows that match, so the whole card is connected at the same time when plugged in. The card then becomes a unit in a larger circuit.

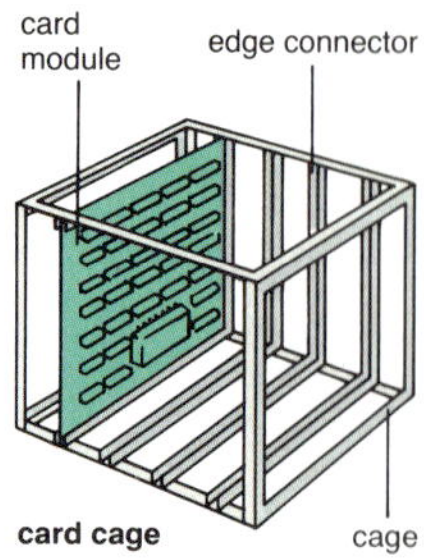


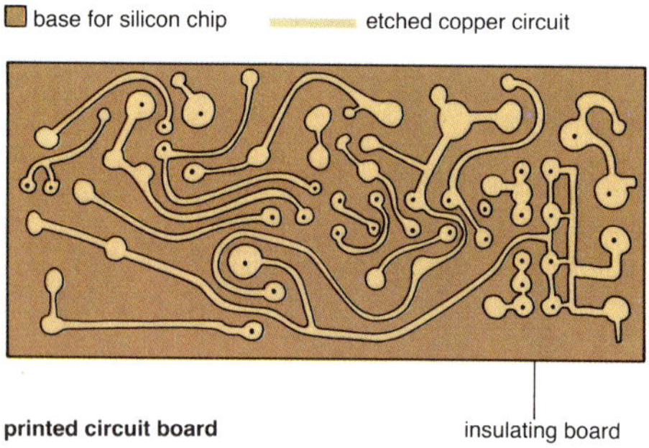


**PC board** an insulating board with a printed circuit on one side in single-sided printed circuits and on both sides in double-sided printed circuits. The insulating single-sided board is covered with copper foil on one side and the unwanted metal is etched (p.138) away, leaving an electrical circuit. Components are put on the other side of the board, and connected, through holes, by solder, to points on the circuit.

module board

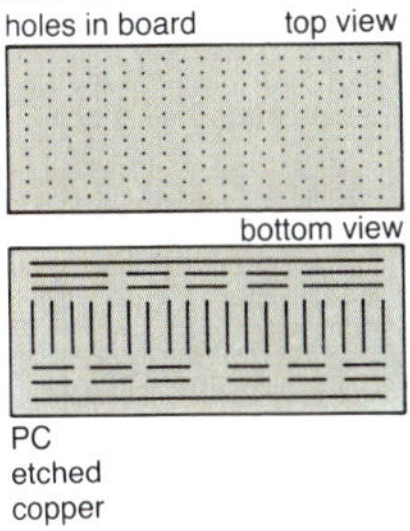


multiboard assembly

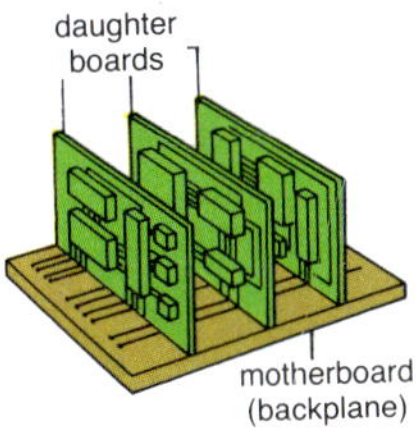


**edgeboard connector** an edge connector (↑) on a PC board (↑).

**breadboard** (*n*) a *temporary* circuit, mounted on an insulating board, consisting of components (p.104), wired together. The purpose is to experiment with the circuit for a device or a process, or to test the architecture (p.13) of a device. *See module board* (↓).

**prototype board** a PC board (↑) or circuit card (↑) that plugs into a backplane (↓). It is used in the design stage of making a microcomputer to test the construction of computer modules (p.11) and their ability to obey program instructions.

**module board** a *blank* module board has a standard printed circuit (p.104). A *plain* module board has neither printed circuit nor holes drilled through it. Components (p.104) are mounted on either type of board to make a breadboard (↑) or prototype board (↑). On plain boards the components are wired together.

**backplane** (*n*) a rigid frame on to which printed circuit modules are fixed. The backplane has a wired circuit to connect the modules. This is a common construction for minicomputers. A backplane is sometimes called a motherboard (↓).

**motherboard** (*n*) a rigid PC board into which various circuit cards, or PC boards, are plugged, using edgeboard connectors (↑).

**daughter board** a circuit card (↑) or PC board (↑) that plugs into a motherboard (↑).

**single-board computer** a microcomputer built on a single board. It uses a single-chip CPU (p.146) unit with memory chips (p.146), a keyboard (p.191), and interface chips (p.219). Many single-board computers are used as controllers of industrial processes.

**SBC** (*abbr*) Single-board computer.

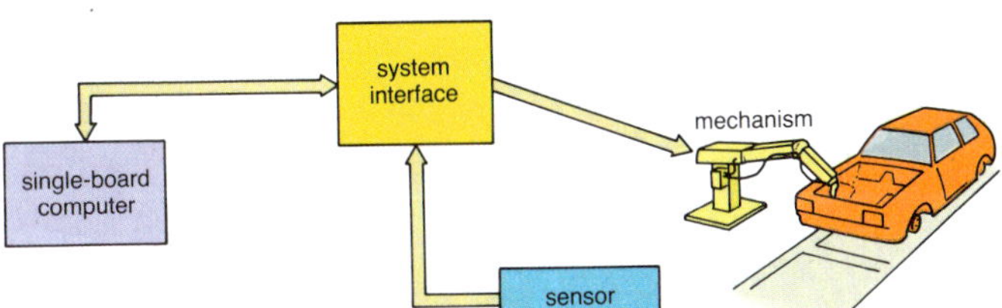


industrial processor

**multiboard system** a computer built from a chassis (↓), with module boards plugged into the backplane.
**chassis** (*n*) a wired frame on which PC boards are mounted.
**kit** (*n*) the hardware, that is, computers, disks, printers, etc., required to supply a complete working system to the end user.
**plugboard** (*n*) a removable board with a collection of sockets connected to different parts of a computer. Connections are made by plugging wire connectors into the sockets, with different programs made by different patterns of connections.
**control panel** alternative term for plugboard (↑).

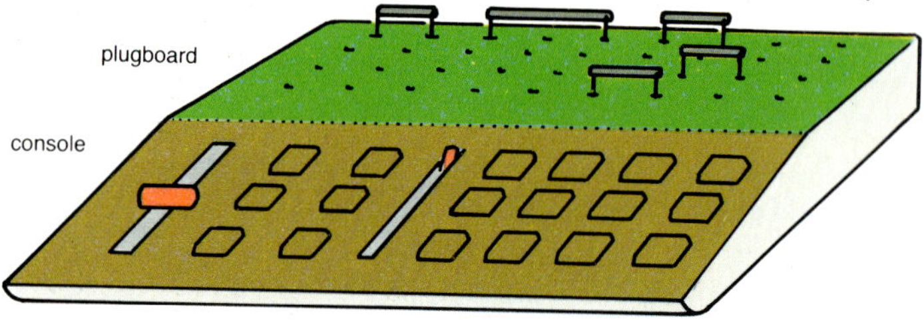


**pinboard** (*n*) a type of plugboard (↑) with fixed connections. A program is changed by replacing one pinboard with another.
**transparent control panel** a dedicated (p.12) control panel (↑) which can be plugged into a CPU (p.146) board; it has its own memory, and is designed for a specific function such as diagnostic routines, program loaders. The panel is plugged in when needed, removed when not needed.
**patchboard** (*n*) a plugboard (↑) with hundreds of sockets allowing a great variety of programs to be made by plugging in patch cords (↓).
**patch cord** a flexible wire connector with plugs, to fit sockets, at each end.
**console** (*n*) a unit with control keys, such as start, stop, and power keys, and switches, for manual control of a computer. Display lights, such as LEDs (p.198) on mainframes, indicate information contained in various registers (p.149). Used by an operator to communicate with, and to control, a computer.

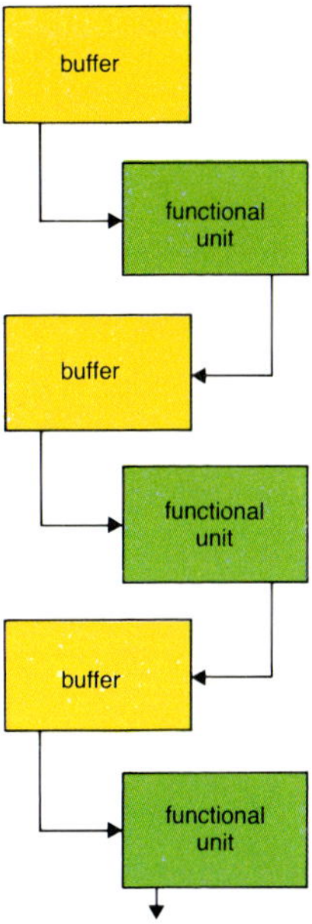


**pipelining**

**wired-program computer** a computer using a plug-board (↑).

**hard-wired** (*adj*) describes a computer, or its component modules, if all the controls are connected by wire to perform specific functions, that is, the computer is not programmable.

**pipeline** (*adj*) pipeline computers execute programs in sequence. A functional unit performs each operation, with the units connected in series, and buffers (p.164) placed between each unit. At any one time a number of operations are being executed, and this speeds up the execution of a program. **pipelining** (*n*).

**synchronous computer** a digital computer (p.9) in which all activities and operations are controlled by equally spaced signals from a clock (p.148).

**asynchronous computer** a digital computer (p.9) in which the completion of one activity or operation produces a signal which starts the next activity or operation. The computer operates at a speed dependent on the electrical characteristics of each circuit in use; this produces a variable time interval between successive operations. Most digital computers use synchronous (↑) working.

**dual processor system** a computer system using two central processing units (p.146). Both units receive the same input, and produce an output. The outputs are compared. This is a costly method of guarding against faults if high reliability is needed. One unit can act in a 'standby' capacity, ready to come into action on failure of the other unit, so that no information is lost.

**microcontroller** (*n*) a microcomputer used to control an industrial process. There are three types: device control operating machine tools; process control (p.262); data control, multiplexing (p.233) data flow.

**sensor**[1] (*n*) a device which responds to an external physical quantity, such as temperature, light intensity, pressure, measures the quantity and generates an electrical signal which is computer readable and which is proportional to the magnitude of the quantity. **sensing** (*v*).

**monitor unit** a device which checks for error conditions during the execution of a program or the operation of a process. When significant errors are detected, either the operator is warned by console (↑) light indicators, or the errors are automatically corrected.

**mode** (*n*) the manner in which an activity or a process is carried out.

**direct mode** a command, which is not part of a program, is entered through the keyboard and the computer executes the instruction when the RETURN key is pressed.

**deferred mode** a command is entered in a line of a program. The instruction is executed as part of the program (p.64).

**execute mode** the command RUN is entered in direct mode (↑) and the program is executed.

**run mode** synonymous with execute mode (↑).

**conversation mode** a conversational (p.12) method of working.

**graphics mode** to produce graphics (p.208) on a screen, a graphics function key must first be pressed. This key changes alphanumeric keys to graphics keys. The computer is then operating in a graphics mode.

**screen**[1] (*n*) the surface of a cathode-ray tube (p.130) on which an information output is displayed. *See character screening (p.204).*

**cursor** (*n*) a position indicator on a screen (↑); normally it indicates the next screen position for an input. The input can be an alphanumeric character, a graphic symbol, or the erasing of a character or symbol. Four keys control the movement of the cursor to any part of the screen.

cursor control keys

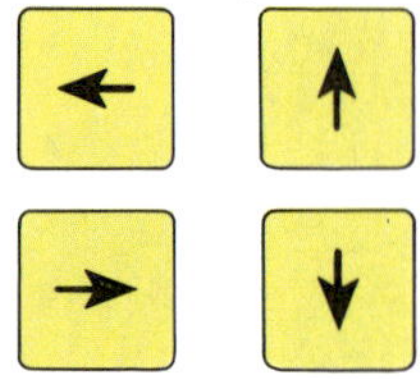

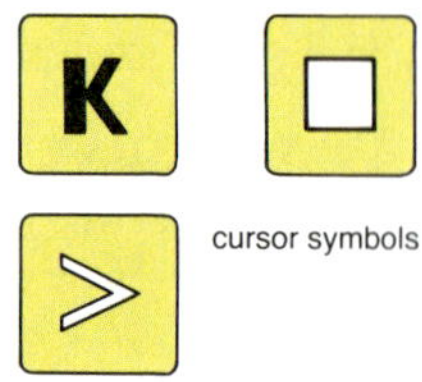


cursor symbols

**cursor**

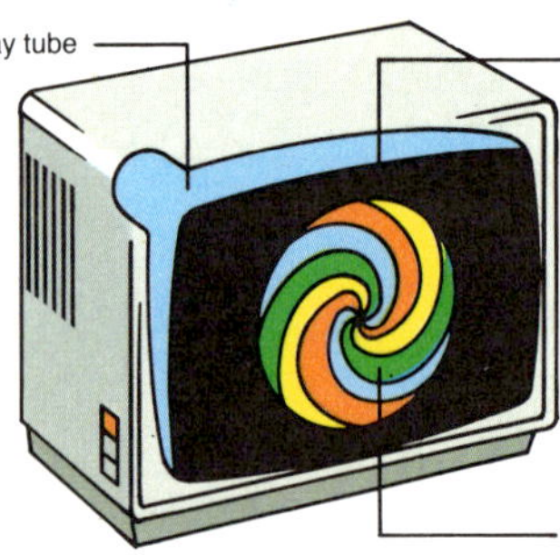


**graphics mode**

**bootstrap** (*n*) a set of instructions, or a device (p.13) which starts the loading of a program (p.64) into a computer. The bootstrap calls other instructions to transfer the program from an input device into the computer.

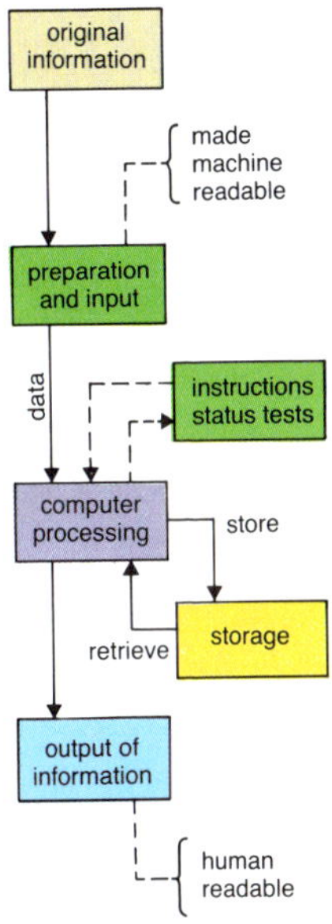


**outline of information processing**

| job no: | date | contract code | cost £ |
|---|---|---|---|
| 1108 | 10 aug | a 184 | 10.69 |
| 1109 | 12 aug | c 107 | 48.31 |
| 1110 | 15 aug | f 233 | 76.90 |

**tabular information**

**one-step operation** a method of operating a computer in which a single instruction or a single step in an operation is executed by the computer. Manual control operates a program, step by step. A patchboard (p.16) is useful for this method of operation; the method allows diagnosis of errors.

**information** (*n*) a microcomputer processes three types of information: instructions, status (p.157) and data (p.244). Instructions tell the computer what processes to carry out; status informs it regarding the state of various parts of the computer; and data are the material on which it operates.

**information storage** information is held in a store, usually called a memory. *See memory (p.165).*

**information retrieval** this concerns the searching for data, its selection from large quantities of data, and its extraction from storage (↑).

**information processing** a description of all the operations on data performed by a computer in accordance with a program. It frequently implies the use of a computer for business purposes obtaining information from files or putting order into files for future retrieval, but is equally applicable to processing mathematical problems.

**information input** carried out by one of several input devices. *See (p.189).*

**information output** information made available of any one of several output devices. *See (p.197).*

**tabular information** the presentation of data in a table, a method particularly suitable to computers.

**calculation** (*n*) computer calculation involves arithmetical operations, trigonometrical and exponential functions and the use of logical operators (p.82).

**I/O** (*abbr*) input/output. Some devices can be used for both input and output, so are called I/O devices.

**I/O chip** a silicon chip controlling I/O facilities in a microcomputer.

**medium** (*n*) the material used for storing information; e.g. magnetic tape, paper tape, printed paper sheets, magnetic ink characters, are examples of media.

**text** (*n*) the words printed, or written, on a sheet of paper or on a screen; the term also includes numbers, mathematical expressions, but excludes diagrams, graphs and pictures. The arrangement of a piece of text is called its format. *See printout (p.199).* **textual** (*adj*).

**fault** (*n*) the cause of a breakdown of a hardware component in a computer, or of an associated unit; e.g. a short circuit, a broken connection, is a fault. The emphasis is on the cause of the computer ceasing to operate. **faulty** (*adj*).

**error** (*n*) an incorrect instruction, process or result in a microcomputer system. The term includes errors due to machine operations and mistakes made by programmers or operators. A machine error can be caused by an incorrect circuit or incorrect firmware (p.173). *Contrast fault* (↑).

**error message** a display on a screen using a code to describe various possible errors in entering a program, e.g. invalid string name (p.68) addressing a non-existent device, insufficient memory, each of which is given an error number.

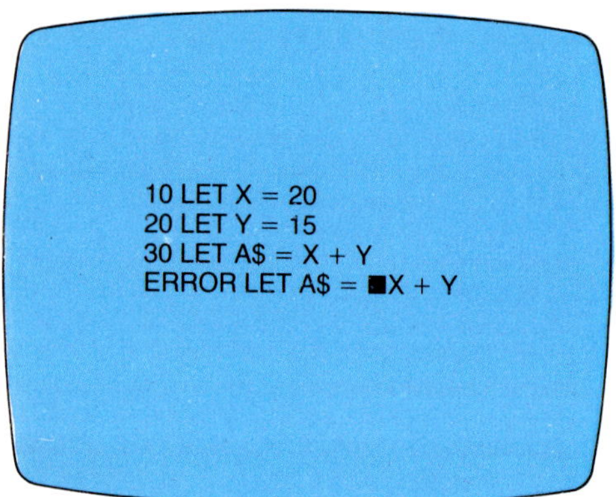


**display of error message (omission of quotes)**

**failure** (*n*) the stopping of a computer from operating due to a defect in hardware (p.12) or software (p.65) or an error (↑) in software or program. A fault or an error causes a failure. The emphasis in failure is on the computer ceasing to function properly. **fail** (*v*).

**fail-soft** refers to computer system which comes to a halt because of a serious failure (↑), but does so with no loss of data. The system is designed to prevent such loss, and the failure is corrected after a temporary interruption of an operation.

**fail-safe** refers to a computer system which comes to a halt because of a serious failure (↑) accompanied by some loss of performance but without loss of data. Fail-safe is less acceptable than fail-soft. However, in some instances, the two terms are considered synonymous.

**graceful degradation** a failure (↑) in a computer system which allows the computer to continue its operation but limits the capabilities of the computer.

**graunch** (*n*) an unexpected error which harms a current program.

**recovery** (*n*) the restoration of a computer to full operation after a failure. Recovery routines (p.61) help to isolate errors and enable a computer to recover from errors. **recover** (*v*).

**automatic checking** automatic checking consists of verifying the accuracy of information transferred, processed, or stored by the use of parity bits (p.39), error detecting codes (p.37) or checks on inadmissible characters or words.

**check register** a register (p.149) for the temporary storage of data to check that when the same data is transferred in a successive operation, the two sets of data match, and hence the item of data has been transferred accurately.

**mean-time-to-failure** the extent in time of continuous operation of a computer, device, or component, that is expected before mechanical failure is observed.

**MTF** (*abbr*) mean-time-to-failure (↑).

**acceptable quality level** computer parts and components are laboratory tested for failure; if more than a certain percentage fail, e.g. more than 1%, then the entire batch is rejected. A failure rate of less than 1% is then the acceptable quality level and the batch is accepted.

**AQL** (*abbr*) acceptable quality level (↑).

**benchmark** (*n*) a performance test in which a computer's characteristics are tested using a set of standard tasks. Both hardware (p.12) and software (p.65) can be evaluated through benchmarks. Characteristics such as operation time on specific operations, accuracy in specific operators, are tested for the comparison of different computers.

**benchmark problem** a problem solved on a computer to evaluate its performance; used for hardware, or software, or both.

**microprocessor system** the basic modules forming a microprocessor system are a CPU module (p.146) and a memory module (p.13). Further modules can be added to this basic system such as a memory interface (p.219) and an I/O interface (p.219) to peripheral devices. A full microprocessor system forms a microcomputer (p.8).

**MPS** (*abbr*) microprocessor system.

**on-line** (*adj*) describes devices under the control of the central processing unit (p.146) of a computer. For example, terminals (p.10) and other devices in interactive communication with a computer. *Contrast off-line* (↓).

**off-line** (*adj*) describes devices not under the active control of a central processing unit (p.146). For example, a computer makes an output to a magnetic tape (p.216). The magnetic tape is used by an off-line printer to produce printed data. Off-line operations are those which are much slower than on-line operations. *Contrast on-line* (↑).

**master/slave system** a system with a master computer (p.11) and a slave microcomputer (p.11).

**master/master system** in this type of system, communication between any two master computers is less frequent than in a master/slave system (↑). Each master is dedicated (p.12) to particular activities and calls on other masters only for supporting data. Contact between masters may be through a common memory (p.165) or may be direct, with access on a priority decided by logical operation decisions.

**real-time** the actual time during which a process is completed. Hence processing information with sufficient speed to give an answer before the process is completed. For example, an automatic gear box on a motor car alters the gears to match the speed, necessary power, and supply of fuel; each adjustment is made in response to the changing conditions produced by the process itself. The information necessary to control the operation is supplied during the operation. This is real-time working.

**real-time operation** a data processing (p.245) operation which allows a computer, or a computer system, to use information, received while the operation is in progress, to modify the process.

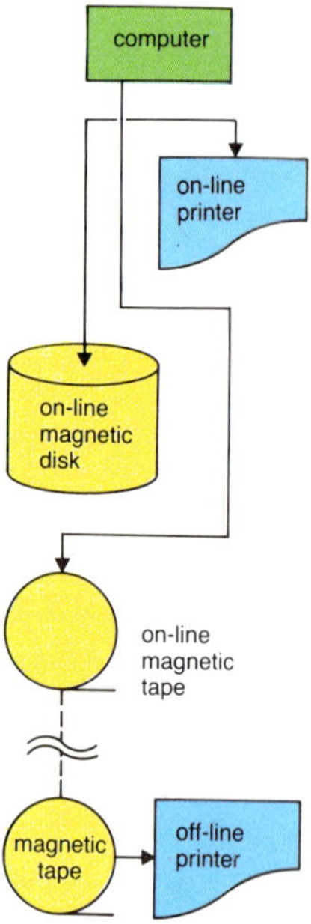


**on-line and off-line devices**

**time-sharing** describes a method in which the facilities of a computer are used by several connected devices at the same time. This is achieved by allowing each device to use the facilities in turn for a short period of time. The high speed of operation of the computer makes it appear that the connected devices use the facilities simultaneously. *See time quantum* (↓).

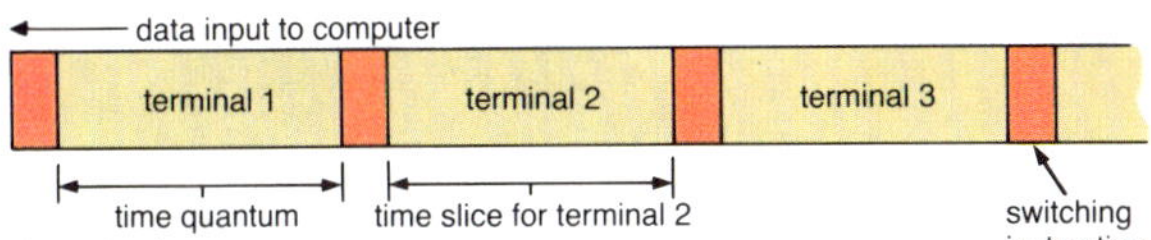


**time-sharing**

**time slice** an interval of time during which a device can be used without interruption. *See TDM* (p.233), *message queueing* (p.24).

**time quantum** the time slice (↑) given to each connected device by a computer during time-sharing (↑).

**networking** (*n*) the interconnection of computers and terminals whether local or remote. Local connections are by cable, remote connections are by telecommunications (p.26). The network function of linking units is mainly performed automatically by the hardware (p.12) of the network units, only a few link control commands need to be added to any particular program. The use of data is thus often user-transparent (p.12).

**network** (*n*) the arrangement of computers and terminals in networking (↑).

**node** (*n*) a point in a network (↑) where the switching of connections between groups of units is done.

**nexus** (*n*) a point in a network (↑) where there are interconnections between units.

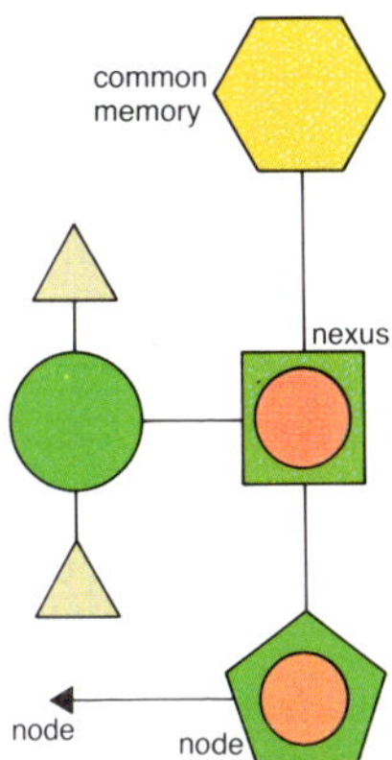


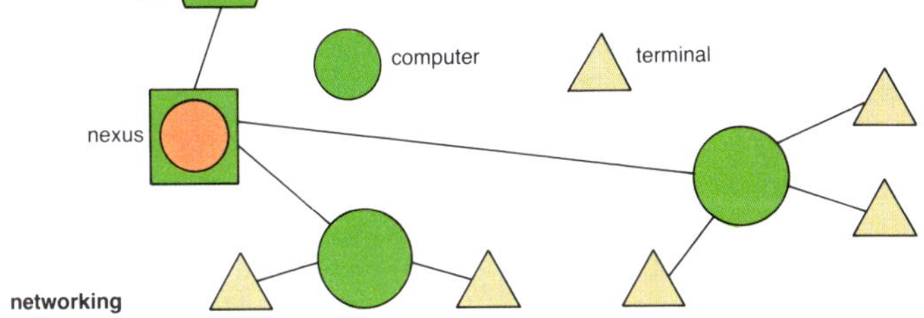


**networking**

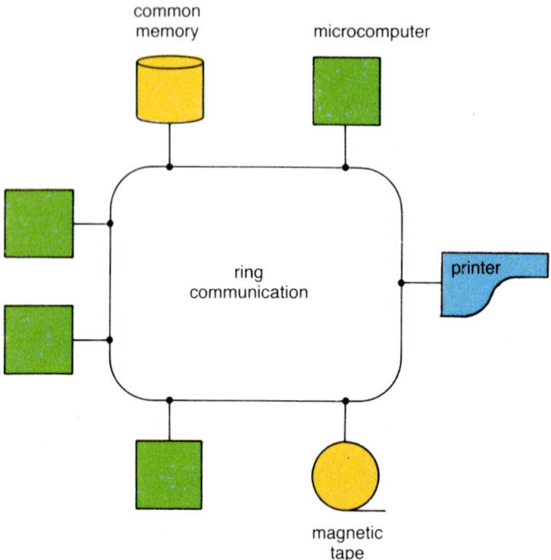


**ring network**

**ring** (*n*) a type of local network (p.23) with units connected by cable in a ring. Each unit on the ring is a microcomputer or a peripheral device (p.13). This forms a computer system with great flexibility and power, equivalent to a much larger computer, but using cheap microcomputers instead of more expensive minicomputers.

**configuration** (*n*) a term for the hardware (p.12) and software (p.65) of a computer system; it includes peripheral devices. It also describes the way in which different units of a computer system are connected in a larger system, e.g. a ring (↑) configuration.

**configured-in** a device in a configuration (↑) which is available for use.

**configured-off** a device in a configuration (↑) which is not available for use.

**configured-out** a device in a configuration (↑) which is available for use only by certain specific devices in the configuration.

**message queueing** a method of controlling messages in a network (p.23). The messages are accepted by a host computer (p.10) and stored until they are processed or transmitted onwards.

**message switching system** in a network (p.23) messages are accepted at a node (p.23) and stored until they can be transmitted onwards.

**packet** (*n*) a group of bits (p.36) consisting of digital coded information, transmitted as a single unit. The group includes control signals and error control bits in addition to data bits. There is an interval between packets to allow access to the memory from which the packet is obtained.

**burst** (*n*) synonymous with packet (↑).

**burst mode** the transfer of bursts of data between a computer and its peripheral devices (p.13).

**packet switching** addressed packets, of fixed length, are transmitted very quickly from node to node (p.23). A channel (p.233) is occupied by the packet for a short time only; because the packet has a fixed length, it can share a channel with other such packets. The path through a network is user-transparent (p.12) and often transparent to the host computer or terminal (p.10) as the packet is rerouted, if a channel fails, by a node.

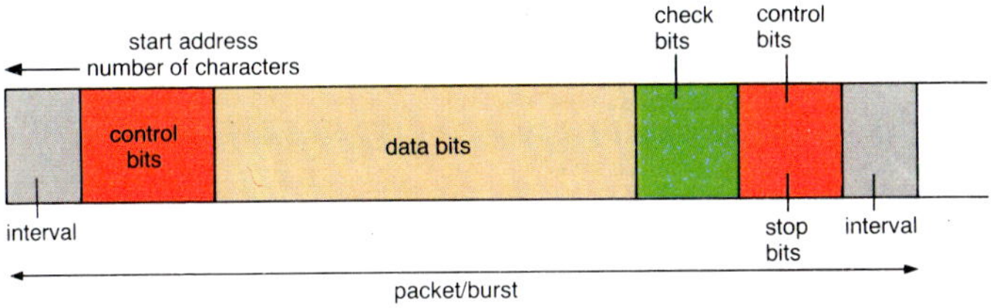


**packet switching**

**packet transmission** transmission of short, standard length packets (↑). Packets are stored temporarily in fast-access memory (p.165) and passed quickly from node to node by packet switching (↑). The error checking codes ensure packets are correctly received at correct addresses, and the codes are so accurate that errors are never greater than 1 bit in $10^{12}$ bits.

**communicating word processors** word processors connected to a network (p.23) with printers as peripheral devices (p.13). These processors provide textual communication at a speed of seconds per page. Printing can be carried out, either on-line or off-line (p.22) as required.

**CWP** (*abbr*) communicating word processors (↑).

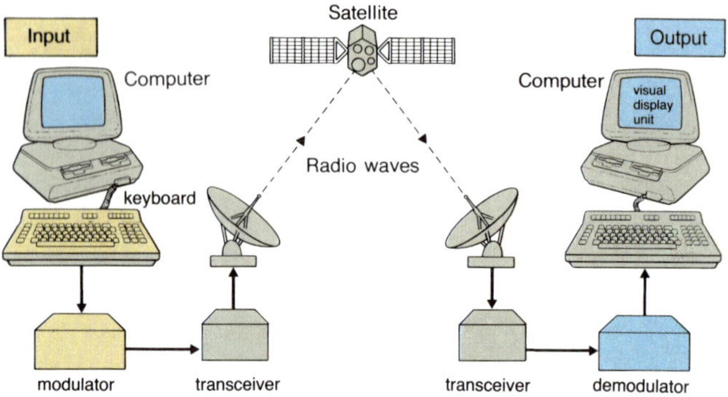


**telecommunication**

**telecommunication** (*n*) the communication of information by electrical signals along wires or by radio circuits using electromagnetic waves (p.131). The original information can be alphabetical, numeric, or pictorial, or it can represent a measurement. The types of telecommunication are telegraphy, radio, television, telemetering and facsimile (↓).

**facsimile** (*n*) pictorial information is scanned (p.195) electronically, converted to electrical signals, and then transmitted. The signals are received then converted back to a picture.

**fax** (*abbr*) facsimile (↑).

**transceiver** (*n*) a device which both transmits and receives telecommunication (↑) signals, either by cable or by radio waves.

**transponder** (*n*) a transceiver (↑) which transmits identifiable signals on receiving a specific signal of interrogation.

**trigger level** the minimum strength of signal of interrogation which causes a transponder (↑) to transmit its identifiable signal.

**teleprinter** (*n*) a device like a typewriter which transmits or receives text by telegraph line and then prints the message.

**telex** (*n*) an international network of teleprinters (↑). Each teleprinter has its own address and any one teleprinter can address any other machine.

**telemeter** (*n*) a device which measures the magnitude of a physical quantity, converts it to a code in electrical signals and transmits it, and also receives a coded message and converts it back to a measurement.

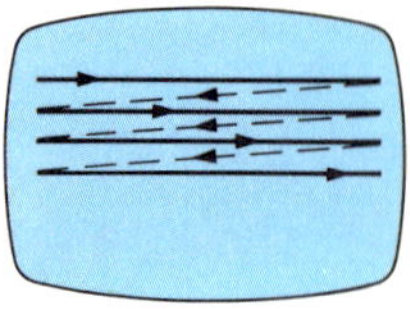

**scanning**

**teleprocessing** (*n*) remote terminals are connected to a central computer, usually by telephone; used for data collection and processing. The term is registered by IBM.

**computer-assisted instruction** a conversational mode (p.18) is used between a computer and a student. The computer program gives information and sets tests. Incorrect student answers are given an explanation of the mistakes involved. The program can be of either a simple linear question and answer form, or a branching form aimed at different levels of ability.

**CAI** (*abbr*) computer-assisted instruction (↑).

**CAL** (*abbr*) computer-assisted learning; uses CAI (↑).

**CML** (*abbr*) computer-managed learning.

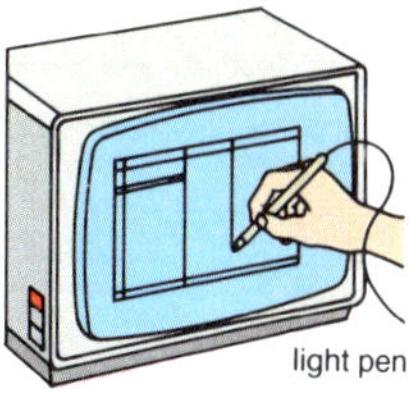


**computer-aided design**

**computer-aided design** the use of a computer in producing designs for industrial, engineering or scientific purposes. The system uses the following peripheral devices (p.13): screen, graphics tablet (p.208), light pen (p.195), graph plotter (p.209). Designs drawn on the screen are stored in memory and can be manipulated by programs to produce the original designs in a different perspective.

**CAD** (*abbr*) computer-aided design.

**automation** (*n*) (1) the implementation of a process or operation by machines which control themselves. (2) the design, development and application of methods of operation by devices that actuate, move and control themselves without the aid of an operator.

robot drilling on car assembly line

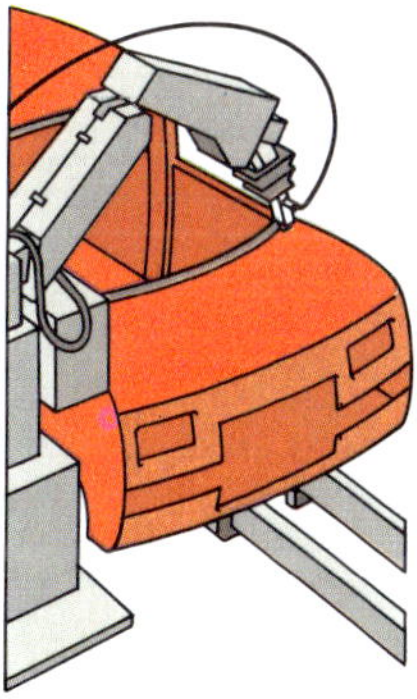

**robot**

**robot** (*n*) a device equipped with sensors (p.17) which detects objects and conditions in its immediate environment. It is programmed to perform repetitive tasks on objects using a mechanism guided by the program which reacts to the sensors' input. Examples of the use of robots include: spraying paint on car bodies on an assembly line, welding and drilling.

**artificial intelligence** the capability expressed by a machine when it can learn, correct itself and adapt to new situations. The emphasis is on the machine's ability to improve its performance on a process through learning from repeated experience.

**robotics** (*n*) part of the study of artificial intelligence (↑). Developed mainly through the use of robots (↑) for repetitive industrial operations.

**turnkey vendor** a supplier who provides a complete computer system with hardware (p.12) and software (p.65) both custom-built (p.141) for a purchaser.

**numeral** (*n*) a symbol representing a magnitude; e.g. 3 is the arabic numeral for three, III is the roman numeral for three. **numerical** (*adj*), **numeric** (*adj*).
**figure** (*n*) (1) synonymous with numeral (↑) (2) a diagram or drawing representing an object.
**number** (*n*) a string of numerals representing a magnitude, e.g. 2047 is a number, 36.23 is a number.
**digit** (*n*) an arabic numeral with a place value in a number; e.g. 312 is a number with three digits. A digit is a numeral with a value smaller than the radix (↓) of its number system. 444 is a number with three different digits but only one type of numeral. **digital** (*adj*).
**integer** (*n*) a whole number; e.g. 66 is a whole number, $6\frac{1}{2}$, 6.5 are not. Zero is an integer. **integral** (*adj*).
**fraction** (*n*) a number less than 1 but greater than 0. For example, $\frac{1}{5}$ is a vulgar fraction, 0.36 is a decimal fraction. **fractional** (*adj*).
**real number** a number with a decimal fraction as part of the number; e.g. 74.63 is a real number, while 74 is an integer and 0.63 is a decimal fraction.
**complex number** a number involving $\sqrt{-1}$. If $i^2=-1$, then $i=\sqrt{-1}$. A complex number is of the form $a+bi$, where *a* and *b* are real numbers (↑); *a* is called the 'real' part of the complex number and *b* is called the 'imaginary' part.
**exponentiation** (*n*) the multiplication of a number by itself a stated number of times, e.g. $6\times6\times6\times6\times6$ is exponentiation.
**power** (*n*) the number of times a number is multiplied by itself in exponentiation, e.g. $6\times6\times6\times6=6^4$ which is 6 to the power 4.
**index** (*n*) (*pl. indices*) in the expression $6^4$, the numeral, 4, is an index. Fractional indices are possible.
**exponent**[1] (*n*) synonymous with index; e.g. in the expression $6^{10}$, the exponent is 10. It is the power to which a number is raised.
**magnitude** (*n*) a point on a scale (p.35) represented by a number. Different points on different scales may represent the same magnitude, e.g. a length of 5.08cm and one of 2 inches both have the same magnitude but different values.
**range** (*n*) the set of magnitudes (↑) any one of which a physical quantity can take; the set has an upper and lower limit; e.g. the range of wavelengths in light is 0.1 micrometre to 1 micrometre.

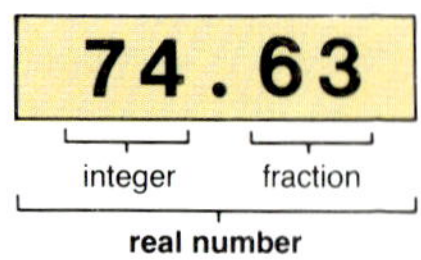


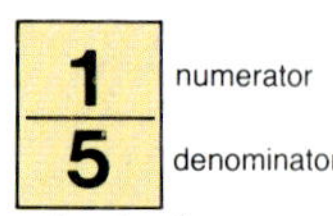

**vulgar fraction**

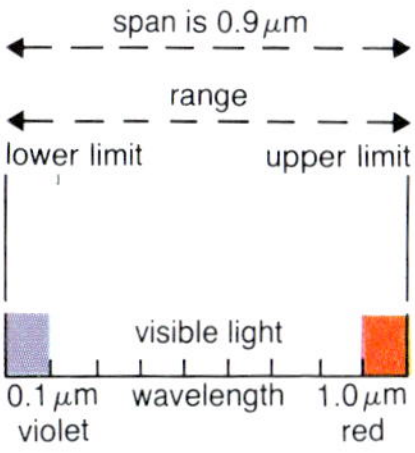


**a particular magnitude**

**span** (*n*) the difference between the upper and lower limits of a range (↑) of magnitudes, e.g. the span of light wavelengths is 0.9 micrometres.

**notation** (*n*) a system of symbols representing information. A numerical notation is a method of representing numbers (↑) by numerals (↑). Other notations include the notation for musical notes.

| no: | notation | radix | decimal equivalent |
|---|---|---|---|
| 1101 | binary | 2 | 13 |
| 1101 | octal | 8 | 577 |
| 1101 | decimal | 10 | 1101 |
| 1101 | hexa-decimal | 16 | 4353 |

**notations**

**positional notation** a number system using digits (↑). Each digit has a place value as well as a numeric value.

**radix** (*n*) a number defining the place value in positional notation (↑). In decimal notation the radix is 10, so digit values range (↑) between 0 and 9, and a factor of 10 moves a digit one place to the left; e.g. 392 represents $3 \times 10^2 + 9 \times 10^1 + 2 \times 10^0$ ($10^0 = 1$). In general, using a radix, *r*, a number 392 is represented by $3 \times r^2 + 9 \times r^1 + 2 \times r^0$.

**base**[1] (*n*) synonymous with radix (↑).

**decimal notation** a radix of 10 is used; the normal representation of a number.

**binary notation** a radix of 2 is used; digits are either 0 or 1. The binary number $1001 = 1 \times 2^3 + 0 \times 2^2 + 0 \times 2^1 + 1 \times 2^0 = 9$ in decimal notation.

**hexadecimal notation** a radix of 16 is used; digits are 0, 1, 2, 3, 4, 5, 6, 7, 8, 9, A, B, C, D, E, F. The symbol F represents 15 on the decimal scale. The hexadecimal number $2C5 = 2 \times 16^2 + 12 \times 16^1 + 5 \times 16^0 = 512 + 192 + 5 = 709$ in decimal notation.

**octal notation** a radix of 8 is used; digits are 0 to 7 inclusive. The octal number 473 in decimal notation = $4 \times 8^2 + 7 \times 8^1 + 3 \times 8^0 = 256 + 56 + 3 = 315$.

**radix point** a symbol which separates the integral (↑) part from the fractional part of a real number (↑). In decimal notation, a decimal point; in English and American usage a dot, elsewhere a comma.

**standard index form** the representation of a number in two parts by $a \times r^b$, where $a$ is a number equal to 1 or between 1 and $r$, the radix of the notation, and b is an integer, the exponent (↓) of $r$. In the decimal system, the standard index form for 457 is $4.57 \times 10^2$; $392.65 = 3.9265 \times 10^2$. In binary notation $1001 = 1.001 \times 2^3$. *See exponent* (↓).

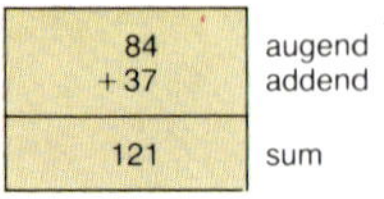


**scientific notation** standard index form (↑).

**mantissa** (*n*) (1) the part of a number in standard index form (↑) which is between 1 and the radix (mathematically $1 \leqslant a < r$); e.g. in $4.57 \times 10^2$, the part 4.57 is the mantissa (2) the fractional part of a logarithm (p.83), 4.3179 is a four-figure logarithm; 4 is the characteristic of the logarithm and .3179 is the mantissa. The mantissa of common logarithms is obtained from a set of tables.

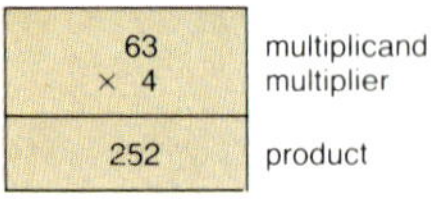


**exponent²** (*n*) the part of a number in standard index form (↑) which is the index (p.28) of the radix; e.g. in $4.57 \times 10^2$, the exponent is 2. The exponent is given the symbol E in computer programs, so 457 could be written as 4.57 E (2). Standard index form is useful with very great numbers; e.g. 6.03 E (23) represents $6.03 \times 10^{23}$. The symbol, E, is always associated with decimal notation in computer usage.

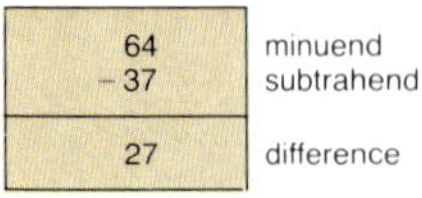


**augend** (*n*) a number to which another number is added. **augment** (*v*).

**addend** (*n*) the number added to an augend (↑).

**sum** (*n*) the result of adding addend (↑) and augend (↑).

**minuend** (*n*) a number from which another number is subtracted.

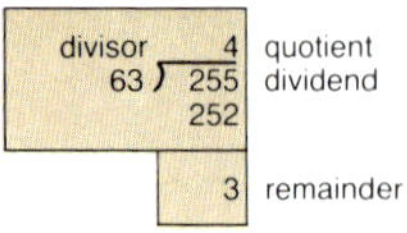


**subtrahend** (*n*) the number subtracted from a minuend (↑).

**difference** (*n*) the result of subtracting a subtrahend (↑) from a minuend (↑).

**multiplicand** (*n*) a number which is multiplied by another number. **multiplication** (*n*).

**multiplier** (*n*) the number which multiplies a multiplicand (↑).

**product** (*n*) the result of multiplying two factors (↓).

**factor** (*n*) a multiplicand (↑) or a multiplier (↑).

**dividend** (*n*) a number which is divided by another number.

**divisor** (*n*) the number which divides a dividend (↑).

**quotient** (*n*) the result of dividing a dividend (↑) by a divisor (↑).

**remainder** (*n*) that part of a result which remains after a quotient has been obtained by division.

| | | |
|---|---|---|
| 3 | 0 | 5 |
| 4 | −1 | 2 |
| −2 | 0 | −3 |

**a 3×3 matrix**

| | |
|---|---|
| 999 | radix − 1 (10 − 1 = 9) |
| 132 | decimal number |
| 867 | complement (nines complement) |
| 868 | true complement (tens complement) |

| | |
|---|---|
| 1111 | radix − 1 (2 − 1 = 1) |
| 1101 | binary number |
| 0010 | complement (ones complement) |
| 0011 | true complement) |

traditional subtraction

| |
|---|
| 364 |
| −132 |
| 232 |

subraction by complement addition

| | |
|---|---|
| 364 | |
| +868 | add true complement |
| 1 232 | |

ignore

**signed number** a number stated to be positive or negative by a sign.

**signum** (*n*) an operator in BASIC (p.52) which gives the result +1 for a positive number, −1 for a negative number and 0 for zero.

**absolute value** the value of a number irrespective of sign, e.g. the absolute value of −16 is 16; the absolute value of +16 is also 16.

**modulus** (*n*) synonymous with absolute value (↑).

**sequence** (*n*) (1) a set of numbers in which each number obeys a rule that allows it to be predicted from the preceding numbers, e.g. 1, 4, 7, 10, . . . is a sequence. (2) a set of items placed in a particular order in accordance with a rule. **sequential** (*adj*).

**factorial** (*n*) a product such as 1×2×3×4×5 is called factorial 5 and written as 5!

**matrix**[1] (*n*) (*pl. matrices*) an arrangement of numbers or variables (p.66), in columns and rows. Mathematical operations can be performed on it, such as the addition of matrices, multiplication of a matrix.

**constant** (*n*) (1) the numerical value of a physical quantity that is unalterable under given conditions; e.g. the freezing point of water is 0°C under standard conditions. (2) in computer programs any value that is fixed and not allowed to alter.

**modulo** (*n*) a division operation in which a number is divided by a modulo number to give a remainder; e.g. 35 modulo 4 = 3 since 35 ÷ 4 = 8 remainder 3.

**modulo-N check** a modulo (↑) number is assigned for checking. Every number to be checked is divided by the modulo number, and the residue, i.e. the remainder, recorded; e.g. let the modulo be 4; then for 35, 3 is recorded. 3 is the residue from modulo 4; this check number has to agree with the modulo-N residue obtained after each operation on the number otherwise a malfunction is reported.

**residue check** synonymous with modulo-N check (↑).

**complement** (*n*) to form a complement, subtract each digit from one less than the radix (p.29). In decimal notation this is a nines complement, in binary notation a ones complement.

**true complement** form a complement (↑) and add 1 to the result. The addition of a true complement to a number is equivalent to a subtraction of the complemented number.

**binary complement** a binary complement is obtained by exchanging zeros and ones. The complement (p.31) of the binary number 0111 is 1000. The binary complement is used in substraction. The subtrahend (p.30) is changed to the binary complement and added, and end-around carry completes the operation.

**binary point** a point which separates the integral and fractional parts of a binary number; it is represented by a dot, e.g. 1011.11 with two digits to the right of the point.

**binary exponent** a binary number written in standard index form (p.30) has an exponent which is the index of the radix (p.29), e.g. 1011 is a binary number; $1.011 \times 2^3$ is the standard index form, the exponent is 3. The exponent of a binary number is contained in a byte (p.36) of 7 bits (p.36) so the highest positive, or negative, exponent is 127.

**binary mantissa** the mantissa (p.30) of a binary number in standard index form, e.g. if $1.011 \times 2^3$ is the number, then 1.011 is the mantissa.

**fixed-point arithmetic** a method of calculation in which the computer operates without regard to the radix point (p.29). The location of the radix point is determined by the program. Fixed-point arithmetic normally operates with integers.

**fixed-point part** synonymous with mantissa (p.30).

**floating-point arithmetic** a method of calculation in which the computer operates with numbers expressed in standard index form (p.30). This method allows numbers to be stored economically with a greater range of magnitudes.

**overflow** (*n*) an arithmetical result producing a number beyond the capacity of a computer location (p.166), because it is too big.

**underflow** (*n*) an arithmetical result producing a number beyond the capacity of a computer location (p.166), because it is too small.

**out of range** when an overflow (↑) occurs in the registers (p.149) of a computer, an error code is reported of number out of range.

**precision** (*n*) a measure of exact definition of a number, which allows the number to be distinguished from other numbers. In decimal notation (p.29) a two-digit integer distinguishes the number from 99 other integers. A high precision, such as using an eight-digit integer, implies a high degree of exactness, but is not necessarily accurate.

**traditional subtraction;**

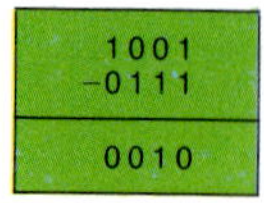


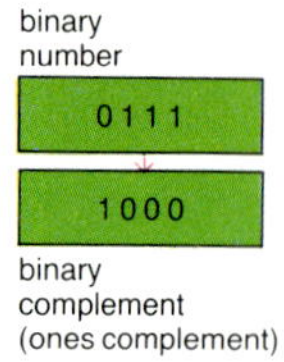


**subtraction by complement addition**

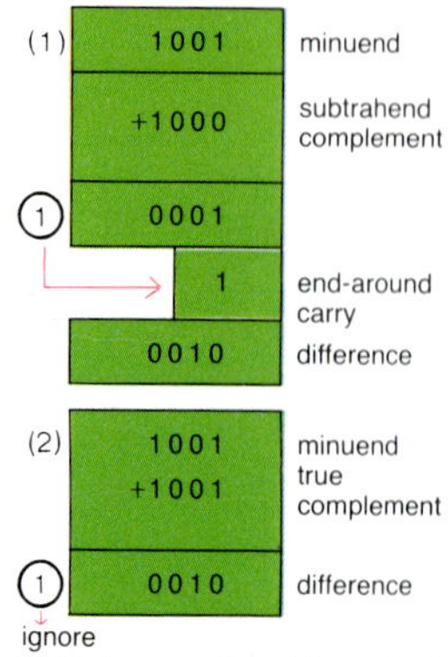


Computers use either of the methods method (2) uses fewer steps.

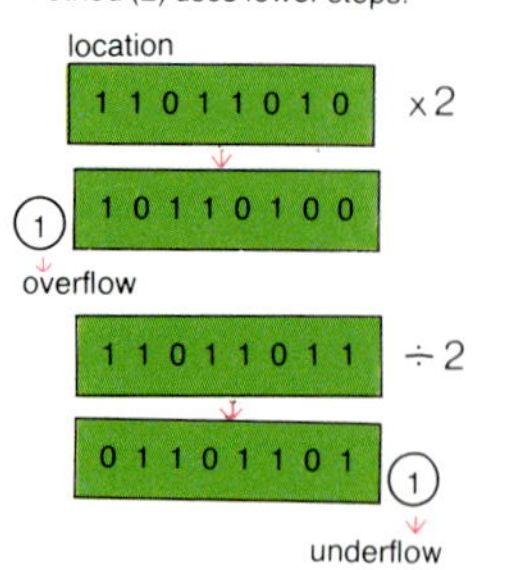


**Overflow and underflow.**

**accuracy** (*n*) a measure of the lack of error in a magnitude. High accuracy indicates a low degree of error. High precision is necessary for high accuracy in most cases, but high precision does not imply high accuracy. For example, a speed of 18326 km/hour is a precise statement, but if the correct speed is 19106 km/hour, the accuracy is low. **accurate** (*adj*).

**single-length precision** (1) the normal method of storing a binary number in a register (p.149). If it is an 8-bit register, then this is single-length precision. (2) the normal representation of a decimal number in output; usually 8 digits are available.

**single precision** synonymous with single-length precision (↑).

**double-length precision** the use of twice the normal length for storing a binary number in a register or the use of twice the number of digits used for single precision. If 8 digits are used for normal representation of a number, then double-length precision gives a 16-digit number.

**double precision** synonymous with double-length precision (↑).

**multiple precision** the use of two or more computer words to represent a magnitude, e.g. for an 8-bit computer, the use of 16, 24, 32 digits to represent a number.

**significant figures** digits which have meaning, in a number, separating accuracy (↑) from precision (↑). For example, to measure temperature with a thermometer and give a result of 25.216°C is precise but the measurement cannot be that accurate; the temperature reading is between 25° and 25½°, i.e. there are only two significant figures in the measurement. 25.216 correct to 2 significant figures is 25.

| | printout | |
|---|---|---|
| | 25.616314 | single-length precision |
| = | $2.5616314 \times 10^2$ | standard index form |
| = | 2.5616314E2 | exponential form |
| ➔ | $2.562 \times 10^2$ | 4 significant figures |
| ➔ | $2.56 \times 10^2$ | 3 significant figures |
| ➔ | $2.6 \times 10^2$ | 2 significant figures |

**significant figures**

**operand**[1] (*n*) a number on which an arithmetical operation is performed.

**binary operation** (1) a mathematical operation using two operands (↑), e.g. add is a binary operation; 2+3 has two operands, 2 and 3. +, −, *, /, are four binary operations. (2) any operation using binary notation (p.29) in its operands.

**dyadic operation** synonymous with binary operation (↑).

**unary operation** a mathematical operation using one operand (↑); e.g. **SQR** 9, where **SQR** is the square root function, is a unary operation.

**monadic operation** a unary operation (↑).

**nullary operation** a mathematical operation with no operands (↑). This can be either a constant, such as **PI**, or in some languages (p.48) **RND**, the command producing a random number (↓).

**priority** (*n*) a definition of the relative importance of mathematical operations. An operation with a high priority is carried out before one of a low priority. The priority order of mathematical operators is: exponentiation; multiply and divide; add and subtract; equals and inequalities. If two mathematical operations have the same priority, then the first in an expression is performed before the second.

**truncation** (*n*) the removal of the less significant digits of a number; this lessens the precision. It often arises because of underflow (p.32); e.g. 36.81437982 is truncated to 36.814379 because only 8-digit numbers can be displayed. **truncate** (*v*).

**random numbers** a set of numbers within a given range such that there is an equal chance of any one number being selected if only one is taken. A sequence of random numbers has no rule for predicting the next member of a sequence (p.31), from the preceding members of the sequence.

**pseudorandom numbers** a set of numbers, produced by an arithmetical process in a computer, such that they satisfy statistical tests for randomness.

**random distribution** an equal distribution of a set of numbers over a given range.

**random variable** a variable (p.66) which can assume a value from a set of values where all have the same chance of selection; e.g. a value assigned to a variable from a pseudorandom number (↑).

**variate** (*n*) synonymous with random variable (↑).

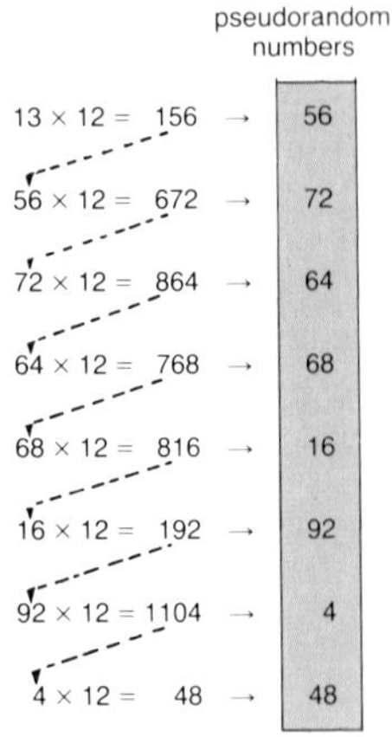


a simple arithmetical process to produce random numbers in the range 1–99, these are pseudorandom numbers

| prefix | symbol | factor | example |
|---|---|---|---|
| mega | M | $10^6$ | 1 MHz =1000000 Hz |
| kilo | k | $10^3$ | 1 kHz =1000 Hz |
| milli | m | $10^{-3}$ | 1 ms =0.001 s |
| micro | μ | $10^{-6}$ | 1 μs =0.000001 s |
| nano | n | $10^{-9}$ | 1 ns =0.000000001 s |
| pico | p | $10^{-12}$ | 1 ps =0.001 ns |

S.I. system of prefixes

frequencies

| | |
|---|---|
| SHF | 3000 — 30000 MHz |
| UHF | 300 — 3000 MHz |
| VHF | 30 — 300 MHz |

radiowaves

**scale** (*n*) a set of numerical steps arising from a low value to a high value.
**unit**[1] (*n*) a well-defined, unvarying, universally-accepted value of a quantity; e.g. the metre is the unit of length in scientific systems of measurement.
**MKS system** a system of measurement based on the metre, kilogram and second.
**SI units** an internationally agreed system of units based on the metre, kilogram, second, kelvin, ampere, candela and mole.
**k** the prefix for *kilo*, meaning 1000, e.g. km.
**K** a symbol used in computer descriptions representing the number 1024, so 4K=4096.
**micron** (*n*) one-millionth of a metre, symbol: μm.
**angstrom** (*n*) a unit equal to $10^{-10}$ metre.
**mil** (*n*) one-thousandth of an inch.
**millisecond** (*n*) 1/1000 of a second, symbol: ms.
**microsecond** (*n*) one-millionth of a second, written as μs.
**nanosecond** (*n*) one-thousandth of a microsecond, i.e. $10^{-9}$ second, written as ns.
**hertz** (*n*) unit of frequency; the frequency of a phenomenon with a periodic time of one second, e.g. 5 Hz is five cycles per second. Symbol is Hz.
**megahertz** (*n*) a frequency of one million cycles per second, written as MHz.
**Hz** (*abbr*) symbol for hertz (↑).
**MHz** (*abbr*) symbol for megahertz (↑).
**radian** (*n*) one radian is the angle subtended at the centre of a circle by an arc equal in length to the radius of the circle. 1 radian=57.296° approximately. 180°=π radians. Most microcomputers operate with radians when using triganometrical functions.
**degree** (*n*) one-ninetieth of a right angle.
**grade** (*n*) one-hundredth of a right angle.
**bel** (*n*) a measurement of power which is a ratio, that is without units. If the power of two sources is $P_1$ and $P_2$, then the relative strength is given by $N=\log_{10}(P_1/P_2)$ and N is measured in bels.
**decibel** (*n*) one-tenth of a bel (↑).
**microwave** (*n*) radio waves of frequency greater than 890 MHz and less than 300,000 MHz.
**VHF** (*abbr*) very high frequency.
**UHF** (*abbr*) ultra-high frequency.
**SHF** (*abbr*) super-high frequency.

**bit** (*n*) an abbreviation for binary digit; it has a value of either 0 or 1. It is the smallest unit of information equal to one binary decision, i.e. true or false, yes or no, available or not available, etc. A bit is a digit (p.28) in binary notation (p.29); it is also the physical representation of a binary digit, i.e. a hole, or no hole, on paper tape, a magnetized spot on tape, a unit in a storage device.

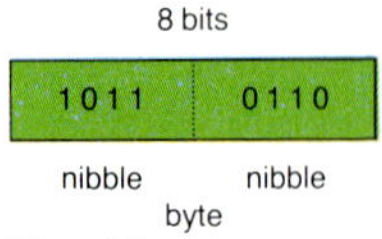


**binary bits**

**byte** (*n*) a group of bits (↑) considered as a single unit. Most microcomputers use a byte consisting of 8 bits; larger computers use 16 bits.

**word** (*n*) a group of bits (↑) considered as a single unit. Generally the largest group of bits that a digital computer (p.9) can operate as a single unit. A word is treated as an instruction (p.48) by a control unit (p.160); it consists of one or more bytes (↑).

**nibble** (*n*) a group of four bits (↑) considered as a single unit. Two nibbles form an 8-bit byte (↑). Nibble operations are associated with binary-coded decimal (↓), or console-controlled operations using LED (p.198) displays.

**gulp** (*n*) a group of several bytes considered as a unit.

**binary-coded decimal** a decimal digit is coded using four bits. The coded value can be recorded in a nibble (↑) or in a column of paper tape or magnetic tape storage.

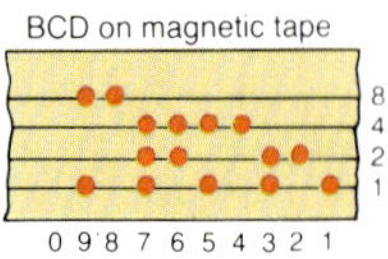


**binary-coded decimal**

**BCD** (*abbr*) binary-coded decimal.

**packed format** the use of BCD (↑) to store two decimal numbers in one 8-bit byte.

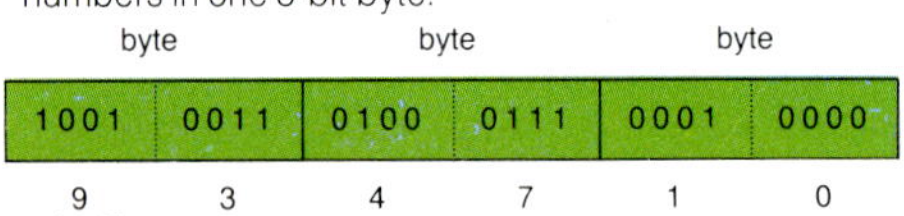


**packed format**

**bit pattern** the representation of characters (↓) by a code using bits (↑).

**most significant bit** the bit which contributes the greatest value to a binary number; in binary notation the digit (p.28) on the extreme left.

**most significant digit** in any numeric notation (p.29) the number on the extreme left.

**MSB** (*abbr*) most significant bit (↑).

**MSD** (*abbr*) most significant digit (↑).

**least significant bit** the bit which contributes the least value to a binary number; in binary notation the digit (p.28) on the extreme right.

**LSB** (*abbr*) least significant bit (↑).

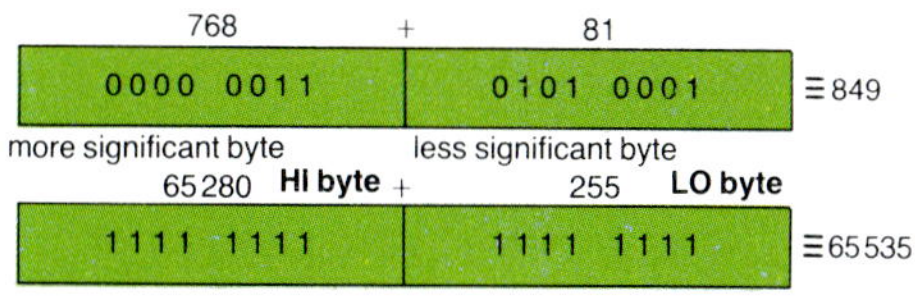


2 byte word

**more significant byte** of two bytes, the one which contributes the greater value to a 2-byte word (↑).

**less significant byte** of two bytes, the one which contributes the lesser value to a 2-byte word (↑).

**HI byte** more significant byte (↑).

**LO byte** less significant byte (↑).

**character** (*n*) a mark in a set of marks, or other physical representations, arranged in order to express information. Man-readable characters include the alphabetical letters, the decimal digits 0 to 9, the punctuation marks, mathematical and logical operators (↓). Computer-readable characters consisting of bytes of binary code.

**numeric character** a character used in numerical notation (p.29). In decimal notation, the characters are the numerals 0 to 9; in hexadecimal notation, the numerals 0 to 9 and the letters A to F are numeric characters.

**alphanumeric character** any letter of the alphabet, any decimal numeral, and any of the additional textual characters such as $, £, @.

**alphameric character** synonymous with alphanumeric character.

**operator**[1] (*n*) a character which defines an operation; e.g. the arithmetical signs (+, −, *, /) are the computer-readable coded signs.

**symbol**[1] (*n*) a character representing, by convention, a physical quantity, a measurement, a relation, an operation, a part of an electrical circuit. Most characters are single symbols. Examples of symbols are: *V* for potential difference; m for metre; > for greater than; ÷ for divide. **symbolic** (*adj*).

**token** (*n*) a coded character representing a word used in programs, e.g. STOP is a word and the one-byte token for it in a BASIC dialect is 250.

**code** (*n*) a system of characters and rules for converting one form of information to another form. Also the representation of information using such a system. A computer uses several different codes in its operations. See ASCII code, machine code, binary code (p.38).

**ASCII** (*acro*) the American Standard Code for Information Interchange. It assigns a bit pattern (p.36) to 96 displayed characters and 32 tokens (p.37). The displayed characters include upper and lower case alphabetical letters, the decimal digits 0 to 9, punctuation marks and operators. The code is used for digital communication between computers, teleprinters, and word processors, over telephone lines. For example, the letter A has the decimal code number 65, in binary this is 1000001; all characters and token are coded by 7 bits (p.36) allowing 128 bit patterns.

**machine code** an operation code (p.41) that instructs a computer to perform a particular operation when reading a particular symbol. The complete machine code defines all the operations a computer can perform. Each computer has a machine code suited to its central processing unit (p.146), but there may be variations between different makes of computer using the same make of CPU. Machine codes use binary notation (p.29); all computers recognize only binary code (↓).

**binary code** a cide in which all characters (p.37), instructions (p.48) and commands (p.48) are assigned a number in binary notation (p.29).

**computer code** synonymous with machine code (↑).

**machine instruction code** synonymous with machine code (↑).

**machine language code** synonymous with machine code (↑).

**object code** the code used for the instructions of an object program (p.53); this usually is machine code (↑).

**command code** the binary code (↑) to start, stop or continue a computer operation; it involves the use of coded status words (p.158).

**mnemonic** (*n*) a word, or group of letters, used to help memory. In computer languages, usually a group of three letters which suggests an operation, e.g. the mnemonic DST suggests 'destination'.

**symbolic code** a code which uses mnemonics (↑) instead of binary code to give instructions to a computer. This makes the task of a programmer easier; for example, using the mnemonic ADD is easier than using the binary code instructing the machine to perform addition. The computer has to convert symbolic code to machine code (↑).

| A | S | C | letter |
|---|---|---|---|
| 65 | 83 | 67 | decimal code |
| 0100 0001 | 0101 0011 | 0100 0011 | binary code |
| 41 | 53 | 43 | hexadecimal code |

**ASCII code**

| byte 1 | byte 2 | byte 3 |
|---|---|---|
| 0010 0010 | 0001 0001 | 1011 1011 |

**example of machine code**

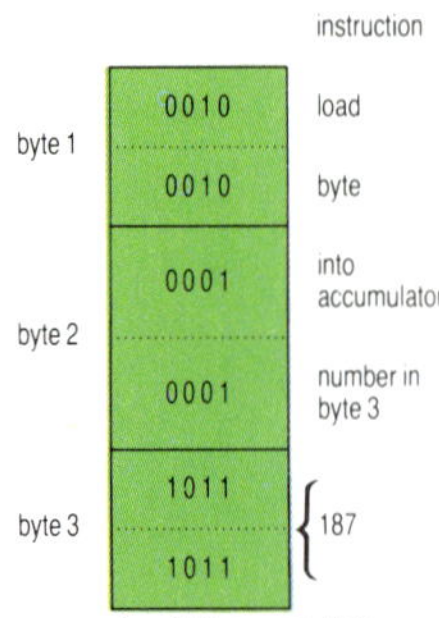


**example of binary code/ machine code**
the number 187, is put in the accumulator

| mnemonics | operand | |
|---|---|---|
| ADD | a, b | add b to a store result in a |
| LD | a, 22h | load accumulator with number 34 |
| INC | b | add 1 to register b |
| NOP | | no operation |

**examples of symbolic code**

**parity** (*n*) the state of being equal. In computer use, making a group of bits (p.36) have an equal format.

**parity check** a check on a word, or array of bits (p.36) to determine whether the number of one's is odd or even. The check is performed before and after the transfer of data (p.244).

**parity bit** a bit (p.36) added, if necessary, to a word, group of bits or array of bits, to make the parity correct for odd or even parity (↓).

**odd parity** the number of one's in a word, group or array of bits (p.36) has to be an odd number. If the word, group or array has an even number of one's, then a 1 is added to make an odd number; this added bit is the parity bit (↑).

**parity bits, column parity**

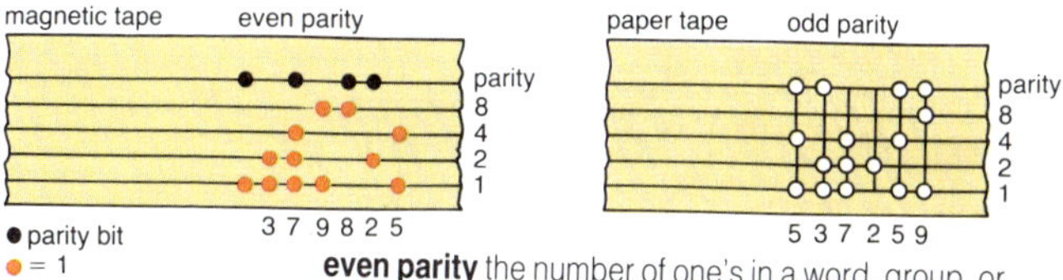


**even parity** the number of one's in a word, group, or array of bits (p.36) has to be an even number. A parity bit (↑) is added, as for odd parity (↑), if necessary to make an even number of bits.

**odd-even check** synonymous with parity check (↑).

**column parity** a parity check is made on each column of bits (p.36) recorded on magnetic or paper tape. Odd or even parity is maintained for each column by adding, if necessary, a parity bit (↑). This is in addition to other parity bits for the array as a whole.

**redundancy check** an automatic check, carried out by the computer's hardware (p.12) by the insertion of bits (p.36) or characters (p.37) in a word, group or array of bits. The bits or characters are redundant, as they can be omitted without loss of information. A parity check (↑) is one form of redundancy check. *See sum check* (p.231), *modulo-N check* (p.31).

**check digit** a digit (p.28) added in a redundancy check (↑).

**check bit** a binary check digit (↑).

**check character** a character (p.37) added in a redundancy check (↑).

**redundant character** synonymous with check character (↑).

**redundant code** a self-checking code in a binary-coded decimal (p.36) using a parity column check (↑) and a row check.

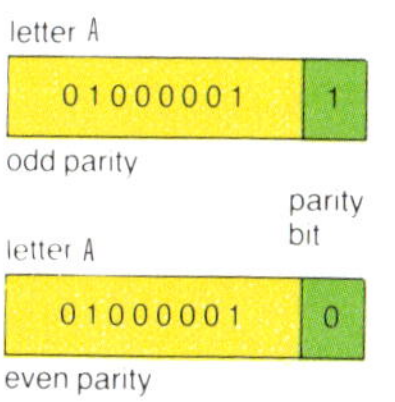


**parity check on a character**

**machine code format** machine code (p.38) is written in 1, 2, 3 or 4 bytes each of 8 bits (p.36). The simplest instructions use one byte, which is divided into 3 fields of 2, 3, and 3 bits each. The two MSBs (p.36) determine the basic instruction type (↓); the next 3 bits may continue the instruction, or indicate a register; the three LSBs indicate a register. With 2-byte instructions, the instruction in the first byte indicates a second byte is needed, similarly with 3- and 4-byte instructions. Examples of machine code format are illustrated below.

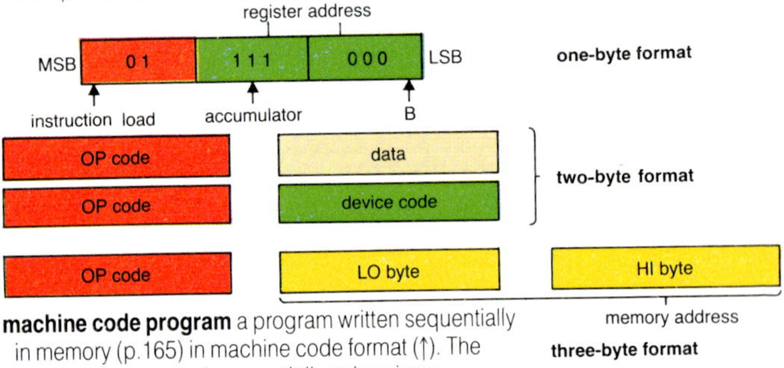


**machine code program** a program written sequentially in memory (p.165) in machine code format (↑). The program is executed sequentially unless jump instructions (p.58) are included in the program.

**instruction types** there are four main types of instruction: (1) data movement, between registers (p.149) and memory (p.165); (2) data manipulation by arithmetical and logical operations (p.161); (3) control and decision, depending on results and conditions; (4) input/output to peripheral devices (p.13).

**operand²** (*n*) any item of data stored in memory (p.165) held in a register (p.149) or entered as an immediate operand (↓).

**immediate operand** an operand (↑) entered by a current program. The machine code format (↑) requires 2 or 3 bytes; the first byte holds the instruction, and the number to be entered is held in 1 or 2 bytes.

**stored operand** an operand (↑) held in memory.

**literal operand** an operand (↑) that is the value of a constant (p.31) and not the address (p.167) storing the constant.

**operation types** there are five types of operation: (1) arithmetical; (2) logical (p.161); (3) data transfer; (4) red-tape (p.161); (5) housekeeping (p.76).

**address mode** the machine code program (↑) defines the method used to locate the address of an operand (↑). The address mode is part of the instruction, and locates operands in registers (p.149) or in memory (p.165). *See address* (p.167).
**op code** abbreviation for operation code (↓).
**operation code** a command (p.48) or part of an instruction (p.48) in machine code (p.38) that causes an operation to be executed by a computer.
**mnemonic operation code** a code using mnemonics (p.38) instead of binary code (p.38) to describe an operation; e.g. LD for LOAD, instead of 01 in binary bits, followed by bits to describe destinations. For example, LD A, B is the mnemonic for a machine code 01 111 000, and the instruction is: load register B into the accumulator (p.150). Mnemonics make the task of programming easier.
**machine-intimate** describes software (p.65), with programs written in machine-readable language, so that interaction between computer and program is close and hence quick.
**intimate** (*adj*) synonymous with machine-intimate (↑).
**prompt** (*n*) a message displayed on a console requiring the operator of the computer to take action.
**word length** the number of bits (p.36) in a word (p.36).
**word mark** some computers have a variable word length (↑), a useful method of saving storage space. A word is distinguished by a word mark at the beginning and at the end of the word.
**start bit** the serial transmission of data, whether of one byte (p.36) or a block (p.217), begins with a start bit. The start bit is always at a positive voltage, it can represent either 1 or 0, depending on the transmission using positive or negative logic (p.42).
**stop bit** the serial transmission of data, begun by a start bit (↑), must end with one or two stop bits. These bits have the opposite code to a start bit.

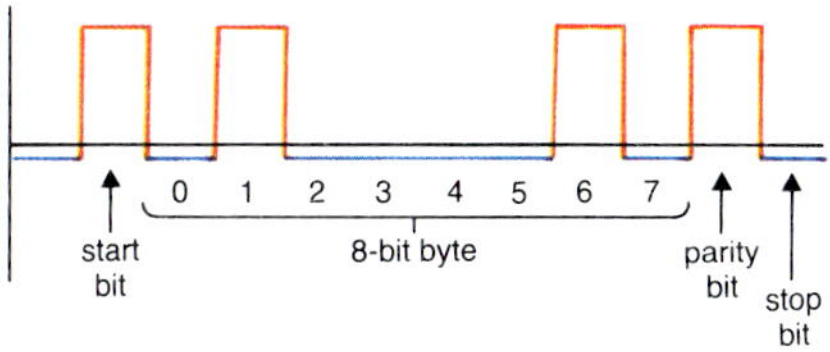


**serial transmission, odd parity ones positive one stop bit**

**bit rate** the speed at which the pulses representing binary digits pass a point in a communications channel.

**baud rate** the number of signal events per second passing a point in a communications channel (p.233). The original baud rate was one half-dot per second in Morse code when transmitted continuously. A baud rate equals one bit per second in serial transmission of binary bits, or two bits per second in four-phase modulation (↓) or three bits per second in eight-phase modulation.

**characters per second** the number of characters per second passing a point in a communications channel (p.233). A character in ASCII (p.38) is transmitted in an 8-bit byte. The byte together with parity, start and stop bits (p.41), requires 11 or 12 bits per character. In serial transmission, a baud rate of 1200 equals 1200/11 = 109cps or 1200/12 = 100cps.

**cps** (*abbr*) characters per sec; cycles per sec.

**negative logic** a signal pulse (p.120) with the binary digit 1 represented by a negative voltage. Most parallel I/O devices use negative logic.

**negative-true logic** synonymous with negative logic (↑).

**positive logic** a signal pulse (p.120) with the binary digit 1 represented by a positive voltage.

**logic levels** the magnitude of the voltages associated with signal pulses for binary 1 and 0.

**carrier wave** an electromagnetic wave (p.131) sent as a radio wave, or along a channel (p.233).

**modulation** (*n*) the variations in a carrier wave (↑) which are a code for signals. A wave can be modulated in three ways: (1) amplitude (2) frequency (3) phase modulated. **modulate** (*v*).

**modulation parameters** amplitude, frequency, and phase of a carrier wave (↑).

**modulation code** the code causing variations in modulation parameters (↑).

**amplitude modulation** a variation in the amplitude of the carrier wave (↑) is used to represent binary 1 or 0. The simplest case is switching the carrier wave on and off.

**frequency modulation** different frequencies are imposed on a carrier wave (↑) to represent binary 1 and 0. This is also called frequency-shift keying and it is the common method used for lower-speed transmission.

**FSK** (*abbr*) frequency-shift keying. *See frequency modulation* (↑).

**carrier wave**

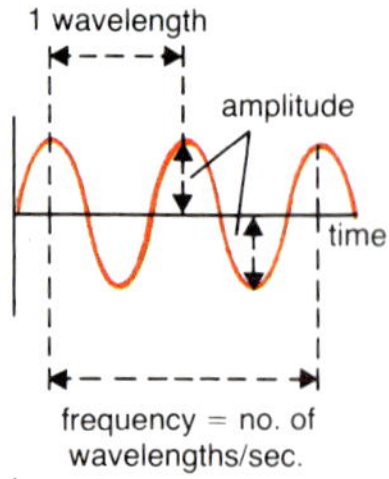


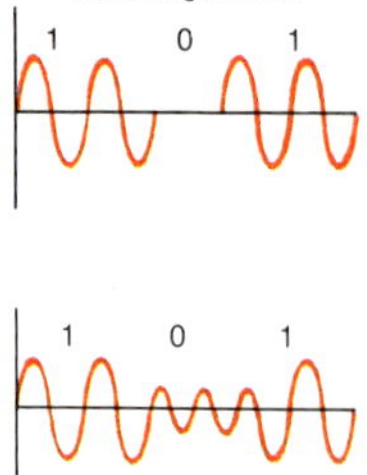


**amplitude modulation**

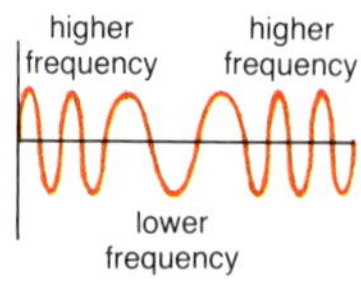


**frequency modulation**

**FSM** (*abbr*) frequency-shift modulation; same as FSK.

**phase modulation** a carrier wave has an associated phase (p.128). This phase can be altered to form a code. The simplest code is formed by one wave in phase and one wave 180° out of phase to represent binary 1 and 0.

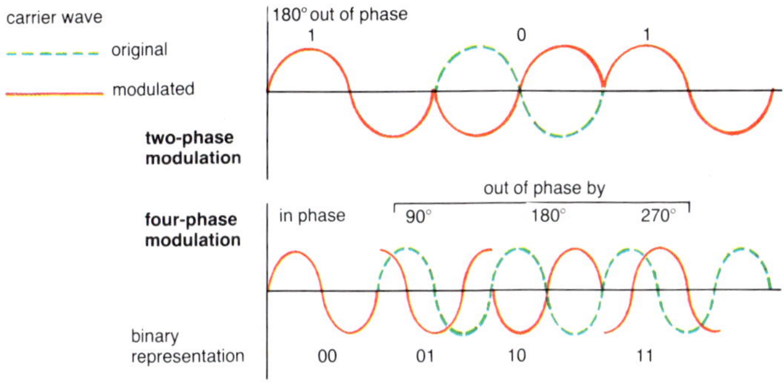


**four-phase modulation** four phase shifts are used: in phase, and 90°, 180°, 270° out of phase. The four different phases represent successively the binary digit pairs 00, 01, 10, 11. One phase signal carries two bits (p.36) hence the bit rate (↑) is twice the baud rate (↑).

**eight-phase modulation** the eight phase shifts are 0°, 45°, 90°, 135°, 180°, 225°, 270°, 315° out of phase, and can represent a trio of binary digits ranging from 000 to 111. The bit rate (↑) is three times the baud rate (↑). *See four-phase modulation* (↑).

**pulse-code modulation** an analog (p.9) modulating signal is sampled periodically and quantized (p.129). The quantized sample is converted to binary digital code and transmitted as pulses (p.120).

**PCM** (*abbr*) pulse-code modulation (↑).

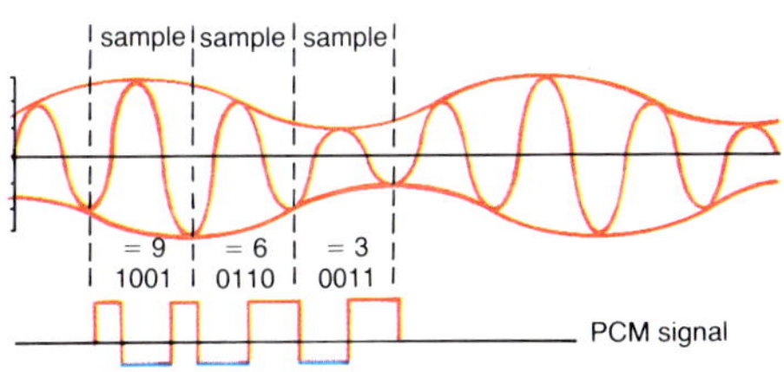

**pulse code** the use of pulses (p.120) of electric current to represent binary digits 1 and 0. Either negative or positive logic (p.42) can be used.
**pulse repetition rate** the average number of pulses transmitted in one second.
**PRR** (*abbr*) pulse repetition rate (↑).
**pulse amplitude modulation** the modulation varies the amplitude of a pulsating current to form an analog (p.9) signal. The pulses are uniformly spaced and of constant width.

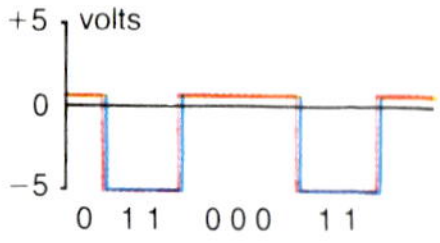


**pulse code negative logic**

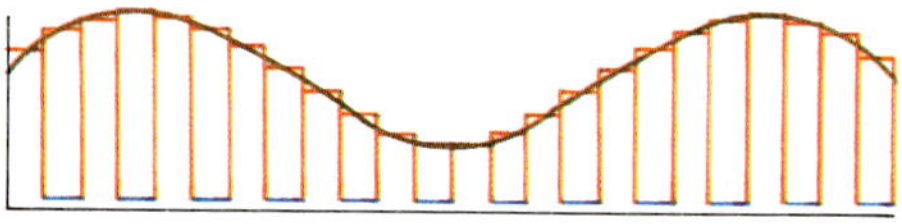

**pulse amplitude modulation**

**pulse carrier** a carrier wave (p.42) which is a uniformly spread, constant width, pulsating current; it is used for pulse amplitude modulation (↑).
**mark** (*n*) indicates a current or a carrier wave; indicates binary 1 in binary code; indicates the actual pulse of current. *Contrasted with space* (↓).
**space** (*n*) represents binary 0 in binary code; indicates an absence of current or a carrier wave; indicates that part of a pulsating current between two successive marks (↑).
**mark-to-space ratio** the ratio of the time taken for transmission of a mark (↑) to that of a space (↑).
**carrier system** a method of sending a number of independent signals along the same channel (p.233). Each signal uses a carrier wave (p.42) of a different frequency; the carrier wave is modulated (p.42) by amplitude, by phase or by FSM (p.42). A modem (p.228) is selectively tuned to separate the frequencies, and each signal, after separation, is transmitted to its destination.

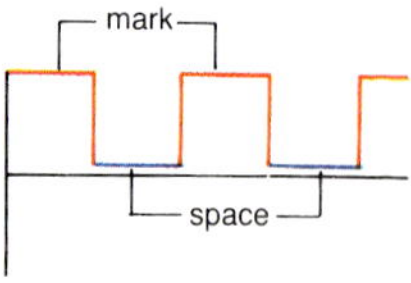


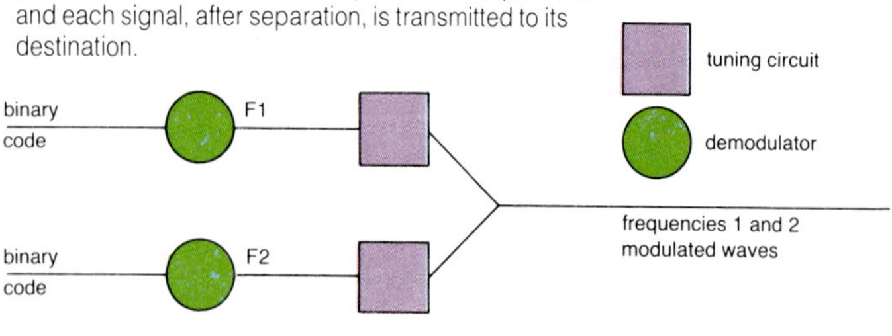

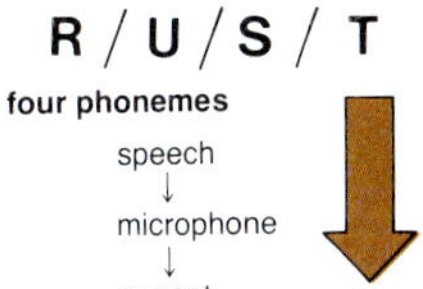


**phoneme** (*n*) a single unit in speech, such as a consonant sound or a vowel sound, with distinctions made for its position in a word, if necessary; two or more phonemes make a syllable. The phonemes are identified for a particular language.

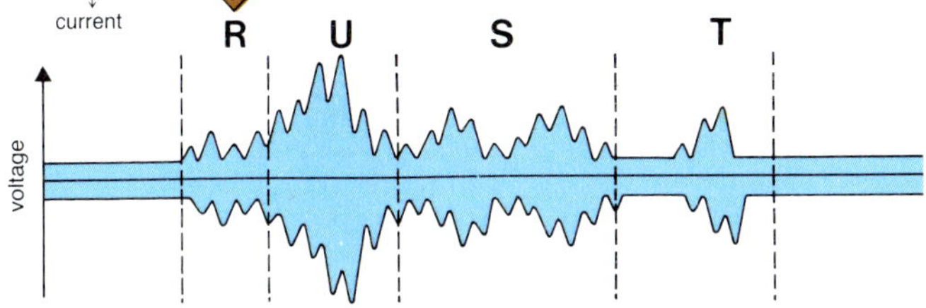


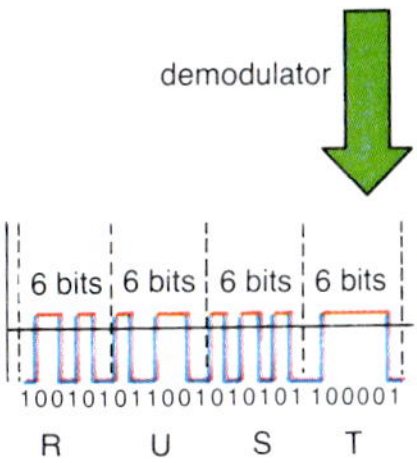


**voice synthesis** one type of synthesis uses phonemes (↑) coded as 6-bit bytes (p.36). An integrated circuit (p.105) selects the phonemes from a keyboard (p.191) typed input, connects them together and generates the sounds for words. For the word to be pronounced correctly, two extra bits are needed for inflection, i.e. emphasis and tone level of a syllable as in the difference between *conduct* (*v*) and *conduct* (*n*).

**voice acceptance terminal** the input accepts audio signals from an operator and generates a digital code. The terminal analyses the spoken word into 32 speech parameters using the characteristics of the audio (↓) wave. The operator speaks a word up to 10 times for recognition by the terminal, and subsequent storage in its memory (p.165). One word requires 32 locations in RAM (p.174) for recognition. Some terminals can recognize 120 words; these words can be joined into sentences of up to 5 words and the sentences recognized as commands.

**voice-response terminal** a voice acceptance terminal (↓) which produces an audio response. This can be used commercially to control order requirements. A vocabulary of 32 words can be used.

**audio** (*adj*) of, or to do with, hearing. **audible** (*adj*), **audibility** (*n*).

**audio response** a spoken output.

**audio-response unit** a device which connects a computer to a telephone to form a voice-response terminal (↑).

**ARU** (*abbr*) audio-response unit (↑).

**Hollerith code** a code used with punched cards (p.211). The card has columns of 12 positions for punching holes. The top 3 positions are zone punches, labelled Y, X and 0 from the top downwards, the bottom nine are labelled 1 to 9. Positions 0 to 9 are for numeric data. The zone punches are used in conjunction with positions 1 to 9 for alphabetic letters and punctuation marks, punching two or three positions in a column.

**zone digits** the top three punching positions on a card, used in Hollerith code (↑).

**bar code** a code consisting of bars of different thicknesses; the code represents numbers 0 to 9. Each commercial article has a coded number such as 76 00189 01309 where 76 represents the country of origin, 00189 is the manufacturer and 01309 is the article. Each digit is then represented by 2 black bars and 2 spaces. The digits are coded on a binary scale, which is an error-detecting code (↓). An example of

bars for bar code

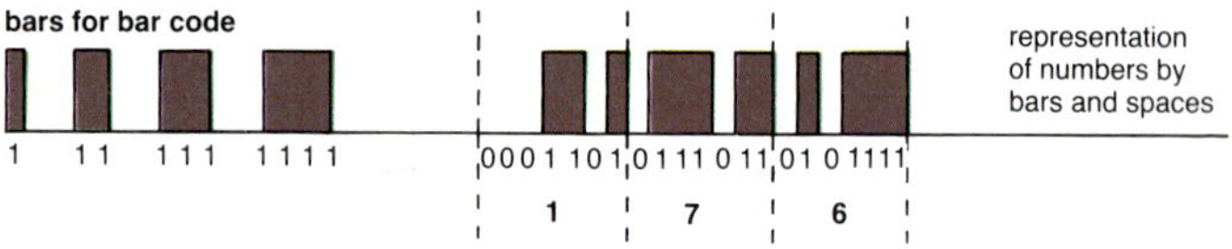


representation of numbers by bars and spaces

such a code uses a 7-bit binary number to represent a digit 0 to 9; it is: (0) 0001101 (1) 0011001 (2) 0010011 (3) 0111101 (4) 0100011 (5) 0110001 (6) 0101111 (7) 0111011 (8) 0110111 (9) 0001011. Black bars represent ones and spaces represent zeros on the bar code. The thickness of the bars corresponds to the number of consecutive one's in the code; the thickness of the spaces corresponds to the number of consecutive zeros in the code. Two longer, thin, bars mark the beginning and the end of the code and also separate the two sections, as shown. The right section uses complemented code numbers, i.e. 1 is represented by 1100110, the left section uses the code above. A check digit is added. The code is used to mark most articles for sale in shops.

**bar-code reader** a device that scans a bar code (↑), by measuring the reflected light from black bars and spaces, and converts the reading to digital pulses in binary code. The binary code is converted by a computer to a VDU (p.203) or printed output. The reader is a box-like device or a hand-held wand.

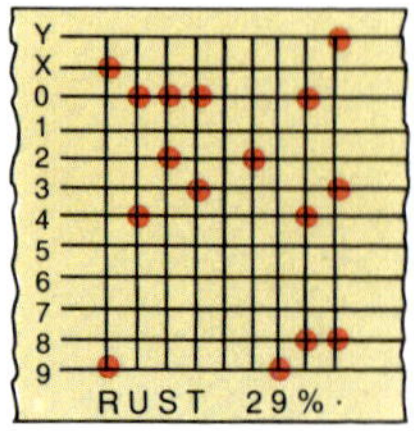


Hollerith code

bar code

| decimal number | Gray code | differ |
|---|---|---|
| 0 | 0000 | |
| 1 | 0001 | |
| 2 | 0011 | |
| 3 | 0010 | |
| 4 | 0110 | |
| 5 | 0111 | |
| 6 | 0101 | |
| 7 | 0100 | 0110 |
| 8 | 1100 | |
| 9 | 1101 | 0111 |

signal distance = 1

| Hamming code |
|---|
| 0000 |
| 2110 |
| 1220 |
| 1101 |
| 0211 |
| 2021 |
| 2202 |
| 1012 |
| 0122 |

signal distance = 3

| biquinary code | binary byte | decimal number |
|---|---|---|
| 0 + 0 | 0000 0000 | 0 |
| 0 + 1 | 0000 0001 | 1 |
| 0 + 2 | 0000 0010 | 2 |
| 0 + 3 | 0000 0011 | 3 |
| 0 + 4 | 0000 0100 | 4 |
| 5 + 0 | 0001 0000 | 5 |
| 5 + 1 | 0001 0001 | 6 |
| 5 + 2 | 0001 0010 | 7 |
| 5 + 3 | 0001 0011 | 8 |
| 5 + 4 | 0001 0100 | 9 |

**biquinary code**

**bar-code optical scanner**[1] a bar-code reader (↑).

**universal product code** a bar code (↑) used in the food industry. There are several versions; a code indicates the version before the main code.

**UPC** (*abbr*) universal product code (↑).

**binary-coded character** any character (p.37) represented by a fixed number of binary digits.

**cyclic code** a group of binary-coded characters (↑) which change by only one bit from one number to a successive number; the signal distance (↓) is 1.

**signal distance** if two binary bytes, or words, have the same number of bits (p.36) the signal distance is the number of digit positions that differ. In the binary words 11010 and 10011, both have five digit positions. They differ in the 2nd and 5th digit position; the signal distance is 2.

**Gray code** a cyclic code (↑) of four binary digits with a signal distance of 1 (↑). The numbers 0 to 9 in Gray code are illustrated. It is one of a group of unit-distance codes.

**cyclic decimal code** synonymous with Gray code (↑).

**Hamming code** a code in which each binary-coded character (↑) has a minimum signal distance (↑) from *every* other character in the code. Each binary-coded character consists of 4 information bits and 3 check bits. An example using ternary digits (radix=3) and a signal distance of 3 is illustrated.

**Hamming distance** synonymous with signal distance (↑).

**error-checking code** a code which is either error-detecting (↓) or error-correcting (↓).

**error-detecting code** a code which is constructed according to particular rules. Certain combinations of digits are not allowed, e.g. in Gray code (↑) 1010 is a forbidden character and is rejected as an error.

**error-correcting code** a code which detects errors, and can correct the error. The Hamming code (↑) is error-correcting, e.g. 2112 is a forbidden character in the illustrated example; it can be corrected to 2110 as it is incorrect in only one digit.

**code element** the physical representation of a binary digit, e.g. a mark or a space (p.44) in a current pulse.

**biquinary code** a notation in which a decimal digit is represented by a pair of numbers (a, b) where a=0 or 5 and b=0 to 4 inclusive.

**language** (*n*) a defined set of characters (p.37) and symbols (p.37) combined together by specific rules. There are high-level (p.51) and low-level languages (↓).

**reserved word** a word which a programmer cannot use as a label (p.67) because it is recognized by the computer as an instruction or command (↓) in a language (↑). A token (p.37) is a code number for a reserved word. Examples of reserved words are: LET, FOR, DIM, PRINT USING.

**dialect** (*n*) a slight variation in the spelling or meaning of a reserved word (↑) as used by different makes of computer. Dialects prevent a program being used by two different computers although both computers recognize the same program language.

**command**[1] (*n*) an electronic signal, or set of signals, the result of a reserved word (↑) which starts, stops, or continues the operation of a computer. Such a command has no operand (p.40). Examples of command words are: RUN, DELETE, CLEAR.

**instruction**[1] (*n*) a program (p.64) step which directs the computer to perform a single operation. The step is in a code recognized by the computer. An instruction is also the set of coded characters causing the operation by the computer. An instruction is not synonymous with command (↑) as it requires an operand (p.40).

**statement** (*n*) the detailed written instructions in a program (p.64) step. It includes reserved words (↑) with operands and is written according to specific rules, called syntax (↓). Statements are narrative, directive, or conditional (↓).

**narrative statement** a statement which assigns values to variables, details the relationship between variables, allocates storage space, specifies printing positions.

**directive statement** a statement containing instructions, which are indirect commands for a computer to perform an operation, e.g. the use of peripheral devices (p.12) is a directive statement. Some commands (↑) can also be written as directive statements, e.g. CLEAR. Examples of reserved words are: PRINT, GOSUB.

**conditional statement** states conditions for following a branching program (p.64) or for stopping a program.

**repertoire** (*n*) (1) the set of instructions, defined by reserved words (↑) that a computer will accept in commands and statements. (2) the set of instructions, defined by machine code (p.38) that a computer can execute.

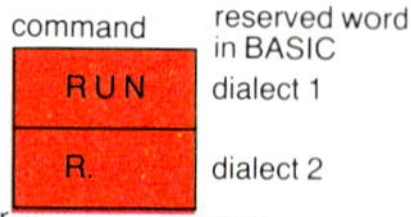

**dialects of BASIC**
a high-level language

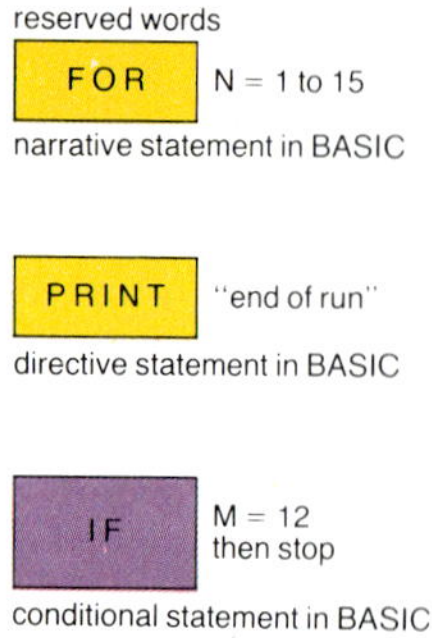

**examples of statements in a program**

**operator²** (*n*) the reserved words which define a logical operation, e.g. AND, OR, NOT (p.85), or a function (↓).

**function¹** (*n*) the operation specified in a command or statement (↑) by an instruction. **functional** (*adj*).

**symbol²** (*n*) the symbols used in a computer language to specify a particular function. Some symbols differ from the mathematical symbols for the same function, e.g. * is used instead of ×; **,^, ↑, are used for exponentiation (p.28) depending on dialect or language. **symbolic** (*adj*).

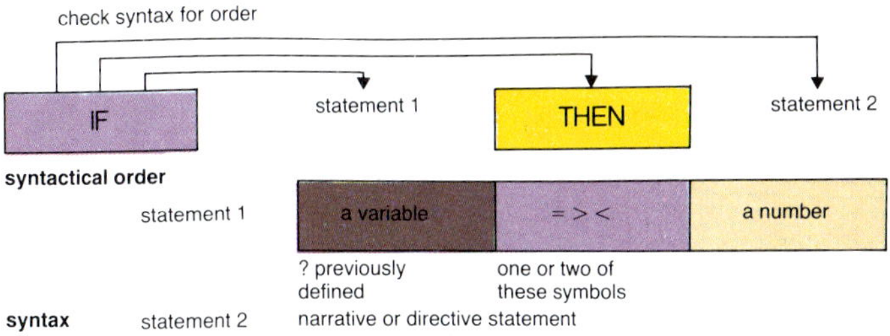


**syntax** (*n*) the rules governing the combination of reserved words (↑), symbols (↑), variables (p.66) and operands (p.40) in a statement. **syntactical** (*adj*).

**lexical errors** written errors in spelling reserved words (↑), or using an incorrect symbol (↑).

**syntactical errors** errors in syntax (↑); they include such errors as the omission of quotes (inverted commas), incorrect use of commas, omission of parentheses (brackets).

**programming languages** there are various languages (↑) in which a program can be written. No all-purpose language exists as yet; each high-level language (p.51) is oriented towards specific problem areas, e.g. scientific use, commercial use, instructional use. Low-level languages (↓) are machine oriented, and hence differ for each type of computer. Most makes of microcomputer operate with one high-level language only, whereas minicomputers and mainframe computers (p.8) offer a limited choice.

**low-level language** a language which is close to machine code (p.38) so that each written instruction in a program can be converted directly to machine code on a one-to-one basis.

**machine language** a language written in binary code. It is almost impossible for a programmer to write a program in machine language without making errors, so all computers convert any written program into a machine language program.

**instruction format[1]** the arrangement of binary digits in machine language (↑) to form a machine instruction. *See machine code format* (p.40).

**assembly language** a low-level language (p.49) using a mnemonic operation code (p.41) which is machine-readable by a particular assembler (p.53). The assembler converts the assembly language into machine language (↑).

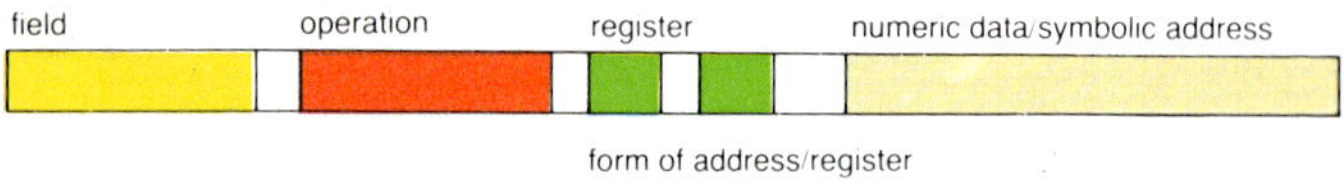


assembly language format

**assembly language format** the format has specific positions for (*a*) a 3-letter mnemonic for a field (p.56); (*b*) a 3-letter mnemonic for an operation; (*c*) a letter designating a register; (*d*) another letter designating the form of address or a second register; (*e*) mnemonic data or a symbolic address. Information is transferred from address or register (*d*) to register (*c*). The complete instruction has a fixed number of characters and spaces, i.e. a fixed length. This enables the assembler (p.53) to recognize, and hence convert, the assembly language to machine language.

**directives** three-letter mnemonic codes written before the beginning of an assembly language (↑) program, and at the end. Written before the program, they reserve space in memory for specific variables or for particular fields (p.56). At the end of a program, they end the program or restore execution to a main, or other, program.

**pseudo-operation** a directive (↑) in assembly language for which there is no equivalent in machine language (↑). It designates a segment of the assembly language (↑) program which will perform a particular task in a field (p.56). No operation is executed by the CPU (p.146).

**pseudo-instruction** a group of characters forming a field label (p.56) which has the same form as an instruction, but is not executed by the computer. It is written in assembly language (↑) and designates the instructions for a particular task.

**quasi-instruction** synonymous with pseudo-instruction (↑).

**microinstruction** (*n*) (1) a single, short command to a CPU (p.146) such as add, shift, compare data. (2) the bit (p.36) pattern, stored in ROM (p.173) which specifies the operation of the individual units in the computer necessary to execute the command.

**microde** (*n*) synonymous with microinstruction (↑).

**macroinstruction** (*n*) a sequence of microinstructions (↑) generated by a single instruction, the macroinstruction. It is a powerful instruction which combines several operations to carry out a commonly used function, such as division. Macroinstructions are provided by the manufacturers; the programmer can also write and label his own instructions..

**macrode** (*n*) synonymous with macroinstruction (↑).

**microprogram** (*n*) a program written in microinstructions (↑), normally user-transparent (p.12). An assembly language (↑) instruction is implemented by a microprogram. A bit-slice microprocessor (p.147) can have a microprogram written for it.

**macrooperation** (*n*) an operation such as multiply, divide, square root, which requires many microinstructions (↑) performed in sequence.

**dictionary** (*n*) a list of directives (↑), produced by a compiler (p.54) from a high-level language (↓). *See also data dictionary* (p.252).

**menu** (*n*) a list of macroinstructions (↑) available to a programmer for macroprogramming (↑). *See also display menu* (p.260).

**high-level language** a language (p.48) consisting of words and symbols which are close to normal English words, and hence readily understandable by a user. High-level languages are oriented to problems or commercial procedures; they are the source languages (p.53) for most programs. A statement (p.48) in a high-level language is converted to assembly language (↑) and finally to machine code (p.38); one statement corresponds to several machine code instructions.

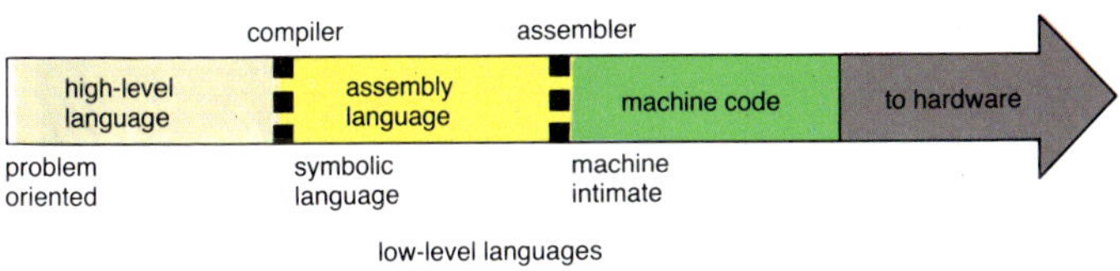

**BASIC** (*acro*) Beginners' All-purpose Symbolic Instruction Code. A high-level language (p.51) used for computers with on-line (p.22) facilities, particularly in a conversational mode (p.18). Almost all microcomputers use BASIC for their program input. There are many dialects (p.48) of the language.

**FORTRAN** (*acro*) FORmula TRANslator. A high-level language (p.51) oriented towards scientific and mathematical problems. Program steps are written as algebraic and arithmetical formulae combined with reserved words for transfer, indexing addresses (p.169) and input/output operations. There are several varieties of FORTRAN.

**COBOL** (*acro*) COmmon Business Oriented Language. A high-level language (p.51) oriented towards business problems. It uses English language statements for the manipulation of business data and problems.

**PASCAL** a high-level language (p.51) which aims at teaching programming in a systematic manner. A program consists of a heading and a block. The heading specifies the variables used; the block specifies labels, constants, types of data, functions and method of execution.

**ALGOL** (*acro*) ALGorithmic Oriented Language. A high-level language (p.51) aimed at concise expression of mathematical and logical processes, and the control of such processes.

**job-control language** a language designed for interactive operation between user and computer. The user specifies the details of operation and the output which is desired.

**JCL** (*abbr*) job-control language (↑).

**APT** (*abbr*) automatically programmed tools. A language designed to operate machine tools using numeric codes.

**APL** (*abbr*) a programming language. A high-level language (p.51) oriented towards mathematical problems, particularly those concerned with arrays (p.69). It is useful for educational work and problem investigation.

**LISP** (*acro*) LISt Processing. A high-level language (p.51) based on functions, some of which are defined, while new functions are defined by the user; these functions are similar to subroutines in FORTRAN (↑).

**LOGO** (*acro*) a dialect of LISP (↑). It builds up a vocabulary of procedures from a small set of simple commands.

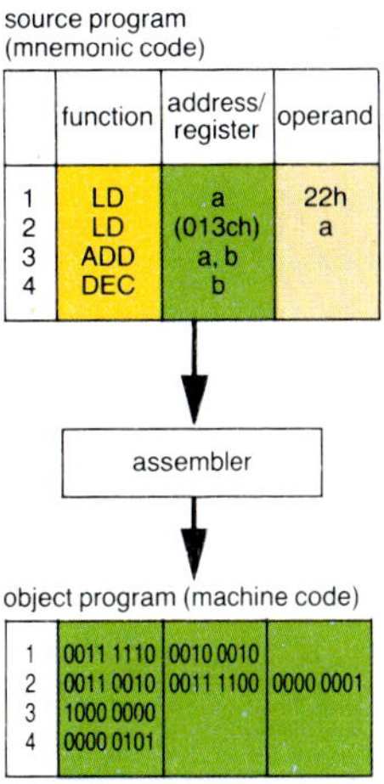


**asembler**
based on Z80 processor

**FORTH** a high-level language (p.51). It uses 16-bit arithmetic; new words can be defined and put in its vocabulary.

**source language** the language used by a programmer for a computer. It can be a high-level language (p.51) or a low-level language (p.49). A source language has to be converted to machine code (p.38) for the instructions to be executed.

**source program** a program in a source language (↑).

**object language** the language produced by the output of a coding operation by a compiler (p.54) or an assembler (↓), from an input of a source language (↑). The object language may be the source language for a further step in coding. It is, however, usually a machine language (p.50) intelligible to a computer.

**object program** a program using object language (↑).

**source code** the code used in a source program (↑).

**target language** synonymous with object language (↑).

**target program** synonymous with object program (↑).

**assembler** (*n*) a program, stored in ROM (p.173), which translates a mnemonic operation code (p.41) into machine code, intelligible to a computer. The assembler converts the mnemonic operation codes and symbolic addresses (p.56) to machine code instructions on a one-to-one basis. *Compare compiler* (p.54). **assemble** (*v*).

**assembler program** synonymous with assembler (↑); also called assembly program.

**single-pass assembler** the source program (↑) is passed once through the assembler.

**two-pass assembler** the source program (↑) is passed twice through the assembler. In the first run, symbolic addresses (p.56) are stored in memory (p.165). On the second run, symbolic addresses are converted to absolute addresses (p.167) and all decimal numbers in the source program are converted to hexadecimal notation, and subsequently to binary notation.

**macroassembler** (*n*) an assembler (↑) which translates macroinstructions (p.51) directly into a sequence of machine code instructions (p.38). A macroassembler program is usually stored in RAM (p.175) and is written in assembly language (p.50).

**disassembly** (*n*) the retranslation of machine code instructions into mnemonic operation code (p.41). This facility is used to help in debugging (p.81).

**translation** (*n*) the process of converting a source language (p.53) to an object language (p.53), or of converting one form of coding to another form, without a significant change in the meaning of the instructions. **translate** (*v*).

**translator** (*n*) any device that carries out translation (↑), e.g. conversion of ASCII code to BCD.

**program scan** the operation by an assembler (p.53) when each line of its source program (p.53) is decoded in sequence. The mnemonics of the source program are stored in memory (p.165) ready for translation into machine code.

**program origin** the absolute address (p.167) of the start of a program. The program can be one of source language or object language (p.53). It is the location (p.166) of the first program step.

**compiler** (*n*) a compiler is a program, stored in ROM (p.173), which effectively translates a high-level language (p.51) into machine code (p.38). The translation program is written in a base language (↓). The compiler performs statement analysis, both lexical and syntactical (↓) on the source program (p.53) and runs through the whole program. During this operation it lists variables, with their types, assigns areas of memory (p.165) to program segments and subroutines, chooses register assignments, and calls library subroutines (↓). The compiler usually includes an assembler (p.53) for the final generation of machine code; it runs through the whole source program before starting to compile machine code. All high-level languages require a compiler or interpreter. *See lexical and syntactical analysis* (↓). **compilation** (*n*), **compile** (*v*).

**base language** the language used in a compiler (↑) program; it is the assembly language (p.50) of the make of CPU (p.146) used in the computer.

**compiler language** a high-level language (p.51) which is intelligible to a particular computer, as the compiler can translate it.

**cross-compiler** a computer is used to compile (↑) machine code from a source language (p.53) in a format suitable for use by a different computer.

**cross-assembler** this has the same purpose as a cross-compiler (↑), which uses assembly instead of compilation.

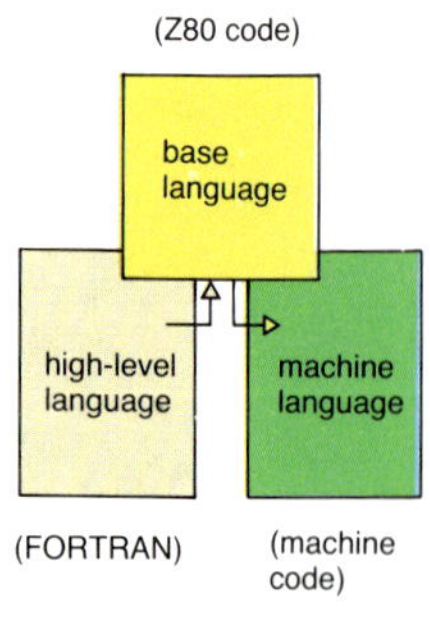

**library subroutine** a subroutine in a set of subroutines, stored in memory (p.165), to perform any one of various small standard processes, the equivalent of a macroinstruction (p.51) in machine code. Some subroutines are supplied by the manufacturer, others written by the computer user.

**program library** the total of library subroutines.

**processor**[1] (*n*) in software (p.65) a computer program used in a compiler (↑) or an assembler (p.53) for translating a specific source language (p.53). Different processor modules perform different functions, such as statement analysis, register assignments, etc.

**lexical analysis** the first processing stage of a compiler (↑); it removes redundant information, condenses statements by eliminating spaces, corrects spelling errors (if possible) and displays error messages for statements that cannot be processed, due to misspelt words, etc.

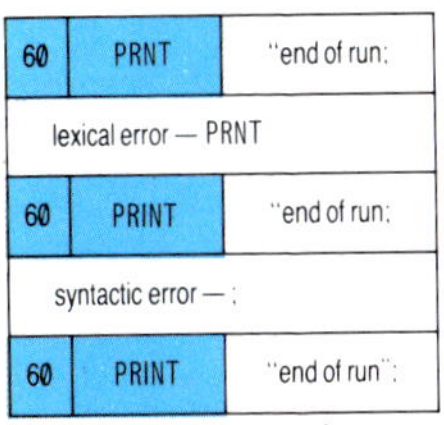


**lexical and syntactical analysis examples**

**syntactical analysis** the second stage of a compiler (↑) in which the syntax (p.49) of each line of a source program (p.53) is tested. It detects errors such as: incorrect order of statements or omissions from statements; misuse of names of variables; incorrect punctuation; conflict with other statements through using the same reference; etc. Error messages are displayed accordingly.

**optimisation** (*n*) a process to increase the efficiency of the object program (p.53). It can be performed before or after the generation of machine code, and on any part of the machine language program (p.50). Optimisation for loops, for example, performs as many tasks as possible outside a loop, to reduce the number of cycles of the loop. Optimisation greatly increases the complexity of the compiler.

**computer-independent language** a high-level language (p.51) which can be used on any computer with a compiler (↑) suitable for translation; it is independent of word length, code representations and symbols, e.g. FORTRAN, COBOL.

**direct-execution language** the architecture (p.13) of some microcomputers is designed to execute instructions direct from a high-level language (p.51). The direct-execution language does not need intermediate translation by compilers (↑). This is useful as debugging (p.81) is easy, and program execution is quick.

**field**[1] (*n*) (*a*) the division of a format into separate sections, called fields, e.g. the division of an 8-bit byte of machine code into 3 separate fields, *see machine code format* (p.40); (*b*) a particular section of a program, such as a loop, or subroutine.
**field label** a 3-character word chosen as a mnemonic to represent a field (↑) in assembly language (p.50). A compiler (p.54) uses the name of a variable as a label for a field stored in the computer's memory (p.165).
**assembler-directive command** instructions in assembly language (p.50) assigned a mnemonic by a programmer, giving him the ability to generate values of variables, and assign data fields (↑).
**register address** each register (p.149) is assigned a letter in mnemonic operation code (p.41) which is its address, and a 3-digit number in machine code (p.38). These codes then become the address of an operand (p.40).
**symbolic address**[1] an address with a 3-character mnemonic, assigned by a programmer in assembly language (p.50) to refer to the memory location (p.166) for a particular item of data, a function, or an instruction.
**deferred address** an address of an operand (p.40) which is stored in the location actually addressed by an instruction. This facility allows the address of the operand to be manipulated by the program during the course of the program.
**relative address**[1] the address part of an instruction which consists of a number which is added to a base address stored in a CPU (p.146) register. A segment of a program can be written with relative addresses, and these changed to absolute addresses (p.167) when the program is run.
**floating address**[1] relative address (↑).
**block transfer** a high-speed serial transfer of a block (p.217) of data to and from magnetic tape or disk (p.213). The blocks may be of either fixed or variable length. The beginning and end of a block is indicated by a block mark (p.231). A sum check (p.231) tests the correctness of the transfer.
**device code** a code identifying a peripheral device (p.12). It is an 8-bit code allowing transfer to a maximum of 256 input/output devices.

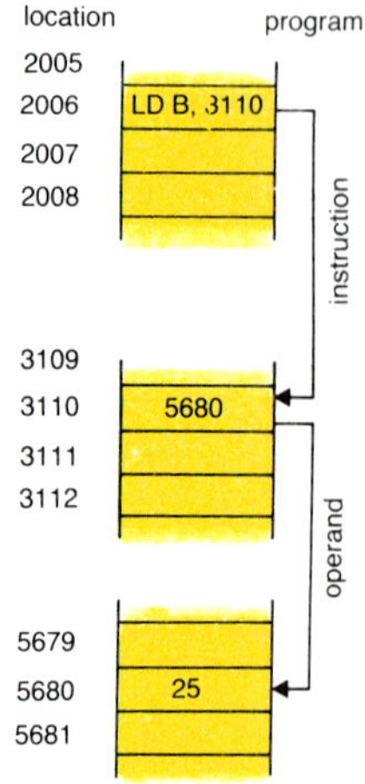

**deferred address**

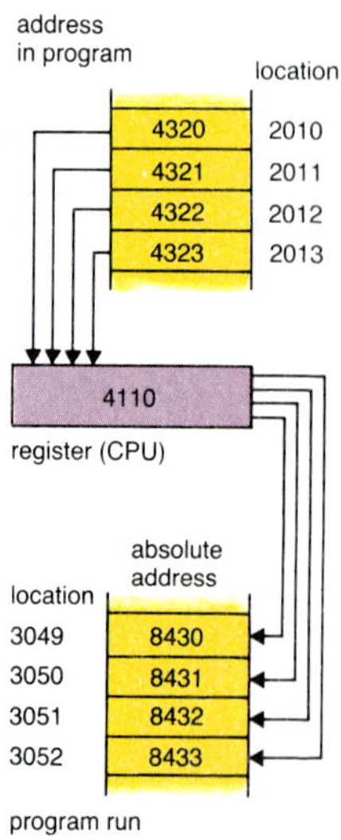

**relative addressing**

**interpreter** (*n*) (1) a program that translates a line of a high-level language (p.51) and executes the instruction before passing on to the next sequential line. It translates the high-level language into machine code. An interpreter is not as efficient as a compiler (p.54), as a particular instruction has to be decoded each time it occurs in a program. It is much slower than a compiler, but requires a much smaller program, hence most microcomputers use an interpreter rather than a compiler as memory (p.165) is conserved. (2) a program that translates pseudo-instructions (p.50) into machine code and executes the instructions as soon as they are translated.

**operation[1]** (*n*) a computer action specified by a single machine code (p.38) instruction, or a pseudo-instruction (p.50). A single step in an arithmetical or logical problem (e.g. +, OR), or a transfer of one unit of data. The computer action producing a result from an operand (p.34).

**instruction[2]** (*n*) a program step instructing a computer to carry out a particular action. It specifies the memory location (p.166) or the register, storing an operand (p.40) and sometimes a key (p.251).

**absolute instruction** an instruction (↑) which specifies completely an operation (↑) and causes the operation to be performed.

**no-op instruction** an instruction (↑) which demands no action by the computer, which then proceeds to the next instruction. It may allow for future program changes, or be used for other purposes.

**dummy instruction** synonymous with no-op instruction (↑).

**blank instruction** synonymous with no-op instruction (↑).

**null instruction** no-op instruction (↑).

**skip instruction** (1) an instruction (↑) which allows a small jump in a program, backwards or forwards, by a few instructions. (2) no-op instruction (↑).

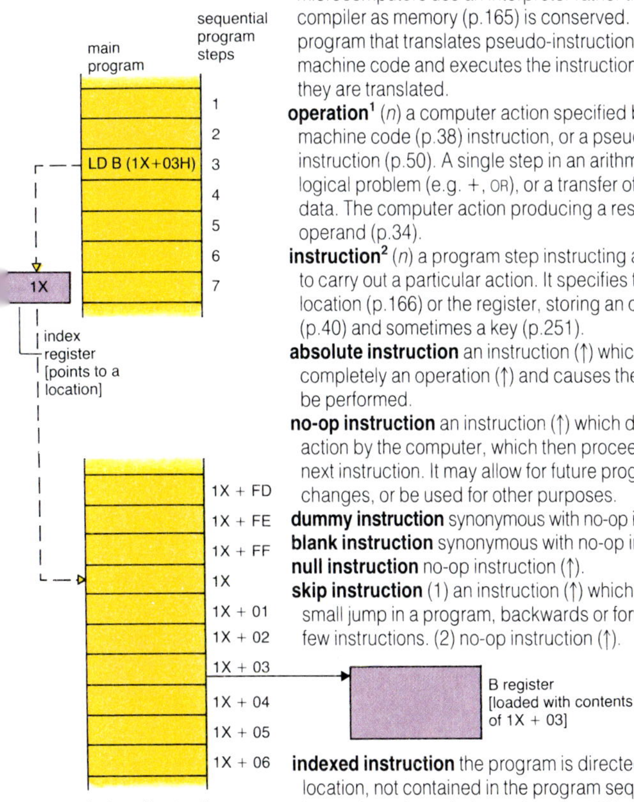

**indexed instruction**

**indexed instruction** the program is directed to a location, not contained in the program sequence of instructions, by an index register (p.156) storing an index. This index can be altered by instructions in other program steps.

**instruction format**[2] an instruction in machine code (p.38) which includes the following: (*a*) an operation code (p.41); (*b*) address of an operand (p.40), either a location in memory (p.165) or a register; some instructions allow more than one operand; (*c*) a modifier (p.71) or displacement (p.169); (*d*) a number; (*e*) address of next instruction. A simple instruction of one byte contains less information than one of four bytes. *See instruction format* (p.50).

**macrocommand** (*n*) a string of related commands used frequently in programming and given a label. The one macrocommand puts the string of commands into the program, reducing programming time.

**load**[1] (*v*) to transfer data into a register (p.149), or a location in RAM (p.175).

**jump** (*v*) to leave sequential following of a program and go to another location, specified by an address, usually depending on the result of an arithmetical or logical operation. Also called branch.

**skip** (*v*) to jump (↑) to an instruction, out of sequence, by passing over one or more intermediate instructions.

**unconditional jump** a jump instruction (↓) which transfers the sequential following of a program to another location, specified by an address without reference to a condition.

**unconditional branch** unconditional jump (↑).

**conditional jump** a jump instruction (↓) which depends on the result of an arithmetical or logical operation.

**conditional branch** a jump instruction (↓) which selects, as a result of an arithmetical or logical operation, one of a number of locations, specified by an address.

**jump instruction**[1] an instruction causing control in a program to go to a location other than in sequential order. If a condition is not met, control continues in normal sequential order.

**call** (*n*) a jump instruction (↑) that remembers the location from which it jumped.

**return** (*n*) an instruction that returns a program to the following statement after the last call (↑) statement.

**increment** (*v*) (1) to add a number to another number; to increase in value or quantity. (2) to increase the value of a binary word in a register by adding 1. **increment** (*n*).

**decrement** (*v*) (1) to subtract a number from another number; to decrease in value or quantity. (2) to decrease the value of a binary word in a register by subtracting 1. **decrement** (*n*).

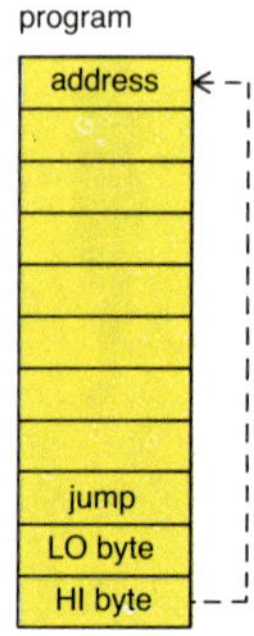


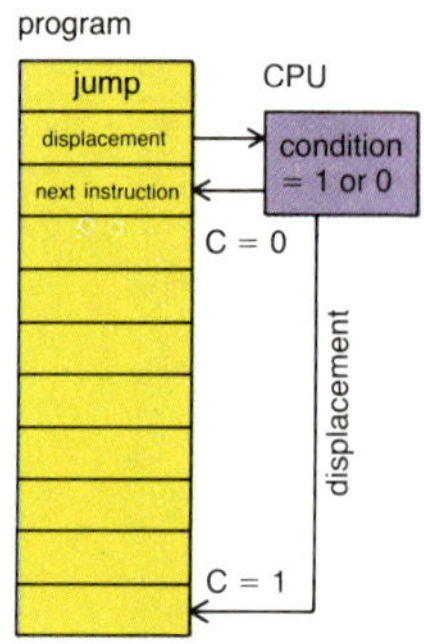


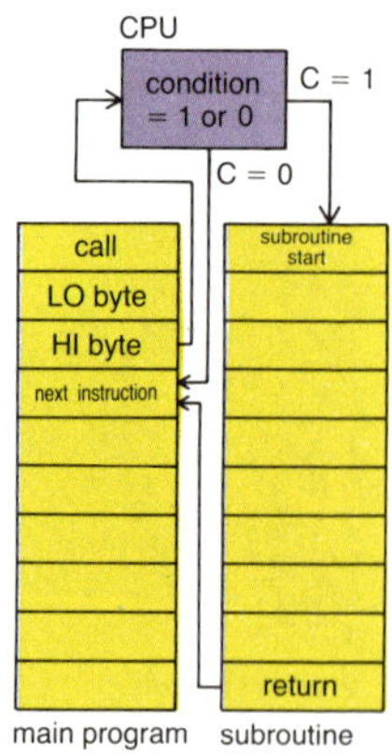


**call and return**

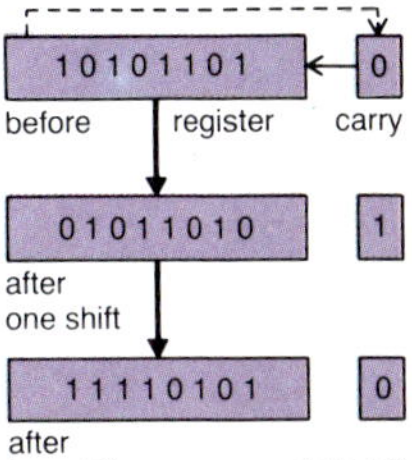

rotate left

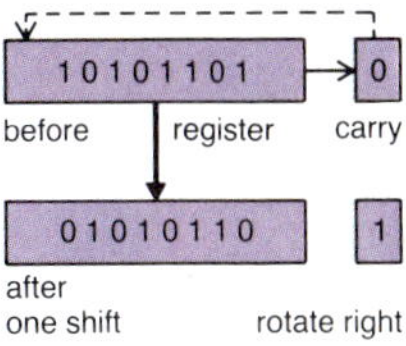

rotate right

**bit manipulation**

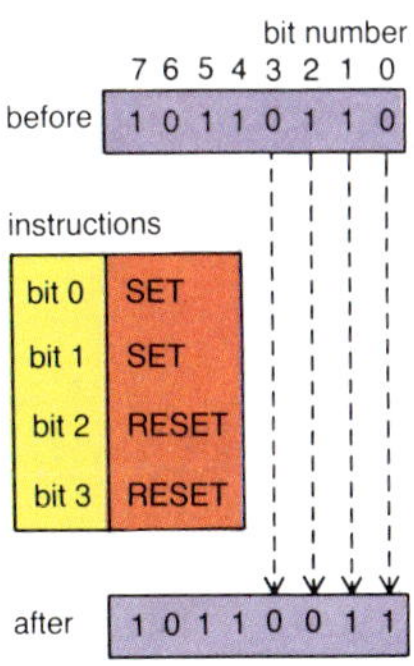


**shift left** to move the binary digits (p.28) in a register to the left. If the digits are moved one place, this is equivalent to multiplying the binary number by 2. If BCD (p.36) digits are moved one place, this is equivalent to multiplying the number by 10. This is an arithmetic shift.

**shift right** to move the binary digits to the right instead of to the left as in shift left (↑). This is equivalent to dividing the binary number by 2. If BCD digits are moved one place to the right, this is equivalent to dividing by 10. This is an arithmetic shift.

**rotate left** to move the binary digits (p.28) in a register to the left, with the most significant digit entering the carry and the carry bit entering the least significant bit position. The carry bit is 0 at the start of the operation. This instruction is used to test the state of a particular bit in a byte. A suitable number of rotates left or right (↓) are performed, and the status of the carry bit is checked.

**rotate right** to move the binary digits (p.28) in a register to the right, with the carry bit entering the most significant digit position, and the least significant digit entering the carry. *See rotate left* (↑).

**cyclic shift** a rotate left (↑) or a rotate right (↑).

**circular shift** synonymous with cyclic shift (↑).

**logical shift**[1] synonymous with cyclic shift (↑).

**end-around shift**[1] synonymous with cyclic shift (↑).

**bit manipulation** machine code (p.38) instructions can set a bit in a register, i.e. make it equal to one; reset a bit, i.e. make it equal to zero; or test a bit to see whether it is one or zero. Each bit in a byte can be addressed and manipulated in this manner. The instructions are independent of the original value of the bit, i.e. if it is originally 0, and it is reset, it remains 0.

**halt**[1] (*n*) the result of a HALT instruction, interrupt command, or the computer reaching the end of a program. The computer stops operating but can be commanded to continue. *See drop-dead halt* (p.72).

**shift left/right**

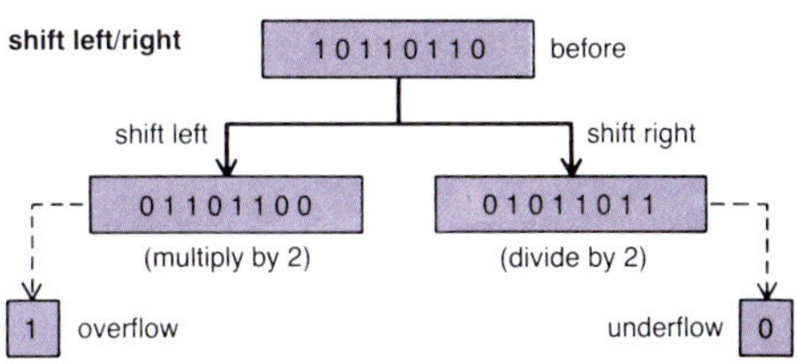

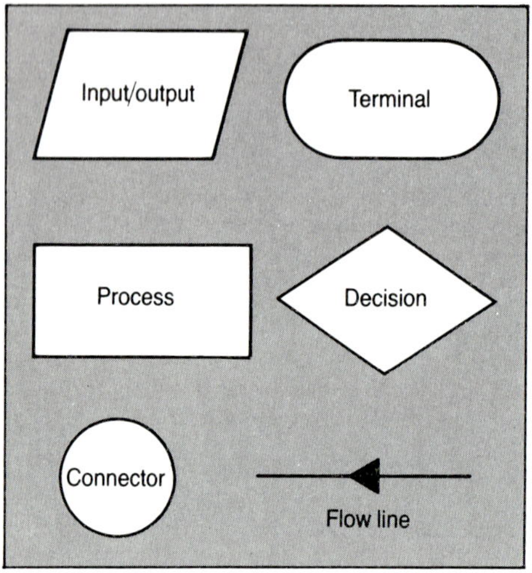


**flowchart** (*n*) a representation of a sequence of operations by conventional symbols showing the flow of information in a solution to a problem. The relationships between the different types of operation are shown in a series of steps; this helps a programmer to design an effective program.

**flow diagram** synonymous with flowchart (↑).

**program flowchart** synonymous with flowchart (↑) but distinguihes it from systems flowchart (p.63).

**flowchart symbols** a set of differently shaped box diagrams representing the basic types of operation executed by a computer.

**terminal box** used at the beginning and end of a flowchart program.

**input/output box** the description indicates use.

**process box** details of instructions are written in the box.

**decision box** an If-Then operation is described; at least two flowlines (↓) must leave the box; usually these are YES/NO lines.

**connector** (*n*) a box labelled with a letter; there are two such boxes showing the link between the connectors.

**flowline** (*n*) the direction of the flow of information is shown by arrowed lines flowing from top to bottom and from left to right.

**typical flowchart – solving a quadratic equation**

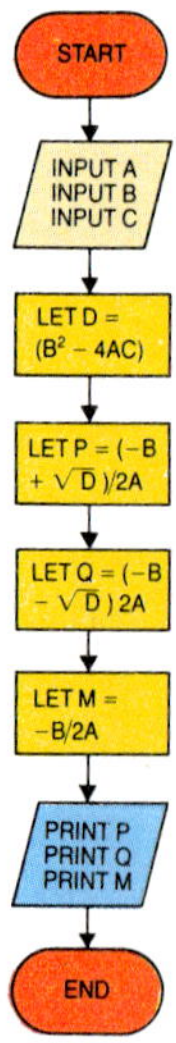

**outline flowchart** a flowchart (↑) indicating the major steps in a complex problem. It ensures all input/output requirements are met; all conditional statements are noted; the program can be divided into suitable segments and subroutines.

**detail flowchart** a flowchart which gives suitable programming steps for the processes given in an outline flowchart (↑). The greatest detail could be expressed in boxes using mnemonic operation code (p.41).

**segment**[1] (*n*) a part of a program (p.64) short enough to be stored completely in memory and run as an entity; it contains conditional or unconditional branches to other parts of the program, or runs sequentially in the program.

**routine** (*n*) a set of instructions (p.57) arranged in sequence and executed sequentially by a computer. It can be considered as part of a program (p.64) but is also used synonymously for a program.

**entry point** a particular instruction (p.57) in a routine (↑) to which other routines or segments can direct the flow of a program; the entry point is usually the first instruction in the routine. A routine can have more than one entry point.

**stop code** the directive statement causing a computer to halt (p.59).

**block**[1] (*n*) a geometrical shape, with or without information written inside it; used to make a diagram of a program, a system, a device, or a computer. Specific shapes have specific meanings, e.g. symbols for flowcharts (↑).

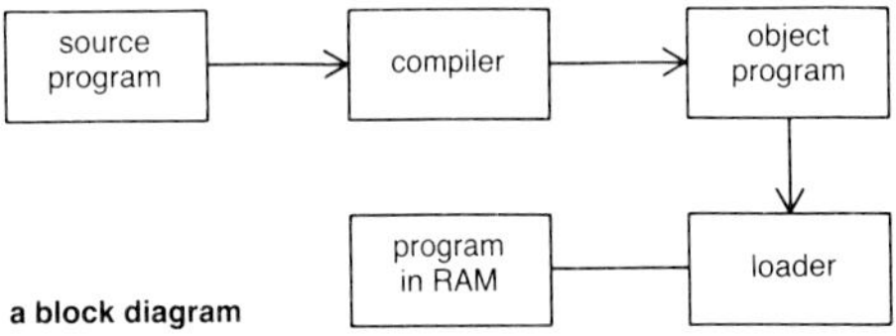


a block diagram

**block diagram** a diagram using blocks (↑).

**macroflowchart** a program flowchart (↑) using blocks (↑). It describes the logical arrangement of a routine (↑) or program (p.64). Less detail is given than in a flowchart.

**logical flowchart** (1) a flowchart using standard symbols (↑). (2) a diagram showing the relationship between logical elements (p.90) using standard symbols.

**logic flowchart** synonymous with logical flowchart (↑).

**decision table** a table, or array, of conditions and actions dependent on the conditions. The basic table consists of 4 sections: (1) stated conditions; (2) value of conditions; (3) courses of action; (4) action taken or value of action. As an illustrated example a decision table is drawn up with entry conditions for a particular task where only males between the ages of 20 and 40 are accepted under the conditions. Decision tables can be used instead of flowcharts (p.60) in the solution of problems.

| | |
|---|---|
| condition ? | value of conditions |
| what action? | value of action |

| | | | | |
|---|---|---|---|---|
| male | N | Y | Y | Y |
| age <20 | – | Y | N | N |
| age >20 | – | N | Y | Y |
| age >40 | – | N | N | Y |
| accept | – | – | + | – |
| reject | + | + | – | + |

N = no Y = yes + = action
– = not significant

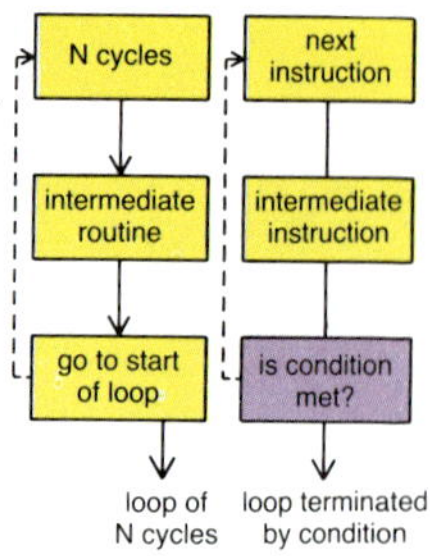


**programming** (*n*) (1) the process of producing a flowchart (p.60) to solve a computer problem; or producing a set of instructions in a high-level or low-level language (p.49) to solve a problem, and testing the instructions to eliminate bugs (p.81); (2) plugging a patchboard (p.16) to form suitable circuits for a computer.

**loop program** a segment of a program which repeats itself until a stated condition is met.

**loop counter** a counter is set to repeat the loop a given number of times.

**loop testing** using a conditional statement (p.48) to test whether the loop function has been completed.

**nesting loops** to enclose one loop inside another; nesting can be at several levels. An inner loop is completed for each unit of an outer loop.

**modification loop** a loop containing instructions which alters data or addresses of instructions.

**loop computing functions** the processes which perform the purpose of the loop as opposed to the initialization (p.67) and housekeeping functions (p.76).

**conditional branch** a branch obeying a conditional statement (p.48).

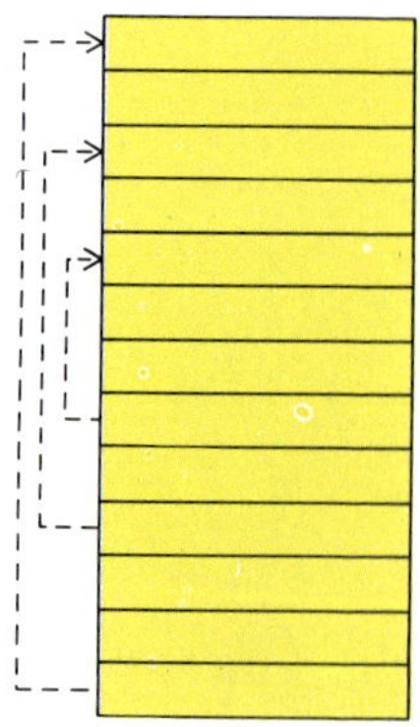

nesting loops

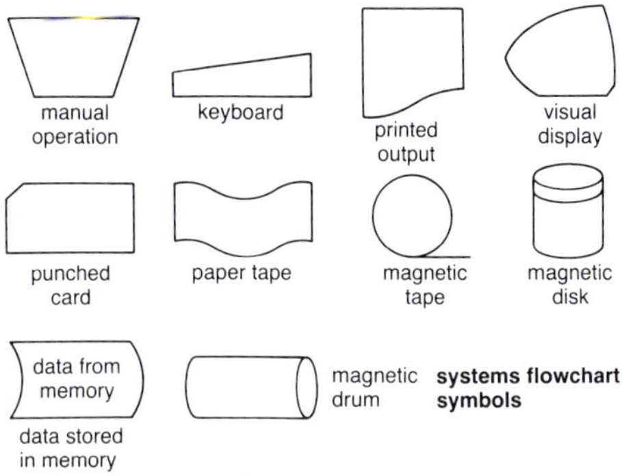


**systems flowchart symbols**

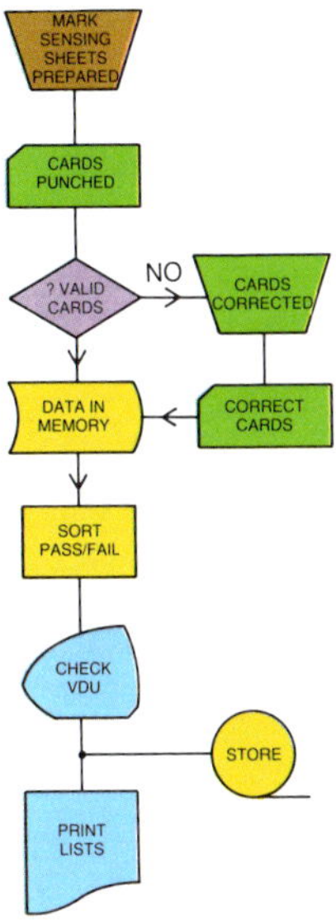


**simple systems flowchart for candidates' results**

**dry run** using a set of simple numbers or characters, to write down the actions undergone by the numbers or characters, when following a flowchart (p.60) or program (p.64). This checks a program before it is used on a computer.

**systems flowchart** a flowchart which shows the input and output devices used, together with the computer procedures for a particular problem. A set of symbols represents the input/output devices, and these are used with the program flowchart (p.60) symbols to form a systems flowchart.

**system chart** synonymous with systems flowchart (↑).

**systems flowchart symbols** a set of differently shaped geometrical figures representing the peripheral devices (p.12) and computer parts used for input/output.

**manual operation symbol** operations carried out by hand, e.g. setting switches, connecting a plugboard (p.16), filling out mark-sensing cards (p.196), coding data by hand.

**keyboard symbol** the QWERTY keyboard (p.191).

**print output symbol** printing on-line or off-line (p.22).

**visual display symbol** a CRT screen (p.204).

**punched card symbol** either a plain or mark-sensing card (p.196).

**paper tape symbol** tape used for either input or output.

**magnetic tape symbol** tape used for input/output.

**magnetic disk symbol** either floppy disk or hard disk.

**data-from-memory symbol** data stored in RAM (p.175).

**magnetic drum symbol** a form of memory little used with modern computers; a drum with a magnetic recording surface. *See* p.184.

**program** (*n*) (1) a set of instructions (p.48) arranged in sequence, prepared for the direction of a digital computer to perform the necessary operations for the solution of a problem or the completion of a task. A program is usually developed from a flowchart (p.60) or a decision table (p.62). (2) to prepare a suitable set of instructions for a computer. **program** (*v*).

**blue-ribbon program** a handwritten program (↑) that is checked to eliminate bugs (p.81) so that it runs successfully the first time.

**program compatibility** the ability of a program to be used on one of several different computers; the program is **compatible** with the computer.

**portability** (*n*) a property of a program (↑) which allows it to be used on more than one computer or more than one computer system. All programs in a high-level language (p.51) should theoretically be *portable*, but dialects interfere with the portability. **portable** (*adj*).

**utilities** (*n.pl*) a group of programs (↑) of general use to carry out standard or routine procedures on files (p.251) such as editing, word processing, copying files, transferring data from one device to another, text preparation. Utilities are used on any computer system. Compare user program (↓).

**package**[1] (*n*) a program which covers a wide variety of uses for solving a general problem, e.g. payroll and taxes. It is usually less efficient than an applications program (↓) but is immediately available and cheaper than an applications program (↓). The main disadvantage of a generalized approach to programming used in a package is that the approach considers a general problem and may not be one that considers a user's specific needs, particularly in payroll or inventory control.

**user program** a program designed for a particular user, or specifically written by him, for a particular purpose. *Contrast utilities* (↑).

**applications program** a program written to solve a specific problem with suitable data processing techniques, e.g. a payroll for a particular firm. A distinction exists between computational applications, requiring mainly numerical computing capacity, and data processing applications, requiring mainly data handling and word processing capacity. *Contrast package* (↑).

| | | |
|---|---|---|
| 5 | REM | to solve equation AX ** 2 + BX + C = O |
| 10 | INPUT | A: INPUT B: INPUT C |
| 20 | LET | D = (B * B) — (4 * A * C) |
| 30 | IF | D < O then 80 |
| 40 | LET | F = SQR(D) |
| 50 | LET | P = (– B + F)/(2 * A) |
| 60 | LET | Q = (– B – F)/(2 * A) |
| 70 | PRINT | P, Q: GO TO 90 |
| 80 | PRINT | "imaginary roots" |
| 90 | STOP | |

**example of a program in BASIC**

| | | |
|---|---|---|
| C | TO SOLVE | equation AX ** 2 + BX + C = ( |
| | READ | (3, 1) A, B, C |
| | FORMAT | (3F8.5) |
| 1 | | B2M4AC = B * B – 4. * A * C |
| | IF | (B2M4AC.LT.O) GO TO 2 |
| | | B2M4AC = SQRT (B2M4AC) |
| | | A2 = 2. * A |
| | | R1 = (–B + B2M4AC)/A2 |
| | | R2 = (– B – B2M4AC)/A2 |
| | WRITE | (6, 3) R1, R2 |
| 3 | FORMAT | (10 HOROOTS ARE, 2F 8.5 |
| | STOP | |
| 2 | WRITE | (6, 4) |
| 4 | FORMAT | (17 HOIMAGINARY ROOT |
| | STOP | |
| | END | |

**example of a progr in FORTRAN**

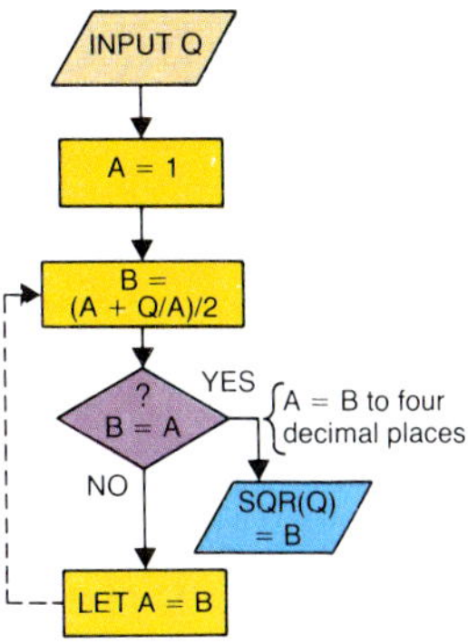


**flowchart for SQR**

Required algorithm, for sequence; $B = \frac{1}{2}(A + \frac{Q}{A})$;

$C = \frac{1}{2}(B + \frac{Q}{B})$; . . .

$E = \frac{1}{2}(E + \frac{Q}{A})$

$\therefore 2E^2 = E + Q \therefore E = \sqrt{Q}$

**applications package** programs (↑) or subroutines to solve particular applications in science, business, etc., e.g. square root subroutines.

**software** (*n*) the programs (↑) including operating systems, procedures, utilities (↑), applications programs (↑), packages (↑) written for a computer system and supplied by the hardware (p.12) manufacturer, or other firms. It includes the various programming aids supplied by the manufacturer. It does not include programs written by the user.

**applications software** available applications programs.

**custom software** applications programs (↑).

**software library** the software (↑) provided by a manufacturer for use with his hardware (p.12). It includes high-level languages, compiler and assembler programs, loaders, utilities (↑) and packages (↑).

**skeleton program** a set of instructions (p.48) parts of which have to be completed when the final program (↑) is generated, e.g. adding variables.

**generator** (*n*) a routine (p.61) that permits a computer to write a specific program (↑) for an operation, starting from a skeleton program (↑) and supplying details or parameters (p.67) of the particular operation. The generator starts with source language (p.53) statements and compiles the program automatically. Generators are of specific types, e.g. a sort generator. **generate** (*v*).

**program generator** synonymous with generator (↑).

**generator program** synonymous with generator (↑).

**checkpoint** (*n*) a point in a program (↑) at which it is possible to store sufficient data and calculated results, so that computation can be restarted from that point. *See checkpoint dump* (↓).

**checkpoint dump** the information recorded at a checkpoint (↑), e.g. input/output records, the contents of important memory locations such as loop counters, instructions register, the address and value of variables. This is useful for a restart (↓).

**restart** (*v*) to continue the execution of a program after an error message (p.20) or a machine fault has disrupted a program. Restarting usually commences at a checkpoint (↑). The use of a restart procedure eliminates a re-run of the whole program, thus saving time when there is a heavy machine schedule. **restart** (*n*).

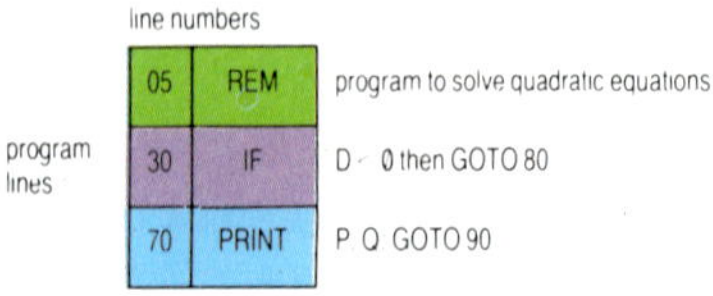


line 05: narrative: comment ignored by computer
line 70: two instructions in one line
D is a variable

**program in BASIC**

**ANSI** (*acro*) American National Standards Institute. An organization that publishes standards for the computer industry; it includes standardization of certain high-level language reserved words (p.48).

**program line** a statement in a program (p.64) usually consisting of one instruction (p.48) but several instructions can be placed on one line.

**program line number** a number identifying a program line (↑). Some high-level languages (p.51) require every line to be numbered sequentially, but not necessarily consecutively. Other languages number lines only if they are to be referenced later in the program.

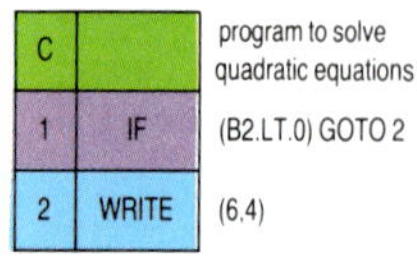


C denotes narrative; comment ignored
B2 is a variable

**program in FORTRAN**

Instructions stored in consecutive locations in memory; machine code used:

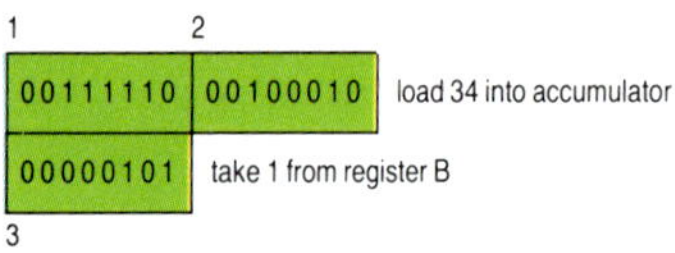


Two operations to be performed by a computer (example from Z80 processor)

**program instructions**

**program instruction** sets of characters defining an operation to be executed by a computer. Types include: mathematical, executive, assignment, halt, loop, jump, macroinstructions, microinstructions, pseudoinstructions.

**program register** a register in the control unit (p.160) of the central processing unit. It stores the address of the current program instruction, such instruction being a microinstruction (p.51), hence it controls computer operation.

**narrative** (*n*) explanations written with program instructions (↑); ignored by the computer.

**comment** (*n*) synonymous with narrative (↑).

**REM** a reserved word (p.48) in BASIC, an instruction ignored by the computer; it heads a line of comment (↑) in a program.

**variable** (*n*) any factor or quantity that can assume different values during the execution of a program run, e.g. temperature, pressure, height, cost, time, speed, acceleration.

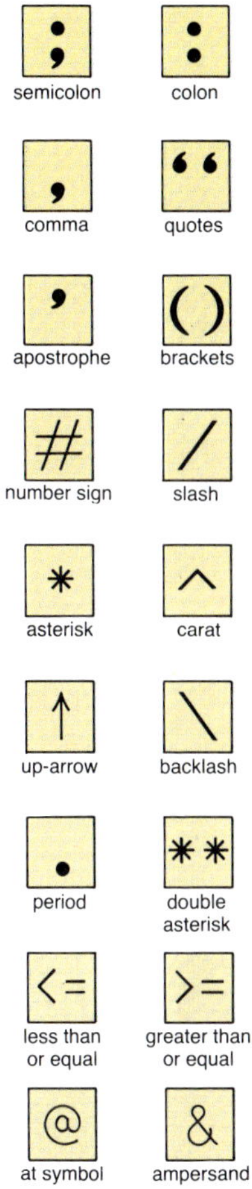


**punctuation and other symbols**

**global variable** a variable which is defined in one routine, or segment, of a program, but is used throughout the whole program.
**local variable** a variable whose use is limited to one routine, or one segment of a program.
**binary variable** a variable which has the values of 1 or 0 only.
**variable name** one or more characters assigned to a variable so that it can be referenced, or used in an algorithm (p.82).
**label** (*n*) a character, set of characters, or a symbol used to identify an item, a file (p.251), a field in an assembly language program (p.56), a record. **label** (*v*).
**tab** (*n*) (1) synonymous with label (↑). (2) abbreviation for tabulate in setting textual information in columns.
**assign** (*v*) to give a value or a name to a variable (↑) or a label (↑) to a field, file or record, etc. To reserve an input/output device for a specific purpose for the whole run of a program. *Contrast allocate* (p.172).
**initialize** (*v*) to set instructions and data at the beginning of a program, e.g. to assign initial values to variables, to state the number of cycles in a loop. The variables will change value during the program, and the instructions will be amended from their initial values. **initial** (*adj*), **initialization** (*n*).
**restore** (1) to return a register (p.149), flag (p.159), counter, switch, variable address, or other computer word to its initial value (↑). (2) synonymous with refresh (p.165).
**parameter** (*n*) a variable (↑) which can assume a range of arbitrary values in association with other variables. A quantity capable of variation within limits; e.g. the modulation parameters of amplitude, frequency and phase are quantities (or variables) alterable in value within limits.
**semicolon** used for printing instructions.
**colon** used to separate statements.
**comma** used for printing instructions.
**quotes** used with alphanumeric characters.
**inverted commas** synonymous with quotes (↑).
**apostrophe** sometimes used instead of quotes (↑).
**brackets** enclose mathematical processes.
**parentheses** synonymous with brackets (↑).
**number sign** specifies double-precision (p.33).
**slash** symbol for division.
**asterisk** symbol for multiplication.
**carat** symbol for exponentiation.

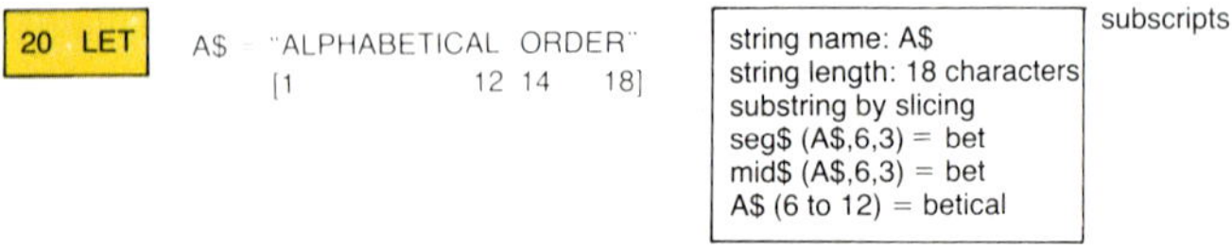


**string** (*n*) (1) a set of characters (p.37) grouped in a sequence according to a rule; e.g. a sentence in English forms a string of letters. A string is enclosed in quotes (p.67). (2) a group of items in sequence according to a rule.

**numeric string** a string (↑) containing numerals only.

**alphanumeric string** a string (↑) consisting of letters and numerals.

**empty string** a string (↑) with no characters.

**null string** synonymous with empty string (↑).

**string name** a string is declared a variable, and then given a variable name; the name is followed by $ (dollar sign), in BASIC, to show the variable is a string.

**string length** the number of characters and spaces, enclosed by quotes, in a string variable; the number of records in a string.

**string value** the result of computing the arithmetical value of a numeric string (↑); alphanumeric strings cannot be evaluated.

**slicing strings** dividing a string (↑) into sections, each of a length determined by the number of characters (p.37) or spaces in the section. Each section is under reference by a subscript (↓) indicating the numbered character in the string.

**substring** (*n*) the result of slicing a string (↑).

**string replacement** a string is sliced (↑) and a substring in the original string is replaced by a short string.

**string comparison** both numeric and alphanumeric strings are compared by using the ASCII code (p.38) for the characters (p.37). Each character in one string is compared in turn with its equivalent character in the second string. This allows numbers or alphabetical words to be sorted into numerical or alphabetical order.

**concatenation** (*n*) linking, or chaining, together, e.g. concatenation of strings, when two or more strings are joined to form one long string.

**catenate** (*v*) to arrange items in a catena (↓).

**catena** (*n*) a set of linked items forming a chained list (p.255); a string of characters (p.37).

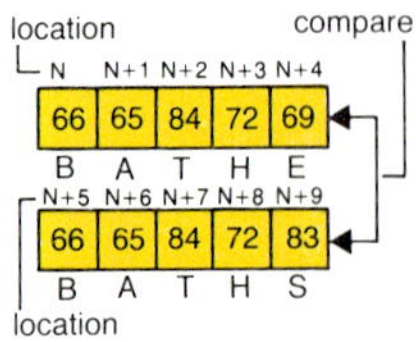


BATHE < BATHS therefore in front alphabetically

```
10 LET   B$ = "ALPHABETICAL"
20 LET   N$ = " "
30 LET   C$ = "ORDER"
40 PRINT B$, N$, C$
```

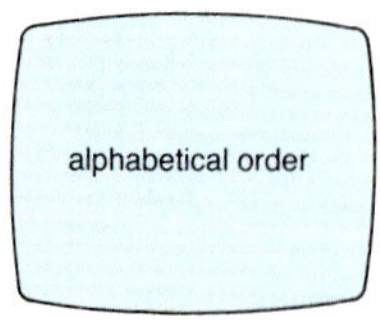


**concatenation of strings**

N$ is an empty string

**padding** (*n*) filling out a block of information; e.g. filling out a string (↑) with blank characters, dummy words, or records to fulfil a fixed length requirement.

**character fill** (*v*) to replace all data in a memory location (p.166) with a repeated specified character, e.g. usually a zero or an X. This is done to overwrite unwanted information and to indicate error conditions. *See garbage* (p.74).

**array** (*n*) a pattern of elements with the pattern having meaning and showing the relationship between individual elements. The structure of the pattern is defined by position indicators. Mathematically, an array is a matrix (↓), subject to the rules of matrix algebra. An array is arranged in columns and rows (↓).

**row** (*n*) a number of items in a line.

**column** (*n*) a number of items arranged one under the other.

**numeric array** an array (↑) with numerals, a numerical matrix (↓).

**alphanumeric array** an array (↑) with letters and numerals forming the elements.

**string array** an array with strings (↑) in the array pattern.

**array dimension** the dimension shows the number of columns, or rows, or items, or, in the case of string arrays (↑), the number of characters in any one array position. A one-dimensional array is a string of characters, i.e. one row with each character representing a column.

**two-dimensional array** (1) a numerical array with numbers arranged in rows and columns; the number of digits in any one position is variable. (2) an alphanumeric array with groups of letters arranged as a list of words; the number of characters must be specified, and cannot be exceeded, in a row.

**three-dimensional array** (1) groups of two-dimensional numeric arrays (↑). (2) a tabular grouping of an alphanumeric array (↑), with words in columns and rows; each word cannot exceed a fixed length.

**subscript** (*n*) (1) a notation (p.29) in which a numeral is written below and to the right of a character to distinguish it from other characters similarly subscripted; (2) a number used to indicate the position of an item in an array (↑).

**matrix²** (*n*) an array of numbers or quantities, subject to operations by mathematical operators or by other matrices.

**one dimensional numeric array**

A =

| | | | | |
|---|---|---|---|---|
| 21 | 4 | 562 | 31 | 6 |

A (4) = 31
(4) is a subscript

B =

| | | |
|---|---|---|
| 5 | 26 | 4 |
| 17 | 3 | 2 |
| 9 | 18 | 41 |
| 7 | 22 | 11 |

row

column

B(2,3) = 2
(2,3) is a subscript

**two-dimensional numeric array**

| | | |
|---|---|---|
| ADD | SUB | NUM |
| DEL | AC | DC |
| GO | LOD | LAB |
| R. | SET | SIN |

**three-dimensional alphanumeric array**

$$\begin{vmatrix} 2 & 4 & -6 \\ -1 & 0 & 3 \end{vmatrix}$$

**a matrix**

**straight-line coding** a computer program (p.64) with instructions that are executed sequentially without looping (↓) or using subroutines, or branching (↓).

**looping** (*n*) using a program (p.64) of a repetitive nature, *see loop program* (p.62). Either a loop counter is used for a specific number of cycles, or the program repeats until a condition is met and a jump instruction (p.58) follow. **loop** (*n*).

**loop increment** the addition of 1 to a loop counter each time a cycle is repeated.

**loop step** the value of an increment in looping (↑); it can be set at any value within the range of the number of cycles; the default value is 1, e.g. for 20 cycles, step 2, the loop repeats 10 times.

**preset** (*v*) to put the contents of a memory location at an initial value. To assign the initial control value of a loop, e.g. N=5 TO 15 where N is preset to 5.

**main routine** the set of instructions which form the basis of a program to be used by a computer in processing data or computing results.

**master routine** a routine (p.61) in a program which includes one or more subroutines (↓) under control of the master routine.

**master control routine** (1) a routine (p.61) that controls the linking (↓) of subroutines; (↓) when a program consists of several subroutines; (2) synonymous with master routine (↑).

**subroutine** (*n*) a routine (p.61) which carries out well-defined mathematical or logical operations and is called (↓) into action on the various occasions when the particular operation is needed; i.e. it is used several times by the master routine (↑) during execution of the program.

**closed subroutine** a subroutine (↑) to which control is transferred from a master routine (↑), and which returns control to the master routine on its conclusion. It requires, as one of its parameters (p.67) a link (↓) with the master routine.

**open subroutine** a subroutine (↑) which is inserted into a main routine (↑) when required instead of being called by a calling sequence (↓).

**calling sequence** the sequence of machine code (p.38) to call a specific subroutine (↑).

**link** (*n*) the address in a branch instruction (p.72) to pass control to the instruction in that address in another part

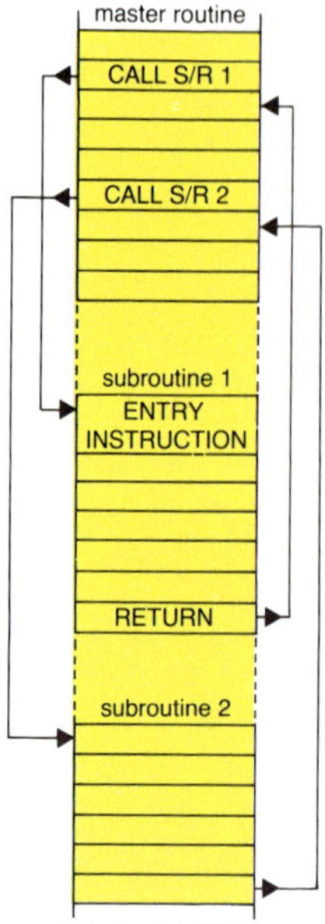

closed subroutine

of the program. Specifically the address in the master routine (↑) to which control passes when the program exits from a closed subroutine (↑).

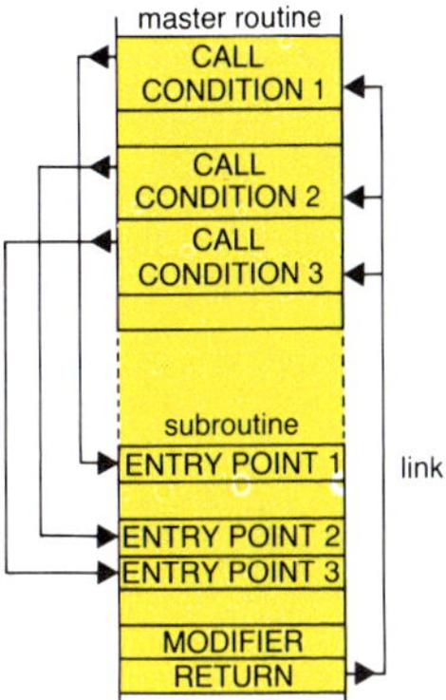


**entry points**

**entry instruction** (1) the first instruction in a subroutine (↑) or program, which is to be obeyed; (2) the instruction at an entry point (p.61).

**entry condition** a specific condition which must be met before passing control to an entry point (p.61).

**modifier** (*n*) a number or word used to alter an address, or instruction, by arithmetic or logical operations. The modifier causes the execution of a different instruction or it directs to a different address, from the original item. The same location in a program, when successively modified, can thus carry out different operations or select different operands (p.40). **modify** (*v*), **modification** (*n*).

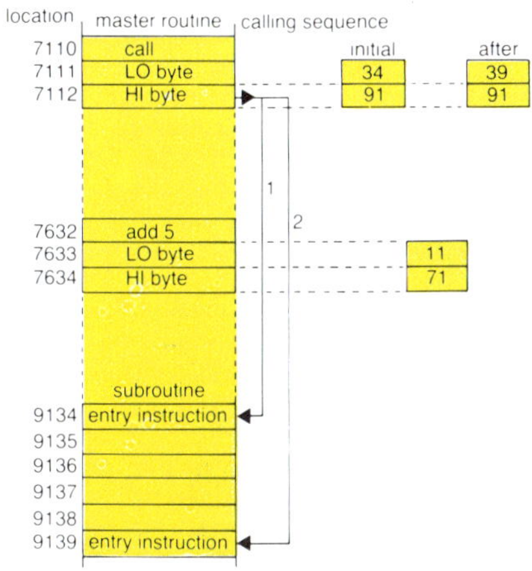


**modifier**

**program modification** the use of a modifier (↑) in a program to alter addresses or instructions.

**master control program** a program which controls the operation of a computer system, limiting intervention by a human operator. The program links subroutines (↑), calls program segments, controls input/output operations, allocates memory for areas of information.

**jump instruction**[2] an instruction (p.48) causing a jump (p.58) in a program to a location other than in the program sequence. It does not use a relative addressing (p.169) mode.

**branch** (*n*) (1) synonymous with jump (p.58); (2) a part of a program not in sequential order; a decision instruction (p.48) in conditional branching, directs control to a new location which can be referenced by any method of addressing. Unconditional branching has no decision to be met. **branch** (*v*).

**branch instruction** an instruction which causes a branch (↑) dependent on a condition being met, unless it is an unconditional branch; the condition is arithmetic or logical, or depends on the state of an indicator (↓).

**discrimination instruction** synonymous with branch instruction (↑).

**control transfer instruction** branch instruction (↑).

**branchpoint** a point in a routine (p.61) where one of two or more addresses is selected for a branch (↑) dependent on the control of the routine.

**exit** (*n*) (1) the last instruction in a routine (p.61); generally a branch instruction (↑) returning control to the master routine or jumping to another segment of the program. (2) the condition for halting a loop routine. **exit** (*v*).

**indicator** (*n*) a signal, or a device such as a register, set by conditions which are controlled by a program. The indicator is tested by an instruction and the result used to initiate subsequent actions; for example, if a process results in a negative number, the indicator is set to −1; on testing, a branch instruction is initiated.

**switch**[1] (*v*) to use a branch instruction (↑) as directed by an indicator (↑). Control can jump to one of a number of locations depending on the setting of the indicator. **switching** (*n*).

**multiple branching** the selection, by the process of switching (↑), of one of a number of addresses of instructions for subsequent control.

**halt**[2] (*n*) the condition of a computer ceasing to operate because of a halt instruction, the ending of a program sequence, an interrupt (p.224) or a hang-up (↓). After a halt, a program can be continued, unless it is a drop-dead halt (↓). **halt** (*v*).

**drop-dead halt** a halt from which a program cannot be continued. It can be a deliberate instruction, or the result of a logical error in programming, e.g. division by 0.

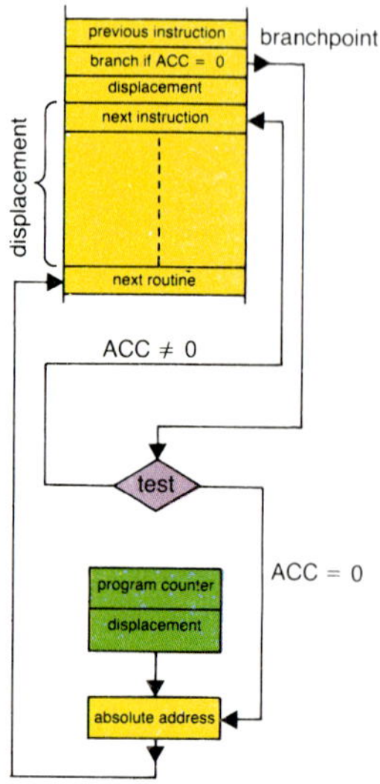


**branch instruction**

**dead halt** synonymous with drop-dead halt (↑).

**hang-up** an unexpected halt (↑) caused by the CPU (p.146) trying to execute an illegal operation (p.162), escape from a closed loop, or use of a non-existent machine code.

**force** (*v*) to intervene in the execution of a program, when the program has halted (↑) because of an error condition, by transferring control to another segment of the program. This is usually done by a branch instruction, either to continue with the program or to force the end of the run.

**default option** an option taken by a computer if no value is given, or decision met; e.g. the default value of a step in a loop is 1.

| decimal | binary | mnemonic | interpretation |
| --- | --- | --- | --- |
| 0 | 0000 0000 | NULL | idle |
| 1 | 0000 0001 | SOM | start of message |
| 2 | 0000 0010 | EOA | end of address |
| 3 | 0000 0011 | EOM | end of message |
| 4 | 0000 0100 | EOT | end of transmission |
| 5 | 0000 0101 | WRU | who are you? |
| 6 | 0000 0110 | RU | are you . . .? |
| 7 | 0000 0111 | BELL | ring bell |
| 9 | 0000 1001 | HT | horizontal tabulation |
| 10 | 0000 1010 | LF | line feed |
| 12 | 0000 1100 | FF | form feed |
| 13 | 0000 1101 | CR | carriage return |
| 21 | 0001 0101 | ERR | error |
| 22 | 0001 0110 | SYNC | synchronous idle |
| 124 | 0111 1100 | ACK | acknowledge |

**control characters: some ASCII codes**

**control character** a character (p.37) which initiates, modifies, or halts a process, or a control function, e.g. starting or stopping actions on a peripheral device (p.13) such as the feed on a magnetic tape unit. It does not affect action on data such as the actual printing, but it does control the paper feed.

**operand**[3] (*n*) the item in a statement on which an operation is carried out by an operator. For example, the number of cycles in a loop is an operand of the iterative operation; the argument (p.83) of a mathematical function is an operand.

**numeric operand** an operand consisting of numerals only.

**alphanumeric operand** an operand (↑) with both numerals and letters, e.g. a string (p.68) can be an operand.

**garbage** (*n*) unwanted or meaningless information, stored in memory (p.165). It may be unwanted because it has been left in memory from a previous job. It may be meaningless because of input errors or program errors. *See character fill* (p.69).

**hash** (*n*) (1) each data item to be stored in memory is given a unique location by means of a hashing algorithm. A good hashing algorithm will spread the data evenly over available memory and allow efficient retrieval. (2) synonymous with garbage (↑).

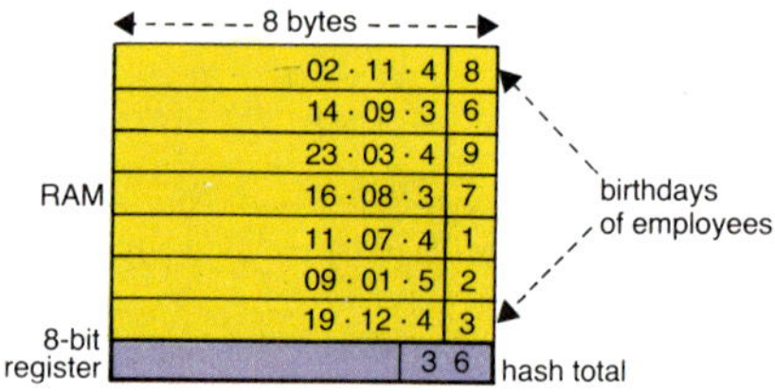


**garbage-in garbage-out** the principle that an input of meaningless information produces an output of meaningless information, i.e. garbage.

**GIGO** (*acro*) Garbage In Garbage Out (↑).

**garbage collection** the removal of unwanted data from memory to make space for new data; the rearrangement of data in memory to improve retrieval.

**gibberish** (*n*) meaningless information, synonymous with hash (↑).

**gibberish total** an addition of specified digits in an area of a file (p.251) where the digits have no meaning as far as information is concerned. The total constitutes a check that all items have been entered, or transferred correctly, during an operation. For example, the last digit of a birth date of all employees could be added to form a gibberish total, to check that all employees have been recorded in a file. Also called hash total.

**program step** one instruction or command in a sequence of instructions; a single operation with the complexity depending on the language level.

**program module** a sequence of instructions forming a unit for an assembler (p.53), a compiler (p.54), a translator (p.54), or a loader (p.78); e.g. a program line in a high-level language is a unit for a translator.

**program segment** *see segment* (p.61). Types of segments include: declaration statements; termination statements; executable statements; directing control between segments; defining variables and constants.

**program run** the execution of a program by a computer; the computer is in run mode or execute mode.

**throughput** (*n*) the total amount of data processed, or passed along a communications channel (p.233) in a specific time. Throughput can be measured for a problem, a program, or a program segment (↑). The speed of throughput can vary from one computer, or device, to another.

**library** (*n*) a collection of programs, standard routines and data files, generally written with symbolic addresses (p.56). **librarian** (*n*).

**library subroutine** a subroutine in a library (↑).

**library tape** a magnetic tape (p.216) storing standard routines, part of a library (↑).

**library track** a track on a magnetic tape or disk (p.213) which stores permanent reference data.

**microcomputer program library** a typical library (↑) collection includes: assembler, translator, keyboard input routine, BCD and binary interconversion, binary arithmetic routines, logic subroutines, loader, control routines for magnetic tape, a DAC, a subroutine for driving.

**multiprogramming** a type of programming designed to keep the central processing unit (p.146) at work as much as possible. Peripheral devices (p.13) operate at much slower speeds than the CPU in processing information. Several programs are run at the same time, so while one program is being processed by the CPU, a second program is taking data from a disk, a third is printing on a line printer; the CPU is thus idle for less time.

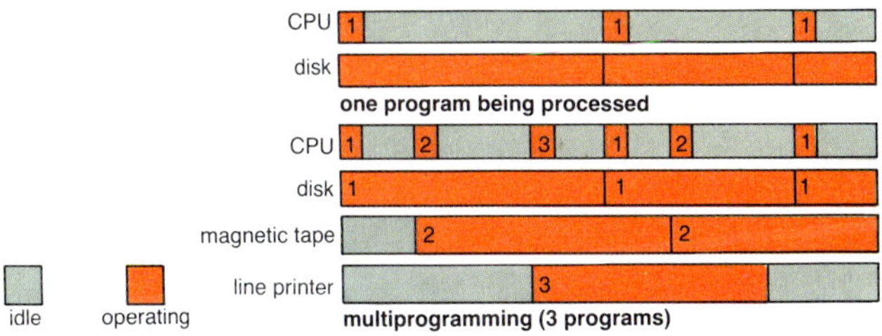

**housekeeping** (*n*) those routines (p.61) which are necessary for the running of a program but are not concerned with the solving of a problem. For example: defining constants; setting up loop counters; initializing (p.67) variables; garbage collection (p.74); assigning names or labels; defining control character (p.73). *Contrast loop computing functions* (p.62).

**menu-driven program** a program which displays on a VDU (p.10) the choice of branching (p.72) at specific points in the program. The operator can then select the next branch instruction manually.

**program storage** the area of RAM (p.175) which is reserved for the storage of programs, routines and subroutines. Protective devices are used in many systems to prevent the accidental alteration of the contents of this area. *See PSU* (↓).

**program storage unit chip** a silicon chip (p.136) used to store programs and certain data constants. The chip can interface (p.219) directly with the central processing unit and may also contain the necessary registers and control units to execute the program such as a program counter (p.153), stack register, interrupt control unit.

**PSU** (*abbr*) Program Storage Unit chip (↑).

**dumping** (*v*) copying the contents of a particular area of RAM (p.175) into a backing store (p.178). This procedure is carried out usually during long runs of computing. *See checkpoint dump* (p.65).

**overlay** (*n*) a technique used when the storage requirements are greater than the capacity of RAM (p.175). The different sections of a program, including relevant data, are held in a backing store (p.178) and read into the program storage (↑) area when each section is needed. At the end of the program run, the program storage area has been used several times, each overlay section being stored at different times.

**overlay system**

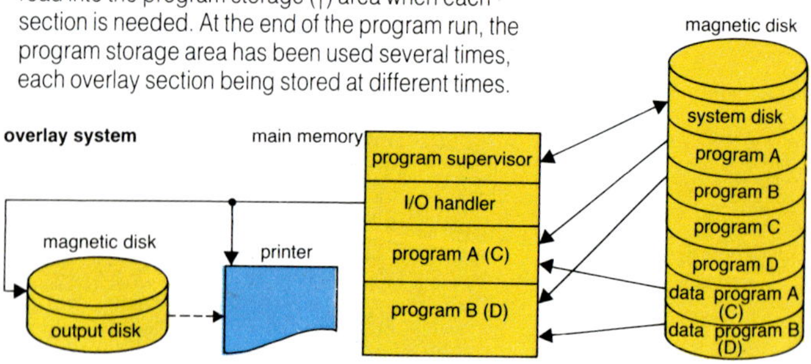

**overlay region** an area in RAM (p.175), where overlay (↑) sections are temporarily stored.

**overlay tree** a graphic diagram showing the relationship of overlay (↑) sections and how they are arranged to use the overlay region (↑) at different times.

**program storage, word determination** all instructions and data are stored in machine code (p.38) and binary code, and hence it is not possible to say whether a particular byte stores an instruction or data. The logical sequence of the computer's program is solely responsible for the correct determination of the meaning of any one byte or word.

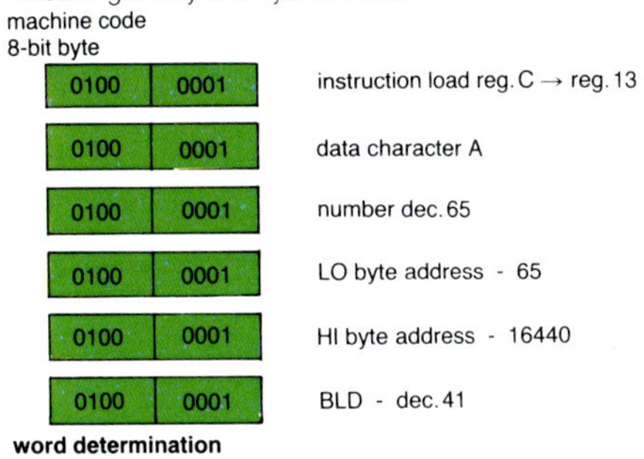


**micro/macro program** an instruction set of macroinstructions (p.51) suited to a particular problem is defined by the programmer. These instructions are included in a high-level language program providing increased speed of operation but needing more complicated programming.

**absolute code** program instructions written in machine code (p.38) using absolute addresses (p.167). Such instructions do not need compiling or assembling, but can be executed directly by a CPU (p.146).

**control program** a sequence of instructions which processes and controls other sets of machine coded (p.38) instructions. It contains many routines for operating input/output devices, handling interrupts from terminals, loading other routines, etc.

**control sequence** in most computers, the sequence of a control program (↑) is consecutive, except for jump instructions.

**control sequencer** a microprogram counter pointing to the microinstruction (p.51) to be executed.

**loader** (*n*) a program, stored in ROM (p.173) that loads a string of bytes from an off-line memory or backing store (p.178) into an input device. It makes a parity check (p.39) on each byte, checks that each word is a valid instruction and converts all addresses to absolute addresses (p.167).
**initial program loader** a routine, stored in RAM, which initiates the procedure of a loader (↑).
**IPL** (*abbr*) Initial Program Loader (↑).
**initial instructions** a routine with the same action as an IPL (↑).
**bootstrap loader** a short routine, held in ROM (p.173), used instead of a loader (↑). Its function is to enter programs into RAM (p.175) from a keyboard or other input device. It contains as few instructions as possible.

flowchart example of a bootstrap loader

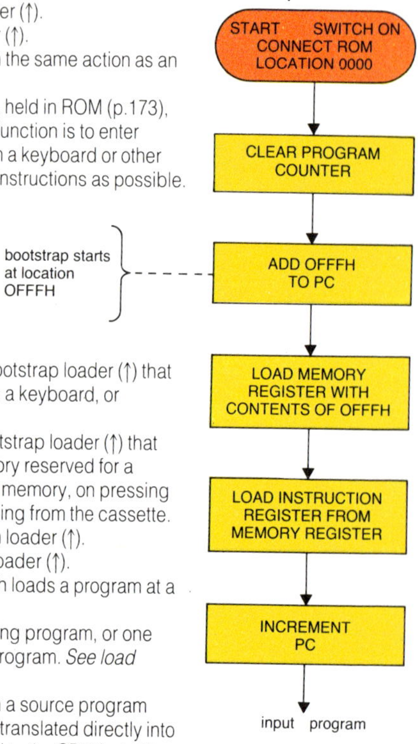


**automatic bootstrap loader** a bootstrap loader (↑) that requires no manual operation on a keyboard, or console, to bring it into action.
**cassette bootstrap loader** a bootstrap loader (↑) that locates the first address in memory reserved for a program, by testing the whole of memory, on pressing the LOAD key. It then initiates loading from the cassette.
**loading routine** synonymous with loader (↑).
**load program** synonymous with loader (↑).
**absolute loader** a loader (↑) which loads a program at a specified address.
**stand-alone program** a self-loading program, or one loaded by another self-loading program. *See load program* (↑).
**load and go** an operation in which a source program (p.53) in a low-level language, is translated directly into machine code (p.38) and passed to the CPU (p.146). There is no other process between loading and execution of the program.
**resident routine** any routine held permanently in memory, that is in ROM (p.173), e.g. a loader (↑), a monitor routine (↓).
**resident program** synonymous with resident routine (↑).

**normal range** a stated range (p.28) of numeric results expected in a computation or in data. Any results outside this range are queried by an error message; e.g. days of the month must be in the range 1–31.

| segment | normal range | error range |
|---|---|---|
| DD | 1 to 31 | >31 |
| MM | 1 to 12 | >12 |
| YY | 24 to 64 | <24 or >64* |

*for age range 20 to 60 in 1984

**example of range of numeric data**

**error range** a stated range (p.28) of values for an item of data, or results from a computation, which cause an error message. The opposite of normal range (↑).
**balanced error** the condition of all errors in an error range (↑) having an equal probability and the average value being equal to zero. *See bias* (↓).
**bias**[1] (*n*) an error range (↑) in which the average value is not zero. *See balanced error* (↑).
**validity check** a check on an error range (↑) to eliminate invalid results.
**diagnostic routine** a routine (p.61) designed to trace coding errors in programs and data, or malfunctions in hardware (p.12) or an operator error.
**diagnostic program** synonymous with diagnostic routine (↑).
**diagnostic test** using a diagnostic routine (↑) while running a machine program to locate malfunctions and potential malfunctions.
**monitor**[1] (*n*) a hardware device (p.12) which examines status in a program to identify error conditions and malfunctions, and verifies instructions, including those to I/O devices.
**monitor routine** a routine (p.61) which checks for error conditions or bugs (p.81) in a program, e.g. check for overflow, accessing prohibited areas of memory, no exit from a loop. It attempts to diagnose and to correct an error; it is part of software (p.65).
**program test** a sample problem, of the same type as the problem to be solved, and with a known result, is run using the program. This allows debugging (p.81) of the program, and a check to be made on the time of execution and the compatability of the program.

**breakpoint** (*n*) a specific point in a program, indicated by a flag or symbol (↓), at which the program may be interrupted for checking. A monitor routine (p.79), or a visual display on a screen, is used, and from the result the program can be modified or corrected. After the interruption, the program returns to the next consecutive instruction and the normal sequence of program instructions is followed.

**breakpoint instruction** a program instruction, put at a breakpoint (↑). It transfers control from the program to a monitor routine, used in a debugging (↓) operation, or it allows other action to be taken, directed by an operator from a console.

**breakpoint halt** the same as breakpoint instruction (↑).

**breakpoint symbol** a symbol included in an instruction to signal a breakpoint (↑).

**leap-frog test** a test designed to discover malfunctions in a computer. A program carries out a series of arithmetical and logical operations on data in a group of locations in memory (p.165). The program and data are then transferred to another group of locations, and the correctness of the transfer is checked; the operations are repeated. A succession of transfers, followed by repeating the operations, is performed until all memory locations have been tested.

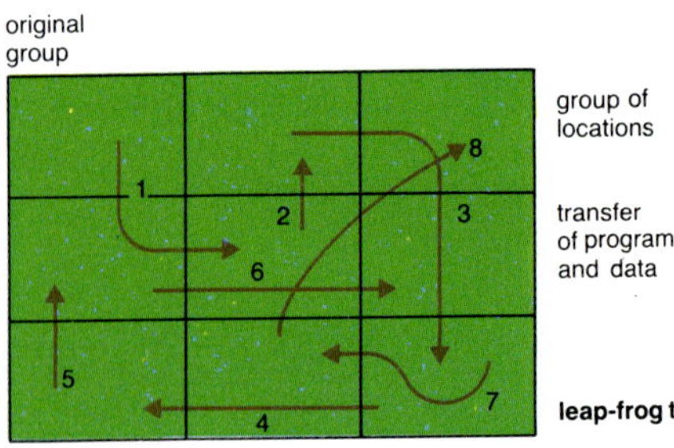


**leap-frog test**

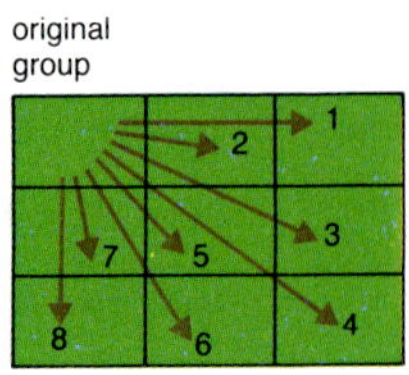


**crippled leap-frog test**

**crippled leap-frog test** a leap-frog test (↑) in which the original program and data remain in the same group of locations, and are successively transferred to other groups of locations for checking. It repeats the test from the original group of locations only.

**TRACE program** a diagnostic routine which instructs the CPU (p.146) to print out the line numbers as each line is executed in a program, together with the results of the instruction. The usual statement in BASIC is TRACE ON to start the procedure and TRACE OFF to end it.

**bug** (*n*) an error, mistake, or a defect in a program; any fault in a computer or systems circuit causing a malfunction. Bugs are detected through diagnostic routines, and program tests (p.79) and can then be eliminated, although this may cause part of a program to be rewritten.

**debugging** (*n*) the removal of bugs (↑) from a program. **debug** (*v*).

**patch** (*n*) a sequence of instructions added to a program by using an unconditional jump (p.58) and then a return to the program. The patch can be used to correct a program, alter a routine, check a routine, or to substitute a program segment. **patch** (*v*).

**bug patch** a patch (↑) used to eliminate a bug (↑). Such patches are recorded, and if they become numerous, they are incorporated in the program and the program is re-assembled.

**erase** (*v*) to remove data from a memory location (p.166) and replace with machine code representing null data. **erasure** (*n*).

**rubout** (*v*) synonymous with erase (↑).

**ignore character** a character which is ignored in memory, i.e. a null character, or one which inhibits an action.

**erase character** synonymous with ignore character (↑).

**program editor** a routine that instructs the CPU (p.146) to locate blocks of data and to alter them; useful in amending an instruction with a bug (↑) when the instruction occurs repeatedly.

**abnormal termination** the stopping of the execution of a program before its completion owing to an error condition or machine malfunction. *See halt* (p.72).

**abend** (*n*) an error condition causing abnormal termination (↑).

**abort** (*v*) to end an activity prematurely because an operator recognizes a fault (p.20) or an error condition.

**crash** (*n*) a breakdown of a program caused by a fault (p.20) or illegal and contradictory instructions. The program cannot be rescued. Crashes are often caused by malfunction of peripheral devices (p.13). **crash** (*v*).

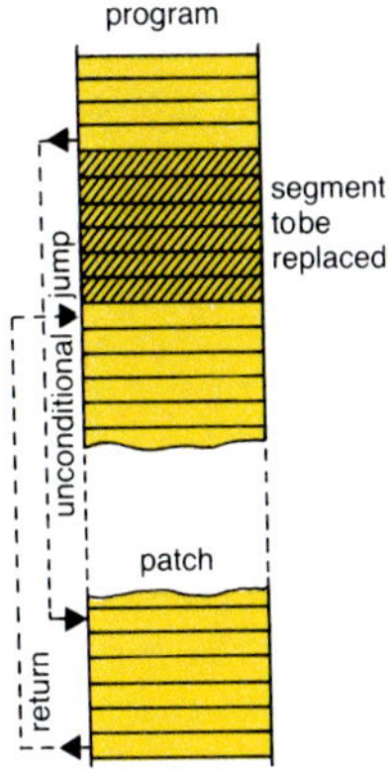


**using a patch**

**expression** (*n*) one or more symbols, which represent quantities or variables (p.66) arranged so that they show a relationship, or a value, or both. For example, $pV=rT$ is an expression where $p$ represents pressure, $V$ represents volume, $T$ represents temperature, and $r$ is a particular constant; the relationship of the quantities is shown. **express** (*v*).

**algorithm** (*n*) a solution to a problem written in a specified number of steps. Each step is written in a high-level language (p.51) using reserved words (p.48) and expressions (↑), with symbols and mathematical or logical operators (↓).

**operator**[3] (*n*) a symbol, or word, which defines an operation to be performed on an operand (p.40). Operators are arithmetic, such as +, −, etc. or logical (↓).

**logical operator** a word or symbol which represents a Boolean operation (p.85). Words used are AND, OR, NOT, etc.

**logic operator** synonymous with logical operator (↑).

**compound operator** a combination of logical operators (↑). This represents an input of several operands giving one output result.

**operation priority** arithmetic and logical operators are assigned a priority value between 1 and 15, giving an order of priority of execution. The operator with the highest value has the greatest priority. If two operators have the same priority, then the first operator in an expression (↑) is computed first.

| operator | priority | operand |
|---|---|---|
| ( ) – brackets | 12 | — |
| SIN LN EXP SQR INT | 11 | unary |
| ** ↑ > | 10 | binary |
| unary minus | 9 | unary |
| * / | 8 | binary |
| + − | 6 | binary |
| > < = > = < = | 5 | binary |
| NOT | 4 | unary |
| AND | 3 | binary |
| OR | 2 | binary |

**specimen priority values**

**iterative process** an arithmetic or logical process which repeats itself until a specified condition is met; e.g. a loop (p.62) is used for iteration.

**iterative routine** a routine performing an iterative process (↑).

**a function**

| input | instruction | output |
|---|---|---|
| x | $3 \times x + 2$ | $y = 3x + 2$ |
| independent variables | function | dependent variables |

**function²** (*n*) (1) an operation specified by an instruction; (2) a set of instructions that will relate one or more inputs to one output.

**argument** (*n*) the independent variable of a function (↑); e.g. if $y = \sin x$, then $x$ is the argument of the function, SIN.

**operand⁴** (*n*) synonymous with argument (↑). All arguments are operands, but not all operands are arguments. *See operand* (p.40).

**exponential function** (1) a typical exponential function is $3^x$, where $x$ is the argument ($x$ is an exponent. (2) a particular exponential function is $e^x$, where $e$ is called epsilon (↓) and $x$ is the argument. This is the value computed by the function EXP; it gives the result of EXP (X) where X is the argument.

**the value of EXP (x)**

$$e^x = 1 + \frac{x}{1!} + \frac{x^2}{2!} + \frac{x^3}{3!} + \frac{x^4}{4!} + \frac{x^5}{5!} + \ldots$$

**epsilon** a constant, symbol $e$, whose value is given by the series $e = 1 + 1/1! + 1/2! + 1/3! + 1/4! + \ldots$ *See factorials* (p.31).

**logarithm** if $y = a^x$, then the logarithm of $y$ to the base $a$ is $x$, that is, $\log_a y = x$. Logarithms can be calculated to any base.

**natural logarithm** a logarithm to the base $e$. If $y = e^x$, then $\log_e y = x$.

**Napierian logarithm** the same as natural logarithm (↑).

**common logarithm** a logarithm to the base 10. If $y = 10^x$, then $\log_{10} y = x$ and $x$ is the common logarithm of $y$.

**trigonometrical ratios** the trigonometrical ratios of an angle A are defined from a rotating arm of unit length forming horizontal and vertical components $x$ and $y$ respectively: $\sin A = y$; $\cos A = x$; $\tan A = y/x$.

**inverse ratio** if $\tan x = y$, then $y = \arctan x$, that is, if $y$ is the tangent of $x$, then $x$ is an angle whose tangent is $y$.

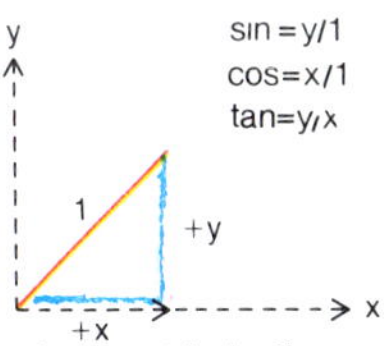


**trigonometrical ratios**

**trigonometrical function** the functions SIN, COS, TAN operate on arguments (p.83) which are angles measured in radians, degrees, or grades (p.35). The result is computed from a power series (↓) where *x* is an angle measured in radians.

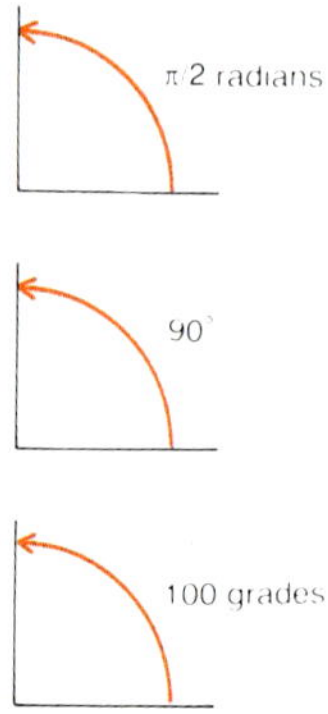


measurement of angles

**ARCTAN** many computers have only one inverse ratio (p.83) that of ARCTAN, which can be computed from a power series (↓). Other inverse ratios are calculated from the ARCTAN value.

**functions library** the set of subroutines which compute common mathematical functions (p.83) using floating point arithmetic (p.32). These are usually provided in ROM (p.173) by the manufacturer. Examples of subroutines include: exponentiation, square root, logarithms, trigonometrical and inverse functions, integer.

**series** (*n*) a set of numbers and letters form an algebraic series if there is a rule which allows the prediction of subsequent terms.

**power series** a set of terms in a series (↑) with ascending powers of a variable; e.g. $1+2x+3x^2+4x^3+\ldots$ is a power series. The numbers 1, 2, 3, etc., are the **coefficients** of the terms. The **general term** is $n\,x^{n-1}$, as replacing *n* by 1, 2, 3, etc. generates the series; the general term can be used in an iterative process (p.82).

$$\sin x = x - \frac{x^3}{3!} + \frac{x^5}{5!} - \frac{x^7}{7!} + \frac{x^9}{9!} \ldots$$

**power series for sin x**

true for all values of x so long as x is in radians

$$\cos x = 1 - \frac{x^2}{2!} + \frac{x^4}{4!} - \frac{x^6}{6!} + \frac{x^8}{8!} \ldots$$

**power series for cos x**

true for all values of x so long as x is in radians

**coefficient** *See power series* (↑).

**general term** *See power series* (↑).

**convergent** (*adj*) describes a power series (↑) in which the numerical value of a term is less than that of the preceding term. The sum of a convergent series can be found to any particular degree of accuracy.

**divergent** (*adj*) describes a power series (↑) in which the numerical value of a term is greater than that of the preceding term. Such a series has no finite sum.

**predict** (*v*) to describe future events if rules are obeyed or conditions fulfilled; e.g. if the rules of arithmetic are obeyed then any succeeding term in a sequence or series can be described from the previous terms.

**Boolean operation** an operation in which the operands have one of two values only, true or false, represented numerically by 1* and 0 respectively. A variable is not a number but represents a statement, with a value of true or false, i.e. a logic value. The operators in a Boolean operation are AND, OR and NOT and combinations of these operators.

**AND operation** a basic operation in which if two operands are true, or each has the value of 1, then the result is true, or has the value 1*. If either operand, or both, is false or has the value of 0, then the result is false or has the value 0. The Boolean statement is A AND B, or A.B; also known as conjunction or intersection. Notice that the operator is written with capital letters.

**Boolean operation: AND**

| A | B | A AND B |
|---|---|---|
| **T** | **T** | **T** |
| **T** | **F** | **F** |
| **F** | **T** | **F** |
| **F** | **F** | **F** |

**Boolean operation: OR**

| A | B | A OR B |
|---|---|---|
| **T** | **T** | **T** |
| **T** | **F** | **T** |
| **F** | **T** | **T** |
| **F** | **F** | **F** |

**OR operation** a basic operation in which if either or both of two operands is true, or has the value of 1*, then the result is true or has the value 1. If both operands are false, or have the value of 0, then the result is false or has the value 0. The Boolean statement is A OR B, or A+B. Notice that the operator is written with capital letters. Also known as inclusive-OR, either-OR.

**NOT operation** a basic operation, with one operand, which changes the operand to its inverse, or complement; e.g. NOT true=false, NOT 1*=0. The Boolean statement is NOT A, written as $\bar{A}$. The operator can be written with other operators, e.g. NOT A AND B. Also known as negation.

**Boolean operation: NOT**

| A | NOT A |
|---|---|
| **T** | **F** |
| **F** | **T** |

| A | B | A.B | A + B |
|---|---|---|---|
| 1 | 1 | 1 | 1 |
| 1 | 0 | 0 | 1 |
| 0 | 1 | 0 | 1 |
| 0 | 0 | 0 | 0 |

**truth table**

*On some machines TRUE is −1 not 1.

**Exclusive-OR operation** a logical operation in which the result is true, or value 1*, if either of two operands is true, or has the value 1. If both operands are true, or value 1, or both operands are false, or value 0, then the result is false or value 0. The Boolean statement is A EOR B, or A⊕B. The operation is derived from the three basic operations: A EOR B = (A OR B) AND NOT (A AND B). (*See* p.85). i.e. $A \oplus B = (A+B).(\bar{A}.\bar{B})$. The operation is used to compare two binary coded numbers; if both are the same number, the result is zero. Also known as anticoincidence, non-equivalence, or inequivalence operation.

**EOR operation** exclusive-OR operation (↑).

| A | B | A EOR B |
|---|---|---|
| T | T | F |
| T | F | T |
| F | T | T |
| F | F | F |

**Boolean operation: Exclusive OR**

| A | B | implications |
|---|---|---|
| T | T | T |
| T | F | T |
| F | T | F |
| F | F | T |

**Boolean operation: *implications***

**conditional implication operation** a logical operation with a result which is false, or value 0, only when operand A is false and operand B is true. For all other values of A and B, the result is true, or value 1*. Also known as inclusion, or if-then operation. The Boolean statement is: A OR NOT B, or $A+\bar{B}$. *See* p.85.

**implication operation** conditional implication operation (↑).

**NAND operation** a logical operation in which the result is true, or value 1*, if one or both operands are false, or value 0. The result is false, or value 0, if both operands are true, or value 1. The Boolean statement is A NAND B, or $\bar{A}.\bar{B}$. Also known as NOT-AND operation; it is the negated AND operation.

Boolean statement: NAND

| A | B | A NAND B |
|---|---|---|
| T | T | F |
| T | F | T |
| F | T | T |
| F | F | T |

| A | B | A⊕B | $A+\bar{B}$ | $\overline{A.B}$ |
|---|---|---|---|---|
| 1 | 1 | 0 | 1 | 0 |
| 1 | 0 | 1 | 1 | 1 |
| 0 | 1 | 1 | 0 | 1 |
| 0 | 0 | 0 | 1 | 1 |
| | | EOR | implication | NAND |

**Boolean statements**

*On some machines TRUE is −1 not 1.

| A | B | A NOR B |
|---|---|---|
| T | T | F |
| T | F | F |
| F | T | F |
| F | F | T |

**Boolean operation: NOR**

| A | B | Exclusive NOR |
|---|---|---|
| T | T | T |
| T | F | F |
| F | T | F |
| F | F | T |

**Boolean operation: Exclusive NOR**

**Boolean statements**

| A | B | $\overline{A \oplus B}$ | $\overline{A \oplus B}$ |
|---|---|---|---|
| 1 | 1 | 0 | 1 |
| 1 | 0 | 0 | 0 |
| 0 | 1 | 0 | 0 |
| 0 | 0 | 1 | 1 |
| | | NOR | Excl. NOR |

**NOR operation** a logical operation in which the result is true, or value 1*, if two operands are false, or value 0. If one or both operands are true, or value 1, then the result is false, or value 0. The Boolean statement is N NOR B, or $\overline{A+B}$.

**Exclusive-NOR operation** a logical operation in which the result is true, or value 1*, if two operands are both true or both false. If the operands are unlike, then the result is false or value 0. The Boolean statement is $\overline{A \oplus B}$. Also known as equivalence or coincidence operation.

**equivalence** a logical operator performing an Exclusive-NOR operation (↑).

**non-equivalence** a logical operator performing an Exclusive-OR operation (↑).

**inequivalence** a logical operator performing an Exclusive-OR operation (↑).

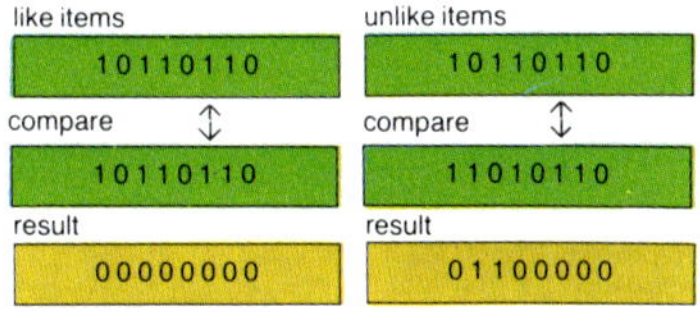


a comparator

**comparator** (*n*) a device which tests whether there is any difference between two binary-coded items. Two different items can be compared, or the same item treated in two different ways, to test the accuracy of transfer. The device uses an Exclusive-OR operation with a zero result if both items are the same.

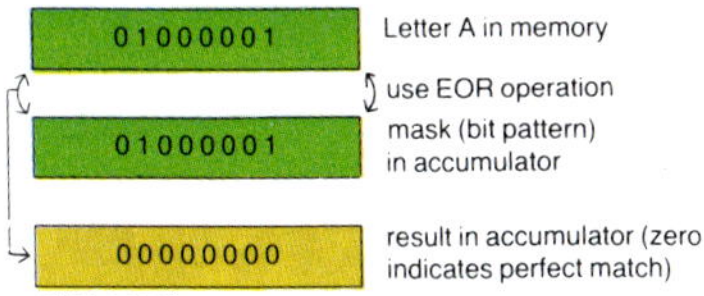


using a mask

**mask**[1] (*n*) a pattern of bits used to select a particular binary code. For example, the letter A is selected by putting the binary number 01000001 (=65d, ASCII for A) in the accumulator (p.150) as a mask and then using an EOR operation. If the two binary codes are a perfect match, the result is zero left in the accumulator. The particular binary code can be used to select processes, extract information from strings, test numbers. **masking** (*n*).

**mask register** a register (p.149) used for masking (↑).

*On some machines TRUE is −1 not 1.

stored in memory

XXXX1010 — male, <21, at university not living at home. X = no information.

**Boolean variable**

| key | 1 | 0 |
| --- | --- | --- |
| sex | M | F |
| age | ≥21 | <21 |
| university | yes | no |
| living at home | yes | no |

**Boolean variable**

**Boolean variable** a binary-coded variable in which each digit represents a true statement by 1* and a false statement by 0.

**Boolean operator** an operator performing a Boolean operation (p.85), e.g. AND, OR, NOT, NAND, NOR.

**monadic Boolean operator** an operator with only one operand, i.e. NOT.

**dyadic Boolean operator** an operator connecting two operands, e.g. AND, OR. A Boolean expression, P OR Q, has two operands connected by OR.

**inverse statement** an opposite statement to a Boolean statement; e.g. if a statement is true, the inverse is false. For example: 'Candidate 231 passed the examination' has as an inverse statement 'Candidate 231 failed the examination', the latter statement being false. The operation is **inversion**.

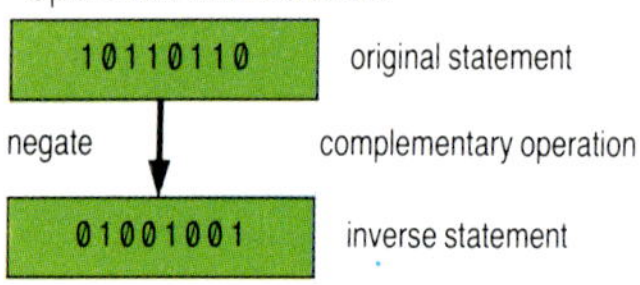


**complementary operation** an operation on a Boolean variable (↑) in which all one's are changed to zeros and all zeros changed to one's; e.g. 1010 by a complementary operation becomes 0101. AND and NAND, OR and NOR, are complementary operations.

**negate** (*v*) to carry out a complementary operation (↑).

**coincidence** (*n*) synonymous with AND operation (p.85).

**anticoincidence** (*n*) synonymous with EOR operation (p.86).

**Venn diagram** a diagram which uses circles, or ellipses, to represent true and false statements. The intersection of the circles, or their exclusion or inclusion, illustrate Boolean operations (p.85).

**universe** (*n*) all possibilities concerning a statement are the universe of that statement. In most cases this means true plus false statements, i.e. a statement and its inverse. A Venn diagram (↑) uses a rectangle to indicate a universe.

*On some machines TRUE is −1 not 1.

**Venn diagram**

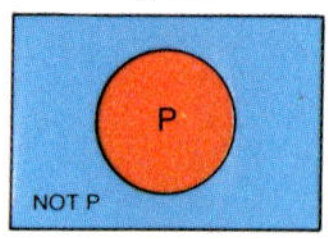


universe

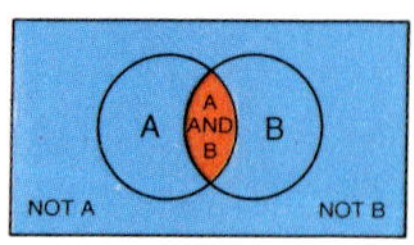


**Venn diagram for AND operation**

**truth table**

$Q = \bar{A}$ and $\bar{B}$ and $C$·
$= \bar{A}.\bar{B}.C$
(let $D = \bar{A}$ and $\bar{B}$)

I = true  O = false

| A | B | $\bar{A}$ | $\bar{B}$ | D | C | Q |
|---|---|---|---|---|---|---|
| 0 | 0 | 1 | 1 | 1 | 0 | 0 |
| 1 | 0 | 0 | 1 | 0 | 0 | 0 |
| 0 | 1 | 1 | 0 | 0 | 0 | 0 |
| 0 | 0 | 1 | 1 | 1 | 1 | 1 |
| 1 | 1 | 0 | 0 | 0 | 0 | 0 |
| 1 | 0 | 0 | 1 | 0 | 1 | 0 |
| 0 | 1 | 1 | 0 | 0 | 1 | 0 |
| 1 | 1 | 0 | 0 | 0 | 1 | 0 |

$Q = \bar{A}.\bar{B}.C$ or $\bar{A}.B.\bar{C}$ or $A.B.\bar{C}$
$= \bar{A}.\bar{B}.C + \bar{A}.B.\bar{C} + A.B.\bar{C}$

| | A | A | $\bar{A}$ | $\bar{A}$ | |
|---|---|---|---|---|---|
| B | 1 | 0 | 0 | 1 | ← $B.\bar{C}$ |
| $\bar{B}$ | 0 | 0 | 1 | 0 | ← $\bar{A}\bar{B}C$ |
| | $\bar{C}$ | C | C | $\bar{C}$ | |

**Veitch diagram for Q**

expression reduces to:
$Q = \bar{A}\bar{B}.C + B.\bar{C}$

| BC \ A | 0 | 1 | |
|---|---|---|---|
| 00 | 0 | 0 | — $\bar{A}\bar{B}C$ |
| 01 | 1 | 0 | |
| 10 | 1 | 1 | — $B.\bar{C}$ |
| 11 | 0 | 0 | |

**Karnaugh map for Q**

expression reduces to
$Q = \bar{A}\bar{B}C + B\bar{C}$

**truth table** a table using 1* to represent true and 0 to represent false for operands and results. The relationship of Boolean operators on variables to give results from combinations of operators is shown. Values of 0 and 1 for more than two variables can also be shown, giving a single result of 1 or 0. If there are *n* variables, then there are $2^n$ combinations unless some variables are described as 'don't care'.

**Veitch diagram** (1) a table of information for results from truth tables (↑) used to design Boolean circuits for logic operations; (2) a graphic technique to solve design problems for logic circuits.

**Karnaugh map** the relationship of Boolean operations to aid in the combinations of logical functions and eliminate duplication of logical operations by listing similar or alternative operations.

**de Morgan's laws** laws showing the mathematical properties of Boolean operators. They are:

$\overline{P+Q} = \bar{P}.\bar{Q}$  NOT (P OR Q) = NOT P AND NOT Q
$\overline{P.Q} = \bar{P}+\bar{Q}$  NOT (P AND Q) = NOT P OR NOT Q

**Boolean operation table** a table giving the values from the logical combination of bits (p.36) in operands; the values of 1* and 0 are interpreted as true or false.

**Boolean operation table**

AND

| | |
|---|---|
| 1100 | 1010 |
| 1010 | 1100 |
| 1000 | 1000 |

OR

| | |
|---|---|
| 1100 | 1010 |
| 1010 | 1100 |
| 1110 | 1110 |

NOT

| | |
|---|---|
| 1100 | 1010 |
| 0011 | 0101 |

*On some machines TRUE is −1 not 1.

**logic** (*n*) related to computers, logic is a mathematical treatment of formal logic using Boolean operators (p.88). It uses a set of symbols to represent operations and laws that can be translated into electrical circuits performing operations on binary-coded Boolean variables (p.88). Formal logic is a science which deals with reasoning and thought. **logical** (*adj*).

**symbolic logic** the study of formal logic (↑) using mathematical symbols and conventions, e.g. A⊕B representing A Exclusive-OR B. *See* p.86.

**logical element**[1] the simplest device which performs a Boolean operation (p.85), e.g. AND operation, OR operation, NOT operation. *See logic element* (p.000).

**logic symbol** a symbol representing a logical, i.e. Boolean, operation (p.85).

**logic diagram** a diagram with logic symbols (↑) representing logical operations on operands.

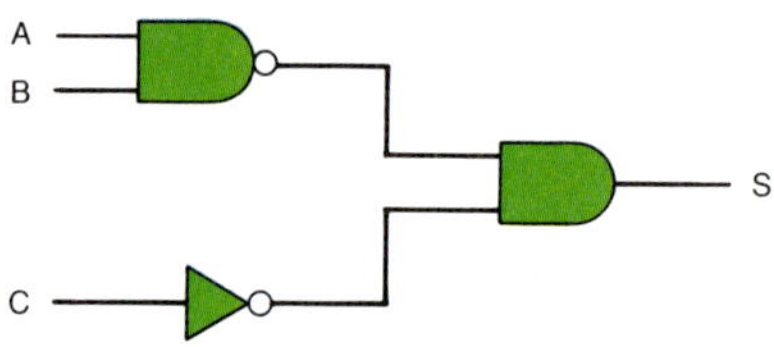


$S = (\overline{A.B}).\overline{C}$

S = (A NAND B) AND NOT C

**logic diagram**

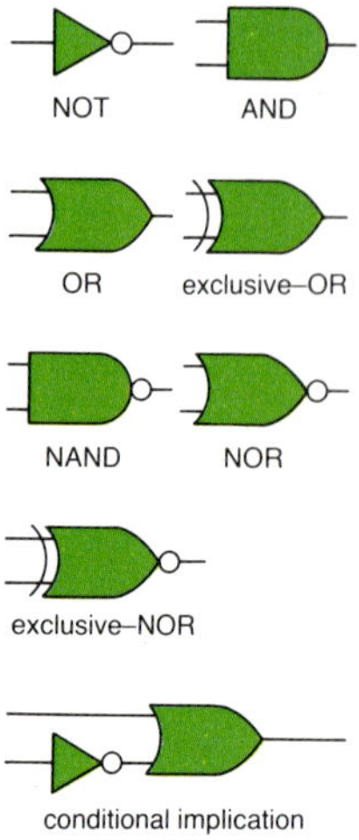


**logic symbols**

**programmed logic array** an orderly arrangement of electrical circuits for AND and OR operations which carries out the decoding of instructions and performs the steps in logical operations.

**programmable logic array** a logic array which can be programmed to perform various logical operations as in a programmed logic array (↑).

**PLA** (*abbr*) a programmed or programmable logic array (↑). PLA integrated circuits are used to replace standard ICs in order to manufacture cheaper microcomputers.

**programmable logic** the application of Boolean operations (p.85) to solve problems using methods ranging from a combination of simple logical operations to complex systems of logical operations controlling business finance and production.

**atom** (*n*) the smallest particle of an element which exhibits the properties of that element. It consists of a nucleus, positively charged, surrounded by electrons, which are negatively charged. An atom is electrically neutral, as the total negative charge of the electrons (↓) equals the total positive charge on the nucleus. The electrons are arranged in shells, and the outer electrons form bonds (↓). **atomic** (*adj*).

**atom**

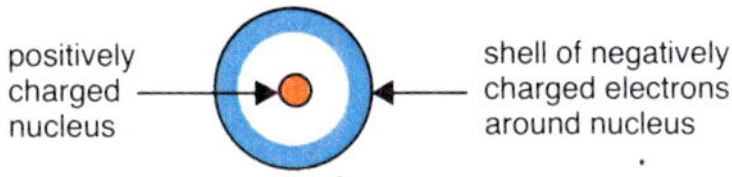


**electron** (*n*) a fundamental particle, found in all atoms (↑). It has a charge of $1.6 \times 10^{-19}$ coulomb, the smallest electric charge (p.92) that can exist. A flow of electrons constitutes an electric current (p.92). **electronic** (*adj*).

**ion** (*n*) an atom, or group of atoms, which has either lost one or more electrons to become a positive ion, or gained one or more electrons to become a negative ion. **ionic** (*adj*), **ionize** (*v*).

**bond** (*n*) a force which holds atoms (↑) or ions (↑) together. There are electrostatic bonds in which ions (↑) are held by the attraction of opposite electric charges. There are covalent bonds in which atoms share electrons, and the shared electrons form a bond.

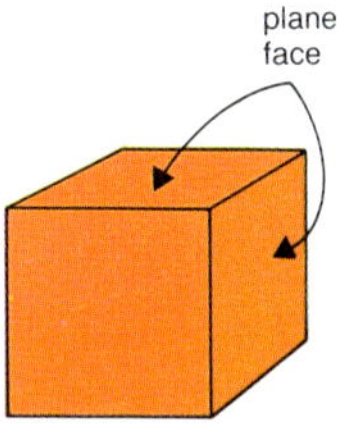


**cubic crystal of silicon**

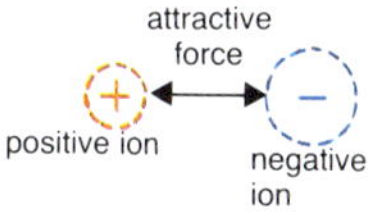


**electrostatic bond**

**covalent bond**

two electrons shared by two atoms

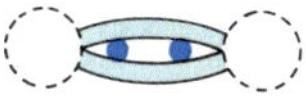

**crystal** (*n*) a solid substance with a regular shape; it has plane faces which are always at the same angle for similar sides in all crystals of the substance. **crystalline** (*adj*), **crystallize** (*v*).

**crystal lattice** a regular arrangement of atoms (↑), ions (↑) or molecules in space with a definite pattern in three dimensions. The pattern reaches to the faces of a crystal (↑) and forms its regular shape. The atoms, ions or molecules are held together by bonds (↑).

**crystal defect** a missing part of a crystal lattice, e.g. a hole which could be occupied by an electron, an ion, or an atom.

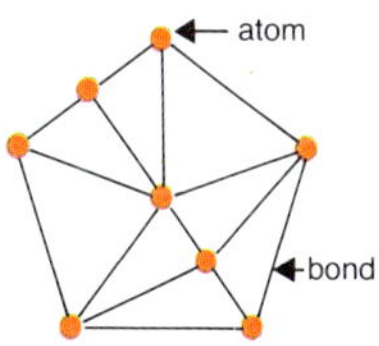


**crystal lattice**

**electric charge** a property of elementary particles, which may be of two kinds, called **positive** and **negative**. Like charges, i.e. two positive or two negative charges, repel each other; unlike charges attract each other. Electrons possess negative charge. The quantity of electric charge is measured in **coulomb**; its symbol is *Q*.

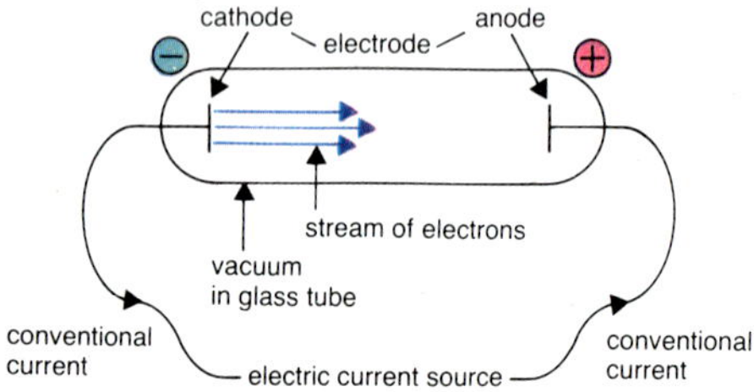


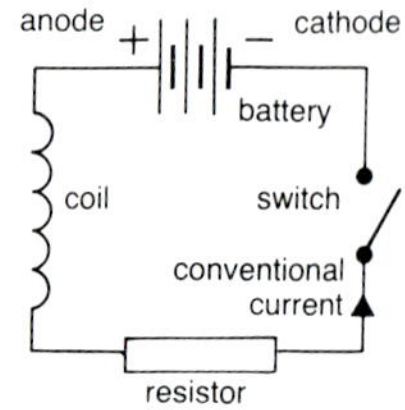


**electrical circuit**

**electric current** a flow of electric charge (↑) forms an electric current. In electrical circuits current is a flow of electrons (p.91), i.e. a flow of negative charge. Electric current is measured in **amperes**; it is the number of coulombs passing a point per second. By convention an electric current is considered to flow from the positive pole of a source to the negative pole; the flow of electrons is in the opposite direction. All electrical circuits use the convention for current. The symbol for electric current is *I*.

**electrode** (*n*) a piece of conducting material (↓) placed in a gas, solution, or molten substance, to enable an electric current to enter or leave.

**anode** (*n*) a positive electrode. Conventional current goes from it, electrons go to it. **anodic** (*adj*).

**cathode** (*n*) a negative electrode. Conventional current goes to it, electrons leave from it. **cathode** (*adj*).

**polarity** (*n*) the condition of possessing positive and negative electrodes, or poles. The polarity of an electrode is either positive or negative. **polar** (*adj*).

**conductor** (*n*) a piece of solid material that permits an electric current to pass through it; e.g. metals are good conductors. **conduct** (*v*), **conduction** (*n*).

**insulator** (*n*) any gas or solid material which does not permit an electric current to pass through it; especially any device preventing a flow of current. **insulate** (*v*).

**semiconductor** (*n*) a substance with conducting properties halfway between those of a conductor (↑) and an insulator (↑). *See* p.94.

**fixed resistor**

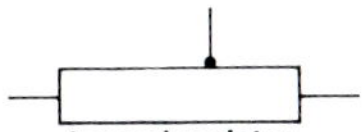

**tapped resistor**

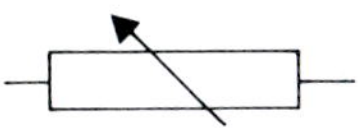

**variable resistor**

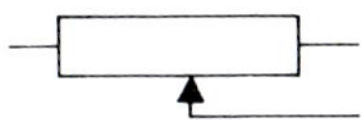

**a parallel plate capacitor**

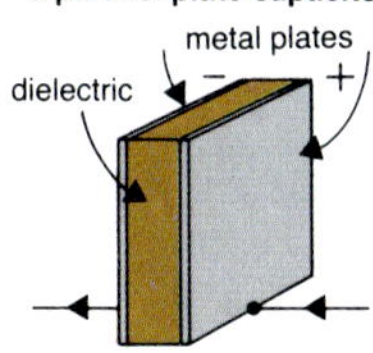


**fixed capacitor**

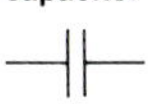

**variable capacitor**

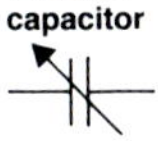

**electrolytic capacitor**

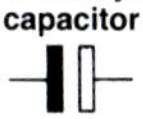

**a.c. supply**

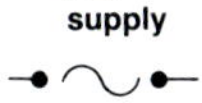

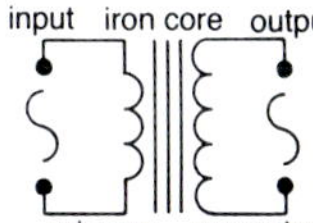


**transformer** (iron cored)

**resistance** (*n*) the flow of electrons through a material is impeded by interaction with the atoms of the material; this causes resistance to the flow of current and dissipates energy in the form of heat. Materials with a low resistance are conductors, those with a very high resistance are insulators. The symbol for resistance is *R*; resistance is measured in ohms.

**resistor** (*n*) a device, in an electrical circuit, which offers resistance to an electric current. The resistance of a metallic conductor (↑) increases with a rise in temperature.

**silicon resistor** a resistor made of silicon, a semiconductor (↑), with an impurity added to decrease resistance. Its resistance does not change appreciably with a change in temperature.

**dielectric** (*n*) an insulating (↑) material placed in a electric field. Electric current cannot pass through it, but an electric field can pass through. An electric field exists between two electrically charged bodies, e.g. two charged metal plates.

**capacitor** (*n*) a capacitor consists of two conductors separated by a dielectric (↑). The simplest capacitor is two parallel metal plates separated by air. (Air is a dielectric).

**capacitance** the property of a capacitor (↑) which allows it to store electric charge (↑). The quantity of stored charge, *Q*, is proportional to the voltage, *V*, between the conductors. The capacitance, symbol *C*, is calculated from $C = Q/V$, and is a constant for a particular capacitor. Capacitance is measured practically in microfarads.

**parasitic capacitance** unwanted capacitance in an electrical circuit caused by the nearness of conductors separated by insulators. Occurs in solid-state circuits (p.105).

$$\frac{\text{output voltage}}{\text{input voltage}} = \frac{\text{turns in secondary coil}}{\text{turns in primary coil}}$$

**voltage relationship of a transformer**

**transformer** (*n*) a device that raises or lowers the voltage of an alternating current supply.

**amplifier**[1] (*n*) an electronic circuit which increases the voltage of the electric current fed into it. *See amplifier* (p.129).

**intrinsic semiconductor** a pure substance used as a semiconductor (p.92). It contains an equal number of holes (↓) and free electrons (↓). The conductivity (↓) is low, and intrinsic semiconductors are not frequently used.

**extrinsic semiconductor** a semiconductor (p.92) with an impurity added. One part in $10^7$ of impurity increases the conductivity by a factor of 1000. Examples of extrinsic semiconductors are silicon with phosphorus or boron added or germanium with arsenic or indium added, as an impurity.

**p-type semiconductor** an extrinsic semiconductor (↑). It has a large number of holes (↓) to carry the electric current; the number of free electrons (↓) is reduced. It is a positive (p-type) semiconductor. An example is silicon with boron added as an impurity.

**n-type semiconductor** an extrinsic semiconductor (↑). It has a large number of free electrons (↓) to carry the electric current; the number of holes (↓) is reduced. It is a negative (n-type) semiconductor. An example is silicon with phosphorus added as an impurity; n-type semiconductors are used more often than p-type as free electrons provide a faster response than holes.

**p-type semiconductor** silicon with boron impurity

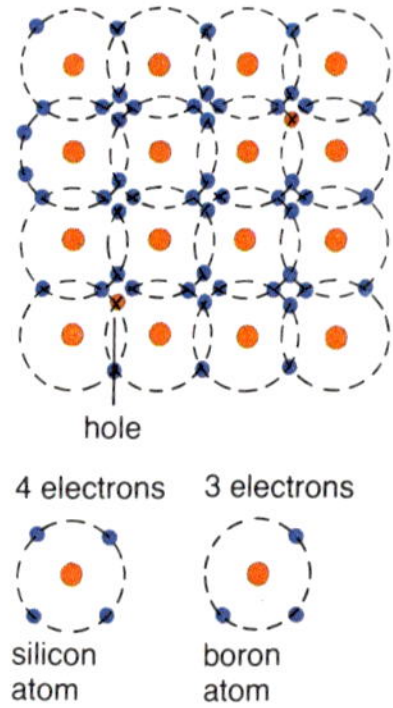


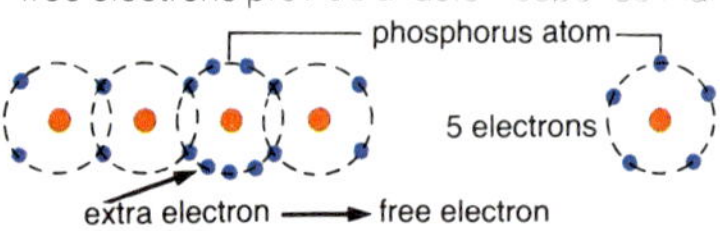


**n-type semiconductor** silicon with phosphorus impurity

**high power semiconductor** a diode, transistor, or integrated circuit using extrinsic semiconductors (↑) which is capable of dissipating more than one watt of power.

**low power semiconductor** a diode, transistor, or integrated circuit using extrinsic semiconductors (↑) which dissipates less than one watt of power.

**high frequency semiconductor** a diode, transistor, or integrated circuit using extrinsic semiconductors (↑) designed to operate at frequencies higher than 3MHz.

**low frequency semiconductor** a diode, transistor, or integrated circuit using extrinsic semiconductors designed to operate at frequencies less than 3MHz.

**semiconductor trap** a crystal defect (p.91) which is a defect in the crystal lattice capable of capturing holes (↓) or free electrons (↓).

**conductivity** the property of a material by which it conducts electric current. The higher the resistance of a device, the lower its conductivity.

**holes as mobile positive charges**

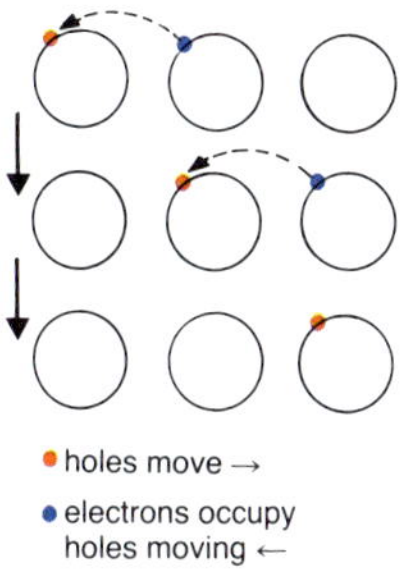


**hole** (*n*) when an electron is given sufficient energy to remove it from an atom, it becomes a free electron and leaves a hole in the structure of the crystal lattice. If an impurity is added with fewer electrons available for bonds than in the intrinsic semiconductor (↑), this also forms a hole. An electron from a nearby atom can fill the hole, creating a new hole. The movement of electrons from hole to hole in one direction is equivalent to a hole moving in the opposite direction. Holes are regarded as mobile positive charges, giving rise to hole conduction.

**free electron** an electron in a crystal lattice (p.91) which is free to move under the influence of an electric field, it forms an electric current. Free electrons are formed when an electron is given sufficient energy to be removed from an atom. If an impurity is added, with more electrons available for bonds than in the intrinsic semiconductor (↑), then this also provides free electrons.

**majority carriers** the current carriers, holes or free electrons, in a semiconductor. In n-type semiconductors they are free electrons (↑). In p-type semiconductors the majority carriers are holes (↑). *See minority carriers* (↓).

**minority carriers** in n-type and p-type semiconductors there are always a few minority carriers; they are the carriers that are not majority carriers (↑), i.e. holes in n-type, and free electrons in p-type semiconductors. The proportion of minority carriers is very small, but rises rapidly if the temperature rises. This limits the use of semiconductors depending on majority carriers for their proper function.

**semiconductor junction**

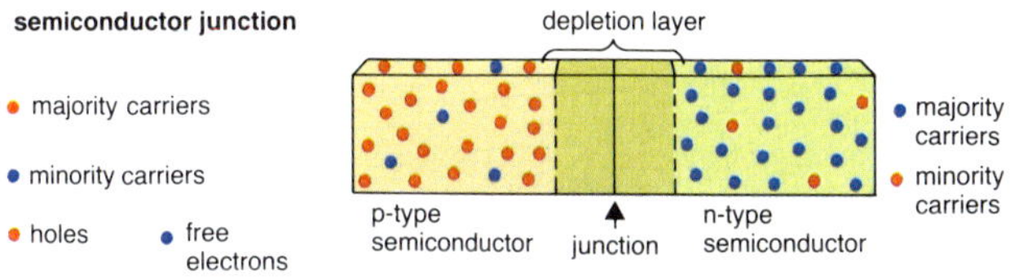


**junction** (*n*) a plane between two different types of semiconductor. Free electrons (↑) and holes (↑) diffuse across the junction and create an electric field.

**depletion layer** at a semiconductor junction (↑) free electrons diffuse from an n-type semiconductor and holes (↑) diffuse from a p-type semiconductor. A narrow depletion layer, with no holes or electrons, is formed on either side of the junction. The n-type layer is left positively charged and the p-type layer negatively charged.

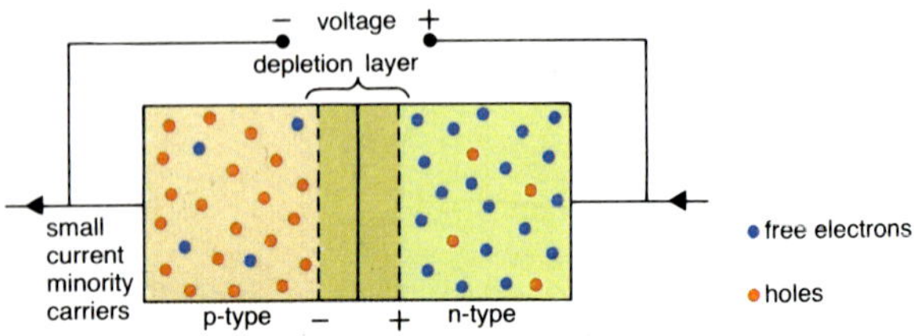


**junction diode** a semiconductor diode consisting of two types of semiconductor material joined at a junction (p.95). If a voltage is applied to the junction diode making the p-type semiconductor positive and the n-type negative, the depletion layer (p.95) is reduced and a current flows across the junction. The current carriers are free electrons from the n-type section and holes (p.95) from the p-type section, i.e. the majority carriers (p.95) in each case. If the voltage is reversed, the depletion layer is increased, and the flow of majority carriers stops. A current from the minority carriers (p.95) does flow, but it is small. The junction diode acts as a rectifier for alternating current, as current flows only when the p-type material is positive; this is called the forward direction.

**diode** (*n*) either a semiconductor diode, i.e. a junction diode (↑), or a thermionic diode.

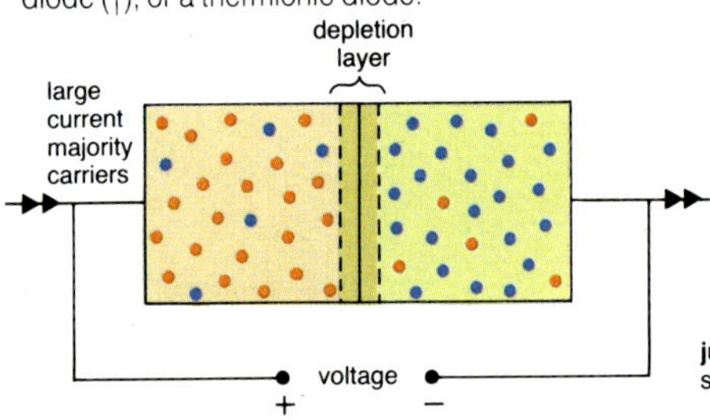


**junction diode** n-p semiconductor junction

**n-p semiconductor junction** a junction (p.95) between n-type and p-type semiconductor material.

**n-n semiconductor junction** a junction (p.95) between two n-type semiconductor materials each with different electron densities, thus having different properties.

**p-p semiconductor junction** a junction (p.95) between two p-type semiconductor materials, each with different hole densities, thus having different properties.

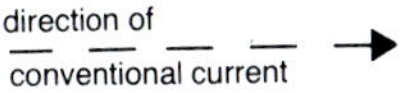


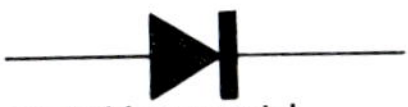
**symbol for a crystal rectifier**

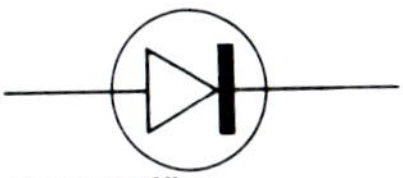
**diode rectifier**

**characteristic for a junction diode**

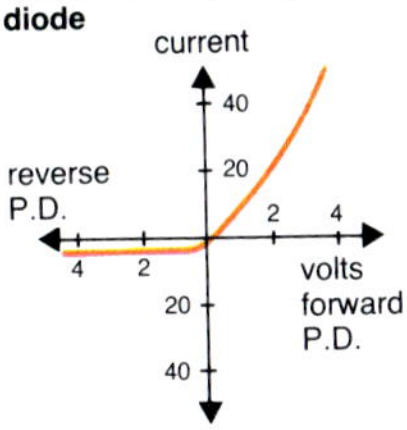


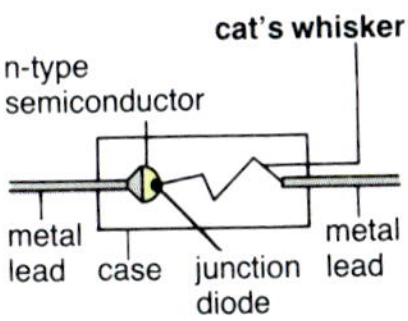

**point-contact diode**

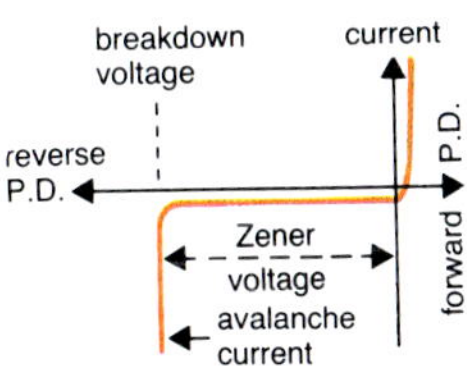

**characteristic for a Zener diode**

**symbol for a Zener diode**

**thermal agitation** the random movement of free electrons (p.95) in a conductor or semiconductor; it produces very small electric currents. When amplified by a circuit, such currents produce noise.

**mobility** (*n*) the drift of free electrons, holes, or ions, caused by applied electric fields. Mobility usually refers to the intrinsic current-carrying properties of doped semiconductors. The mobility of free electrons is 2.5 times greater than that of holes (p.95), so n-type transistors are faster than p-type.

**diode rectifier**[1] a rectifier consisting of a junction diode (↑). It converts alternating current to direct current, as it allows current to flow in one direction only. The symbol and the direction of current flow are shown in the diagram.

**characteristic curve** a graph representing the relationship between two quantities which is characteristic of a device. The most common characteristic curves show the relationship between potential difference (i.e. voltage) and current for electronic devices. Usually called characteristic.

**crystal rectifier**[1] a rectifier formed from a wafer of a semiconductor in contact with a metal.

**point-contact diode** an n-type semiconductor is in contact with a **cat's whisker** (a springy metal wire). A relatively high current is passed forming a thin layer of p-type semiconductor at the point of contact. This produces a junction diode (↑) which can be used for high-frequency alternating current.

**Zener diode** a type of silicon junction diode (↑) with a specially treated pn junction. It has a relatively low reverse breakdown voltage. When the breakdown voltage is exceeded a large current, called an **avalanche current**, passes. The diode at this point has a low resistance, and the voltage across the junction remains constant for a large range of current values. The breakdown voltage of a Zener diode can be any voltage between 2.7V and 200V. Zener diodes are used in voltage stabilization circuits.

**avalanche diode** a Zener diode (↑).

**Zener voltage** the breakdown voltage of a Zener diode (↑).

**avalanche current** *see Zener diode* (↑).

**voltage regulation diode** a Zener diode (↑) used to regulate voltage in a circuit.

**Schottky diode** a diode with a junction of metal against an n-type semiconductor. It operates at very high speed because of a very short recovery time from forward to reverse voltages.

**Schottky barrier diode** a Schottky diode (↑) used with high-frequency alternating currents for high-speed switching.

**transistor** (*n*) a device consisting of two semiconductor junction diodes (p.96) joined together to form an n-p-n or a p-n-p structure.

**emitter** (*n*) the region in a transistor (↑) from which current carriers flow, either free electrons in n-type regions or holes in p-type regions.

**collector** (*n*) the region in a transistor (↑) into which current carriers flow. It is the same type of semiconductor as the emitter (↑).

**base**[2] (*n*) a thin piece of one type of semiconductor material placed between two pieces of semiconductor material of opposite type. The voltage applied to the base controls the current flow through the transistor.

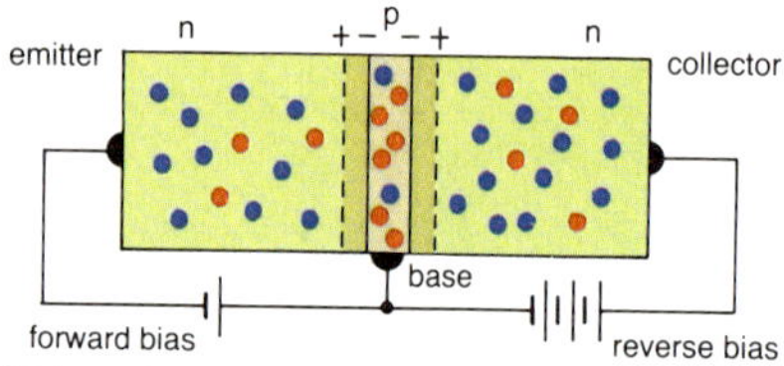


**bias on a n–p–n transistor**

**bias**[2] (*n*) a voltage applied to one semiconductor junction diode (p.96) in a transistor. If the bias reduces the depletion layer (p.95) it is called **forward bias**; if it enlarges the depletion layer, it is **reverse bias**.

**n-p-n transistor** a transistor in which the emitter (↑) and collector (↑) are n-type semiconductor material and the base is p-type. Forward bias (↑) is applied to the emitter-base junctions and reverse bias (↑) to the collector-base junctions. The forward bias is at a low voltage, with a negative voltage applied to the emitter. Current movement is almost entirely by free electrons from the emitter to the base. If the base is thin, the electrons diffuse across it. The reverse bias is at a higher voltage, with the collector made positive, and the free electrons are attracted rapidly to the collector. The emitter-base circuit has a low resistance, the base-collector circuit a high resistance. The magnitude of the

B = base
C = collector
E = emitter

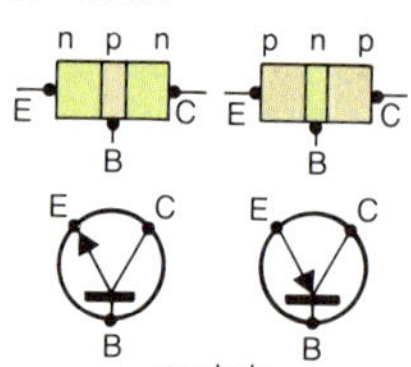


**n–p–n transistor** **p–n–p transistor**

collector current depends on the forward bias applied to the base. Most transistors are n-p-n type.

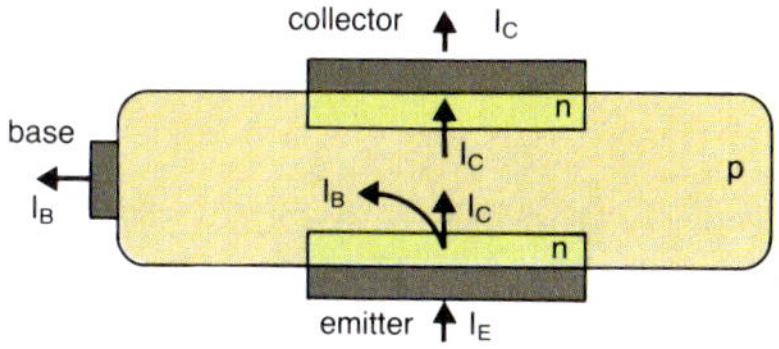


**current flow in an n–p–n transistor**

electron flow →

**p-n-p transistor** a transistor (↑) in which the emitter and collector are p-type semiconductor material and the base is n-type. Bias is applied as for an n-p-n transistor (↑) with the voltages of opposite polarity. Current movement is almost entirely by holes (p.95). The method of action is similar to that of the n-p-n transistor.

**transistor characteristics** current enters a transistor through the emitter ($I_E$). In an n-p-n transistor the current is a flow of electrons from the emitter to the base. The current divides with a small fraction (about 1 per cent) flowing to the base, forming a base current ($I_B$) and the remainder flowing to the collector and leaving as a collector current ($I_C$). $I_E = I_C + I_B$ and $I_C = 100\ I_B$. The base current $I_B$ is the controlling factor in a transistor. The characteristic curves show the collector current for different values of the base current when using different voltages applied between the emitter and collector ($V_{CE}$). $V_{CE}$ = (forward bias) + (reverse bias).

**output characteristics of a transistor**

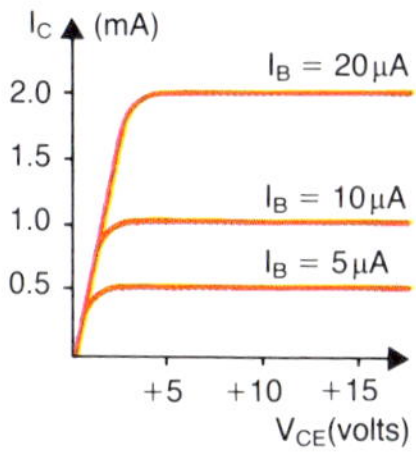


**amplification factor** a transistor amplifies currents. The amplification factor (β) is given by $\beta = I_C/I_B$ where $I_C$ is the collector current and $I_B$ is the base current. The input and output in a common emitter transistor circuit are shown in the diagram. The voltage between collector and emitter is usually about 15 volts, positive to collector for n-p-n types and negative for p-n-p types.

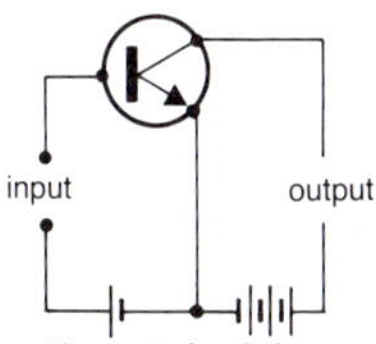


**input/output circuit for an n–p–n transistor**

**leakage current** a current results from free electrons and holes (p.95) formed by thermal agitation (p.96). This is a leakage current ($I_{CO}$) and it is small and additional to the collector current ($I_C$). If β is the amplification factor (↑) and $I_B$ is the base current, then $I_C = \beta I_B + I_{CO}$. The leakage current increases with rise in temperature. *See thermal runaway* (p.103).

**reverse recovery time** the time required for the current or voltages to change round after switching from a forward bias condition to a reverse bias condition.

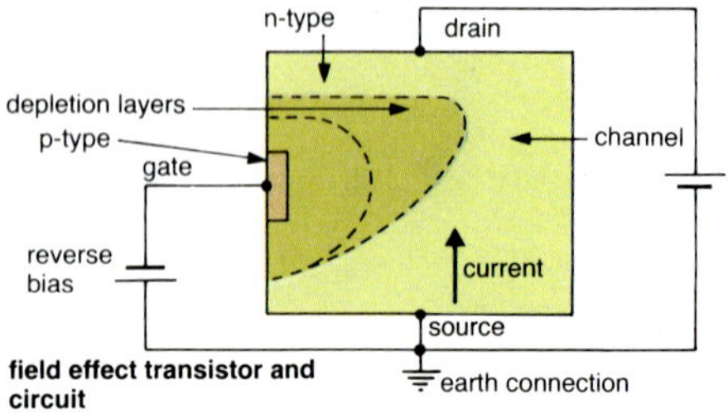


**field effect transistor and circuit**

**field effect transistor** a device consisting of a bar of n-type semiconductor with a layer of heavily-doped p-type semiconductor on one side. Connections are made to a source and a drain on the n-type material and to a gate on the p-type. This is the most common field effect transistor, called an n-type. A p-type transistor has a bar of p-type semiconductor with a gate of n-type. Current is carried by majority carriers (p.95), i.e. free electrons, for an n-type transistor.

**FET** (*abbr*) field effect transistor (↑).

**source** (*n*) the contact through which majority carriers enter an FET (↑).

**drain** (*n*) the contact through which majority carriers leave an FET (↑).

**gate**[1] (*n*) reverse bias (p.98) is applied to the pn junction at the gate contact; this produces a depletion layer.

**channel**[4] (*n*) the region at the side of the gate (↑) between the source (↑) and the drain (↑).

**FET characteristics** a depletion layer (p.95) is formed at the pn junction of an FET (↑). The greater the reverse bias on the gate (↑) the wider is the depletion layer. The effective width of the channel (↑) decreases as the bias increases. For a fixed source-to-drain voltage, the drain (↑) current is a function of the reverse bias voltage. Eventually a drain-source voltage is reached when the channel is 'pinched off', and drain current is almost constant for increasing voltage. Finally a maximum drain-source voltage is reached at which breakdown occurs and an avalanche current (p.97) flows. For small values of drain-source voltages, an FET acts as a simple semiconductor resistor, and the drain current is directly proportional to the drain-source voltage.

**MOSFET** metal-oxide-semiconductor FET (↑), also called an insulated-gate FET (↓).

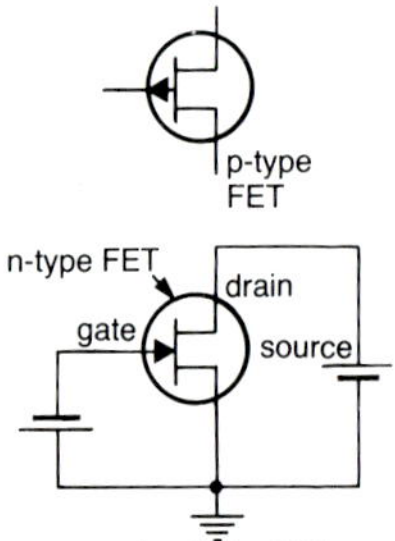


**circuit for FET**

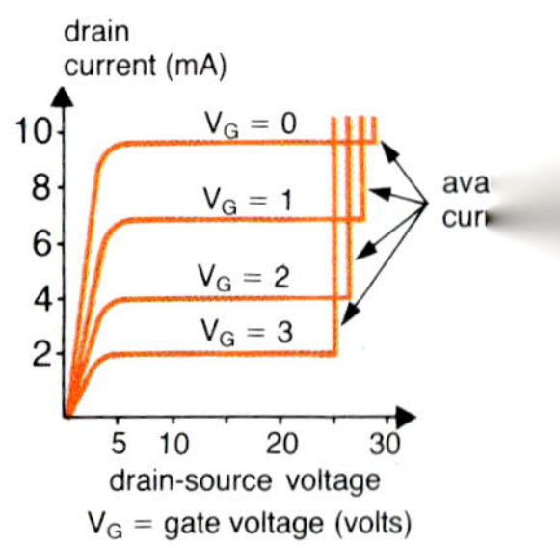


**common-source drain characteristics** (n-type FET)

**insulated-gate FET** a lightly-doped substrate of p-type semiconductor has two heavily-doped n-type regions diffused into it. A thin layer of silicon dioxide, an insulator, is grown over the surface. Holes are cut in the insulator layer for contacts to the source and the drain. Aluminium is deposited on the oxide layer to form the source, gate and drain.

**insulated-gate FET/ enhancement MOSFET**

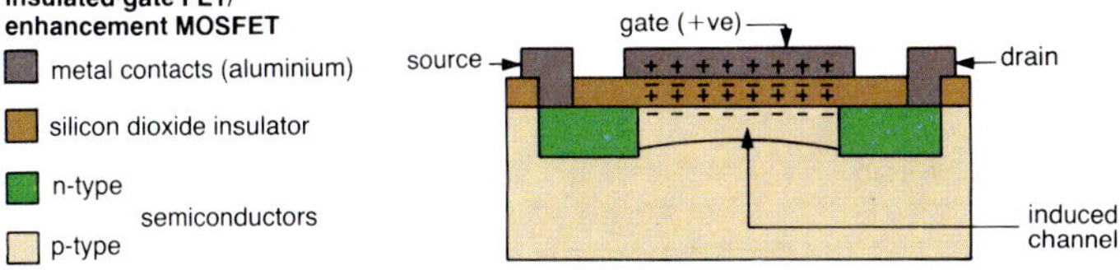


**enhancement MOSFET** the substrate is connected to earth and the gate made positive. An electric field is directed perpendicularly through the insulator. Negative charges are induced in the substrate below the gate and between the source and drain. The induced negative charge (i.e. electrons) is increased as the gate voltage is increases. Current flows from source to drain through the induced channel.

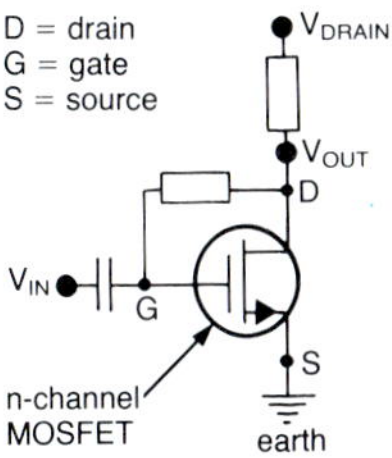


**bias, drain to gate for a MOSFET**

**depletion MOSFET** an n-type semiconductor channel is diffused between the source and the drain. If the gate voltage is made negative, positive charges are induced in the induced channel and conductivity is reduced. If the gate voltage is made positive, then negative charges are induced and the conductivity of the induced channel is increased.

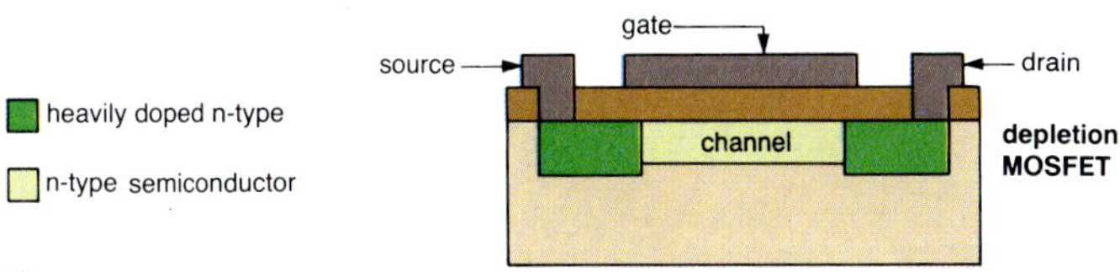


**depletion MOSFET**

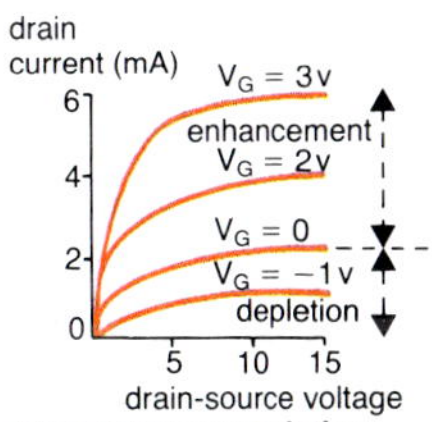


**MOSFET characteristics**

**MOSFET characteristics** an enhancement MOSFET (↑) and a depletion MOSFET with positive bias have similar characteristics, with the depletion type producing a higher drain current. The depletion MOSFET operates with negative bias (e.g. $V_G = -1V$) to produce lower currents. With maximum drain voltages, both types produce avalanche currents (p.97). All MOSFETs have extremely high input resistances. The gate, insulator layer and semiconductor channel form a capacitor.

**unijunction transistor** a bar of n-type silicon semiconductor has two metal contacts on one side at each end. On the opposite side of the bar, an aluminium rod, about 0.01mm diameter, is alloyed to the bar. This forms a pn junction. The n-type silicon forms a base with two electrodes $B_1$ and $B_2$. The aluminium rod is an *emitter*. The main difference between this type of transistor and an FET is the gate (*see* p.100) surface of this type is very much smaller.

**unijunction transistor circuit**

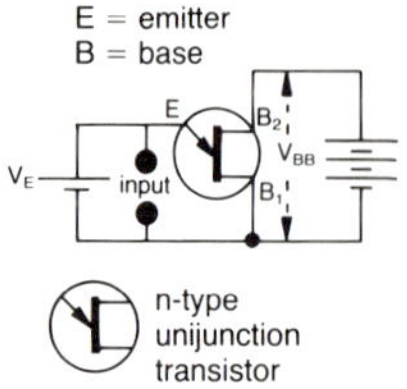


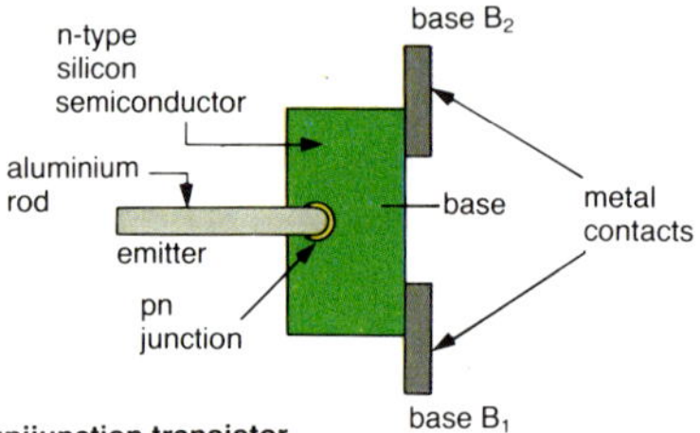


**unijunction transistor**

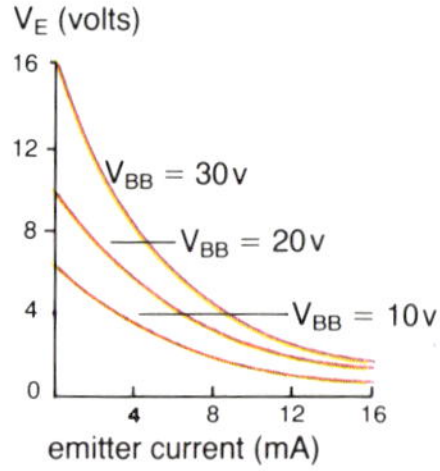


**UJT characteristics**

**UJT** (*abbr*) unijunction transistor (↑).

**UJT characteristics** a fixed voltage, $V_{BB}$, is applied between the two base contacts, $B_1$ and $B_2$. A voltage is applied to the emitter, suitable for the working conditions. An input voltage is added to the emitter voltage. The characteristics show the emitter current for different emitter voltages at various fixed-base voltages ($V_{BB}$). Each characteristic has a negative resistance value, i.e. current decreases as voltage increases. The main application of UJTs is as a switch for the rapid discharge of a capacitor (p.93).

**JFET** (*abbr*) junction field effect transistor, usually called FET (p.100).

**IGFET** (*abbr*) insulated gate field effect transistor, usually called MOSFET (p.101).

**unipolar transistor** a transistor which depends on the flow of majority carriers (p.95) only. All field effect transistors, FET (p.100), MOSFET (p.101) and UJT (↑) are unipolar transistors.

**bipolar transistor** a transistor which depends on the flow of both majority and minority carriers (p.95). Conventional transistors (p.98) of the n-p-n and p-n-p types are bipolar transistors.

**cascade amplifier**

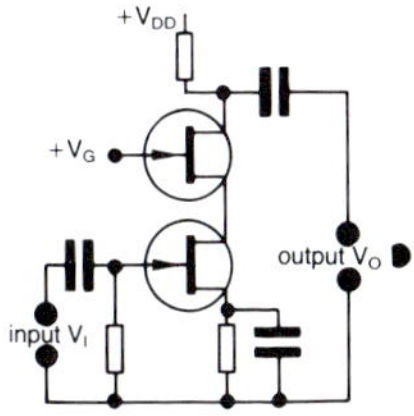


**common emitter circuit for load line**

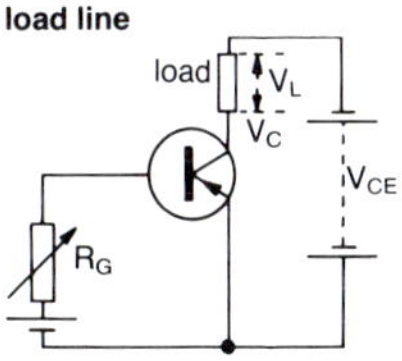


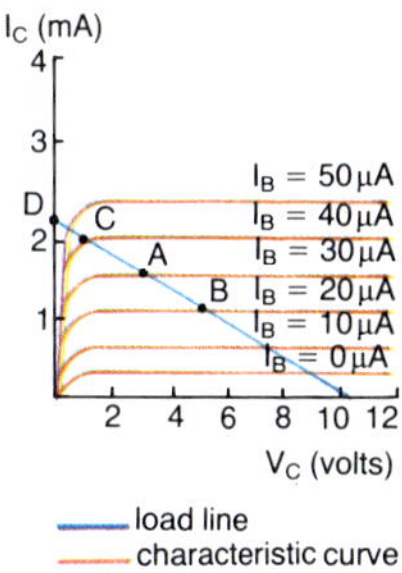


**load line** common emitter amplifier)

**cascode amplifier** two transistors, usually FETs (p.100) are used. The amplification gives the same gain as using one transistor, but it eliminates the unwanted capacitance (p.93) effect of an FET.

**load²** (*n*) the power consumed by an electric circuit, or a machine, when performing its work. For an electric circuit, the load can be represented by a theoretical resistance equivalent to the load.

**load line** a transistor, whether unipolar or bipolar (↑) delivers current to a load (↑). A load line shows the relationship between the current and voltage as determined by a load; the load line is drawn on the characteristic curves for a transistor. A simple circuit for a load line uses a variable resistor to alter the base current and a resistor to represent the load. A working point is selected (point A) with a base current ($I_B$) of 30μA. A fixed voltage, $V_{CE}$, is applied to the collector and emitter through the load. The voltage drop across the load is $V_L$ where $V_L = I_C R_L$ ($I_C$ = collector current, $R_L$ = resistance of load). The collector voltage, $V_C$, is determined by $V_C = V_{CE} - V_L$. The slope of the load line is $1/R_L$, so the load line can be drawn through point A. If the base current is reduced to 20μA, the collector current falls to 1 mA, the value of $V_L$ falls so the magnitude of $V_C$ rises. If the base current rises, $V_L$ rises, and $V_C$ falls.

**bottomed** (*adj*) as the base current ($I_B$) increases, the load line (↑) indicates that the collector voltage decreases, and the collector current ($I_C$) increases. The graph indicates a point D, the highest collector current theoretically possible for the given working conditions. Point D cannot be reached as there is no characteristic curve at that point. When $I_B$ reaches a point, near D, where the collector voltage is almost zero, further increase in $I_B$ is impossible and the transistor is said to be *bottomed*. **bottom** (*v*).

**thermal runaway** if the temperature of a transistor rises above a critical value, the leakage current (p.99) becomes excessive and the transistor is destroyed. The heat developed by current passing through a transistor raises the temperature, which increases the leakage current, and the cumulative effect leads to *thermal runaway* which destroys the transistor.

**heat sink** a block of metal which conducts heat away from a transistor or other electrical device. A heat sink helps to prevent thermal runaway (↑).

**circuit** (*n*) a connected path which can be followed by an electric current; it begins and ends at a source of electromotive force (↓). It consists of components (↓) connected together by conductors (p.92).

**component** (*n*) an electrical device used in a circuit, e.g. resistors, capacitors, diodes, transistors, electric cells, meters for measurement, switches.

**electromotive force** the force of an electric cell (p.125) which drives a direct current round a circuit. It is measured in volts.

**potential difference** an electric current flows from a higher to a lower positive potential (by convention). A potential difference drives a direct current round a circuit. Potential difference is measured in volts.

**voltage** (*n*) the electromotive force (↑) or potential difference (↑) applied in a circuit.

**series connection** the connection of components (↑) so that the same value of electric current flows through each component. Components are then connected **in series**.

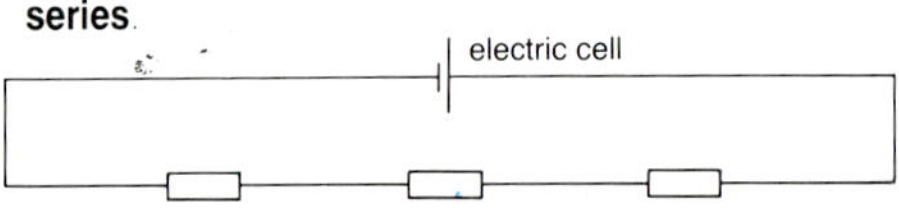


**three resistors in series**

**parallel connection** the connection of components (↑) so that the value of electric current in each component is only a proportion of the total current in the complete circuit. Components are then connected **in parallel**.

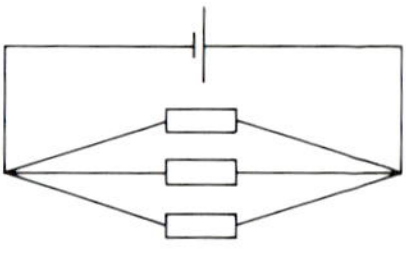

**three resistors in parallel**

**short circuit** if two points, A and B, in a circuit have components (↑) situated between A and B, then there is a definite resistance between the points. If A and B are now connected by a conductor of low resistance, current flows directly between A and B to form a short circuit. The components are short circuited.

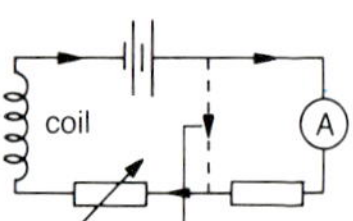


**jumper** (*n*) a short length of a conductor used to complete a circuit temporarily or to bypass one or more components in a circuit.

**printed circuit** a circuit with the conductors, for connecting components, printed on an insulating board. An insulating board is covered with a thin coat of copper. The circuit design is covered photographically with a protective film. The unprotected copper is removed by an acid solution leaving the circuit etched on the board.

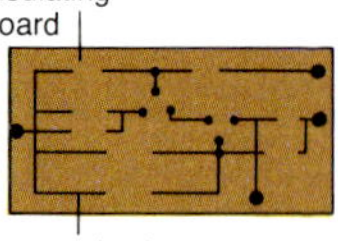


**a printed circuit board**

**PC²** (*abbr*) printed circuit (↑).

**integrated circuit**

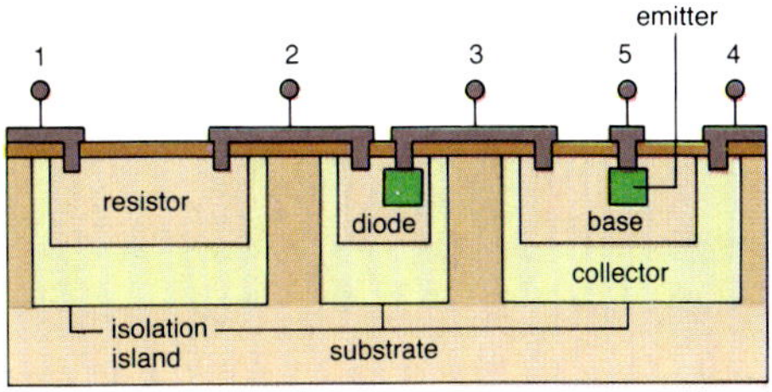


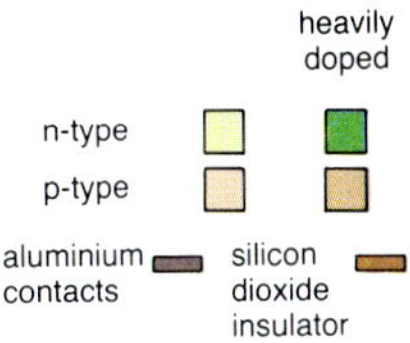


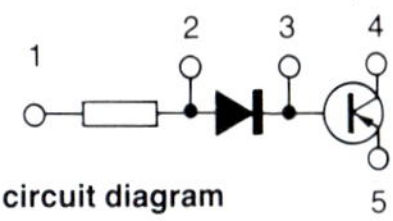


**circuit diagram**

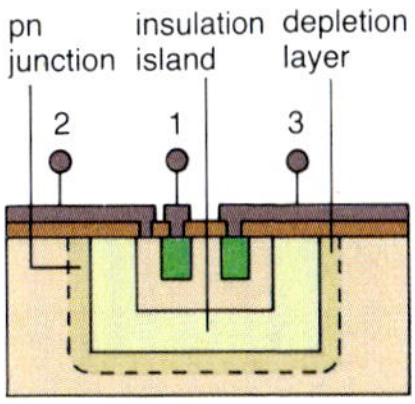


negative voltage

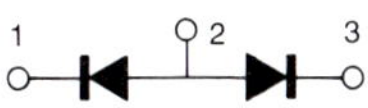


two diodes back to back

**circuit diagram**

**integrated circuit** the combination of a number of components (↑) such as resistors, capacitors, transistors, into a complete circuit made from a single piece of semiconductor material and containing both active and passive devices and their connections. The construction of such a device from n-type and p-type semiconductors, silicon dioxide insulators and metal conductors is illustrated in the diagram. The construction gives increased reliability over a conventional circuit connected by conductor wires. The manufacture of an integrated circuit is described under silicon chip (p.139). It is manufactured from a substrate of p-type semiconductor material.

**IC** (*abbr*) integrated circuit (↑).

**solid-state device** a device that consists of solids only and has no heated filaments, vacuum gaps or connecting wires. All semiconductor devices are solid state, but not all solid state devices are semiconductors, e.g. transformers are solid state devices but are not semiconductor devices.

**solid-state circuit** an integrated circuit in which only solid state devices are used.

**isolation island** an n-type semiconductor region surrounding an integrated circuit component. Two isolation islands are separated from each other by heavily-doped p-type semiconductors, usually labelled $p^+$-type. The purpose of an isolation island is the electrical isolation of the component. The p-type substrate of an integrated circuit is held at a negative voltage with respect to the isolation islands. The pn junctions of substrate and isolation island are thus reverse biased (p.98) forming a depletion layer (p.95) of high resistance and hence a good insulator.

**isolation region** alternative term to isolation island (↑).

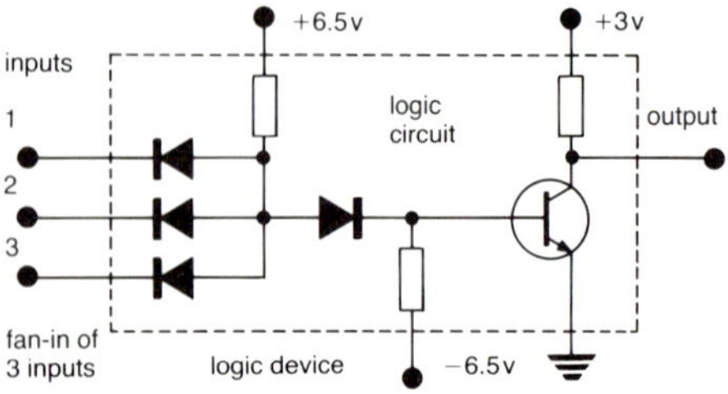

**fan-in of a device**

**logic element** the simplest device which can be represented by a Boolean operator (p.88).

**logic circuit**[1] (1) the circuit for a logic element (↑); (2) a set of logic elements (↑) connected to carry out the design of a particular process; it is part of the total logic design of a computer.

**fan-in** the number of inputs permitted to a logic element (↑).

**fan-out** the number of circuits that can be driven from the output terminal of a circuit or device. This is determined by the power available from the output and the power required for each input in the number of circuits.

**astable circuit** the circuit usually consists of two transistors each connected to an oscillator circuit of a resistor and a capacitor *(see diagram)*. The transistors are connected so that the output of one transistor is fed directly back into the input of the other transistor. The two resistors, $R_L$, form a collector load (p.103). The collector current in transistor $T_1$ increases until the transistor is bottomed (p.103), that is, switched off. The capacitor $C_1$, connected to the collector of $T_1$, discharges and provides an input to transistor $T_2$. The collector current of $T_2$ increases until $T_2$ is bottomed. The process is repeated with $T_1$ and $T_2$ alternatively being switched off. This produces an output from $T_2$ (the collector of either $T_1$ or $T_2$ can be used) of the waveform (p.128) shown. The period of each oscillation is 0.69CR. Using identical transistors and making $C_1R_1 = C_2R_2$, a square waveform can be produced.

**multivibrator** a device using an astable circuit (↑) to generate non-sinusoidal waves (p.128).

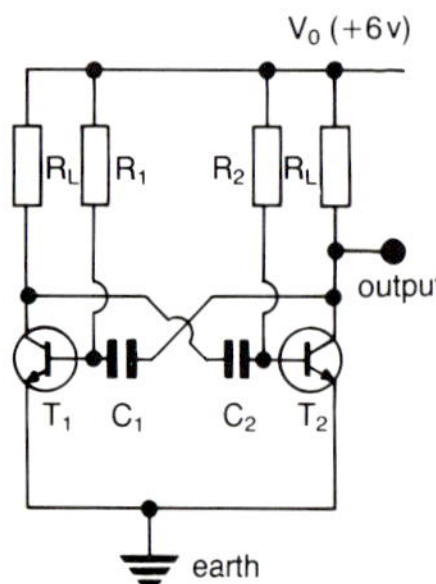

**astable circuit (multivibrator)**

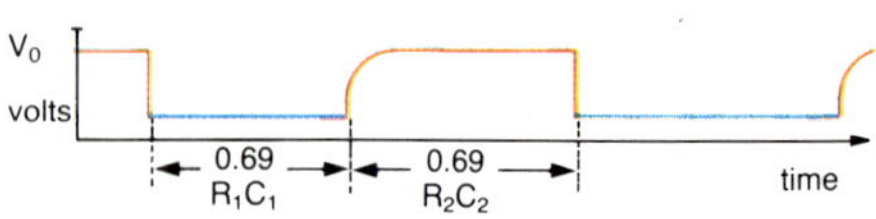

**waveform from multivibrator**

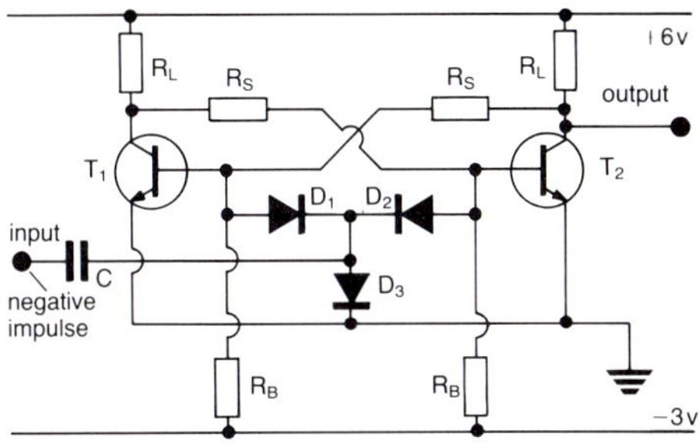


**simple bistable circuit**

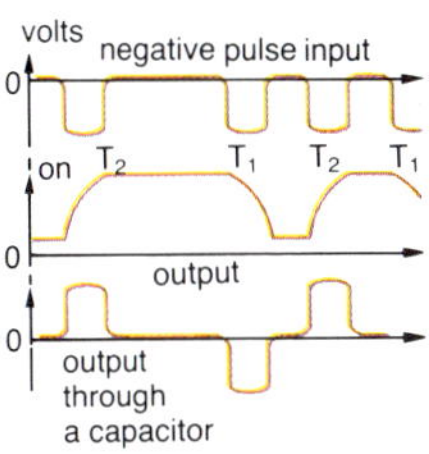


**bistable circuit output**

**bistable circuit** the circuit contains two transistors with the output of one fed back into the input of the other *(see diagram)*. The two resistors, $R_L$, form the collector load. Let transistor $T_1$ be conducting, i.e. ON. The base of $T_1$ is slightly positive, so a collector current flows and this increases the base current of $T_2$ until $T_2$ is bottomed (p.103) and the collector voltage of $T_2$ becomes almost zero. $T_2$ is then effectively OFF and its base is reversed bias with a negative voltage. Now apply a negative pulse at the input. As the base of $T_2$ is negative the pulse current cannot pass through diode $D_2$, so it goes through diode $D_1$ and applies reverse bias to $T_1$. $T_1$ starts to switch off, its collector voltage falls to zero, collector current flows and the base voltage of $T_2$ becomes slightly positive so $T_2$ is ON. A negative pulse thus changes the circuit from $T_1$ ON and $T_2$ OFF to $T_2$ ON and $T_1$ OFF and further negative pulses reverse the process each time. The resistors, $R_S$, stabilize the circuit so that two stable states can exist. The diode, $D_3$, short circuits any positive pulse to earth. The capacitor, C, allows only current pulses to pass, i.e. current increases or decreases, and blocks any direct current. The output produces a positive voltage when $T_2$ is ON, and a less positive voltage when $T_2$ is OFF and $T_1$ is ON. As the pulse needs a specific positive voltage to overcome the negative voltage applied to the bases through resistors $R_B$, the lower collector voltage has the same effect as a negative voltage. The effect of successive negative pulse inputs is shown in the graphs.

**storage circuit** a bistable circuit (↑) that can be switched from one stable state to another. The two states can record binary 1 and 0. *See flip-flop* (p.114).

**component density** the number of discrete circuit components in a solid-state circuit (p.105) divided by the volume of the circuit assembly. Expressed in components per cubic inch or per cubic centimetre.

**microcircuit** (*n*) an electronic circuit made of elements interconnected so that they are inseperable and miniaturized.

**microelectronic device** a device, such as a resistor, capacitor, transistor or similar component, interconnected with other such devices on a single semiconductor substrate (p.136).

**printed element** a device, such as a resistor, capacitor, or line connector, that is formed on an insulating circuit board by depositing metal or etching the design.

**back-to-back devices** two semiconductor devices connected in parallel but in opposite directions. This allows current control without rectification.

**inverse-parallel connection** connection of back-to-back devices (↑).

**terminal**[2] (*n*) a metal projection, at the end of a wire or line connector or connected to an electrical device, used to make a connection with an electrical circuit. The connection is made by using a nut on a thread, by a plug (↓) and jack (↓), by a wirewrap connection (↓), or by soldering a connecting wire to the terminal.

**wirewrap** (*adj*) a terminal (↑), which is a square pin, has wire wrapped round it many times to make contact. Used with PC boards (p.14).

**accordion** (*n*) a connector used with printed circuits. It is a springy piece of wire, shaped like a letter Z, which can be stretched to connect two terminals (↑).

**socket** (*n*) a terminal (↑) consisting of metal in the shape of a small cylinder. Connector lines or wires are soldered to it. A plug (↓) fits in the socket.

**plug** (*n*) a pin-shaped piece of metal which fits into a socket. Connector lines or wires are fastened to it. Insertion of the plug completes an electrical contact.

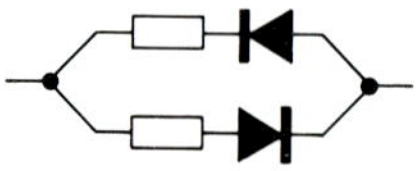
two diodes connected back to back
**inverse parallel connection**

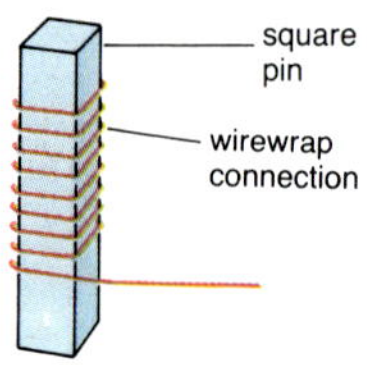


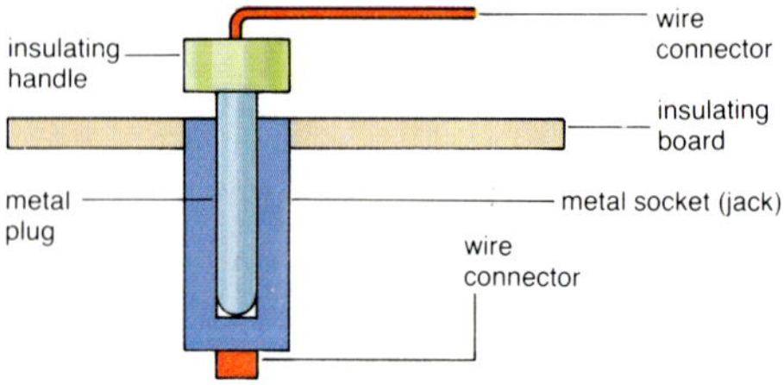


**plug and socket connection**

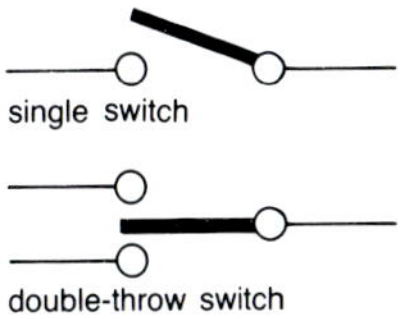

**symbols for switches**

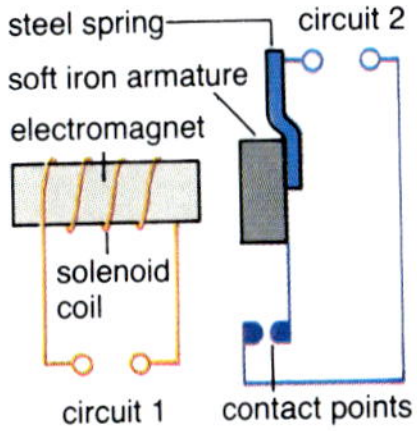

**electromechanical relay**

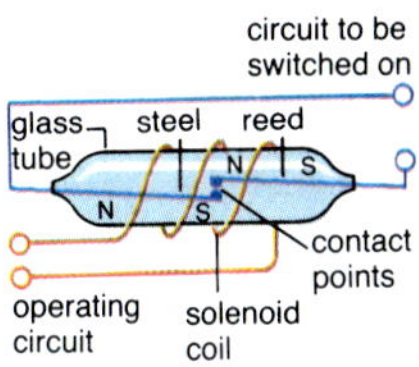

**reed relay**

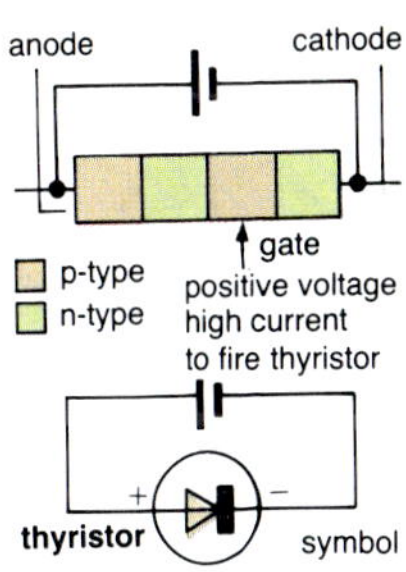

**thyristor**

**switch²** (*n*) a device for connecting one part of an electrical circuit to another part. When the switch is closed, current flows in the circuit. When the switch is open, an open circuit is formed and no current flows. Some types of switch can connect a component, or a circuit, to either one of two alternative circuits. This is a double-throw switch.

**toggle** (*n*) (1) a manually operated ON-OFF switch (↑); (2) a flip-flop (p.114).

**toggle switch** an ON-OFF switch (↑) with a snap action, as in an electric light switch.

**relay** (*n*) a device by which electric current flowing in one circuit can open or close a second circuit, i.e. switch the current ON or OFF in the second circuit.

**electromechanical relay** the operating circuit (circuit 1), *see diagram*, is connected to a solenoid coil wound round an iron core. A current in the coil forms an electromagnet which attracts the soft-iron armature. This brings the contact points together, circuit 2 is closed and current flows. When circuit 1 is switched off, the steel spring returns the armature to the open position and current in circuit 2 is switched off.

**reed relay** two steel reeds are sealed in a glass tube. A solenoid coil is wound round the tube. When the operating current is switched on, the solenoid coil magnetizes the reeds. Unlike magnetic poles are opposite at the contact points, so the points are attracted, and the secondary circuit is switched on. When the operating current is switched off, the reeds spring apart, break contact, and the secondary circuit is switched off. Reed relays are made as make, break, or changeover switches.

**chatter** (*n*) the rapid closing and opening of the contact points of a relay (↑). This wears out the points and reduces the life of the relay.

**thyristor** (*n*) a semiconductor device used as an electronic switch (↑). It consists of four layers of semiconductor, p-n-p-n, and has three electrodes, anode, cathode and gate. It is similar to an ordinary pn diode (p.96) but conduction and rectification takes place only when a signal is given. The signal is a sufficiently high current with an applied positive voltage; this fires the thyristor. Once fired the thyristor keeps conducting even though the gate current is cut off. Conduction is stopped by removing the anode voltage or reducing it to a low value.

**switching circuit** a transistor is used in a switching circuit, *see diagram*. When the input is earthed, i.e. an input of 0 volts, the base has a negative voltage, depending for its magnitude on the values of $R_I$ and $R_B$. The transistor is reversed biased (p.98) and no current flows. The collector current is zero, there is no voltage drop over resistance $R_L$, so the collector voltage is +6 volts. If the input is a voltage of +6 volts, then there is a positive voltage applied to the base. If this is sufficiently high, the transistor is bottomed (p.103) and the collector voltage is effectively zero. The collector current is switched off and on by an input of 0 volts and +6 volts respectively.

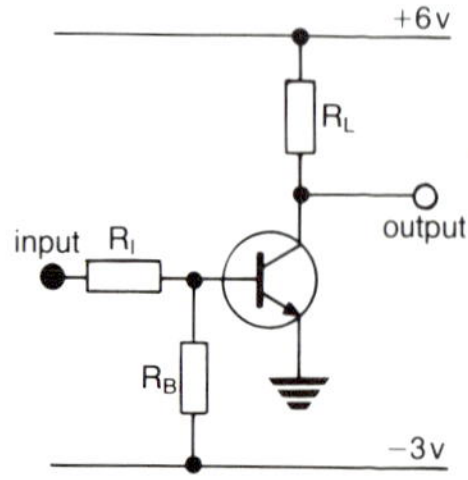

**switching circuit (transistor)**

**logical high** a high value of voltage representing binary 1 with zero volts, i.e. earthed circuits, representing binary 0. The voltage can be either positive or negative. *See logic level* (p.42).

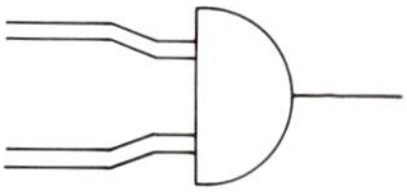
**basic gate symbol**

**stepping switch** a switching device, or electronic relay, having a number of discrete positions. The device advances from one position to the next on receiving an input pulse.

**gate**[2] (*n*) an electronic switch which may have more than one input but only one output. The output is energized when certain input conditions are met.

**logical element**[2] another term for a gate (↑).

**logic gate** another term for gate (↑).

**gate circuit** an electronic circuit forming a gate (↑).

**gate equivalent circuit** a measure of the relative complexity of a digital circuit. It is the number of individual gate circuits that would have to be interconnected to perform the same logical function.

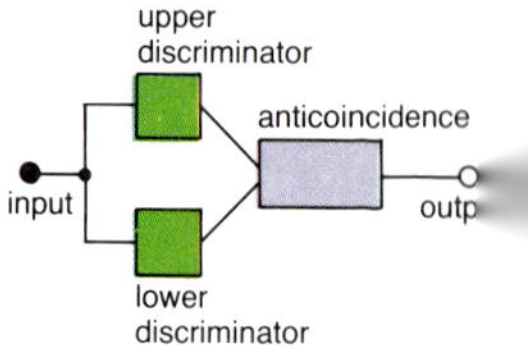


**gating circuit** a circuit operating as a switch, allowing an output only during specific time intervals or when the magnitude of a signal pulse is within specified limits.

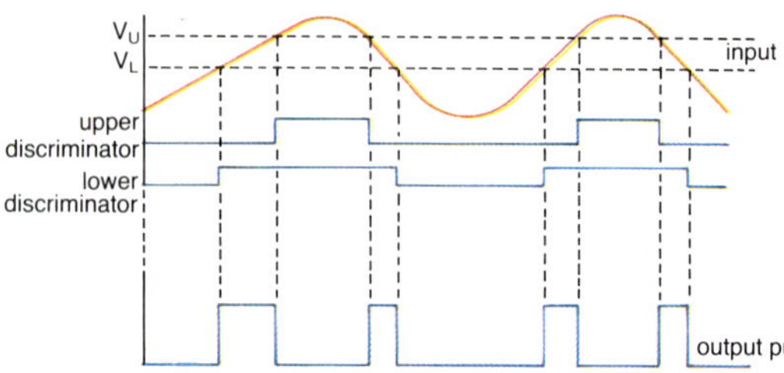

**gating circuit**

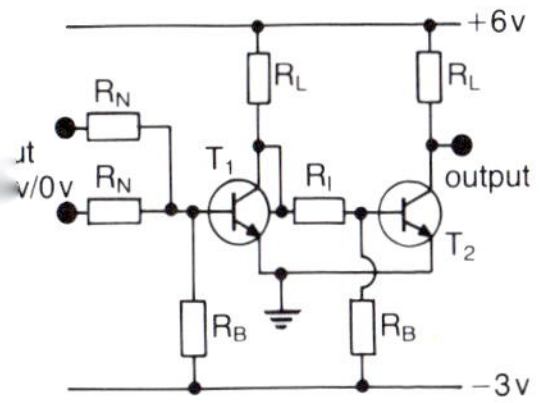


**OR gate circuit**

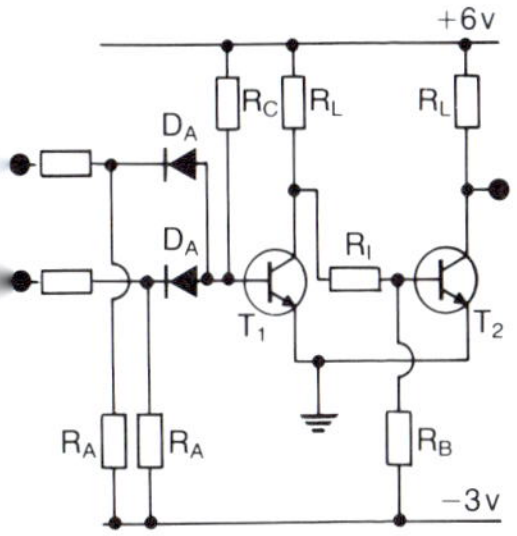


**AND gate circuit**

**NOT gate** a gate (↑) with one input and one output. The output is energized only if the input is not energized. It alters the value of a Boolean variable (p.88) to its opposite value, i.e. from 1 to 0 and vice versa. An inverter (↓).

**inverter** (*n*) (1) a device which inverts polarity, i.e. from positive to negative or vice versa; (2) a transistor switching circuit (↑) is an inverter, as logical high (↑) is inverted to logical low. A NOT gate (↑) is an inverter.

**negation gate** a NOT gate (↑).

**OR gate** a gate (↑) with two (or more) inputs and one output *(see diagram)*. If both inputs are at zero volts, the base of transistor $T_1$ is slightly negative, i.e. reverse biased (p.98) and non-conducting. The collector is at a potential of +6 volts, i.e. the output of $T_1$. If either input is at +6 volts, the base of $T_1$ is positive. The resistors $R_N$ and $R_B$ are of such values to make the positive voltage sufficient to bottom the transistor. The collector potential is zero volts. An OR operation (p.85) requires a value of 1 if either input has a value of 1, so an inverter (↑) is added to the circuit. Transistor $T_2$ is the inverter, using the output of $T_1$.

**conditions in OR gate circuit**

| input | base $T_1$ | transistor $T_1$ | output $T_1$ | output $T_2$ |
|---|---|---|---|---|
| or | slightly negative | non conducting | +6v | 0v |
| +6v | positive | bottomed | 0v | +6v |

**NOR gate** an OR gate (↑) without the inverter. The output is taken from the collector of transistor $T_1$.

**AND gate** a gate (↑) with two (or more) inputs and one output *(see diagram)*. If both inputs are at zero volts, current flows from the positive supply (+6V) through $R_C$, through the diodes, $D_A$, through resistors $R_A$, to the negative supply. $R_L$ and $R_A$ are of such values that the base of transistor $T_1$ is slightly negative, so $T_1$ is non-conducting, and its output is +6V. If one input is at +6V, the other input keeps the base of $T_1$ slightly negative and the output is +6V. If both inputs are at +6V, no current passes the diodes, $D_A$. Current flows from the positive supply through $R_C$, through $T_1$ to earth. The base is positive and $R_C$ is chosen so that the transistor is bottomed. The output is 0 volts. An inverter, using $T_2$, converts this to +6 volts. The four conditions for an AND gate are shown in the diagram.

**NAND gate** an AND gate (↑) without the inverter. The output is taken from the collector of transistor $T_1$.

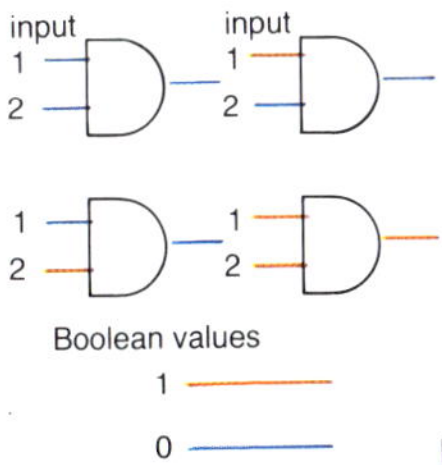


**results from AND gate**

**Exclusive-OR gate** this logic gate uses two NOT gates and three NAND gates, that is, five transistors in the circuit. The connections are shown in the diagram. If the input consists of two unlike variables, i.e. 1 and 0, the output is 1. *See Exclusive-OR operation* (p.86).

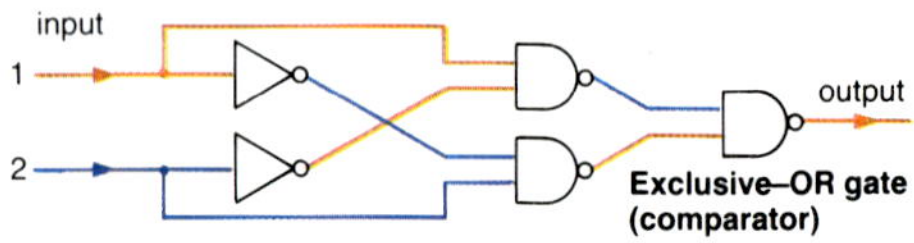


**comparator gate** an Exclusive-NOR gate (↑).
**CP gate** a comparator gate (↑).
**Exclusive-NOR gate** this logic gate uses two NOT gates, two NAND gates and an AND gate. It is an Exclusive-OR gate (↑) followed by an inverter (p.111). If the input consists of two like variables, the output is 1.

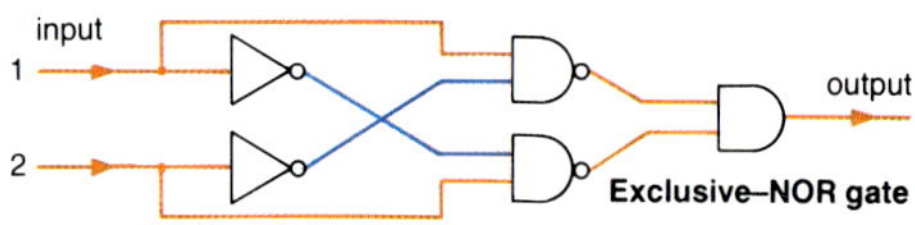


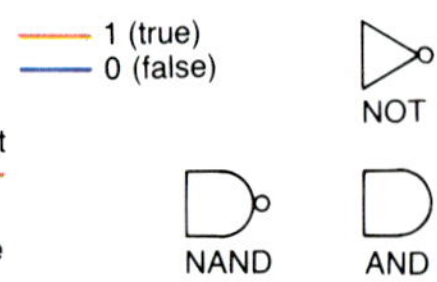


**threshold** (*n*) the minimum value of an input signal needed to energize the output of a threshold element (↓).
**threshold element** a logical element (p.110) with several input signals and one output. Each input signal has a specific magnitude. The output signal depends on the threshold value (↑) of the signals added together.
**decision element** a threshold element (↑).
**majority element** a threshold element (↑) in which the sum of the input signals must be greater than half the total possible input signal. For example, if there are *n* signals, each with a magnitude of 1, then the threshold value is $(n+1)/2$.
**matrix switch** an array of electronic devices, such as transistors, diodes, resistors, capacitors, interconnected to perform a logical function. The devices form gates (p.110) for logical functions such as decoding and encoding number systems, word translation, etc.

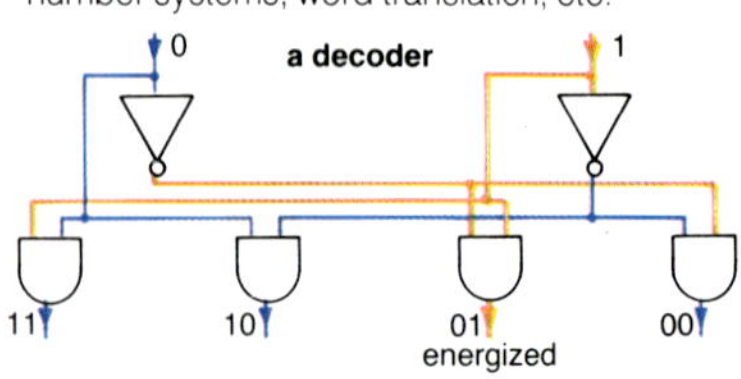

**resistor-transistor logic** a logic circuit (p.106) with resistors performing the logic and transistors producing an inverted output. The OR circuit on p.111 is an example.

**RTL** (*abbr*) resistor-transistor logic (↑).

**diode-transistor logic** a logic circuit (p.106) with diodes performing the logic and transistors producing an inverted output *(see diagram)*.

**a diode-transistor logic circuit**

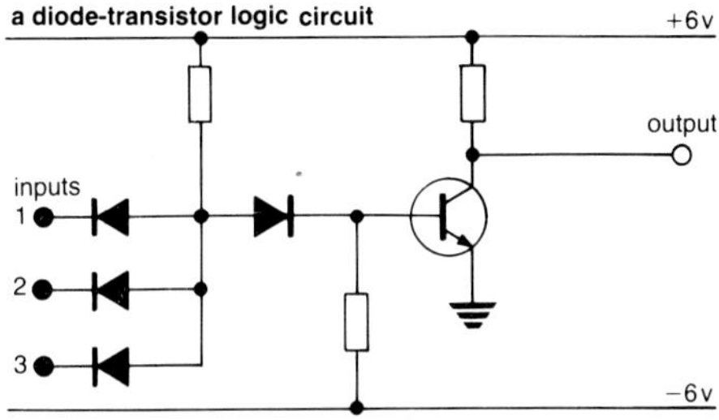


**DTL** (*abbr*) diode-transistor logic (↑).

**transistor-transistor logic** the most common logic circuit (p.106). It uses transistors to perform the logic. Bipolar transistors (p.102) are usually faster, but are more expensive than unipolar transistors (p.102) and their construction in integrated circuits is more complicated. Using n-channel MOSFETs, however, the same speed as bi-polar transistors can be obtained. Transistors can also be used as resistors, and diodes in logic circuits; n-channel MOSFETs are compatible with most memory devices.

**TTL** (*abbr*) transistor-transistor logic (↑).

**emitter-coupled logic**[1] a logic circuit (p.106) preventing transistor saturation. This increases the speed of operation and propagation delays are typically reduced to 2ns per gate. Simple OR gates can provide both inverting or non-inverting outputs. Power dissipation is higher than for TTL circuits. ECL circuits are mainly used in mainframe computers.

**ECL**[1] (*abbr*) emitter-coupled logic (↑).

**TRL** (*abbr*) transistor-resistor logic; synonymous with resistor-transistor logic (↑).

**sleeping sickness** the failure of a transistor caused by moisture collecting on its base.

**binary cell** a bistable circuit (p.107) used as a storage element. It stores one binary digit, that is, a 1 or a 0.

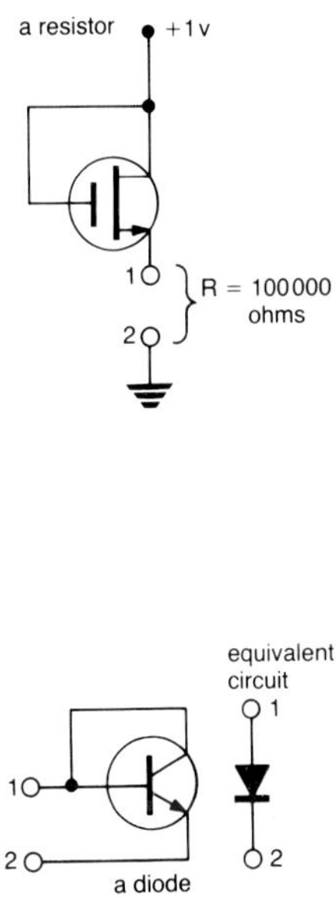


**transistors in TTL logic**

**flip-flop** (*n*) a bistable circuit (p.107) which can assume one of two stable states; these states represent 1 or 0. The flip-flop can thus store one bit (p.36) of binary code. A flip-flop can have two input terminals corresponding to each of the two stable states, or one input which allows it to act as a single stage binary counter (p.117).

**binary pair** a flip-flop (↑).

**bistable device** an electronic device capable of assuming two stable states, i.e. a flip-flop (↑).

**R-S flip-flop** a flip-flop (↑) which consists of two NAND gates cross-coupled so the output of one provides one input for the other. Each gate has another input, one gate is marked R and the other marked S. There are two possible outputs, P and Q. Q is the designated output. Initially the flip-flop is at stable state 0 with P = 1 and Q = 0. Using n-p-n transistors, a positive voltage represents 1 and a low, or negative, voltage represents 0. In a stable state, both R and S have a high, or positive, voltage *(see diagram)*. A negative pulse can be supplied to either R or S, and the output is taken from Q.

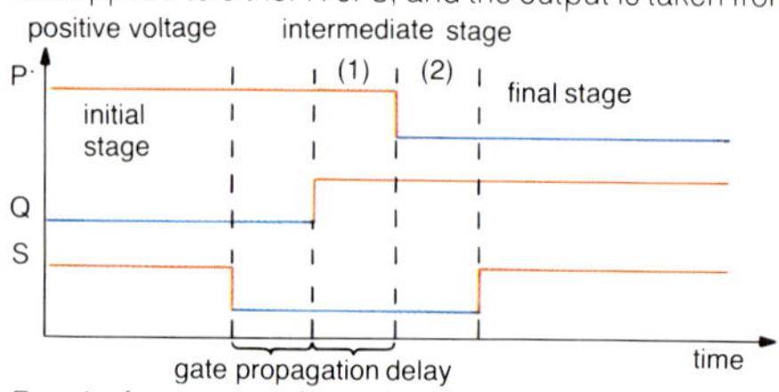


Results from a negative pulse input are given below:

| *initial state* | *input* | *result* |
|---|---|---|
| Q = 0 | negative pulse S | Q = 1 |
| Q = 1 | negative pulse S | Q = 1 |
| Q = 0 | negative pulse R | Q = 0 |
| Q = 1 | negative pulse R | Q = 0 |

A negative pulse at S makes Q = 1 whatever the initial state, while a negative pulse at R makes Q = 0. The action of the gates is shown in the diagram. A propagation delay occurs when a negative pulse is put in; this delay is characteristic for a particular transistor. R-S stands for reset-set (↓). An R-S flip-flop can also consist of two NOR gates.

**reset** (*v*) to give a flip-flop a value of 0.

**set** (*v*) to give a flip-flop a value of 1.

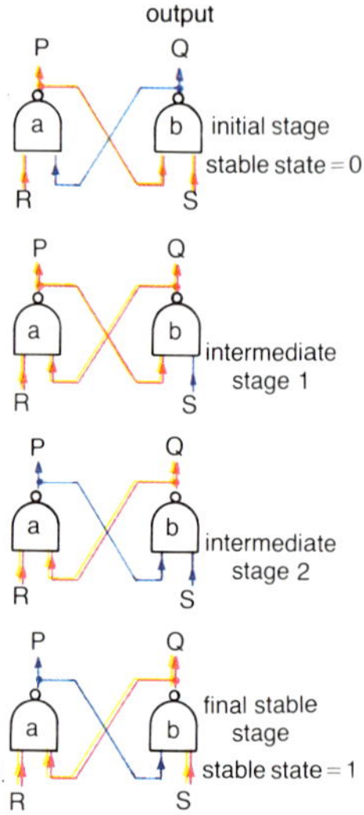


an R–S flip-flop

positive = 1
negative = 0

time sequence for R–S flip-flop

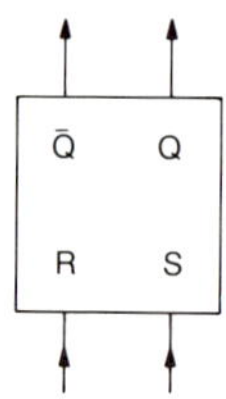


symbol for R-S flip-flop
output taken from Q
Q represents current value

**T flip-flop**

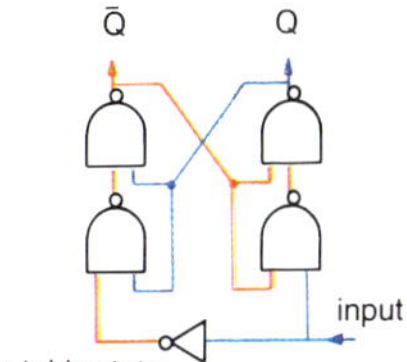


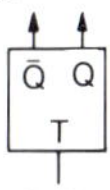


**symbol for T flip-flop**

**T flip-flop** a T flip-flop has only one input. A positive pulse on the input reverses the state of the flip-flop from 1 to 0 or 0 to 1. The flip-flop consists of an R-S flip-flop (↑) controlled by two NAND gates and a NOT gate on the input. The truth table for a T flip-flop is:

| | | | | | | | | |
|---|---|---|---|---|---|---|---|---|
| K | 0 | 0 | 1 | 1 | 0 | 0 | 1 | 1 |
| J | 0 | 0 | 0 | 0 | 1 | 1 | 1 | 1 |
| initial Q | 0 | 1 | 0 | 1 | 0 | 1 | 0 | 1 |
| new Q | 0 | 1 | 0 | 0 | 1 | 1 | 1 | 0 |

A positive pulse, (1), is used to trigger the change.

**toggle flip-flop** T flip-flop (↑).

**J-K flip-flop** a flip-flop which behaves similarly to the R-S flip-flop (↑) but overcomes the difficulty of the R-S flip-flop when pulses are supplied simultaneously to the R and S inputs. On the R-S flip-flop this would produce an uncertain result as the flip-flop can set in either way. In a J-K flip-flop simultaneous inputs on the J and K lines reverse the state of the flip-flop, i.e. toggle it, so that 1 becomes 0 or 0 becomes 1. The truth table uses a positive pulse (= 1) for an input. No input on J or K leaves the state unchanged. An input on the J line sets the flip-flop and an input on the K line resets it. J-K flip-flops are used in preference to R-S flip-flops because of their toggling action.

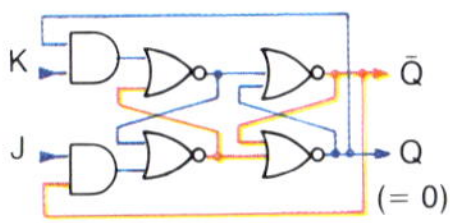


**J-K flip-flop**

**truth table for J–K flip-flop**

| | | | | |
|---|---|---|---|---|
| initial Q | 0 | 1 | 0 | 1 |
| T | 0 | 0 | 1 | 1 |
| new Q | 0 | 1 | 1 | 0 |

**symbol for J-K flip-flop**

**R-S-T flip-flop** the R-S-T flip-flop combines the actions of the R-S flip-flop and the T flip-flop. Two OR gates receive the input, so an input from the T-line provides a pulse for both K and J. This input reverses the state of the flip-flop for each input. Lines R and S are used to reset and set, respectively, the output of the flip-flop.

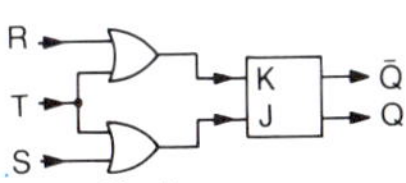


**R-S-T flip-flop**

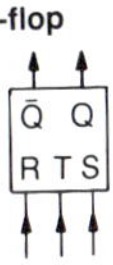


**symbol for R-S-T flip-flop**

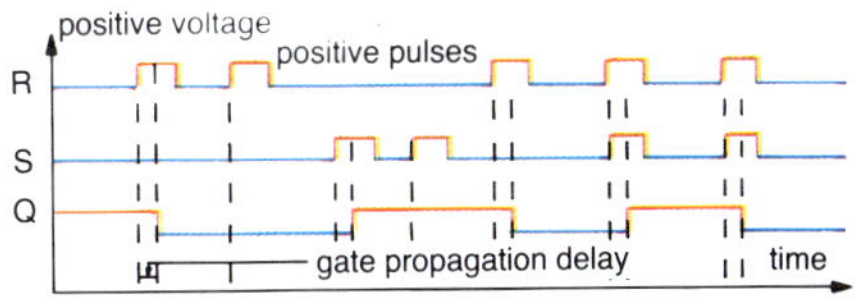


**time sequences for R-S-T flip-flops**

**trigger** (*v*) to start an action by an impulse (p.120) supplied by an external device, to a device which then continues to function under its own control.

**D flip-flop** R-S flip-flops (p.114) have their own individual times for propagation delay (↓) and it is difficult to design a computer to function correctly under these circumstances. Most microcomputers use synchronous circuits, controlled by a regular positive pulse from a clock, and logic circuits use a D flip-flop. The D flip-flop consists of four NAND gates, and one NOT gate, connected as shown in the diagram. There are two inputs, one for data and one for the clock. When the clock input is negative (or low) any signal on the data line is ignored. When the clock input is positive (or high) the signal on the data line becomes the output, after the gate propagation delay time. The clock pulse is kept short, so that the data input does not change during the sampling period. D flip-flops are used in registers (p.149) with parallel transmission.

**D flip-flop**

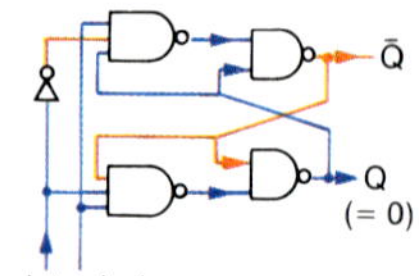


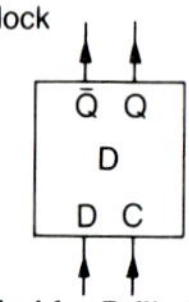


**symbol for D flip-flop**

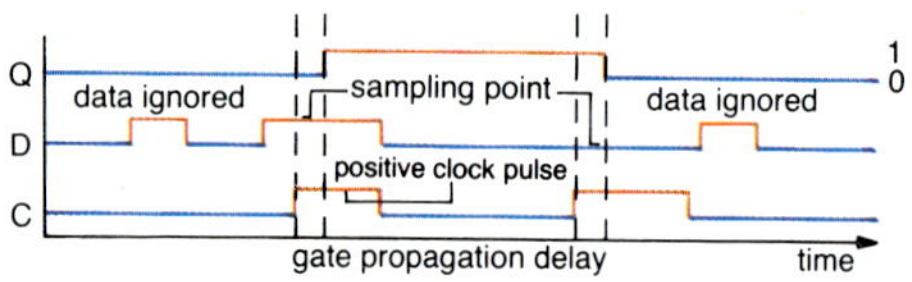


**time sequence for D flip-flop**

**gate propagation delay** the small period of time between a flip-flop receiving an input and making an output.

**propagation delay** gate propagation delay (↑).

**J-K-T flip-flop** a J-K flip-flop which is clock-controlled for a toggle action. An R and an S input allow the flip-flop to be reset or set overriding all other data. With the J and K lines set, the clock impulse reverses the state of the flip-flop, i.e. a toggling action from 1 to 0 or 0 to 1. The flip-flop also acts as a memory unit transferring the J and K values to the output. The S and R lines cannot both be positive (or high) as this input cannot be used with the R-S stage. Finally, the device acts as a normal J-K flip-flop with synchronous action. The circuit is thus useful for many functions.

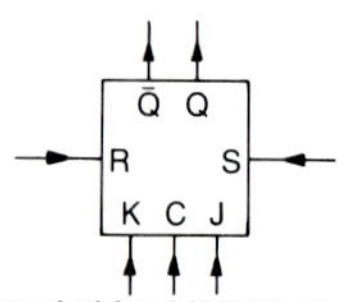


**symbol for J-K-T flip-flop**

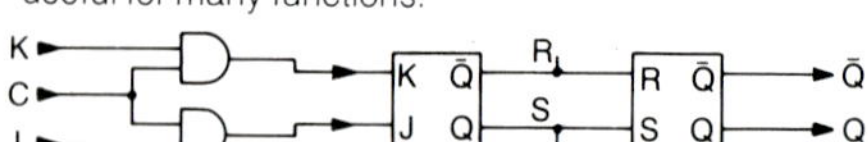


**J-K-T flip-flop**

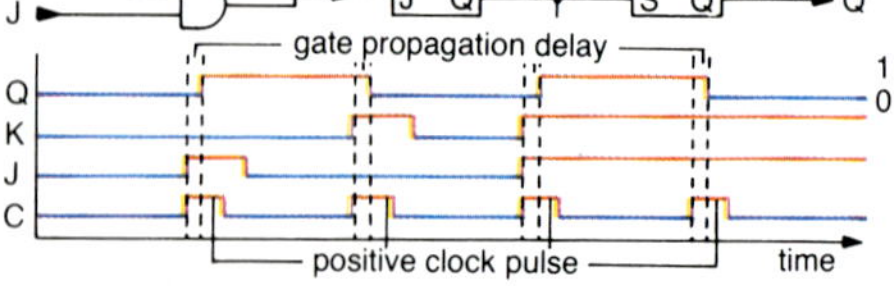


**time sequence for J-K-T flip-flop**

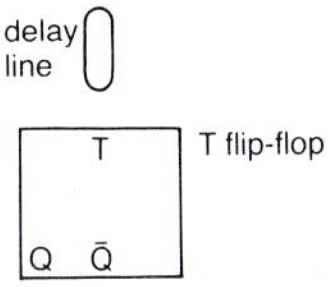


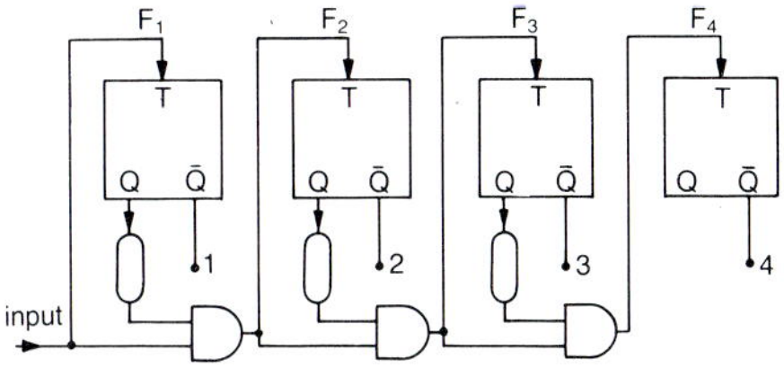


**binary counter**

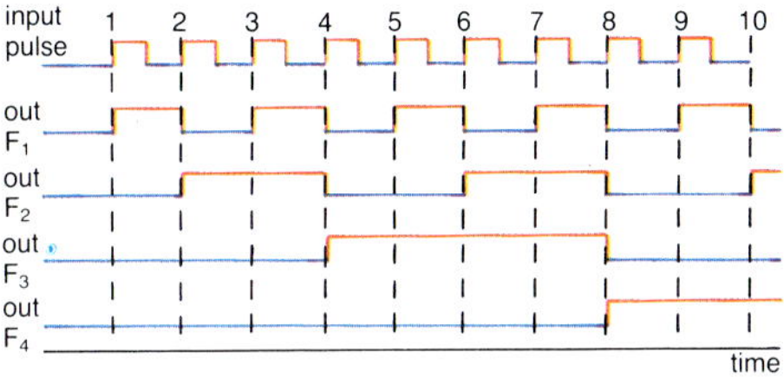


**time sequence for binary counter**

**binary counter** a binary counter consists of T flip-flops (p.115) connected in series through AND gates. The input is a series of positive pulses which are to be counted. The first pulse switches the first flip-flop ($F_1$ *in diagram*) to 1. A delay line (p.230) prevents this being an output to the AND gate at the same time. By the time the second input arrives, the input to the AND gate from the flip-flop has risen to 1. The second input pulse and the flip-flop pulse pass a positive pulse to flip-flop $F_2$. $F_2$ changes to 1 and $F_2$ resets to 0. The delay line prevents the output from $F_2$ presenting a positive pulse to the second AND gate. The first AND gate has a 0 pulse from $F_1$ and an input pulse, so the result is 0 and the second AND gate has a result of 0. The third input pulse changes $F_1$ to 1, passes no pulse to $F_2$ which remains at 1. The sequence of changes is shown in the time sequence graph. After 10 input pulses the readings of the four flip-flops are 1010, i.e. 10 on the binary scale. Outputs from the flip-flops are labelled 1, 2, 3 and 4. These have to be inverted to pass the binary count to a register (p.149) or a memory location (p.166). A cascade (↓) of flip-flops can be used to produce any required binary number.

**cascade connection** two or more similar devices connected in series so that the output of one is the input of the following device. For example, the T-flip-flops in a binary counter (↑) have a cascade connection.

**decimal counter** this is a 4-digit binary counter (p.117) with an additional circuit that stops counting at 9 and sets all the flip-flops to zero. J-K-T flip-flops are used so that any recorded digit can be overridden and set to 0. The diagram shows the situation at a count of 9. A positive input pulse at the AND gate *d* produces a resulting positive pulse which resets all flip-flops and provides a positive pulse for the 'carry' terminal. The device then counts up to 9 again. The four outputs (1 to 4) provide a BCD reading (p.36). These devices can be connected in tandem (↓) to count tens, hundreds, etc.

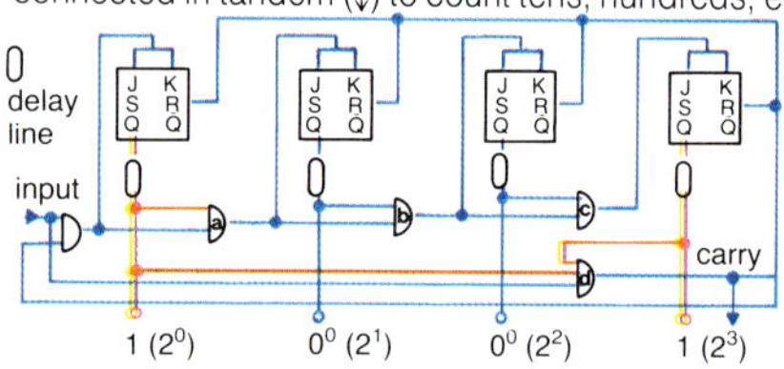


decimal counter producing binary-coded decimal

**tandem connection** (1) two or more similar devices connected so that the output of the preceding device controls the succeeding device; (2) two devices connected so that the output of one provides the input of the other.

**ring counter** a counter consisting of R-S flip-flops connected by AND gates; it has as many distinct states as there are outputs. With every pulse the flip-flop which is set is reset and the succeeding flip-flop is set. The diagram shows a ring counter with three outputs and the second output is set. A negative input pulse resets flip-flop 2 and sets flip-flop 3; the next pulse resets 3 and sets 1. Discrete counts can be taken from a ring counter to control other devices with no further logic devices required.

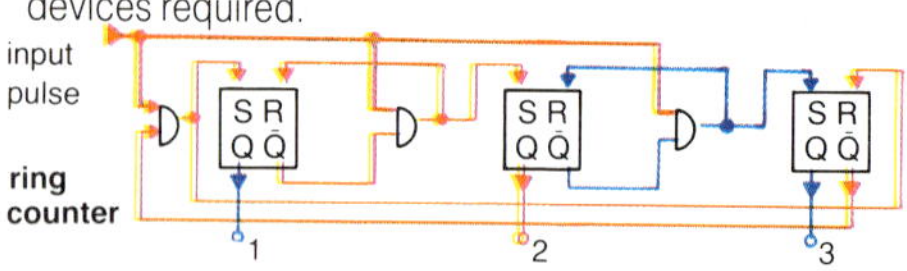


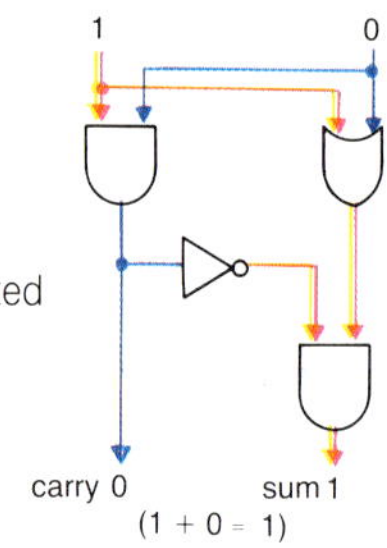


half adder

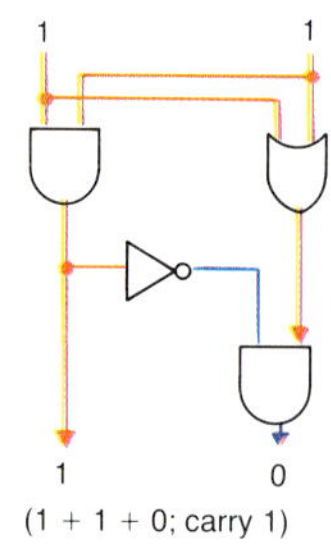


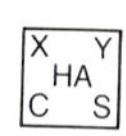


symbol

**half adder** a logic element (p.106) that accepts two binary digits as input and delivers two outputs, a sum and a carry (↓). It consists of 4 gates.

**full adder** half adders (↑) in parallel are connected by OR gates. The full adder accepts two binary numbers and delivers one binary number, the sum, and a carry (↓).

**adder** (*n*) a full adder (↑).

**full adder** (four digit)

```
  1001
+ 1010
carry 1  0011
```

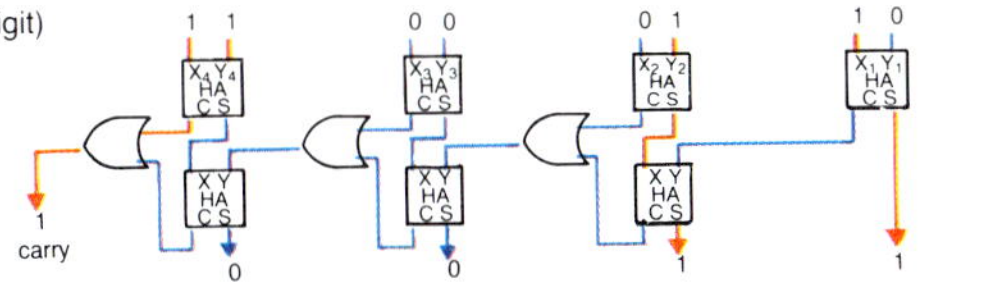


```
  10
+ 11
 101
   1 carry
 110
```

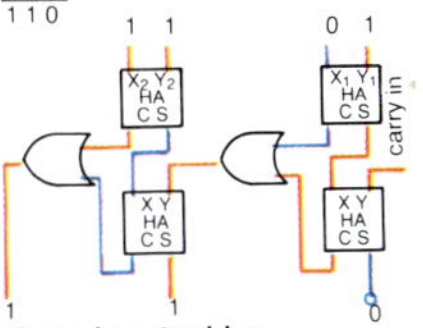


**three-input adder**

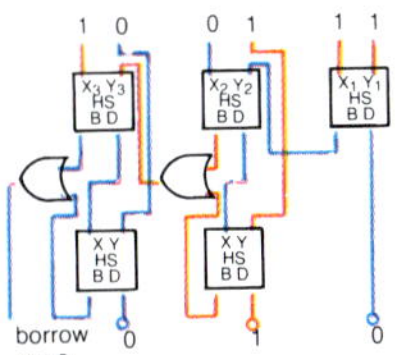


```
  101
- 001
  010
```

**full subtractor** (3 digits)

**halfsubtractor**

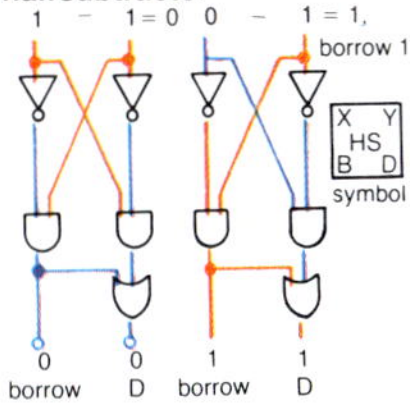


**subtractor** (using complementary addition

```
 101      101
−011  =  +100 + 1
          001
            1
          010
```

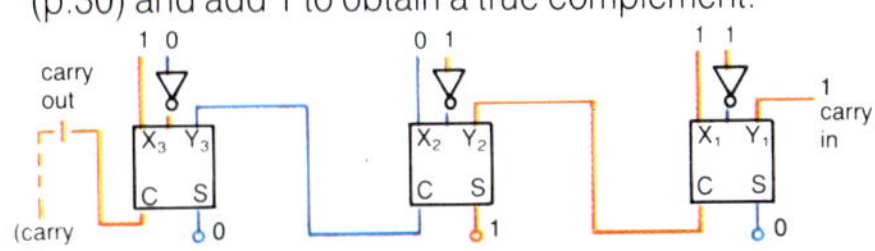


symbols

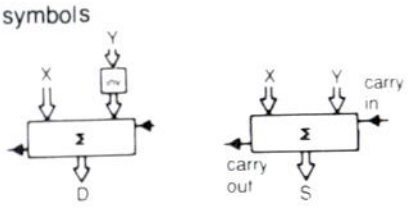


**three-input adder** a full adder (↑) with three inputs, two binary numbers and a carry from another adder. It delivers two outputs, sum and carry (↓).

**parallel adder** a chain of full adders (↑) which carries out addition for the word length (p.41) of a computer. There is a carry propagation delay (↓) in the action, which must be allowed for in the computer design.

**carry**[1] (*n*) the overflow which may arise when two binary digits are added, i.e. if both digits are 1, then the sum is 0 with a carry of 1.

**carry propagation delay** there is a propagation delay (p.116) for each gate in the adder (↑). In general, if there are *x* bits in a binary addition, there will be 2*x* propagation delays.

**half subtractor** a logic element (p.106) that accepts two binary digits as input and delivers two outputs, a difference and a borrow. It consists of 5 gates.

**full subtractor** half subtractors (↑) in parallel are connected by OR gates. The full subtractor accepts two binary numbers and delivers one binary number, the difference, and a borrow.

**subtractor** (*n*) this is either a full subtractor (↑) or a device using complementary addition to perform subtraction. The binary complement (p.32) of a number is made by inverting each digit by a NOT gate. The result is added to the minuend (p.30) and 1 is added to the sum. Most subtractors use this method, as the same device can be used for both addition and subtraction with a small additional circuit to invert the subtrahend (p.30) and add 1 to obtain a true complement.

**borrow** (*n*) the subtraction of 1 (in the binary number system) from the next more significant digit.

**clear**[1] (*v*) to put every flip-flop (p.114) or storage device (p.165) into a state of zero or blank.

**pulsating current** a direct current which undergoes regular changes in magnitude from a constant value. The changes are either in current or in voltage.

**pulse** (*n*) one variation in current or voltage of a pulsating current. Ideally it should have a square wave form. As produced by electronic circuits it has a rise, a duration and a decay. The pulse has a leading edge and a trailing edge.

**pulse amplitude** the magnitude of the pulse above the normally constant value. This is a general definition and more exact definitions are used with the variety of pulsating currents.

**rise time** the interval between the instants of the amplitude of a pulse (↑) going from its lower to its higher limit, usually measured for the leading edge to go from 10 per cent to 90 per cent of the pulse amplitude.

**pulse rise time** rise time (↑).

**decay time** the interval between the instants of the amplitude of a pulse (↑) going from its higher to its lower limit, usually measured for the trailing edge to go from 90 per cent to 10 per cent of the pulse amplitude.

**pulse decay time** decay time (↑).

**return from zero time** decay time (↑).

**impulse** (*n*) (1) a pulse (↑) whose duration is so short it can be considered to be infinitesimal; (2) synonymous with pulse.

**spike** (*n*) an impulse (↑) in a pulse train (↓).

**pulse train** a sequence of equally spaced pulses of similar characteristics.

**pulse repetition frequency** the number of pulses transmitted in one second in pulse-code modulation (p.43).

**chopper** (*n*) a device which interrupts the transmission of a current or a beam of light to produce a pulsating current (↑) or signal.

**polar** (*adj*) describes a coding method in which binary 1 is represented by current flowing in one direction and binary 0 by current flowing in the opposite direction. This is achieved by using negative and positive pulses (↑).

**delay element** a device that delays a pulse (↑) for a fixed period of time, e.g. a delay line (p.230).

**one-shot multivibrator** with no input to the circuit *(see diagram)* $T_2$ conducts normally from the supply line at +V volts, through the emitter and collector to earth. $T_1$ is off, bottomed (p.103) by the bias to its base. When a positive impulse is applied at the input, $T_1$ is switched

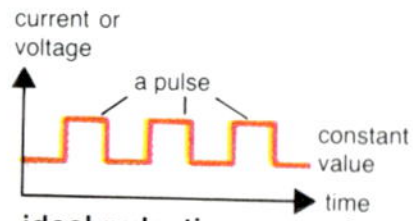

**ideal pulsating current**

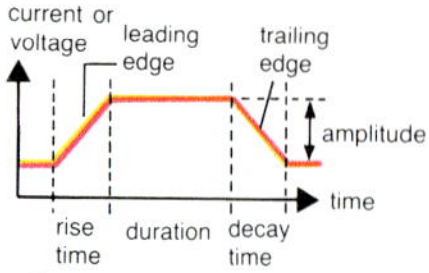

**characteristics of a pulse**

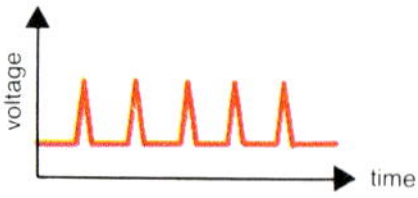

**train of spikes (impulses)**

on, resulting in a drop in its collector voltage. The capacitor, C, connects this voltage drop to the base of $T_2$, which is switched off. This causes the voltage on $T_2$ collector to rise. The capacitor has become charged, and then leaks the charge through resistor R. The time factor for the constant RC determines the period for which $T_2$ is switched off. When the bias on $T_2$ becomes too low, $T_2$ switches on again. The output is a pulse initiated by a spike impulse (↑) at the input.

**one-shot multivibrator circuit**

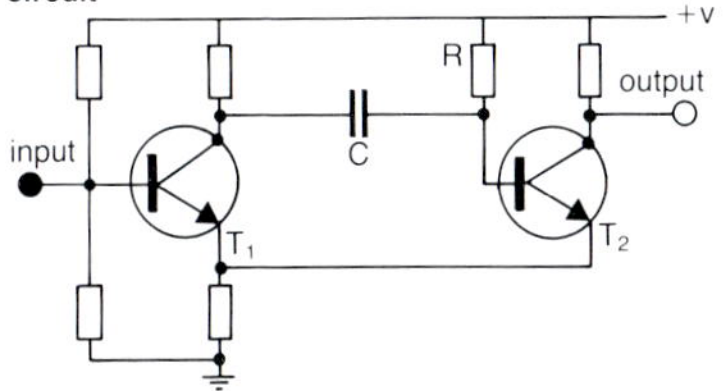


**action of one-shot multivibrator**

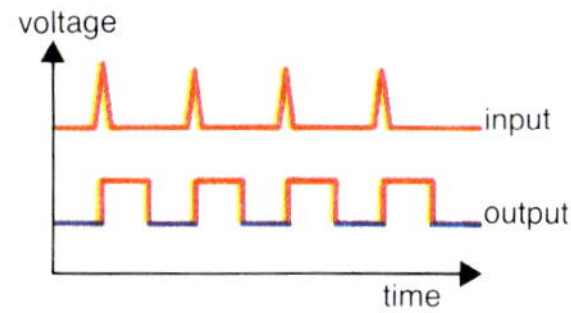


**resistance characteristics of a transistor**

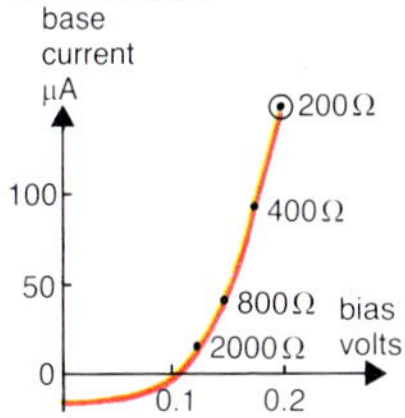


**pulse stretcher**

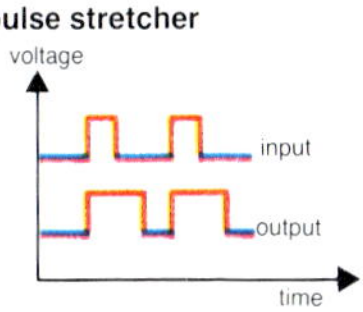


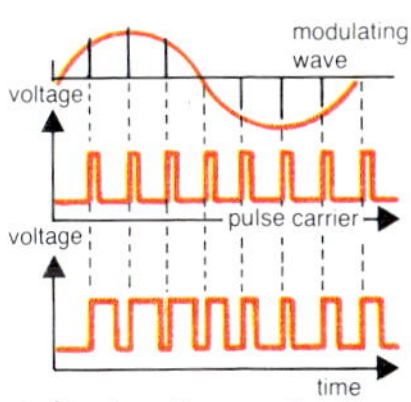


**pulse duration modulation**

**pulse stretcher** a one-shot multivibrator (↑) circuit with the resistance, R, replaced by a transistor acting as a resistor. This allows the factor RC to be altered so that the length of the pulse (↑) depends on the value of R. The duration of the output pulse is always longer than the duration of the input pulse. The diagram shows a typical variation of input resistance with base current and bias for a transistor.

**pulse duration modulation** a modulating wave (*see diagram*) is to be transmitted by a pulse carrier, a regular pulsating current with pulses of equal width. The modulating wave is sampled at regular intervals, and a voltage generated proportional to the amplitude of the modulating wave. This voltage is fed into a pulse stretcher (↑), and a pulsating current is produced with pulse widths proportional to the amplitude of the modulating wave. For maximum negative amplitude of the modulating wave, the stretch is nil. For accuracy of modulation the pulse repetition frequency should be high compared with the frequency of the modulating wave.

**PDM** (*abbr*) pulse duration modulation (↑). *Compare pulse amplitude modulation* (p.44).

**race** (*n*) in sequential and parallel circuits, unequal propagation delays (p.116) in logic circuits (p.106) supplying a common gate can result in a spurious pulse (↑). This is a logic hazard, and races in circuits may affect the final result.

**bounce** (*n*) a mechanical switch, such as a toggle, push-button or contact switch, may not be fully and finally closed for a few milliseconds, and during this time several separate impulses (p.120) may be generated by the contact. These impulses are contact bounce, and cause glitches (p.237). This is a logic hazard and has to be eliminated by a debouncing circuit (↓).

**contact bounce** bounce (↑).

**debounce** (*v*) to remove bounce (↑) ensuring a single sharp switching action.

**debouncing circuit** a switch is connected to an R-S flip-flop (p.114) as shown in the diagram; the flip-flop uses two NAND gates. When the switch is set, input S is high (positive voltage). When the switch is reset, input S is low (zero). A zero output (=0) indicates an OFF position and a positive output indicates ON. If bounce (↑) occurs, positive impulses are delivered at S; the output remains positive, i.e. this is the state of the flip-flop which remains unaltered. However many contact impulses are received, the output remains positive and thus eliminates bounce.

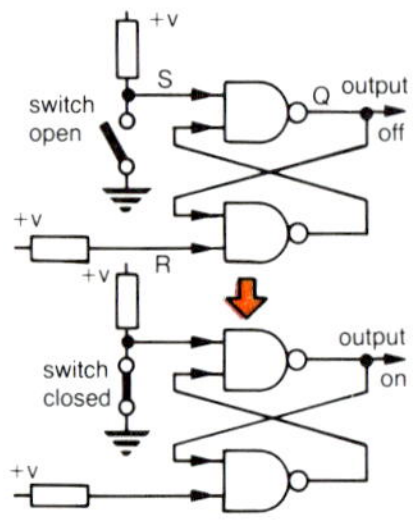

**debouncing circuit**

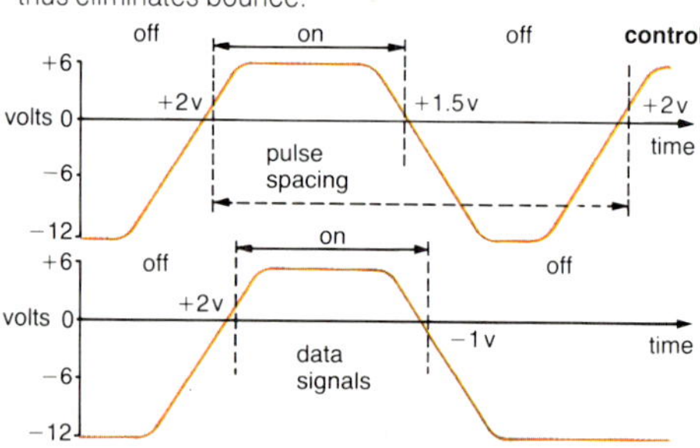

**pulse response**

**pulse response** a pulse (p.120) shape is non-ideal when produced by an electronic circuit. The leading edge of the pulse passes through a voltage which is sufficient to operate a gate or a flip-flop *(see diagram)*. Similarly on the trailing edge, there is a point at which the pulse ceases to activate a device. These voltages differ for control signals and for data signals.

**pulse spacing** the time interval between the corresponding instants of two pulses *(see diagram)*.

**pulse jitter** very small variations of pulse spacing (↑) in a pulse train (p.120).

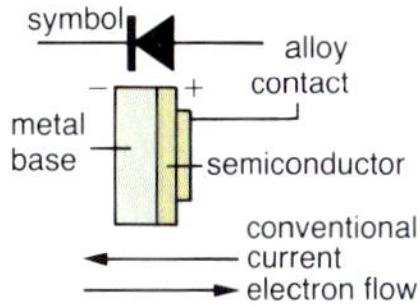

**metal rectifier**

**half-wave rectifying circuit**
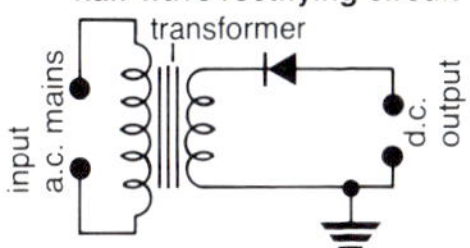


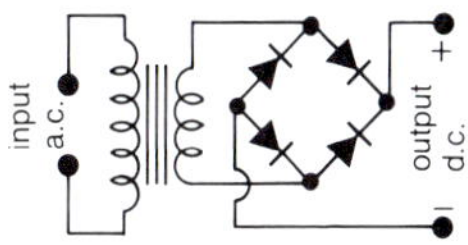

**full-wave rectifying circuit**

**rectifier** (*n*) a device which converts alternating current to direct current. Common devices are metal, crystal and diode rectifiers. **rectification** (*n*), **rectify** (*v*).

**metal rectifier** a rectifier consisting of a semiconductor (p.92) in contact with a metal base. A rectifier used for large-scale power rectification.

**crystal rectifier**[2] a point-contact diode, used as a rectifier.

**diode rectifier** a junction diode (p.96), used as a rectifier.

**power-supply operation** modern power supplies for microcomputers use solid-state components which include a transformer, a rectifier (↑), a filter (p.124) and a voltage regulator (p.124).

**rectifying circuit** a simple rectifying circuit produces half-wave rectification *(see diagram)*. A full-wave rectifying circuit rectifies both positive and negative voltages of alternating current. The transformer in each circuit reduces the a.c. voltage to the required d.c. voltage.

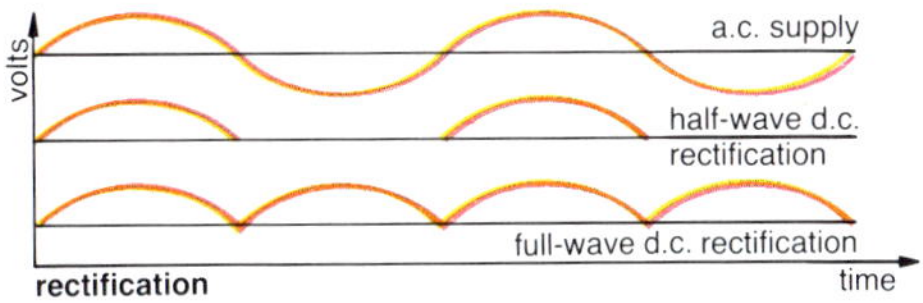

**rectification**

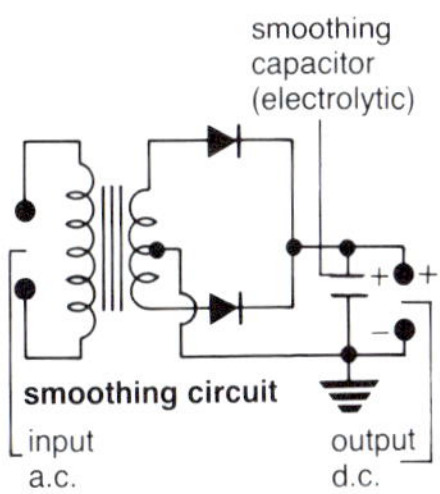

**smoothing circuit**

**smoothing circuit** full-wave rectification produces a voltage with a series of peaks. To overcome this, a smoothing circuit is used, usually a large capacitor connected in parallel with the output. The storage capacity of the capacitor never allows the voltage to reach zero, as it is charged by an increasing voltage and discharges when current is drawn from it.

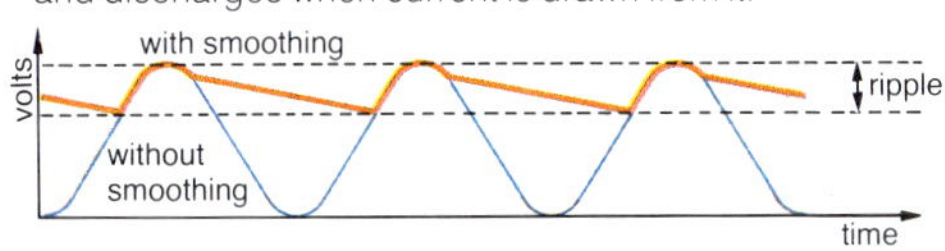


**ripple** (*n*) the variation in voltage, an a.c. component from rectification, which is small in comparison with the d.c. voltage from the rectified output.

**ripple filter** a low-pass filter (p.124) which reduces the ripple current while passing the direct current output from a rectifier. It uses an inductor, L, a coil which suppresses ripple, and a capacitor. Choosing suitable values for the components, ripple is reduced to 0.1 per cent of the d.c. voltage.

**ripple filter**
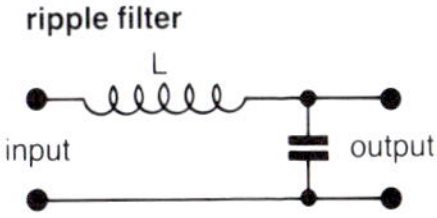

**filter** (*n*) a device using a capacitor and an inductor to remove certain frequencies of an alternating current. If *L* is the inductance of the inductor and *C* is the capacitance of the capacitor, then the cut-off frequency, *f*, of the circuit is given by $f = 1/2\pi\sqrt{LC}$. For a high-pass filter, frequencies below *f* are reduced; for a low-pass filter, frequencies above *f* are reduced. A simple filter circuit does not have a sharp cut-off point.

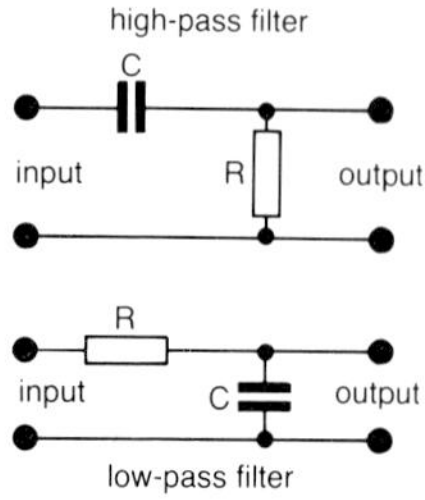

**filter circuit**

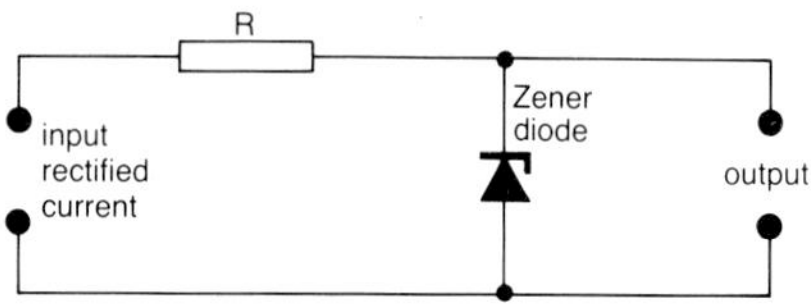

**simple voltage-regulator circuit**

**voltage-regulator circuit** a Zener diode (p.97) can be used to stabilize the voltage of a rectified current. The circuit, under working conditions, uses the avalanche current of the diode, stabilizing the voltage at the diode's breakdown voltage. A Zener diode is not always able to provide a large enough current to meet the demands of a computer, as the current rating may be exceeded.

**voltage-stabilizing circuit** voltage-regulator circuit (↑).

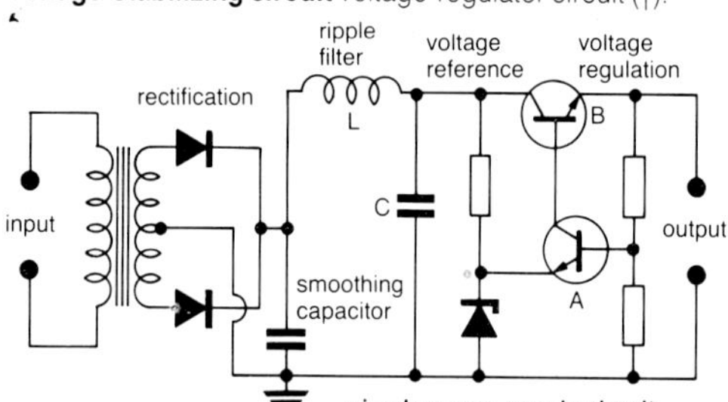

**simple power-supply circuit**

**power-supply circuit** a simple basic circuit is shown in the diagram, with a Zener diode providing a voltage reference, but passing a small current only. Transistor A compares the output voltage with the Zener voltage and controls the current passed by transistor B so as to keep the output voltage constant.

**warm-up time** the period of time between switching on an energy supply to a device, and the device supplying its rated output characteristics.

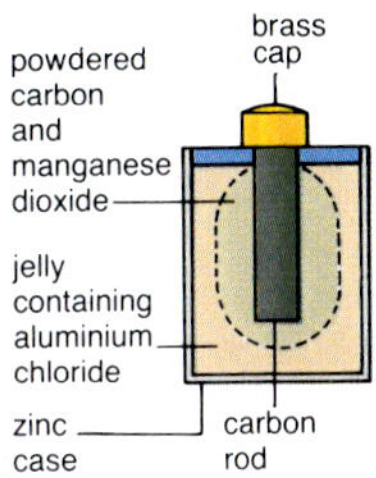


**dry cell**

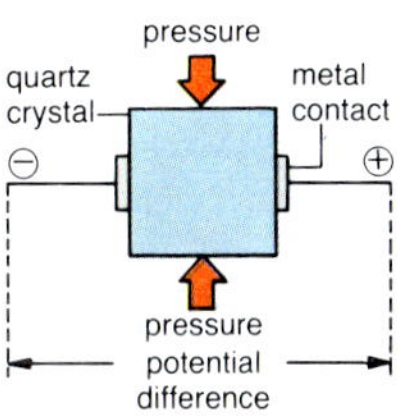


**piezoelectric effect**

**electric cell** a source of electrical energy; it provides electric potential at a specific voltage for a particular cell.

**battery** (*n*) two or more cells, usually connected in series.

**dry cell** the normal dry cell (incorrectly called a battery) is a Leclanché cell with a zinc and a carbon electrode. The electrodes are in contact with a jelly containing ammonium chloride as an electrolyte. The carbon rod is surrounded by a depolarizer, manganese dioxide. The cell delivers 1.5 volts. Its action consumes the zinc case, and it cannot be recharged.

**nickel-cadmium cell** a cell with a cadmium cathode and an anode of nickel oxide held in pockets of perforated steel. The electrolyte is potassium hydroxide. The cell delivers 1.2 volts and can be recharged.

**cadmium cell** a nickel-cadmium cell (↑).

**nickel-iron cell** a cell with an iron cathode and an anode of nickel oxide. Both electrodes are made of perforated steel with the electrode material held in powder form in pockets of the electrode. The electrolyte is potassium hydroxide. The cell delivers 1.2 volts and can be recharged.

**NiFe cell** a nickel-iron cell (↑).

**accumulator**[1] (*n*) an electric cell (↑) which can be recharged.

**electrostriction** (*n*) the changes in the physical dimensions of a crystalline dielectric (p.93) that appear when an external electric field is applied.

**piezoelectric effect** when pressure is applied to certain crystals, positive and negative charges are produced on opposite faces. These charges give rise to a potential difference between the faces. This effect is the opposite of electrostriction (↑).

**piezoelectric crystal** a crystal that exhibits the piezoelectric effect (↑).

**quartz** (*n*) natural crystalline silicon dioxide; it is a dielectric (p.93) and a piezoelectric crystal (↑). Quartz crystals are used in clock (p.148) devices.

**crystal electrostriction** electrostriction (↑).

**crystal oscillator** an oscillating circuit whose frequency is determined by a piezoelectric crystal. A quartz crystal is normally used as the piezoelectric crystal. Crystal oscillators have a high order of accuracy for their frequency of oscillation.

**ferromagnetic material** a material whose permeability (↓) is much greater than that of a vacuum; the permeability varies with the strength of the external magnetic field (↓). Ferromagnetic materials exhibit hysteresis (↓). Iron, nickel, cobalt, manganese, and alloys of these metals are common ferromagnetic materials.

**magnetic field** a field of force which exists as a result of a conductor carrying an electric current or from the presence of a permanent magnet. It has magnitude and direction.

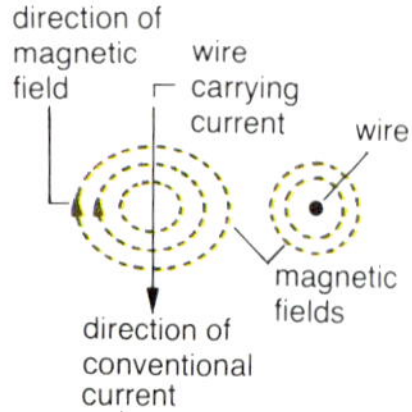


**magnetic fields**

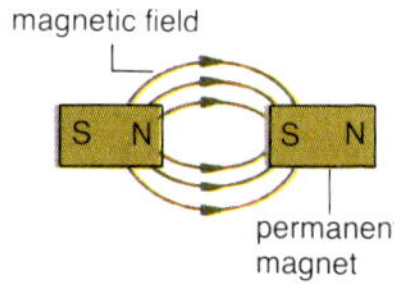


**magnetic flux** a measure of the strength of a magnetic field (↑). It is equal to the force per unit area acting on one metre of wire carrying a current of one ampere. It is measured in **tesla**.

**permeability** (*n*) a property of a material or medium which determines the magnitude of the magnetic flux (↑) in it. The relative permeability of a material or medium is the radio of the magnetic flux in it divided by the magnetic flux in a vacuum of the same area. The permeability of a vacuum is 1.

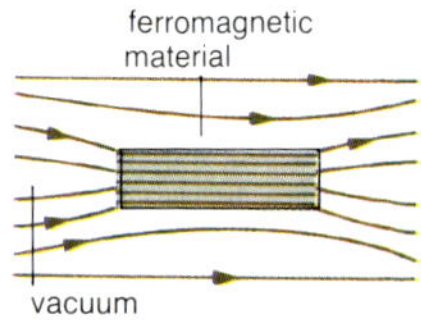


**magnetic flux in a ferromagnetic material** (representation of permeability)

**magnetic permeability** permeability (↑).

**magnetic-field interference** interference induced in electric circuits due to the presence of magnetic fields arising from conductors carrying electric current.

**magnetic hysteresis** the property of a magnetic material which causes the magnetic flux in the material to depend on the previous history of magnetization. On magnetizing a material a magnetic flux is formed in the material; on reducing the magnetizing field, the loss in magnetic flux lags behind in reduction. A hysteresis cycle is formed by a complete cycle of variation of the applied magnetic field.

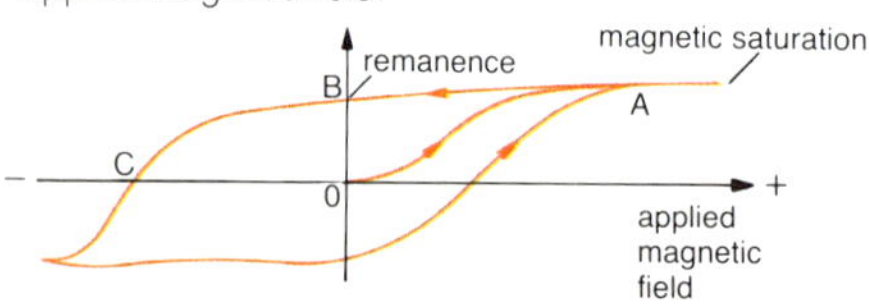


**hysteresis cycle**

**magnetic saturation** the state in which an increase in strength of the applied magnetic field produces no further increase in the magnetization of a material. Point A *(see diagram)* of the hysteresis cycle.

**remanence** (*n*) the residual magnetic flux in a material when the applied magnetic field is reduced to zero. Point B *(see diagram)* of the hysteresis cycle.

**reluctance** (*n*) the property of a piece of material to resist a magnetic flux passing through it. It is the reciprocal of the relative permeability multiplied by the area of the material.

**ferromagnetics** (*n*) a study of the storage of information in computers by the use of magnetic materials as binary storage elements.

**electromagnetic induction** when a changing magnetic flux (↑) passes through a coil, an electromotive force is induced in the coil producing a potential difference between the ends of the coil. An induced current flows in the coil.

**induction in a coil**

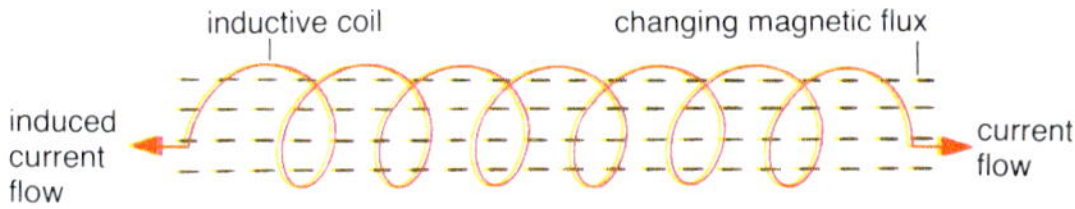


**induction** (*n*) electromagnetic induction (↑).

**inductance** (*n*) a changing current in a coil produces a changing magnetic flux. The changing magnetic flux results in an induced current which opposes the original current flowing in the coil. A coil thus inhibits the flow of alternating current, and is consequently called a choke. An iron core in the coil increases the effect. Inductance is a measure of the effect of induction.

**choke**

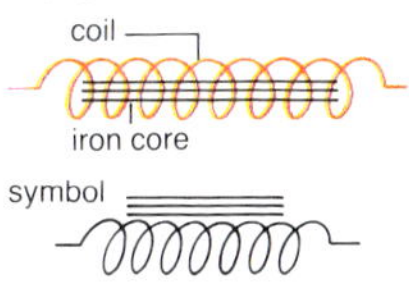


**choke** (*n*) *see inductance* (↑).

**magnetic striction**

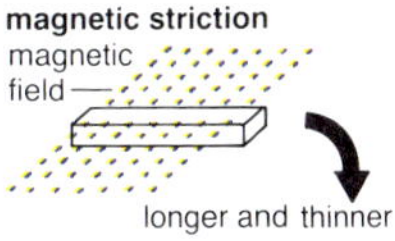


**magnetic striction** the effect by which placing a ferromagnetic material (↑) in a magnetic field (↑) makes it longer and thinner. The change in shape is very small.

**Curie point** the temperature at which a material loses its ferromagnetic properties.

**Hall effect** when an electric current flows through a conductor and a magnetic field is applied to the conductor at right angles to the current, then a potential difference develops across the conductor which is perpendicular to both the magnetic field and the current. The effect is very small for metals, but about 0.1V in semiconductors.

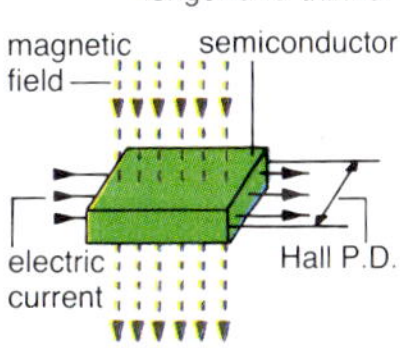


**Hall effect**

**Hall coefficient** the potential difference developed by the Hall effect (↑) is proportional to the magnetic flux density, the current density, and the width of the conductor. The constant of this proportionality is the Hall coefficient. It is positive for p-type semiconductors and negative for n-type.

**Hall constant** Hall coefficient (↑).

**waveform** (*n*) the graphic representation of a wave indicating the frequency and the variation of amplitude with time. Typical waveforms are: sine, rectangular, sawtooth, pulse; these are ideal waveforms. Non-ideal pulses, and outputs from multivibrators (p.106), and flip-flops (p.114), have their own particular waveforms.

**amplitude** (*n*) the displacement between the zero position and a crest or a trough of a wave.

**frequency** (*n*) the number of crests, or troughs, of a wave passing a point in one second. Frequency is measured in hertz (Hz).

**sinusoidal wave** a wave which changes in amplitude (↑) with time according to a sine curve; e.g. $y = \sin x$ produces a sine curve. Alternating current has a sinusoidal waveform.

**non-sinusoidal wave** any waveform which is not sinusoidal (↑).

**square wave** a series of pulses with a mark-to-space ratio of unity.

**phase**[1] (*n*) points in a waveform are in phase if their displacements are of the same magnitude and moving in the same direction. If the crests of two waves coincide in time, the waves are in phase.

**phase angle** the difference in phase between two waveforms (↑) is measured by a phase angle, $\phi$. (Greek letter phi). The method of obtaining a phase angle is shown in the diagram. Waveform $W_1$ **leads** on $W_2$ or $W_2$ **lags** on $W_1$. If $\phi = 90°$ the crest of one wave is coincident in time with a zero displacement of the other. If $\phi = 180°$, the crest of one wave coincides with the trough of the other.

**phase difference** *see phase angle* (↑).

**LCR circuit** a circuit with a capacitor, C, an inductor, L, and a non-inductive resistor, R, which uses alternating current. C is the capacitance of the capacitor, L is the inductance of the inductor, and R is the resistance of the resistor. Using a capacitor, the voltage lags 90° on the current, using an inductor, the voltage leads 90° on the current, while with a non-inductive resistor, voltage and current are in phase. Using all three, a voltage is developed out of phase with the current by an angle $\phi$, where $\phi = \tan^{-1}(4\pi^2 f^2 LC - 1/2\pi fRC)$ and $f$ is the frequency (↑) of the wave.

**phase shifter** a device from which the output voltage differs in phase from the input voltage. LCR or capacitor circuits, are used to produce the phase difference.

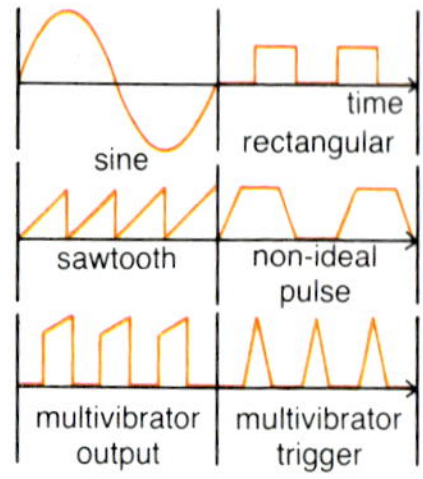

**waveforms**

**characteristics of a wave**

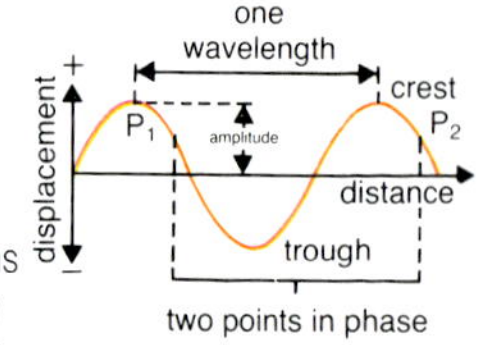


**phase differences**

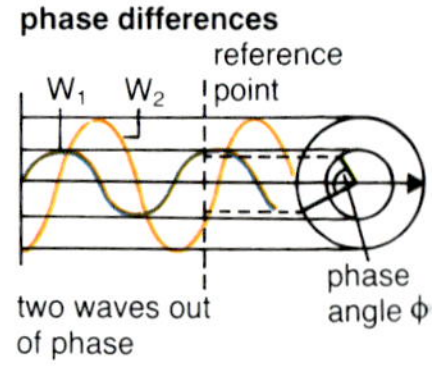


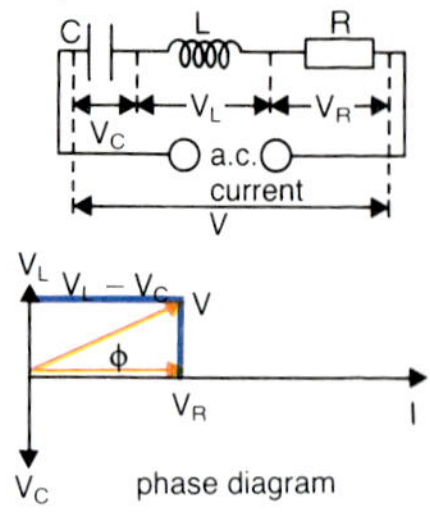

**LCR circuit**

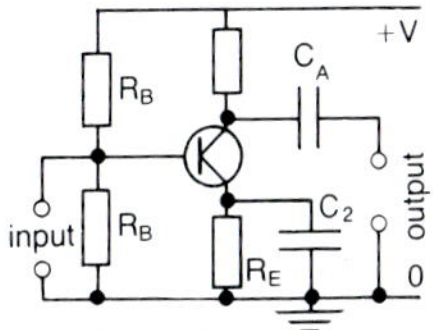

amplifier circuit

symbol for amplifier

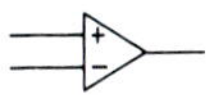

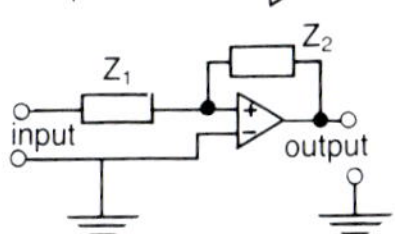

operational circuit

**amplifiers**

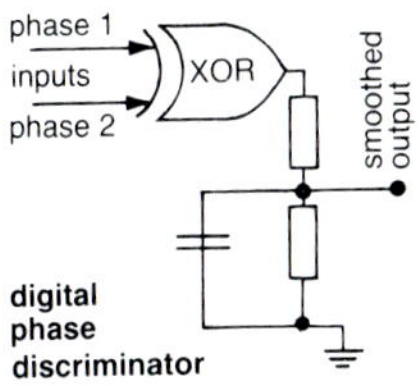

**digital phase discriminator**

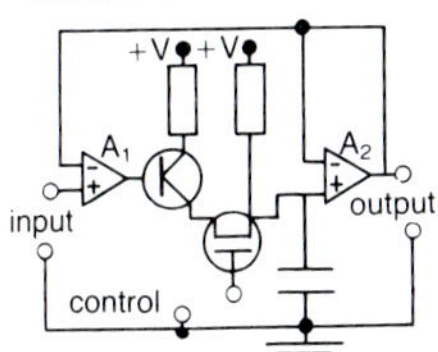

**track-and-hold circuit**

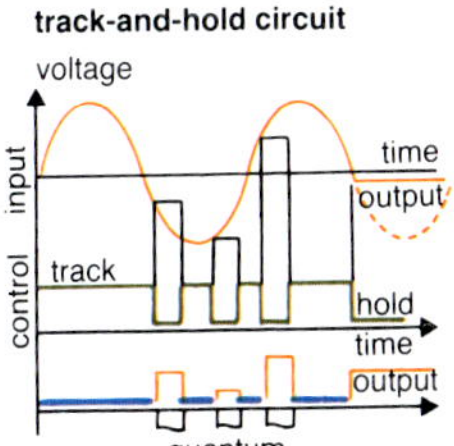

track and hold with **quantization**

**phase splitter** a device which has an output of two or more waves which have a phase difference from the input wave.

**amplifier**[2] (*n*) an amplifying circuit, using an n-p-n transistor, is shown in the diagram. The two resistors, $R_B$, provide bias for the base at the operating condition of the transistor. Capacitor $C_A$ blocks direct current to the output. $C_2$ is a by-pass capacitor to prevent the emitter voltage fluctuating at the signal frequency. $R_E$ is a stabilizing resistor. An operational amplifier has two resistors connected to the amplifier as shown in the circuit. If the resistances (↓) of these resistors are $Z_1$ and $Z_2$ *(see diagram)* then the voltage amplification is $Z_2/Z_1$, providing the impedance of the amplifier is very high.

**impedance** (*n*) if the voltage across an LCR circuit is V and the current passing through it is I, then the impedance, Z, is given by $Z = V/I$. Impedance is the effective resistance of capacitors and inductors to alternating current.

**phase discriminator** a device in which phase variations produce amplitude variations in the output. A digital phase discriminator can be made with an Exclusive OR gate, as shown in the diagram. The waveform produced by the gate is a rectangular wave whose mark-space ratio is proportional to the phase difference between the input square waves. The output wave is applied to a suitable low-pass filter to produce a d.c. voltage, which is proportional to the phase difference of the inputs.

**track-and-hold circuit** with the control OFF *(see diagram)* the signal passes straight to the output. With the control ON, the signal is held. The FET (p.100), is ON for tracking and OFF for hold. The output and the control can be used with an AND gate to produce an amplitude modulated pulse corresponding to the analog signal. This circuit is also known as a clamping circuit.

**quantization** (*n*) a process by which a signal wave is divided into a number of equal parts and a quantized value assigned to each part. Each part is a **quantum**. The quanta are separated by a space. A track-and-hold circuit (↑) uses a control signal to define the quanta, and the analog signal is converted to an amplitude modulated pulse, with the amplitude being the assigned quantized value.

**quantum** (*n*) (*pl: quanta*) *see quantization* (↑).

**transducer**[1] (*n*) a device which receives an input of energy in one waveform (p.128) and supplies waves in another form to an output. The waves can be voltage, current, signal impulses, sound waves, pressure waves, light waves, or any other form of wave energy. A microphone, a piezoelectric crystal, a phase shifter (p.128) are examples of transducers.

**clamp** (*v*) to hold an input signal to a transducer (↑) at an instantaneous level, e.g. the 'hold' action in a track-and-hold circuit (p.129).

**radio frequency** the frequency of an electromagnetic wave approximately between 10kHz and 100 000MHz.

**RF** (*abbr*) radio frequency (↑).

**voice frequency** the frequency of a sound wave, approximately between 20Hz and 3.5kHz.

**audio frequency** a frequency that can be heard by the human ear; it is between 15Hz and 20kHz.

**cathode rays** a stream of electrons emitted by a cathode (*a*) when the cathode is heated or (*b*) when it is bombarded by positive ions, in a partial vacuum.

**cathode-ray tube** a vacuum tube, specially constructed with a glass screen. It consists of an electron gun, electron lenses, and a fluorescent screen. The electron gun produces a stream of electrons, focused by an electric field into a beam. The electron beam is deflected horizontally and vertically by (*a*) an electric field formed between two sets of metal plates, or (*b*) a magnetic field formed by two sets of coils carrying current. The pairs of metal plates are fixed at right angles to each other inside the neck of the tube, and these electrostatic tubes are used for oscilloscopes. The two sets of coils are fitted at right angles to each other outside the neck of the tube, and these electromagnetic tubes are used for VDUs and TV receivers. The screen is coated with phosphors which emit light when bombarded by electrons.

**CRT** (*abbr*) cathode-ray tube (↑).

**afterglow** (*n*) the action of a phosphor, a phosphorescent material, continuing to glow after excitation by electrons.

**persistence** (*n*) the length of time for afterglow (↑).

**touch tablet** a small rectangular tablet operated by putting a finger on it. A cursor (p.18) on a CRT (↑), moves to follow the movements of the finger on the tablet. Items displayed on the CRT can then be manipulated by commands.

**cathode-ray tube**

1. electron gun
2. negatively charged electrode
3. heated cathode
4. anodes
5. electric field plates
6. vertical deflectors
7. horizontal deflectors

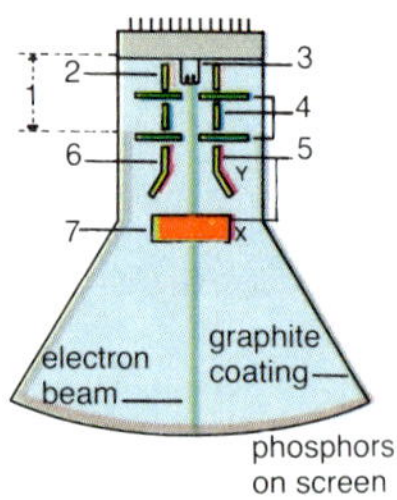


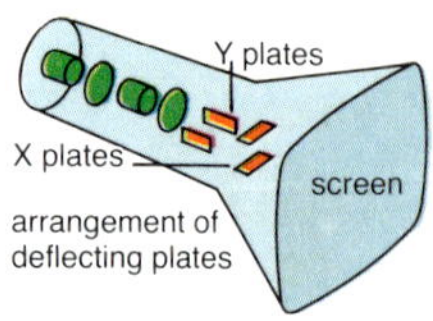


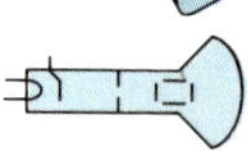
symbol for CRT

**emission** (*n*) the liberation of electrons or electromagnetic waves (↓) from a surface. Emission can be caused by heat, light, bombardment by atomic particles, radiation (↓), etc. **emit** (*v*), **emissive** (*adj*).

**radiation** (*n*) energy travelling in the form of electromagnetic waves (↓), electrons, alpha particles or neutrons.

**electromagnetic waves** sinusoidal waveforms produced by electric and magnetic fields perpendicular to each other and to the line of propagation. All frequencies have the same speed in a vacuum, or space; it is approximately $3 \times 10^8$ m/second. Electromagnetic waves can be reflected, refracted and polarized. The intensity and the speed of propagation are both reduced when the waves pass through a dense medium. The lowest frequencies are used as radio waves, the highest frequencies are gamma rays which are emitted by radioactive substances. The electromagnetic spectrum *(see diagram)* is composed of all the frequencies; the boundaries are not sharp, as each type of wave emerges into the next.

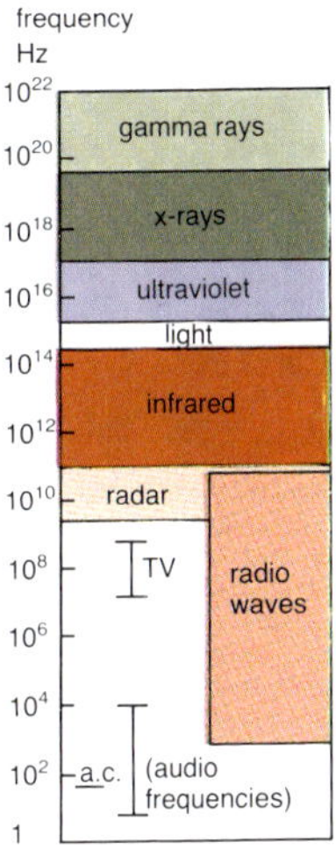


audio frequencies are voice frequencies modulating radio waves

**electromagnetic spectrum**

**electromagnetic radiation** electromagnetic waves (↑).

**ultra-violet radiation** electromagnetic radiation (↑) of higher frequency than violet light. It has a chemical, that is ionizing, effect on many materials, and is used with PROMs (p.173). The radiation causes burns on skin and eyes.

**UV** (*abbr*) ultra-violet, as for radiation (↑).

**ultra-violet lamp** a lamp emitting ultra-violet radiation.

**infra-red radiation** electromagnetic radiation (↑) of lower frequency than red light. It is emitted by hot bodies; the higher the temperature of the body, the higher the frequency of the waves.

**IR**[1] (*abbr*) infra-red, as for radiation (↑).

**laser** (*acro*) Light Amplification by Stimulation of Emission of Radiation. For example, the atoms in a ruby rod are stimulated by a flash tube *(see diagram)* and a sharply defined beam of intense light is emitted. The repeated reflection of the atoms in the rod builds up their energy which is transformed into light energy. Other lasers use: (1) helium-neon gas in tubes instead of a ruby rod; (2) semiconductor diodes producing a **coherent** output in the infrared (↑) range.

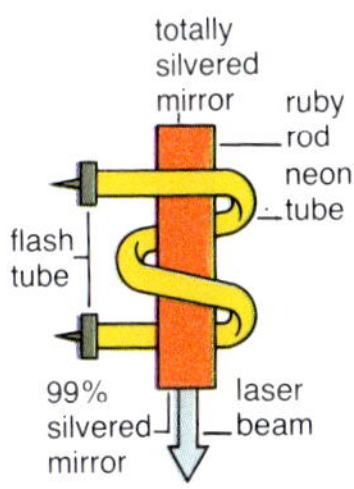


**laser**

light from flash tube excites atoms in ruby rod. Energy reflected to and fro between mirrors. When energy sufficiently high, laser beam emitted.

**photoelectricity** (*n*) the phenomenon of electrons being emitted from the surface of a material when light, ultraviolet radiation (p.131) or X-rays are directed at the surface. The intensity of the radiation must exceed a certain energy level for any one material. **photoelectric** (*adj*).

**photo-emissive** (*adj*) describes any surface exhibiting the phenomenon of photoelectricity (↑).

**photoconductivity** (*n*) the effect of increasing the conductivity, i.e. reducing the resistance, of a material when the intensity of electromagnetic radiation falling on it is increased. Such materials are usually semiconductors (p.92).

**photoelectric cell** the cell consists of a curved cathode and a small anode. The cathode is coated with a photo-emissive (↑) material, e.g. selenium, caesium oxide. When light, or ultraviolet radiation, falls on the cathode, electrons are emitted. When a positive potential is applied to the anode, the electrons are attracted to it, and a circuit is completed, with current flowing in the circuit. A photoelectric cell can also use the photovoltaic effect (↓), but usually it is the photo-emissive type. The characteristics *(see diagram)* of the cell show it can be used to measure the intensity of a radiation.

**photocell** (*n*) a photoelectric cell (↑).

**photovoltaic cell** a layer of a semiconductor (p.92), e.g. selenium or silicon, is fused on a base plate of metal, usually iron. The semiconductor is covered with a thin film of gold, and a circular metal contact is fitted round the edge. Electrons from the metal drift into the semiconductor, making it negative, while the metal becomes positive. When light falls on the cell, electrons are set free in the semiconductor, and repelled across the junction, a voltage is generated, and current flows. The semiconductor contact is negative and the metal base is positive. This cell generates its own voltage and no voltage is applied. It is more sensitive than a photocell (↑) and the current is proportional to the logarithm of the intensity of radiation.

**photovoltaic sensor** a photoelectric cell (↑). It has a good time of response between 1 and 100 microseconds, and the time can be reduced by suitable biasing. Photovoltaic sensors are used for light meters and in tape or card readers.

**photoelectric cell**

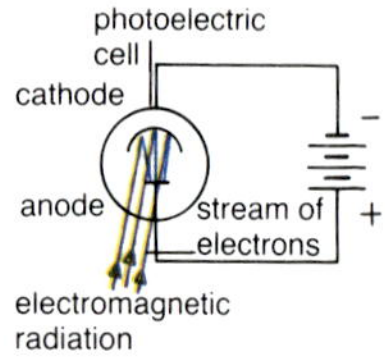


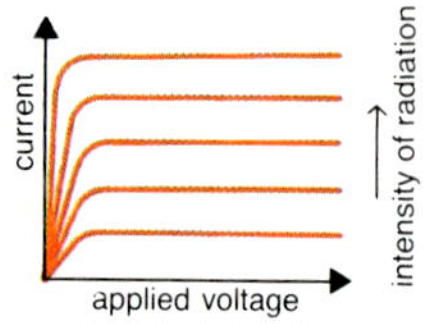


**characteristics of a photoelectric cell**

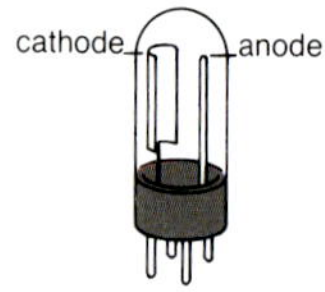


photocell

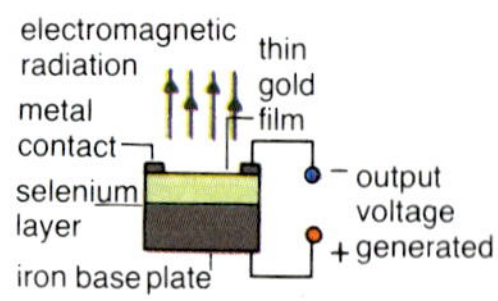


**photovoltaic cell**

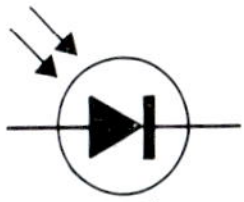

symbol for **photodiode**

**photodiode** (*n*) a junction diode (p.96) which can be illuminated by light. The diode is reverse biased (p.98). Light falls on the junction, and the resistance is lowered due to photoconductivity. A current then flows, which may be used to operate some form of detector.

**photoconductive diode** photodiode (↑).

**phototransistor** (*n*) an ordinary n-p-n or p-n-p transistor is used with a transparent case. This functions as a photodiode (↑) with current amplification, using the amplification factor of the transistor. A circuit showing the use of a phototransistor connects it to a relay. When light falls on the phototransistor, current flows and closes the relay. The resistor between base and emitter reduces the leakage current. The diode connected in parallel with the relay coil prevents any induction producing a high voltage and damaging the transistor, as any induced current is shorted.

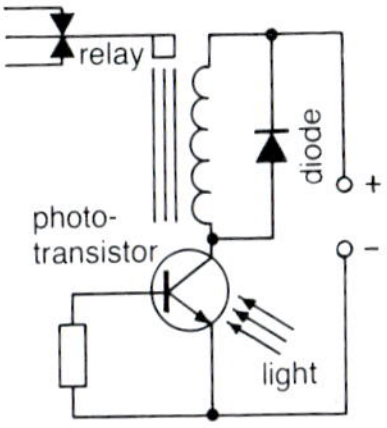


**phototransistor**

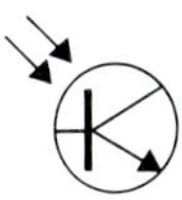

symbol for transistor

**photomultiplier** (*n*) a device which uses electron multiplication. Light falls on a cathode coated with a photo-emissive (↑) material, e.g. a semiconductor. The electrons from the photo-emissive surface bombard an electrode with a specially treated surface. The electrode emits up to four electrons for each electron bombarding it; this is called **secondary emission**. Such an electrode is called a **dynode**. With four dynodes $4^4$ (=256) electrons reach the anode of the device. Each dynode is given a successively increasing positive voltage to accelerate the electron, resulting in a much stronger current than in a photoelectric cell (↑).

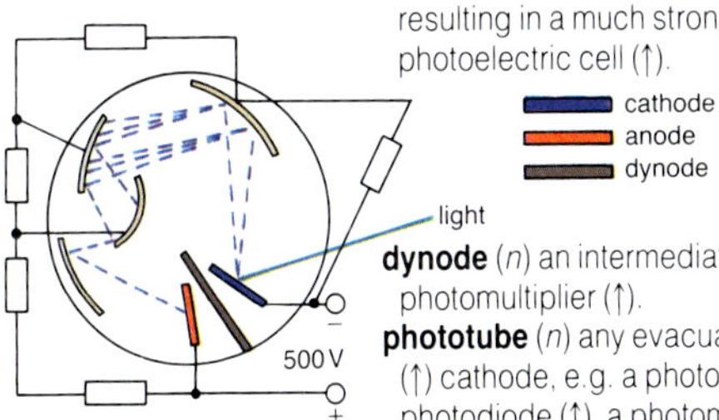


**photomultiplier**

**dynode** (*n*) an intermediate electrode in a photomultiplier (↑).

**phototube** (*n*) any evacuated tube with a photo-emissive (↑) cathode, e.g. a photoelectric cell (↑), a biased photodiode (↑), a photomultiplier (↑).

**photocell matrix** a two-dimensional array of small photocells, on which a lens projects an image of an optical character (p.194). The horizontal and vertical components of the character are recorded by the matrix. The matrix is then scanned to read the character.

**thermoelectric effect** the production of a potential difference etween two junctions of two different metals when the junctions are at different temperatures. The potential difference is of the order of a few millivolts.

**thermocouple** (*n*) a pair of junctions are made from two different metals. One junction is heated and the other is cooled. A potential difference is generated, the magnitude of which depends on the particular metals used. A copper-iron thermocouple produces a standard potential of 1.5mV; a thermocouple of copper-nickel over 20mV.

**Peltier effect** this is the converse effect of the thermo-electric effect (↑). If an electric current is passed through two junctions of two different metals, then one junction becomes hot and one becomes cold.

**thermionic emission** the emission of electrons from hot metals. It is used in cathode-ray tubes, X-ray tubes, discharge tubes, electron guns and thermionic valves (thermionic tubes).

**thermionic valve** a device using thermionic emission (↑). A heated cathode emits a stream of electrons which are attracted to the positive anode; the circuit is completed and current flows. The electrons can cause secondary emission of electrons from the anode, so the electron stream is slowed down by a negatively charged grid. Variations in the grid potential cause variations in the anode current.

**thermionic tube** thermionic valve (↑).

**static error**[1] static electricity is produced when two non-conducting surfaces are rubbed together. Plastic surfaces in particular produce static electricity; e.g. walking on a vinyl floor or on a synthetic fibre carpet can produce static voltages of 4,000–12,000 volts, although the charge is very small. A static charge of 500 volts, with a very small charge, can produce erroneous data on a transmission line or in memory locations. These are static errors. Static-free surfaces should be used in the vicinity of a computer and its peripheral equipment.

**dielectric isolation** in integrated circuits, parasitic capacitance (p.93) effects may appear due to semiconductor components being separated by insulation areas which act as dielectrics. These capacitances are not acceptable, and are eliminated by insulating each component with a dielectric layer. An isolation island (p.105) is used to achieve dielectric isolation.

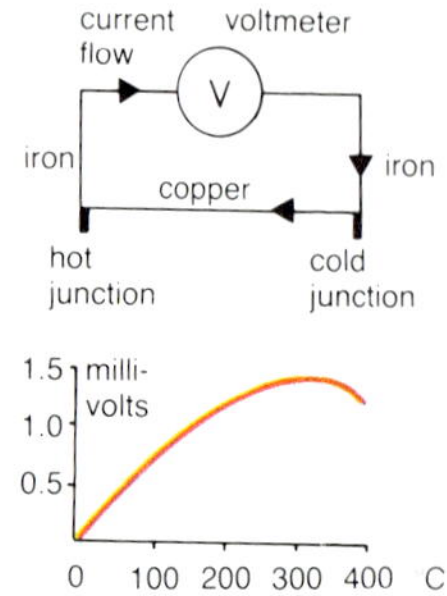


**thermocouple**

thermoelectric potential gainst temperature for an iron-copper thermocouple

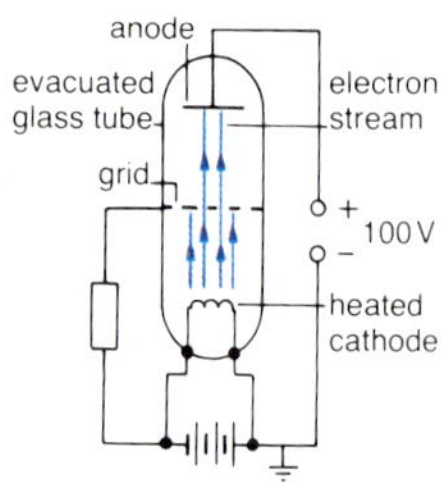


**thermionic valve**

**amplitude distortion** the effect produced by an amplifier, or other device, in which the output amplitude is not directly proportional to the input amplitude. The amount of distortion is usually measured with a sinusoidal (p.128) input under steady state conditions (↓).

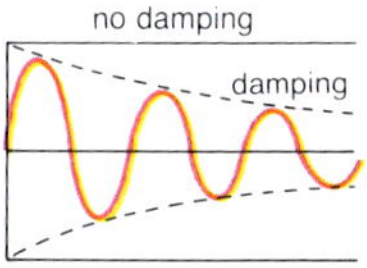


**damping** with a sinusoidal wave

**damping** (*n*) a gradual reduction in the amplitude and frequency of an oscillating circuit. The damping of a sinusoidal wave is shown in the diagram, the amplitude is reduced exponentially, but the frequency remains the same. Discharging a capacitor, for example, results in the production of an oscillatory voltage. Energy is dissipated in heating the circuit and emitting radio waves, so the amplitude is damped. If a large resistance is put in the circuit with the capacitor, the voltage charge is heavily damped so that there are no oscillations.

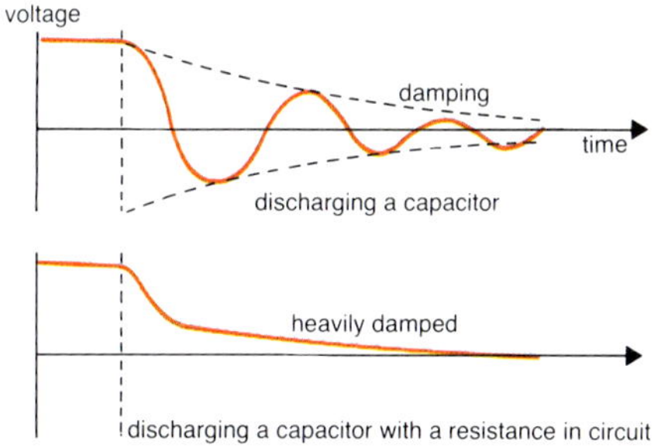


**steady state** a state in which current and voltage remain constant after all initial fluctuating or oscillating conditions have settled down.

**attentuation** (*n*) the reduction in signal strength between emission and reception.

**loss** (*n*) attenuation (↑).

**propagation loss** attenuation (↑).

**shielded line** a line or a circuit that is protected from external electric or magnetic fields by a sheath which is of conducting or ferromagnetic material.

**electrostatic screen** a grounded shield of conducting material surrounding an instrument or device to prevent interference by external electric fields.

**drift** (*n*) a slow gradual change in the output of a circuit. It is usually produced by heat causing changes in component values and/or characteristics. The heat is usually generated by the components themselves.

**chip** (*n*) a very small piece of a semiconductor, usually silicon, on which microscopic electronic devices are formed. The devices form one or more electrical circuits, which, when connected by leads to external devices, form an integrated circuit (p.105). The size of a chip is about 4–6mm square, and it is hermetically sealed in a plastic case.

**chip architecture** the interrelationship between the parts of a chip. A microprocessor chip has an ALU (p.150), registers (p.149) and a control-bus device. These are connected to pins which allow connection to other parts of the computer. The arrangement and connection of these circuits on the chip form the chip architecture.

**substrate** (*n*) the material on which an integrated circuit (p.105) is formed. It provides a solid support for the IC and may provide an electrical or a thermal function for the circuit as well. Silicon is the substrate for a silicon chip.

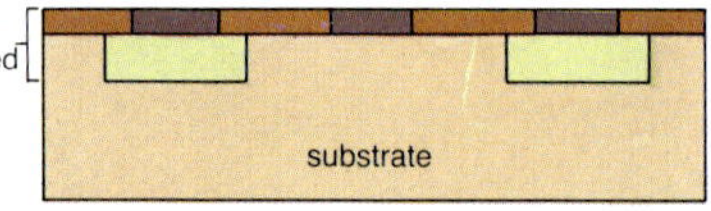


**chip size** the size describes the number of gates per chip (↑) in an integrated circuit (p.105) or the number of bits per chip that can be stored for a memory. For integrated circuits, *see LSI* (p.145). For memory chips, a chip recording 64000 bits is available. Chip size continues to grow, but growth produces problems of defects in manufacture, e.g. defects in photomasks (p.138), defects in semiconductor crystals, dust producing errors in etching. Chips range in size from 4mm to 6mm square.

**probe** (*n*) a test lead, with a fine point for contact on a particular point on an integrated circuit to test a chip after its manufacture.

**chip yield** the percentage of good, usable chips from a wafer (p.138). As manufacturing of chips is cheap once the necessary masks (p.138) have been prepared, a low yield is acceptable. All chips on a wafer are tested by probes (↑). Those which are unusable are marked before the wafer is cut up, and then rejected.

**chip carrier** a small, flat insulator on which a chip is mounted with fine aluminium wires attached to the contacts on the edge of the chip.

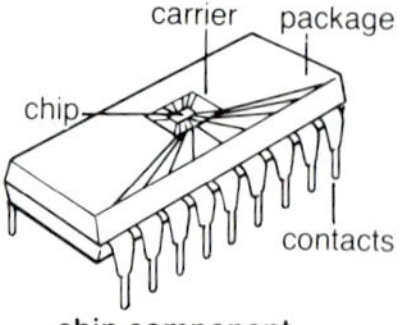


**chip component**

**package²** (*n*) the plastic, metal or ceramic base on which a chip carrier (↑) is mounted. The chip contacts are wired to pins on the package.

**chip component** a chip carrier mounted on a base with connecting leads to pins which provide contacts to other parts of a computer system.

**monolithic** (*adj*) describes a single silicon substrate (↑) on which an integrated circuit (p.105) is manufactured.

**silicon-on-sapphire** a substrate (↑) of artificial sapphire has a thin layer of silicon grown on it. The silicon layer is then processed to form an integrated circuit (p.105). Sapphire is a true insulator, hence the substrate is inert, and small silicon islands on the substrate form the circuit. This type of chip reduces parasitic capacitance (p.93) and reduces leakage currents (p.99). Sapphire and silicon have almost exactly equal coefficients of thermal expansion, so any heating during working of the circuit does not cause the silicon layer to separate from the sapphire substrate; sapphire is also an excellent conductor of heat.

**SOS** (*abbr*) silicon-on-sapphire (↑).

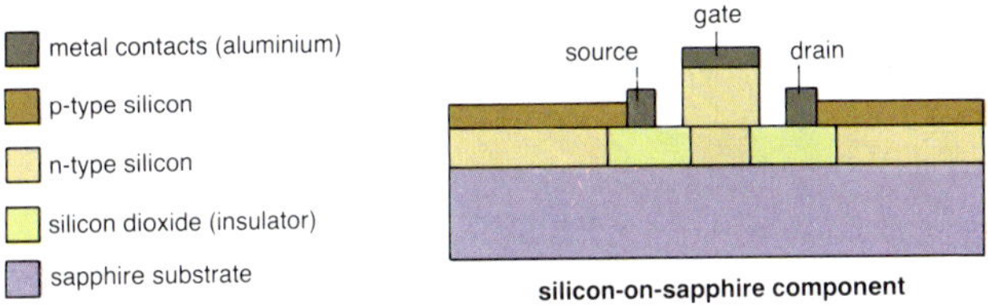


**silicon-on-sapphire component**

**microprocessor chip** a silicon chip (↑) on which is an integrated circuit (p.105) that contains all the essential parts of a central processing unit (p.146). The microprocessor chip is combined with a memory chip and an input/output chip to form a microcomputer. By itself, a microprocessor chip cannot function, it needs the other chips to form a viable system.

**microprocessor chip characteristics** the chip has the following general characteristics. (1) a byte (p.36) of 8 bits; (2) more than 70 instructions (p.48); (3) general-purpose registers; (4) arithmetic and logic functions; (5) memory locations for ROM (p.173); (6) clock and timing circuits; (7) a 2μs instruction cycle time; (8) interrupt handling; (9) power-on circuits. Chips with 16 data-bits and 32 data-bits are available.

**slab** (*n*) a crystal of p-type silicon usually, but n-type can also be used. It is produced from molten silicon doped (↓) to form an extrinsic semiconductor.

**wafer** (*n*) a thin slice of silicon cut from a slab (↑). A wafer is 7.5–10cm in diameter and circular or square in shape; it is about 0.45mm thick.

**slice** (*n*) a wafer (↑).

**lap** (*v*) to polish one side of a wafer (↑) to produce an optically flat surface.

**art work** a large-scale drawing of the different layouts of layers of semiconductors, insulators and connectors needed to make an integrated circuit. The drawing is reduced in size to make a mask (↓) for individual chips.

**mask²** (*n*) the pattern from artwork (↑) printed photographically on glass to define the areas on a chip to form windows (↓). The pattern is repeated a sufficient number of times to cover a wafer (↑); it contains about 500–1,000 repeated patterns.

**photomask** (*n*) a mask (↑).

**projection aligner** a device to fix a mask (↑) in its correct position over a wafer (↑) so that the correct areas on each individual chip are made into windows (↓).

**photoresist** (*n*) a material which is photosensitive and resistant to an etching material. It is used to cover a wafer and then is covered by a mask (↑). Ultraviolet radiation is shone on it. The exposed parts can be washed off, the parts covered by the mask are not removed. The photoresist is hardened in a furnace.

**etch** (*v*) to remove unwanted material from a surface, usually by using concentrated acid. In a silicon chip, silicon dioxide is usually removed.

**window** (*n*) the exposed semiconductor layer left after a silicon dioxide layer has been etched away. Windows are made for diffusion (↓) processes.

**dopant** (*n*) a substance added to a semiconductor to increase its conductivity. Dopants produce p-type or n-type semiconductors (p.94).

**doping** (*n*) the process of adding a dopant (↑) to a semiconductor. **dope** (*v*).

**diffusion** (*n*) the process by which a dopant (↑) spreads from the surface into a substrate (p.136) of semiconductor material. In the manufacture of silicon chips, a wafer (↑) is heated in a furnace in an atmosphere of the dopant. The dopant penetrates the surface of the substrate through a window (↑). **diffuse** (*v*).

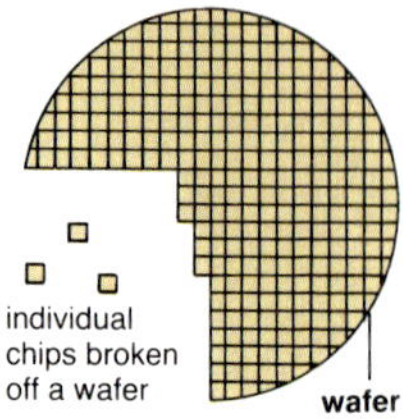

a mask for an individual chip

1. a layer of silicon dioxide is formed top and bottom of a wafer

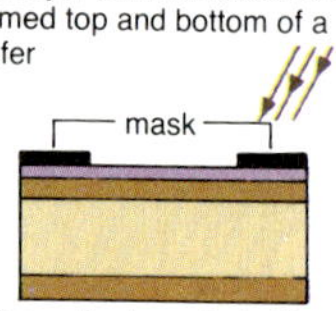


2. the wafer is coated with photoresist and exposed to ultraviolet radiation through a mask

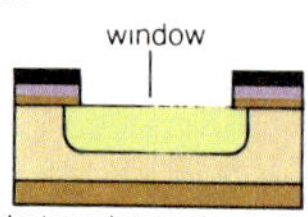


3. photoresist washed off leaving a window. Dopant diffused into substrate

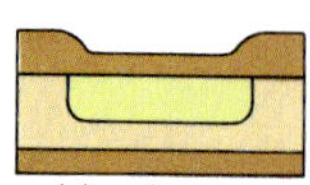

4. remaining photoresist removed. Reoxidized surface

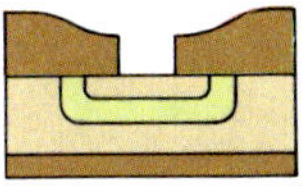

5. stages 2 and 3 repeated diffusing dopant to make a third layer

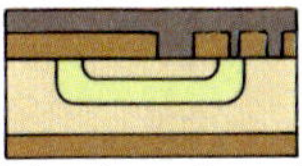

6. windows formed by another mask and photoresist. Whole surface covered with metal

pnp transistor

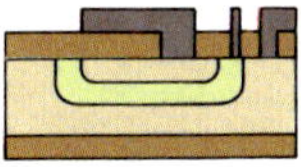

7. metal etched away using further mask and photoresist to leave contacts

- p-type silicon
- n-type silicon
- silicon dioxide
- photoresist
- metal

**using photolithography to make a silicon chip**

**absorption** (*n*) the taking in of a gas, a liquid, a radiation, or energy into a solid or a liquid, e.g. the absorption of heat and light by black surfaces.

**silicon** (*n*) an element with the properties of a semiconductor (p.92). Steel containing 3.5 per cent silicon makes a magnetic material used in the iron cores of chokes and transformers.

**silicon dioxide** the substance formed by heating silicon in oxygen. Silicon dioxide is an insulator. It occurs in crystalline forms such as quartz, and is the main constituent of sand and many rocks. Silicon dioxide is called silica.

**donor impurity** an element with more valency electrons than the semiconductor material to which it is added. It greatly increases the number of electrons available to conduct current and produces an n-type semiconductor (p.92). About one part in $10^7$ is added.

**acceptor impurity** an element with fewer valency electrons than the semiconductor material to which it is added. It greatly increases the number of holes available to conduct current and produces a p-type semiconductor (p.92). About one part in $10^7$ is added.

**p-type silicon** silicon with boron as an impurity, or dopant (↑).

**n-type silicon** silicon with phosphorus as an impurity, or dopant (↑).

**alloy** (*n*) a material composed of two or more elements, one of which must be a metal. The result is an homogenous mixture, similar to a solution. The properties of an alloy are often similar to those of its constitutents, but generally an alloy is harder than its chief constituent.

**metallization** (*n*) the pattern of metal, usually aluminium, on the surface of a silicon chip, that provides the conducting connections of the integrated circuit (p.105). The chip is covered with metal, then photoresist (↑), then a mask. A window (↑) is formed and the unprotected metal is removed by etching (↑), leaving the circuit connections.

**laser annealing** the removal of ionic impurities by heating a semiconductor surface by a laser (p.131). It is more efficient than annealing by heating.

**UV light** ultraviolet radiation (p.131).

**photolithography** (*n*) the use of photoresist (↑) masks, and etching in the manufacture of integrated circuits on chips.

**epitaxial growth** a wafer (p.138) of silicon is heated to 1200°C and vapours containing free silicon atoms are passed over the crystalline silicon. These silicon atoms are deposited on the wafer and extend the crystal structure of the silicon, forming a layer, or film. Impurities can also be introduced to dope (p.138) the silicon.

**epitaxial film** a film of semiconductor material formed by epitaxial growth (↑).

**thick film** a film manufactured by applying a paste, or solid, coating through a mask on to a ceramic substrate, and heating it in a furnace to form the film. Successive layers are applied to build up components of an integrated circuit. The result is a microminiaturized circuit on the insulating substrate. Thick films are cheaper to make than thin films (↓) but of poorer quality. They are usually more than 5µm thick.

**thin film** a film manufactured on a glass or ceramic substrate. Metal, or other materials, are deposited on the substrate, then a design formed on them using a mask and photoresist (p.138). Unprotected materials are etched away leaving an electrical circuit. The thickness of the film is 1 µm or less.

**two-dimensional circuitry** circuits formed from thin films (↑).

**hybrid integrated circuit** a circuit formed from semiconductor and other material on an insulating substrate such as ceramic materials or glass.

**channel**[1] (*n*) a region of a semiconductor between two electrodes with an electric field applied at right angles to the region. Current flows in the channel with the current strength controlled by the electric field.

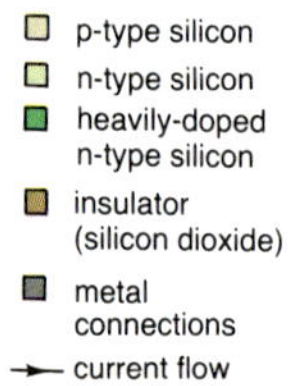


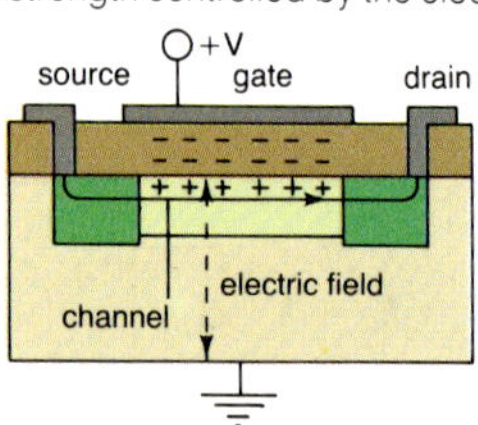


**channel in a semiconductor**

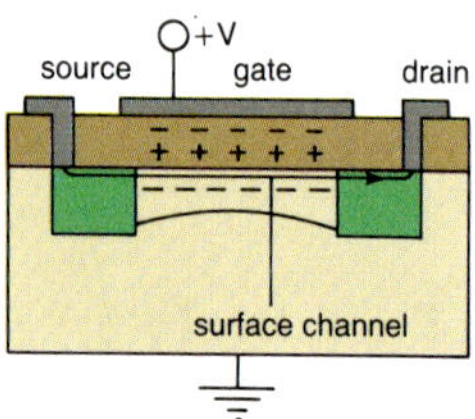


**surface channel**

**surface channel** a channel (↑) created by induction at the interface of a semiconductor and an insulator. As the electric field is increased, so is the current flowing at the interface.

**passivation** (*n*) the formation of an insulating layer, usually silicon dioxide, over a silicon semiconductor to prevent atmospheric contamination.

**planar** (*adj*) describes a device, used in an integrated circuit (p.105) in which all the electrodes are in the same plane. The different regions of semiconductor material are also in the same plane, or in a plane only slightly different.

**planar process** the process for manufacturing a silicon chip, using photolithographic (p.139) processes. Other planar processes are: thin-film deposition; surface passivation (↑); epitaxial growth.

**planar transistor** a transistor formed by etching and diffusion of semiconductor material and provided with electrodes that are all in the same plane.

**planar transistor**

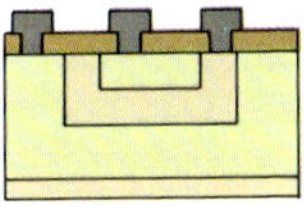



**metal-insulator-silicon** a silicon substrate is doped with phosphorus to produce the required conductivity. The substrate is then covered with silicon dioxide, etched to form the required circuit and then provided with metal electrodes.

**MIS** (*abbr*) metal-insulator-silicon (↑).

**silicon integrated circuit** an integrated circuit formed on a silicon wafer (p.138), consisting of layers, one on top of the other, of silicon semiconductors and metal. The circuit patterns are now designed down to a minimum width of 3 micrometres.

**SIC** (*abbr*) silicon integrated circuit (↑).

**purpose built** (*adj*) describes a silicon integrated chip (↑) designed by the manufacturers for a particular purpose, for example a silicon chip (p.136) for a digital watch, a portable digital thermometer, a small pocket calculator.

**custom built** (*adj*) purpose built (↑).

**dedicated**[2] (*adj*) a chip (p.136), a machine, a program, a transmission line, designed or set aside for one particular use.

**undedicated** (*adj*) a standard chip (p.136) which is not dedicated (↑). A transmission line used for general purposes.

**wired logic** a system using a printed circuit board (p.104) with standard chips, usually SSI or MSI (p.145), to provide required functions such as a microprocessor (p.147), memory chip, interface chip (p.219). It is the simplest and cheapest way of producing a purpose-built (↑) computer.

**uncommitted logic array** a chip (p.136) containing an array of gates (p.110) which are complete in themselves, but not connected to form a circuit. A manufacturer can add metallic connections to produce an appropriate circuit. Manufacture is cheap and quick. The circuit is limited in design by the logic array, and the final circuit may not be the optimum one.
**ULA** (*abbr*) uncommitted logic array (↑).

**uncommitted logic arrays**

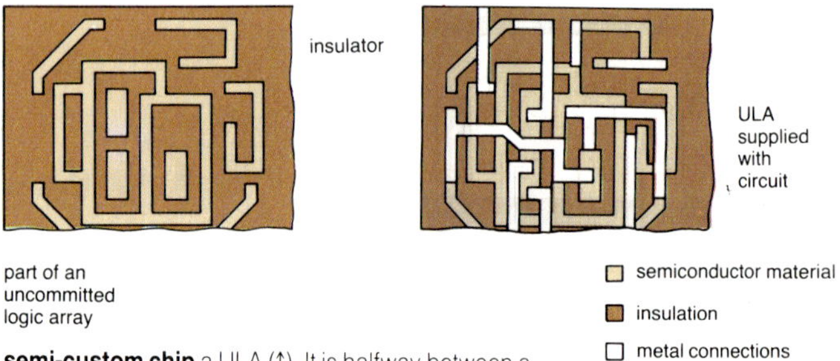


part of an uncommitted logic array

**semi-custom chip** a ULA (↑). It is halfway between a custom-built chip (p.141) and a standard, mass-produced chip.
**metal-oxide-semiconductor** a type of integrated circuit based on insulated-gate field effect transistors (p.100). The layers on a substrate are metal, silicon dioxide insulation (oxide layer) and semiconductor layers. The manufacturing process requires fewer stages than bipolar transistors (p.102), and more devices can be put on a given area than for bipolar devices. For example, a similar bipolar device needs ten times the area of an MOS device. MOS integrated circuits suffer from parasitic capacitance (p.93), are slower than bipolar circuits, require higher voltages than bipolar circuits for working. MOS and bipolar devices are not compatible, usually, in the same circuit. *See FETMOS gate* (↓).
**MOS** (*abbr*) metal-oxide-semiconductor.
**FETMOS** (*abbr*) field effect transistor metal-oxide-semiconductor.
**FETMOS gate** a FETMOS circuit for a logic gate is given in the diagram. It shows the simplicity of the circuit for a logic result of A NOR (B AND C). The absence of resistors and capacitors is to be noted.
**PMOS** (*abbr*) MOS (↑) with p-type silicon channel (p.140).

**metal-oxide semiconductor transistor**

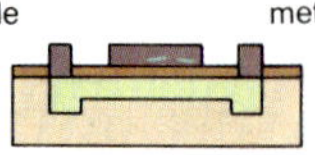


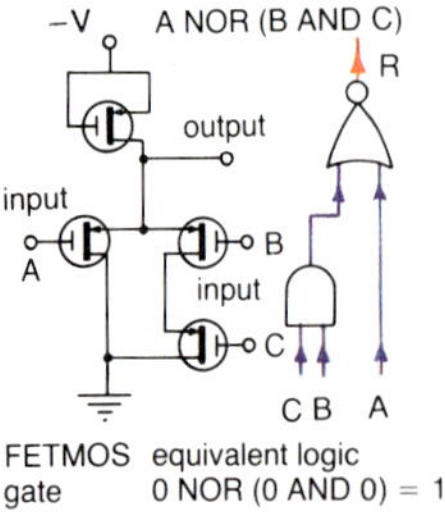


**FETMOS device**

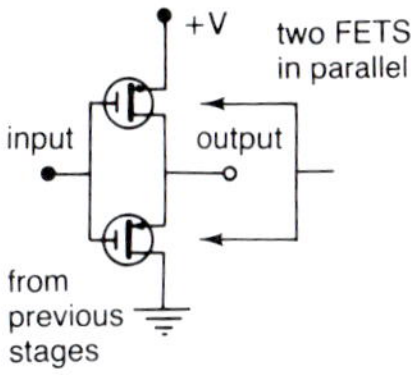

**complementary MOS**

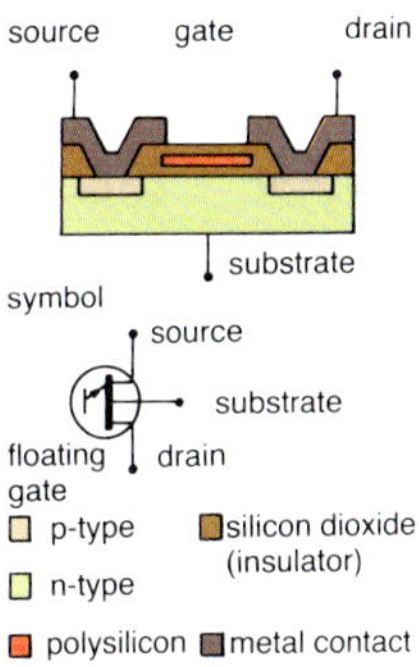

**silicon gate FET (p-channel)**

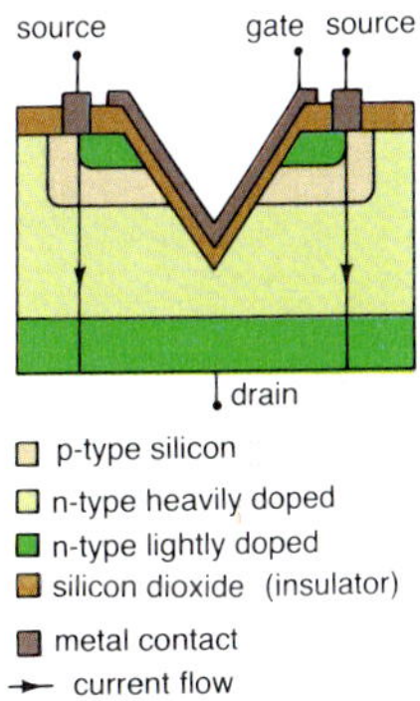

**VMOS transistor**

**NMOS** (*abbr*) metal-oxide-semiconductor (↑) with n-type silicon channel (p.140).

**complementary MOS** this type of integrated circuit (p.105) differs from an MOS circuit (↑) only in the last or output stage. It has complementary p-channel and n-channel FETMOS (↑) in parallel. When one transistor is ON, the other is OFF, so power consumption is limited to the actual switching time between the two states, i.e. very small consumptions. CMOS circuits can be used as non-volatile memories (p.165), as small batteries can be used to supply sufficient power when the main power source is switched off.

**CMOS** (*abbr*) complementary MOS (↑).

**BiMOS** (*abbr*) a new technology that uses bipolar (p.145) and MOS (↑) devices in the same circuit. A high density of devices is possible. *See VMOS* (↓).

**high-performance MOS** a new process with NMOS chips (↑). Improved methods of photolithography, using electron beams to fabricate masks, has produced a very high device density such as 29000 transistors on a chip 6mm square.

**HMOS** (*abbr*) high-performance MOS.

**silicon gate FET** this is a field effect transistor (FET) which is used in memories (p.165). It uses an insulated polysilicon (p.146) gate *(see diagram)*. If the gate is given a charge, the transistor will conduct. As the gate is insulated, the transistor continues to conduct after the charging voltage is switched off. The gate is charged by a voltage pulse of approximately −50V between the substrate and the drain. Applying a low negative voltage to the drain reads out the state of the FET.

**VMOS** (*abbr*) a FETMOS (↑) in which current flows vertically through a silicon chip and not horizontally across the plane of the chip. An n-type silicon substrate is given an epitaxial growth of lightly doped n-type silicon. The epitaxial layer has n-type and p-type channels diffused into it. A V-shaped groove is then etched through the diffused regions, and the whole surface then covered with a silicon dioxide layer. Metal contacts are then etched on the chip. A VMOS device can produce a high density circuit as current flows vertically from source to drain. The V-shaped groove insulation breaks down under high voltage conditions. This defect is eliminated by using a U-shaped groove. VMOS devices are used in BiMOS (↑).

**emitter-coupled logic²** the bottoming (p.103) of a transistor prolongs the time for switching to another state. Emitter-coupled logic increases the speed of passing signals through gates by preventing transistor saturation. Propagation delays are reduced to 2 nanoseconds per gate. Logic 1 is represented by −0.75V and logic 0 by −1.60V, although the supply voltage is about 5 volts. Such circuits consume more power than TTL circuits (p.113), but the speed is useful for arithmetic units and larger computers.

**ECL²** (*abbr*) emitter-coupled logic (↑).

**collector diffusion isolation** bipolar devices (↓) require more space than MOS devices (p.142). Close packing of bipolar devices is improved by using isolation islands (p.105) of heavily doped semiconductors of the same type as the collector electrode.

**CDI** (*abbr*) collector diffusion isolation (↑).

**integrated injection logic** a simplification of bipolar circuits (↓) is achieved by using integrated injection logic which removes the need for resistors and the isolation of transistors (p.105). The architecture of an IIL chip is shown in the diagram together with the corresponding circuit. Fewer masking and diffusion steps are needed to manufacture an IIL gate, and the packing density of the devices approaches that of MOS gates (p.142). The device consists of a p-n-p transistor forming a current source for a multicollector p-n-p transistor. The input is to the collector-base connection of the circuit. The outputs can be used for different functions. An IIL gate has the speed of a bipolar gate, and one-hundredth of the power consumption of normal TTL circuits (p.113).

**IIL** or **I²L** (*abbr*) integrated injection logic (↑).

**tristate logic** a variety of TTL logic (p.113) which has the normal inputs and output of a gate, together with a control signal. High and low voltages signal a 1 and a 0 respectively with low impedance. With the control signal, a 1 is signalled and the gate is switched ON with a high impedance. The high impedance is used when several gates are connected together, i.e. in data highways (p.164), and is used to prevent more than one gate putting data on to a data bus line (p.238) at one time.

**small-scale integration** integrated circuits (p.105) containing up to 20 logic gates on a chip. Usually used with wired logic (p.141).

**SSI** (*abbr*) small-scale integration (↑).

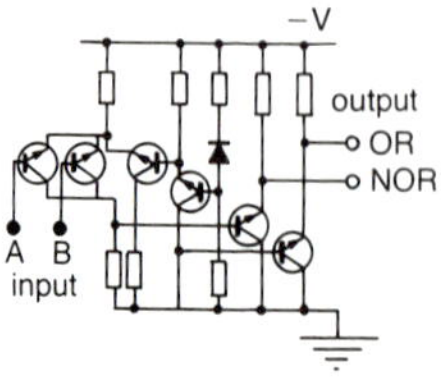

emitter-coupled logic (ECL) for OR/NOR gates

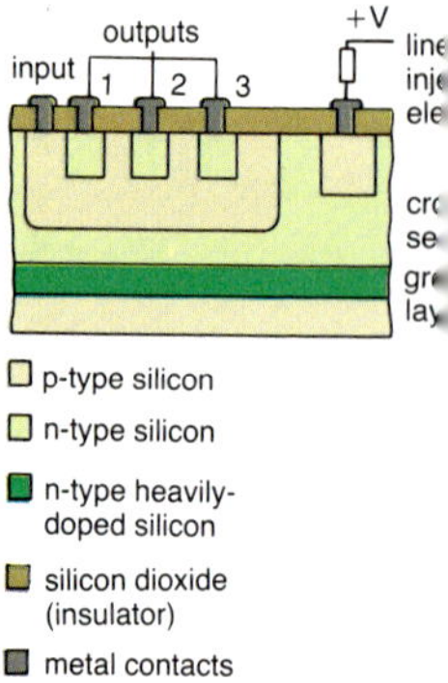


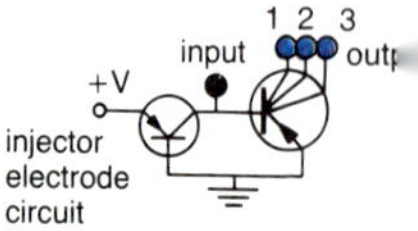

integrated injection logic transistor

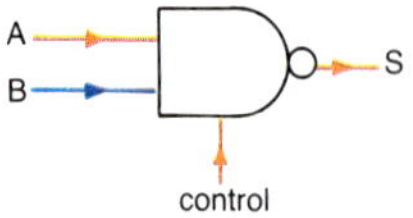

tristate logic

**medium-scale integration** integrated circuits (p.105) containing 20–100 logic gates, or less than 1000 memory bits on a chip. Usually used with wired logic (p.141).

**MSI** (*abbr*) medium-scale integration.

**large-scale integration** integrated circuits (p.105) containing 100–10000 logic gates or 1000–16000 memory bits on a chip.

**LSI** (*abbr*) large-scale integration (↑).

**very-large-scale integration** integrated circuits (p.105) containing more than 10000 logic gates per chip.

**VLSI** (*abbr*) very-large-scale integration (↑).

**super-large-scale integration** the largest chips which contain up to 100000 components.

**SLSI** (*abbr*) super-large-scale integration (↑).

**bipolar** (*adj*) (1) describes a circuit that uses positive and negative voltage; (2) describes a transistor that uses positive and negative charge carriers. *See bipolar transistor* (p.102).

**bipolar integrated circuit** a circuit that uses devices connected to positive and negative voltages. *See OR gate circuit* (p.111). A circuit that uses level logic (↓).

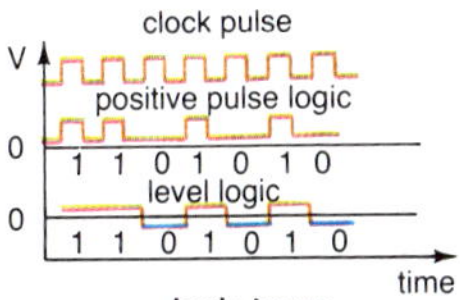


**logic types**

**level logic** the voltage level defines the value of a bit as 1 or 0. Changes in the voltage occur only when the bit changes from 1 to 0 or vice versa. Level logic can be similar to positive or negative logic (p.42) as one level can be ground; it can also have positive and negative voltage levels *(see diagram)*.

**bipolar microprocessor** a microprocessor using bipolar integrated circuits (↑).

**chip resistor** a thick- or thin-film (p.140) chip used in hybrid integrated circuits (p.140). The film forms the resistance, and is sand-blasted or scraped to adjust the resistance to the required value.

**IOP chip** a specialized chip that controls input and output from a microprocessor (p.147) to peripheral units. It functions separately from the microprocessor, i.e. CPU (p.147), as the latter processes data only. Using an IOP chip increases the capability of a system.

**maths chip** chips designed specially for processing numbers such as arithmetic, logarithmic, trigonometric numbers by floating point notation (p.32). The performance is up to one hundred times quicker than that of the same process carried out by a standard CPU (p.146).

**memory chip** there are three kinds of memory chips, RAM, ROM and programmable ROM. The memory chips constitute the greater part of a microcomputer system.

**master chip** a standard chip containing a fixed number of electronic devices which are unconnected. For example, a ULA (p.142) is a master chip. Master chips are used in semi-custom (p.142) manufacturing processes.

**support chip** a chip used with a microprocessor chip or CPU chip to provide help with computer functions, e.g. an IOP chip (p.145), a maths chip (p.145), a chip for a timer circuit, a chip for direct memory access.

**discrete device** a single device, such as a transistor, a capacitor, a gate, in an integrated circuit.

**FAMOS transistor** a floating gate avalanche injection metal-oxide-semiconductor transistor *(see diagram)*. The floating gate is charged by applying a high voltage pulse between the drain and the substrate. This charges the gate and it remains charged because it is insulated. The transistor is then conducting, representing a logical '1'. The floating gate can be discharged by exposure to UV radiation. The storage is thus programmable, and non-volatile (p.165). The logic state is read out by applying a low voltage to the drain. FAMOS transistors are used in PROMs (p.173).

**control gate** this gate in a FAMOS transistor (↑) inhibits, or otherwise, the read-out of the logic state.

**transistor capacitance** the gate and the conducting channel of an insulated-gate FET (p.100) form a capacitor, which is not required in the circuit. Such capacitative effects lead to power losses and reduction in the speed of operation.

**surface leakage** a small current along the surface of an insulating material. The current strength depends on humidity, surface contamination, etc.

**polysilicon** (*n*) a crystalline form of silicon composed of single crystals randomly oriented.

**central processing unit** the unit of a computer that controls all other units. It consists essentially of an arithmetic unit, a control unit, and an internal memory. A minimum requirement is three registers, a decode and control section, an adder and two memory buffers. The control of other functions is exercised through the interpretation and execution of instructions. The diagram indicates the flow of information through the CPU.

**CPU** (*abbr*) central processing unit (↑).

**two discrete devices in an IC**

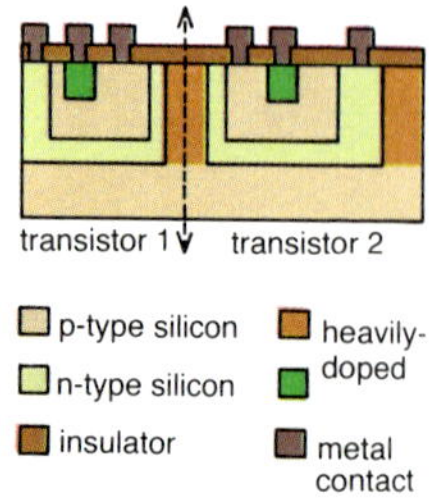


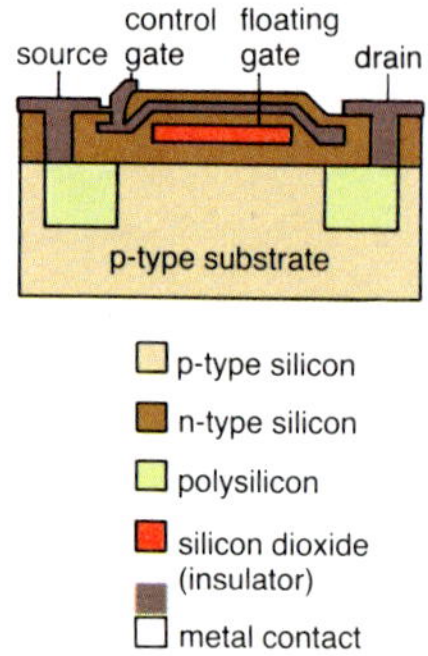


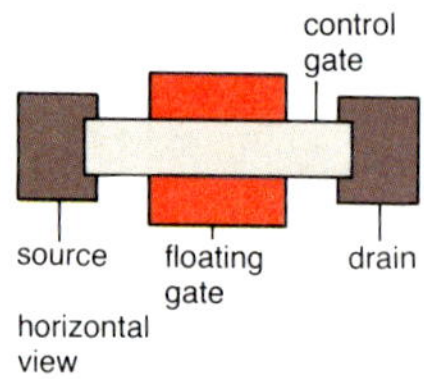


**FAMOS transistor**

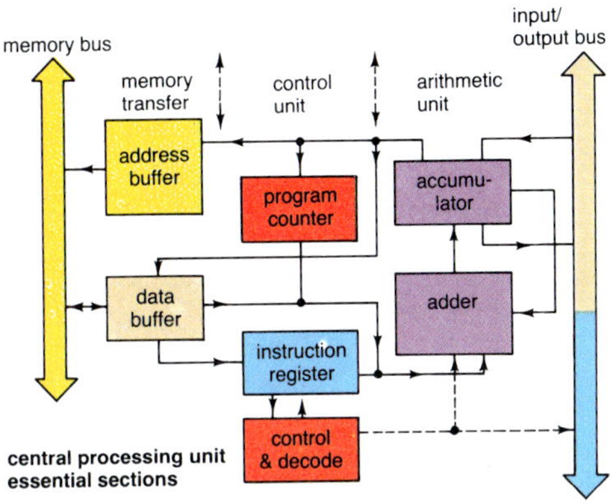

**central processing unit essential sections**

**central processor** central processing unit (↑).
**processor²** (*n*) central processing unit (↑).
**mainframe** in large data processing units, the CPU (↑) is sometimes called the mainframe. It is more usual to restrict this term to describing the whole system.
**central processing element** a 2-bit, 4-bit or 8-bit element which passes through the whole of the CPU (↑). CPEs can be connected in parallel to form a CPU of any desired word length which is a multiple of the bit elements. The CPE structure permits functions to be performed at greater speeds than if the whole word structure were used; it also reduces the size of the microprogram (p.77) memory.
**CPE** (*abbr*) central processing element (↑).
**microprocessor** (*n*) the CPU (↑) of a microcomputer, usually available on a single silicon chip (p.136). A dedicated (p.141) microprocessor consists of a control unit and an arithmetic unit with a fixed instruction set. An undedicated microprocessor usually contains an internal memory as part of the chip.
**microprocessing unit** a microprocessor with a RAM and ROM (p173), interface devices for input/output, a clock circuit, together with driving circuits, buffers and some passive circuit elements. It is a microcomputer without peripheral devices such as keyboard and display unit.
**MPU** (*abbr*) microprocessing unit (↑).
**microprocessor architecture** the constitutents of a microprocessor together with their arrangement. A specimen microprocessor architecture is shown in the diagram.

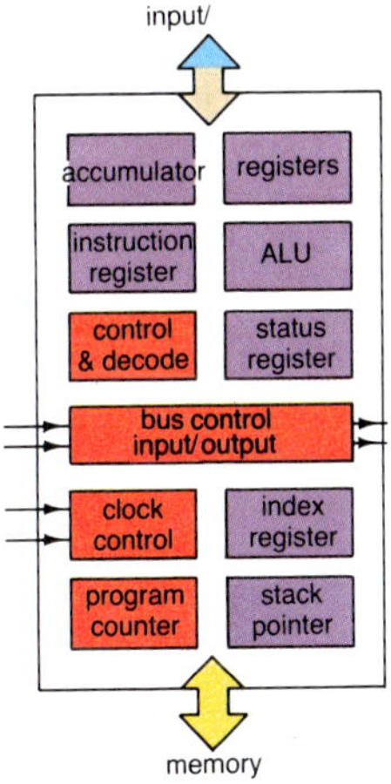

**microprocessor architecture**

**microprocessor 'slices'** most microcomputers use a fixed word length of 8 or 16 bits. A variation is to use 2-bit or 4-bit 'slices', which can be used to build 8-bit, 16-bit or even 32-bit words. The shorter bytes use smaller circuits and smaller memories while allowing the longer words to be used for addressing memory and coding instructions.

**bit-slice microprocessor** a microprocessor using 'slices' (↑). All registers, and buses, are expandable from one slice to multiples of the slice. Each bit slice is controlled by microinstructions (p.51).

**multiprocessor** a computer with more than one arithmetic and logic units (p.150), so that two or more arithmetic and logic processes can be carried out simultaneously, one on each ALU.

**clock** (*n*) an electronic circuit generating periodic signals, used to synchronize all actions in a computer. It is also used for counting, measuring frequencies and transferring information from input to storage in flip-flops (p.114). The circuit is shown in the diagram. The output is a series of pulses (p.120).

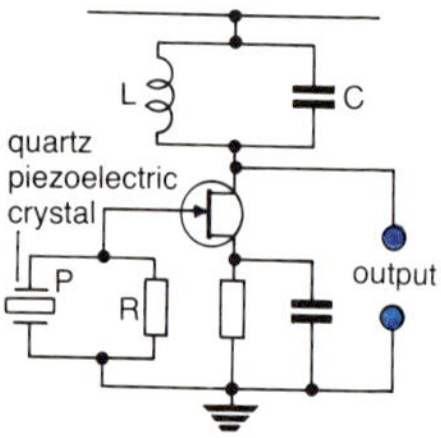


clock electronic circuit

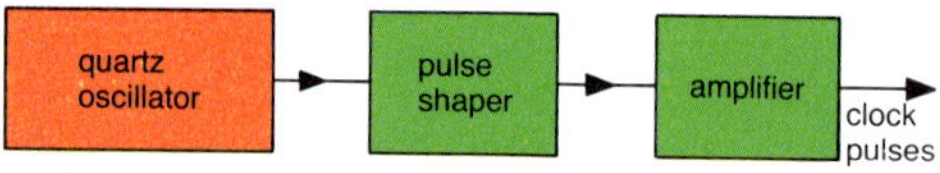


clock generator

**clock generator** a device consisting of a quartz oscillator, a pulse shaper, and an amplifier. The oscillator controls the periodicity of the signals. The pulse shaper, or pulse generator, produces a pulse of requisite length from the oscillator impulse. The amplifier supplies a sufficiently high pulse amplitude.

**clock-pulse generator** this consists of NAND gates with two routes for the input. The propagation delay (p.116) of the gates produces the required pulse length.

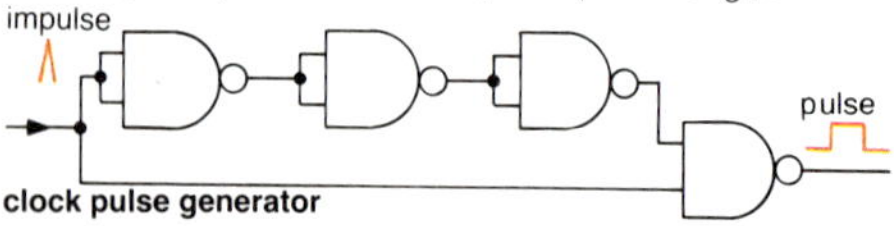


clock pulse generator

**clock rate** the frequency of the pulses produced by the clock-pulse generator (↑).

**clock, programmable** the use of the clock rate (↑) to measure intervals of time such as between events, to synchronize the computer with an external event, to cause time-measured delays in a program.

**register** (*n*) a device in digital computers for the temporary storage of data, with a capacity which is the length of one byte (p.36) as used by the CPU (p.146). The majority of computers use D flip-flops (p.116) in registers with one bit kept in each flip-flop. Most microcomputers use 8-bit registers.

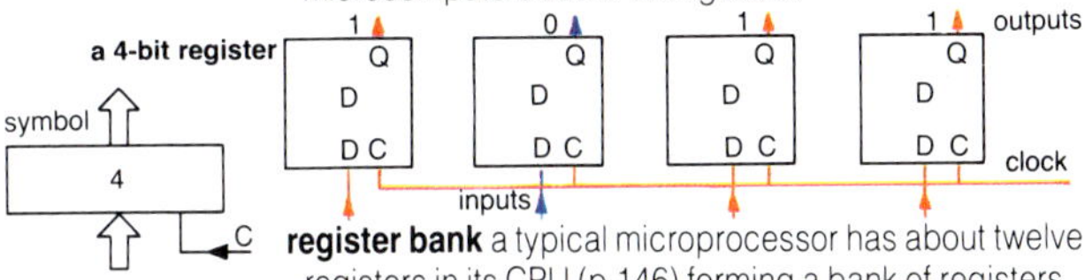


**register bank** a typical microprocessor has about twelve registers in its CPU (p.146) forming a bank of registers. Some are special registers, used for one purpose only, the remainder are for general use.

**general-purpose register** a register (↑) used for binary arithmetic, logical processes, modification of addresses. It stores binary numbers to be used in these processes, and also results for further operations.

**general register** general-purpose register (↑).

**GPR** (*abbr*) general-purpose register (↑).

**paired registers** two registers that can function as a single register. Two 8-bit paired registers form a single 16-bit register. Suitable microinstructions (p.51) connect the two registers. 16-bit registers are needed for memory addresses (p.167) as these are in the range 1K–64K, and 16-bits are required to define 1 to 64K addresses.

**temporary register** a 12-bit register that provides temporary storage for results from an ALU (p.150) before it is sent to a results register. This avoids race conditions (p.121).

**TEMP** (*abbr*) temporary register (↑).

**external register** locations in RAM which hold variables (p.66) or constants, and are given references in a program. The data held in the external register is available for computation, testing, or other processes.

**pseudoregister** (*n*) a location in RAM, i.e. an external register (↑), or a location in a universal asynchronous receiver/transmitter. It contains data concerning baud rate, word length, and the number of stop bits.

**console display register** a set of indicator lights on a console (p.16), which displays the contents of various registers. It uses binary code with a '1' shown by a light shining and a '0' by no light.

**arithmetic and logic unit** the section of the CPU that executes arithmetic and logical operations. Its essential constitutents include an accumulator (↓), a shift register (↓), a results register, a bank of registers (p.149) for holding intermediate results, and an AND and an OR logical gate. Control logic is necessary to decode instructions and to perform the operations. A multiplexer (↓) is generally used to feed the operands (p.34) into the registers and gates. **ALU** (*abbr*).

**arithmetic unit** the structure of a simple unit is shown in the diagram. An operand (p.34) can be directed from the accumulator to be either an A or a B operand. Multiplication and division are performed by the use of the shift register (↓). All arithmetical operations reduce to an addition in the results register. The result is directed back to the accumulator so that iterative operations can be performed.

**basic arithmetic unit**

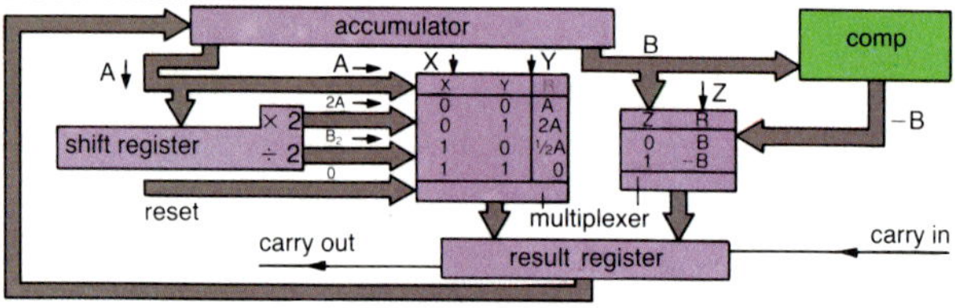


**multiplexer** (*n*) a device which selects one from a number of alternative signals for onward transmission. The diagram shows a multiplexer with four operand (p.34) inputs and one output channel. There are two control inputs, X and Y. When a control input presents two one's at a gate, then the input is passed on. Three control inputs are needed for eight operand inputs, four controls for sixteen inputs.

**mill** (*n*) an older term for the interconnected registers and controls of the arithmetic unit, as numbers go round and round the system to achieve a result.

**accumulator**[2] (*n*) the most important register in an ALU (↑). All data to and from memory (p.165) pass through the accumulator. In microprocessors it is usually a 16-bit register or it consists of two paired 8-bit registers. The result of an arithmetic operation is passed to, and held in, the accumulator. Using the arithmetic unit (↑), the contents of the accumulator can be cleared, complemented, incremented, decremented, rotated, or tested.

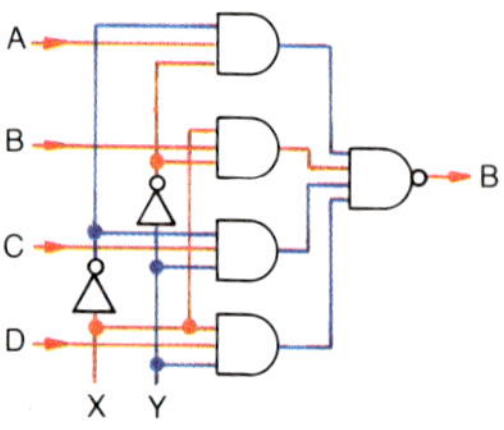


when X and Y = 1, gate is enabled

**multiplexer**

**accumulator register** accumulator (↑). **ACC** (*abbr*).

**shift register** a register that shifts bits, or digits, either to the right or to the left. With binary digits, shifting to the right is equivalent to dividing by 2, while shifting to the left is equivalent to multiplying by 2. In either shift, a zero must be entered to replace the end digit or bit removed by the shift. The shift can be made by a series shift or a parallel shift *(see diagram)*.

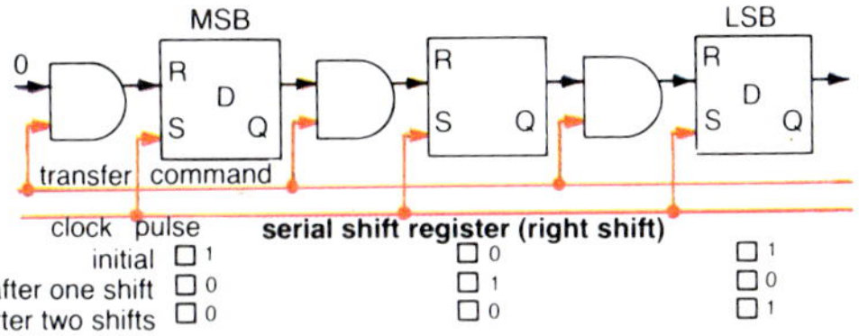


**serial shift register (right shift)**

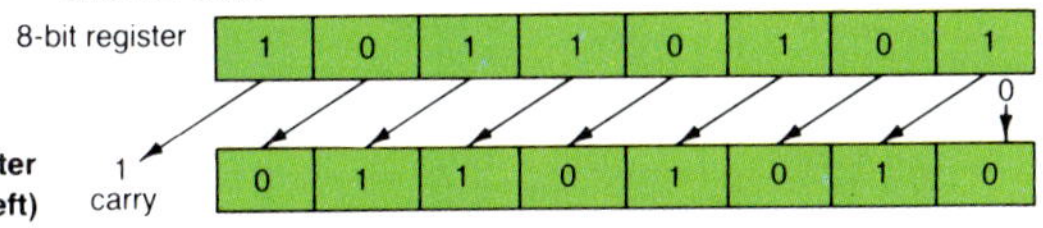


**parallel shift register (shift left)**

**accumulator shift instruction** an instruction that shifts the contents of an accumulator (↑) to the right or left.

**shift** (*v*) to move elements of a set of characters, bits or digits one place to the right or left. **shift** (*n*).

**shift pulse** a control pulse that operates a shift (↑).

**arithmetic shift** a movement of the digits of a number which multiplies or divides the number by its radix (p.29). In binary notation, the radix is 2.

**circulating register** a shift register (↑) in which the digit moved out of one end is entered at the other end; e.g. if a register holds the binary code 1011 after a circulating shift to the left, it holds 0111. *See cyclic shift* (p.59).

**add register** a register which is an adder (p.118).

**overflow indicator** a bistable circuit (p.107) which changes state when an overflow (p.32) occurs in an addition operation. The indicator can be interrogated or reset to zero.

**subtract register** a register which is a subtractor (p.119). Usually an add register is used with an inverter to form a complement (p.31) of the subtrahend (p.30).

**serial adder** one number is stored in a shift register (↑), the other in an ACC (↑). Each number is shifted right, one digit at a time, through a 1-bit adder (p.118). The sum for each two digits is stored back in the ACC, and the shifting operation continued.

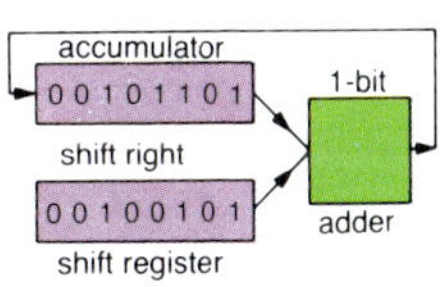


**serial adder**

**logic circuit²** a circuit using a combination of AND-OR gates or NAND-NOR gates to perform a particular logical operation (p.161). The circuit illustrated is for P AND Q AND R AND S=X.

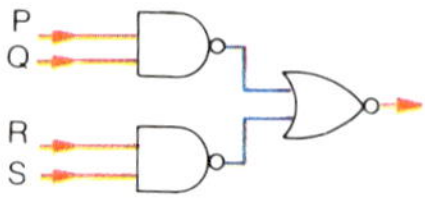


**result register** a temporary store for the output from an arithmetical or logical operation performed in other registers. In many computers the operation is conducted in the accumulator (p.150) and the result held there.

**carry²**(*n*) if the sum of two or more digits is greater than the radix (p.29) of the number system, then an overflow is produced, and this overflow must be added to the next more significant digit. This overflow is a carry in an addition process. Performing this process sequentially on each digit produces a **complete carry**. **carry** (*v*).

| A | B | CARRY in | CARRY out | sum |
|---|---|---|---|---|
| 0 | 0 | 0 | 0 | 0 |
| 0 | 0 | 1 | 0 | 1 |
| 0 | 1 | 0 | 0 | 1 |
| 0 | 1 | 1 | 1 | 0 |
| 1 | 0 | 0 | 0 | 1 |
| 1 | 0 | 1 | 1 | 0 |
| 1 | 1 | 0 | 1 | 0 |
| 1 | 1 | 1 | 1 | 1 |

**results for binary digit adder**

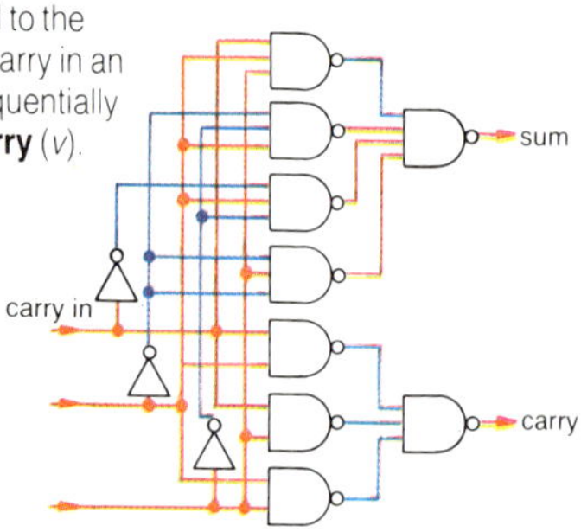


**binary digit adder**

**carry time** (1) the time required for a carry operation (↑) from one digit position to the next; (2) the time for all carries to be completed in the addition of two bytes or two words.

**partial carry** a method used by parallel adders (p.119) in which all carries (↑) are temporarily stored, instead of being transferred immediately.

**carry cascade** the use of a partial carry (↑) in parallel addition with the partial carry process repeated until no new carries are produced.

**carry types** complete carry (↑) from one digit to the next; partial carry (↑); carry cascade (↑); high-speed carry (↓); end-around carry (↓).

**high-speed carry** if a carry into a digit position results in a carry out from that position, and the register circuit performs this as one action, with the carry transferred through two digit positions, then this is a high-speed carry.

**end-around carry** a carry in which the most significant digit of a byte is transferred directly to the least significant digit.

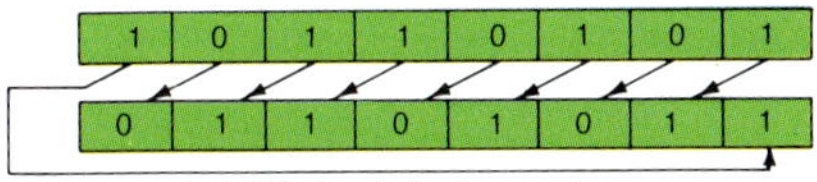

end-around shift (left)

**end-around shift**[2] the digits in a register are moved from right to left or left to right; the digit moved out of one end is moved into the other end, using an end-around carry (↑).

**logical shift**[2] end-around shift (↑).

**complemented** (*adj*) the number in a register after an original number has been changed into its true complement (p.31). Each digit is negated (1 changed to 0 and 0 to 1) and 1 is added to the result. (This is a two's complement.)

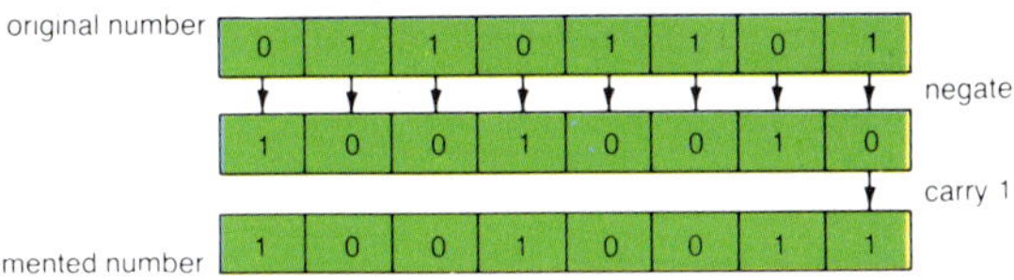


**cleared** (*adj*) every location in a memory, or every digit position in a register, is put in a non-programmed state, usually zero. A space character may also be used instead of zero.

**program counter** the program counter is a register which holds the address of the next instruction byte. It is automatically incremented after a byte has been fetched from memory. The increment is 1. An unconditional jump in the program stops the automatic increment, and the address specified by the jump instruction is put in the program counter. A conditional jump is tested, and if the condition is met, the procedure for an unconditional jump is followed. During interrupts (p.224) the program counter saves the instruction address.

**PC**[3] (*abbr*) program counter (↑).

**instruction address register** a register which holds the address of the next instruction, whether a sequential address, or one determined by jump instructions (p.58), halts, subroutines or interrupts (p.224). It is used in the process of retrieving instructions from memory.

**sequence control register** (1) a register which acts as a counter and determines the sequential order in which instructions are executed. It is subject to branching, execute and interrupt instructions (p.224); (2) program counter (↑).

**sequence register** sequence control register (↑).

**sequencer register** a register that controls the sequence of instructions.

**instruction register** a register that holds the instruction which is currently being executed by the CPU (p.146). The instruction is in binary code and has been fetched from a location in memory. The contents of the instruction register can be modified by arithmetic processes, giving flexibility in a program depending on previous instructions. The instructions are decoded for action by an instruction decoder (p.156). A set of microprograms in ROM can be used through a microprogram controller (↓) instead of a decoder. **IR²** (*abbr*).

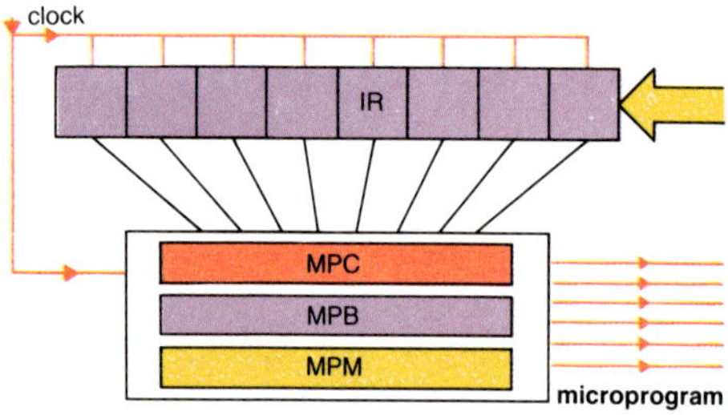


**microprogram controller**

**microprogram controller** the ROM contains a number of microprograms (p.51) each consisting of a number of microinstructions. These microprograms implement the actions of the logic units. A counter (MPC) controls the sequence of the microinstructions. A buffer (MPB) is needed to provide temporary storage for the instructions. A memory (MPM) stores the initial addresses of each microprogram in ROM. Control lines connect to logic units. The rate at which the microprograms are processed is governed by a clock pulse. The logic units in the ALU (p.150) execute the instructions.

**control register** (1) instruction register (↑); (2) a register which controls the transmission of data to peripheral devices. It determines (*a*) baud rate of transmission (*b*) data word length (*c*) number of stop bits (p.41).

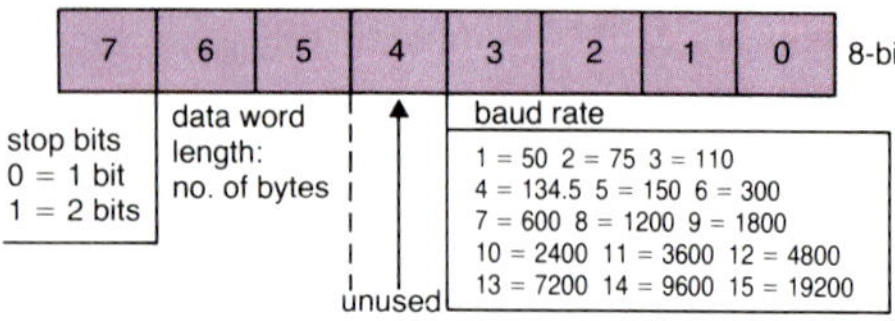


**control register**

**command register** a register which controls the transmission of data to peripheral devices. It determines (*a*) handshake status (p.242); (*b*) full or half duplex transmission (p.233); (*c*) type of parity (p.39).

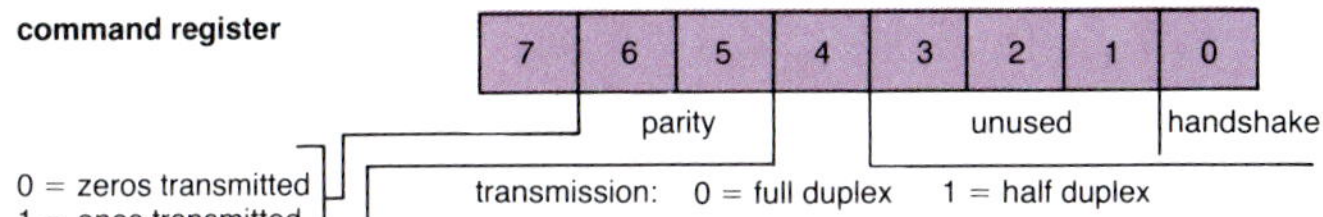


**memory-address register** a register which contains the address of the current program instruction for reading or writing into RAM (p.175).
**MAR** (*abbr*) memory address register (↑).
**memory register** a register that transfers data and instructions between memory, the arithmetic unit, and the instruction register (↑). In some computers it can be addressed. The contents of the register can be modified by addition or subtraction, and the contents are held until the register is cleared.
**address register** a register which stores an address, e.g. MAR (↑), PC (↑).
**store address register** memory address register (↑) or a register which stores the current address for transfer to the decoder where more than one address is used in an instruction.
**SAR** (*abbr*) store address register (↑).
**memory-data register** a register that stores the last data byte or word which has been read from memory or written into memory. The location in memory is obtained from the MAR (↑). **MDR** (*abbr*).
**store data register** memory data register (↑) or a register that stores the last data byte or word read from memory.
**SDR** (*abbr*) store data register (↑).
**memory cycle** (1) a computer operation consisting of a complete sequence of operations of reading from and then writing into memory; (2) the time taken to complete this cycle of operations.
**memory buffer register** a register in which all data entering or leaving memory are stored before onward transmission. It acts as a buffer (p.164) to allow for time differences in the execution of instructions in other parts of the computer, including peripheral devices.
**modify** (*v*) to alter the binary code of an instruction or data resulting from other instructions in a program. For example, instructions to a loop which alter data.

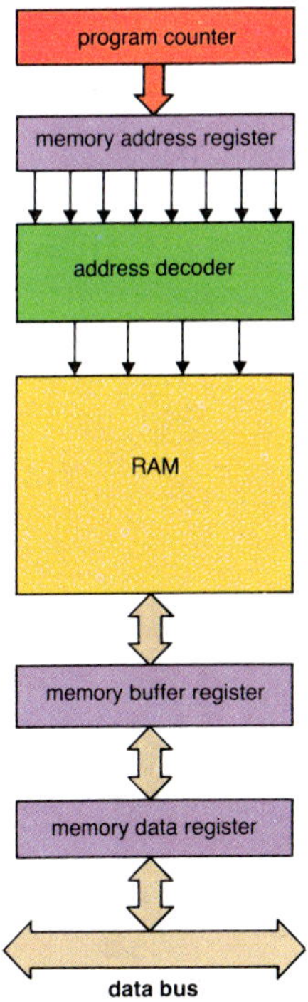

**address decoder** the binary code in an address register activates a set of gates which selects an address line. Three address lines are neeeded to address sixty-four K locations in RAM; they are labelled (1) A0–A6, (2) A7–A13, (3) A14; A15. Three decoders supply the necessary number of lines.

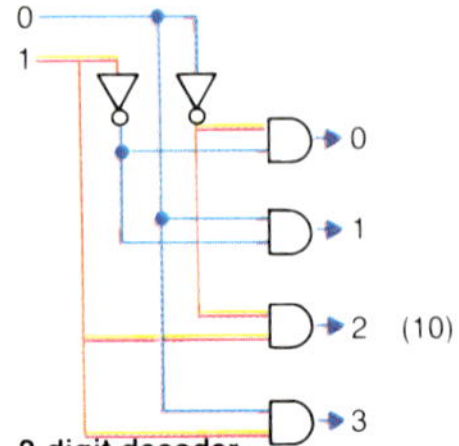

**2-digit decoder**

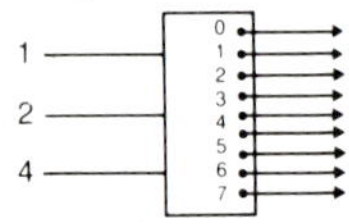

**symbol for an address decoder**

**instruction decoder** the binary code in the instruction register is broken down into its separate fields. The decoder selects one or more output lines which initiate the computer operation based on the signal from the binary code. The method of operation is similar to that of an address decoder (↑).

**index register** a register which is used to modify an instruction. The contents of the index register are added to the instruction counter (↓) to modify the instruction. See index addressing (p.169) in which the memory address is modified. The index register is also used in a count mode in which it controls the number of steps in an operation.

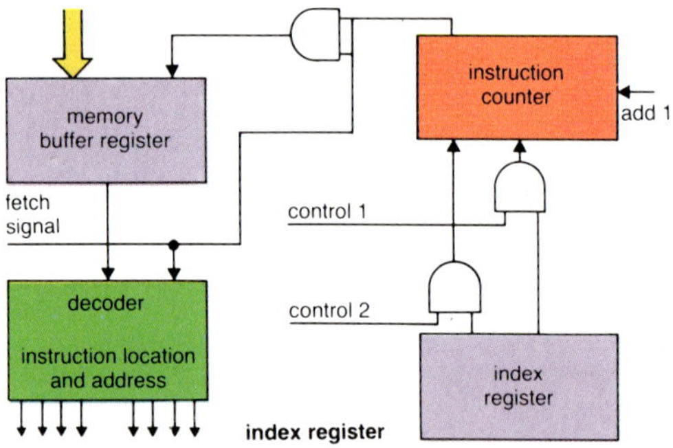

**index register**

**instruction counter** a register which stores the address of the current instruction; it is the input to the memory-address register (p.155).

**index word register** an index register (↑) used for modifying addresses.

**B-register** index register (↑).

**IR³** (*abbr*) index register (↑).

**stack pointer** a register which holds the address at the top of a stack (p.180). The contents of the stack pointer can be transferred to the index register (↑). The stack pointer is decremented by 1 for each byte stored in the stack.

**pushing a byte on a stack pointer**

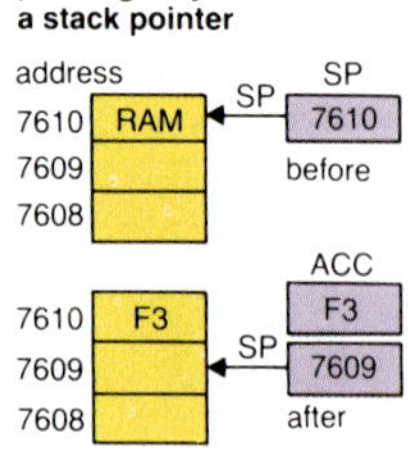

**SP** (*abbr*) stack pointer (↑).
**push** (*v*) to add a byte to a stack.
**pull** (*v*) to remove a byte from a stack.
**pop** (*v*) to pull (↑).
**data I/O register** a register used for the temporary storage of data before it is transferred to or from the data bus (p.238). It is an 8-bit register storing one byte of data.
**input register** a register which receives data from peripheral (p.13) or other external devices at a slow speed, stores it, and then transfers the data at a high speed to the ALU (p.150), the control unit register, or to RAM.
**output register** a register which receives data from the ALU (p.150), or RAM, at a high speed, stores it, and when signalled transmits it at a slow speed to a peripheral or other external device.
**data buffer register** a temporary storage register in a CPU (p.147) or a peripheral device (p.13). It can receive data and then transmit it at a different speed to suit the device to which it is sending the data. A register of this type is usually situated between the CPU and devices operating at slower speeds, e.g. a printer.
**direct-memory access** a form of data transfer between memory and high-speed peripheral storage devices such as disks (p.213). The transfer takes place directly along an input/output channel at high speed between memory and the device. The CPU initiates the transfer on a DMA request from the device and thereafter is not involved in the operation.
**DMA** (*abbr*) direct-memory access (↑).
**data break** direct-memory access (↑).
**word-count register** a register which is loaded with the number of words to be transferred in an I/O transfer. It is decremented for each word transferred and tested for zero. On reaching zero, it generates an interrupt signal to inhibit the operation.
**status** (*n*) information about the conditions of a device. For example: does a register contain a positive or a negative number of zero; does an addition result in a carry; is the syntax of a statement correct, so that the interpretation can be continued, or is an error signalled? The status of a computer unit is recorded in a number of parameters which characterize the system or a particular operation.

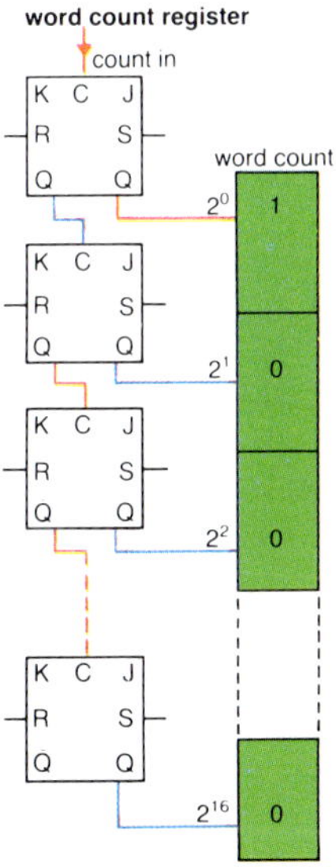

A pulse on in toggles the first J–K–T flip-flop. Each successive pulse decrements the word count

**status register** a register which contains the status (p.157) of a functional unit of a computer or a peripheral device, e.g. the status flags (↓) for the control and arithmetic units, the status of a handshake or interrupt, the quantity of paper remaining in a printer.

**status word** a word which contains the status (↑) of related devices, or the different statuses of a register or device, e.g. the statuses of an accumulator (p.150), such as zero or not zero, positive or negative, overflow or not.

**status word register** a register which contains the present status (↑) of a microprocessor recorded in binary code: it holds a status word (↑).

**SWR** (*abbr*) status word register (↑).

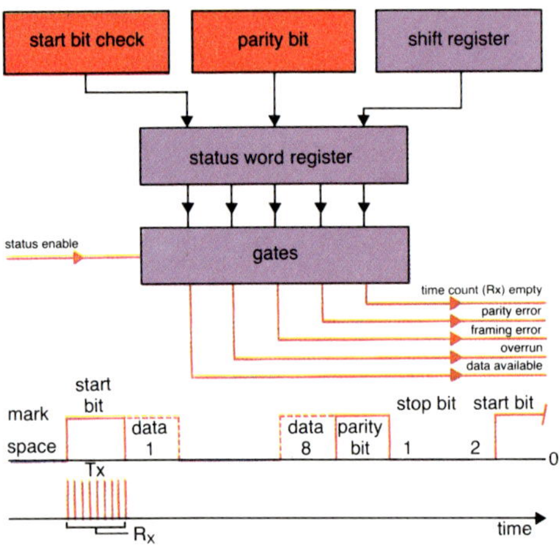


Tx is time cycle for machine
Rx is time cycle for pulse

**status word register**

**program status word** a status word (↑) used to control interrupts (p.224) in the processing of programs, and the status of a computer generally in relation to the program being processed.

**PSW**[1] (*abbr*) program status word (↑).

**device status word** a status word (↑) which contains the status (↑) of devices, including peripheral devices.

**DSW** (*abbr*) device status word (↑).

**status bits** the bits in a status word (↑) indicating the particular condition of a register or device, e.g. a status bit to show whether a register contains a number or zero, the status bits to show the type of parity.

**condition code** a code for status bits (↑) giving information on the result of the last CPU (p.146) operation. For example, a bit, designated Z, is 1 for a zero result, 0 for any other result; a bit, designated N, is 1 for a negative result, 0 for a positive result.

**condition code register** a register containing status bits (↑) for a limited number of arithmetical processes, e.g. borrow, carry, overflow, negative/positive, zero/not zero.

**CCR** (*abbr*) condition code register (↑).

**flag** (*n*) a bit, or bits, that stores one item of information, represented by 1 or 0. It indicates a condition being present or absent, when the condition is to be used in a subsequent step of a machine program. A flag implements action in either hardware or software.

**flag register** a register which contains flags (↑) concerned with the same process in a part of a program.

**sentinel** (*n*) (1) a flag (↑). (2) a symbol used to mark the beginning or the end of a particular piece of data, e.g. start bits, stop bits.

**carry flag** a flag which is set (= 1) for a carry from the most significant bit of a byte.

**zero flag** a flag which is set (= 1) if the contents of a register, usually the accumulator (p.150), is zero.

**sign flag** a flag which is set (= 1) if the number in a register, usually the accumulator (p.150), has the most significant bit equal to 1. If the register holds a signed number, this is interpreted as a negative number.

**parity/overflow flag** a flag which is set for overflow when using a SUBTRACT register. A flag which signals whether the number of digits in the value of logic one is odd or even.

**half-carry flag** a flag which is set for a carry from the less significant nibble (p.36) to the more significant nibble in a binary-coded decimal (p.36) arithmetic addition process.

**subtract flag** a flag which is set for overflow from the more significant nibble (p.36) to the less significant nibble in a BCD (p.36) arithmetic subtraction process.

**control** (*n*) the parts of a computer which execute instructions according to a program sequence, set flags (↑) from results and interpret the signals from flags to proceed with a process interpreted from a machine code program.

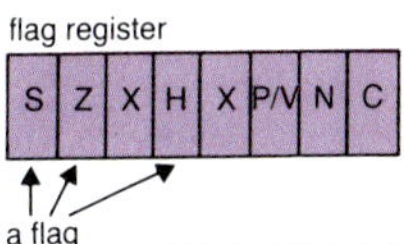


| | |
|---|---|
| C | carry flag |
| N | sign flag |
| P/V | parity/overflow flag |
| H | half-carry flag |
| Z | zero flag |
| S | subtract flag |
| X | not used |

**flag register**

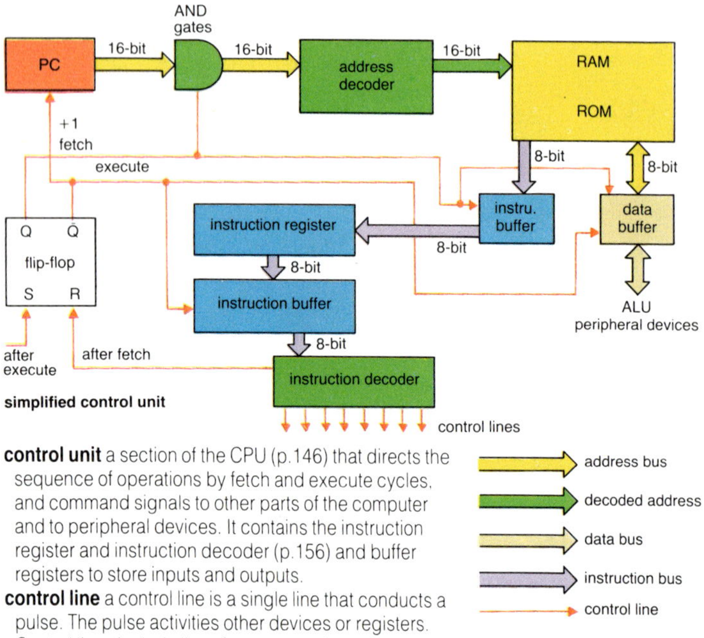


simplified control unit

**control unit** a section of the CPU (p.146) that directs the sequence of operations by fetch and execute cycles, and command signals to other parts of the computer and to peripheral devices. It contains the instruction register and instruction decoder (p.156) and buffer registers to store inputs and outputs.

**control line** a control line is a single line that conducts a pulse. The pulse activities other devices or registers. Control lines include lines for commands such as clear, set, reset, and enable (p.163).

**control block** the circuits that form the control unit, including circuits for gates, registers and decoders.

**instruction control circuit** the entire circuit that forms the control block (↑).

**fetch signal** a signal pulse from a flip-flop that controls the fetch cycle (↓). Several pulses are needed to activate, in turn, each part of the control unit.

**execute signal** a signal pulse from a flip-flop that controls the execute cycle (↓). Several pulses are needed to activate, in turn, each part of the control unit.

**fetch cycle** the program counter sends the address of the next instruction, controlled by AND gates, and then decoded, to ROM for instructions, and to RAM for data. The contents of the memory locations go to the two buffers. The fetch signal, suitably delayed, activates the buffers, and instructions are passed to the instruction register or data are passed to the ALU (p.150) or to peripheral devices.

**execute cycle** when the fetch cycle (↑) is finished, the flip-flop is reset; this activates the execute signal. The instruction byte is sent to the instruction decoder. The control lines needed for the operation are activated and the operation executed. The execute signal increments the program counter to update it. When the operation is completed, the part of the CPU executing the process sends a signal to the flip-flop which is set. This activates the next fetch signal.

**send signal** an execute signal (↑) which sends data to peripheral devices.

**command²** (*n*) an electrical pulse which causes an operation to start, stop or continue. It is not the same as an instruction. An instruction, such as 'jump if zero', initiates a process which needs several commands.

**program control unit** that part of the control unit (↑) that organizes the execution of the computer instructions and their sequence of operations (↓).

**program controller** program control unit (↑).

**operation²** (*n*) the action executed by a single logic element (p.106). It may not necessarily produce a result.

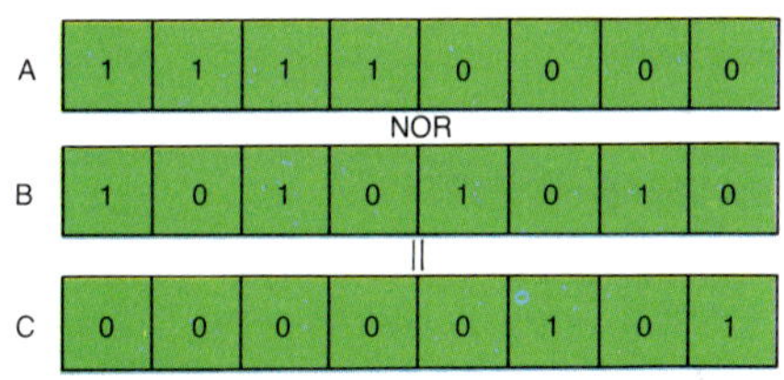


A NOR B = C
**a logical operation**

**logical operation** an operation (↑) on a Boolean variable (p.88), using logical operators. The process does not involve arithmetic; each digit has a separate meaning which describes a particular characteristic as present or absent.

**red-tape operation** an operation which does not itself contribute directly to a result in the processing of data, but is necessary for the actual processing, e.g. initializing a counter. *See housekeeping operation* (p.261). Red-tape operations are usually restricted to use in one application.

**transfer operation** an operation involving the transfer of data by a transmission line between terminals (p.10) and computers. The rate of the transfer operation is measured in baud (p.42).

**illegal operation** the result obtained when a computer attempts to execute an illegal instruction (↓). Either the computer cannot perform the operation or the operation produces incorrect or undesired results.

**illegal instruction** an instruction (p.48) not recognized from the set of instructions available in the computer.

**operation cycle** the part of a machine cycle (↓) during which the actual execution of the instruction takes place.

**operation time** the time needed to complete an operation cycle (↑).

**clock cycle** if the clock rate (p.148) is 5MHz, then the number of cycles per second is 5 million and the time for one cycle is 1/5 million = 0.2μs or 200 nanoseconds. This is the **cycle time** of the computer clock, during which time one clock cycle is completed.

**cycle time** see clock cycle (↑). It is the minimum time interval between two successive accesses to one storage location.

**T-state** an external clock cycle; the cycle time (↑) of a computer. It is used in calculating the time required to complete one instruction.

**execution cycle** operation cycle (↑).

**execution time** the time required (1) to execute, or run, a program or (2) to carry out an execution cycle.

**machine cycle** the shortest complete action or process that is repeated or carried out in turn in the execution of an instruction. For example, transferring a number into a memory location specified by a register in the CPU requires three machine cycles which take up ten T-states (↑); incrementing a register requires one machine cycle taking up four T-states. An instruction for division requires several repetitions of the same action, together with testing for completion.

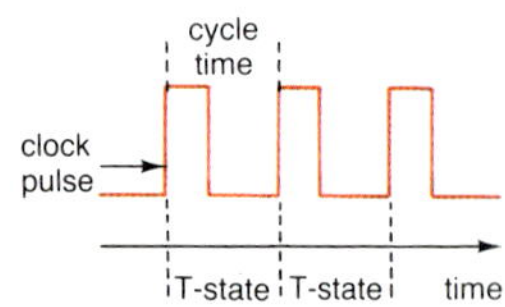

**clock cycle and T-state**

$T_1$–$T_7$ 7 T-states
$M_1$–$M_2$ 2 machine cycles
$F_1$–$F_5$ 5 fetch phases/cycles
$EC_1$–$EC_2$ 2 execute/operation times

instruction time = $F_1 + F_2 + F_3 + F_4 + F_5$
= (total time) − ($EC_1 + EC_2$)

instruction: add register R to accumulator

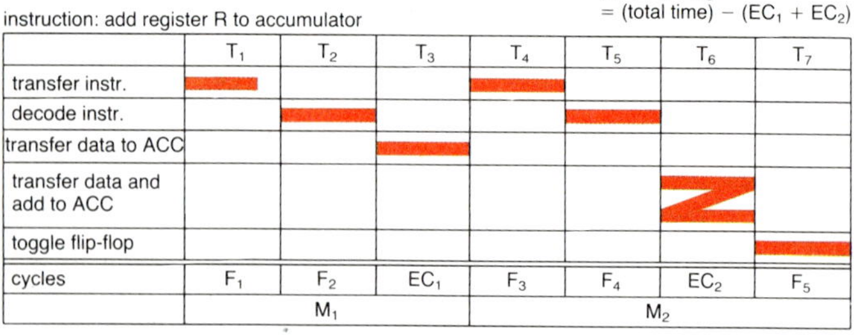

**M-cycle** machine cycle (↑).

**instruction time** the time required to process one instruction and step to the next instruction less the execution time (↑). The time to complete one step in a machine code program equals instruction time + execution time.

**compilation time** the time required to translate a high-level language (p.51) to machine code (p.38) and compile the machine code program. Contrast execution time (↑), the time taken to run the program.

**addition time** the time required to add the contents of one register to the contents of another register. This time is often used as an estimate of the speed of a computer for processing data. It should not be taken as the only criterion of speed, as some microprocessors use only an accumulator (p.150) for addition processes. An alternative addition time is the time required for adding the contents of a memory location to the accumulator of a CPU.

enabling signal on enable line sets gates to transmit data on data bus.

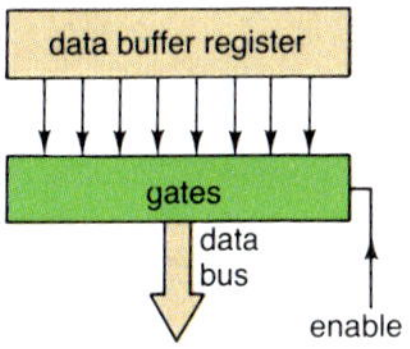


**enable** (*v*) (1) to set a device into a circuit, so that it can be used. This is usually done by a control enable line activating a gate, a buffer or the device itself; (2) to restore a device to its normal operating condition after an inhibit signal (↓). **enable** (*n*).

**inhibit** (*v*) to prevent a signal from being transmitted; to prevent a specific process occurring or changing state. The opposite of enable (↑).

**disable** (*v*) to make a peripheral device inoperative, that is, ceasing to function, although requests to use it are allowed to queue until the device is enabled (↑) again.

**disarm** (*v*) to make a peripheral device inoperative, so that requests to it are lost, e.g. the interrupt facility of a device is completely lost when it is disarmed. *Compare disable* (↑).

**suppress** (*v*) to eliminate certain constituents of an output when certain specified conditions occur, e.g. to suppress zeros to the left of digits in a number.

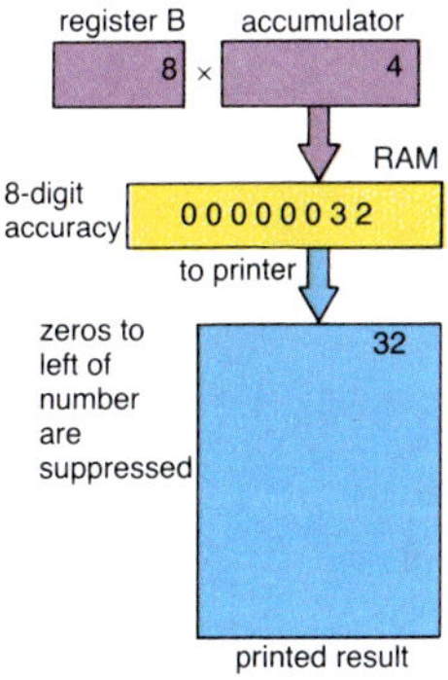


**masking** (*n*) using a bit pattern in a mask (p.87) to inhibit (↑) certain actions and to enable (↑) others.

**arm** (*v*) to make a peripheral device operative, and thus allow interrupts (p.224) to take place in accordance with specified conditions.

**enabling signal** a signal which allows an operation to take place when the operation has been previously set up.

**highway** (*n*) a common signal path, used in parallel mode (p.104) for the transmission of information signals, shared by several sources and several acceptors. It is used to transmit bytes or words and hence has as many lines as there are bits in the bytes or words. A highway is usually reserved for internal communication in a CPU.

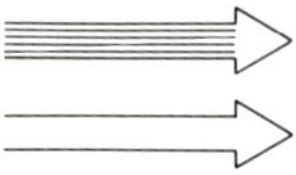

**symbols for a highway**

**data highway** a highway (↑) for transferring data. Most microprocessors use an 8-bit byte of data, so the highway consists of eight parallel transmission lines.

**data input bus** in some microcomputers, a single highway (↑) with the microprocessor, or CPU, the memory, and the input/output interfaces (p.222) all using the data input bus. The data input bus is used to transfer address information and data between any two of the processor, memory and input/output interfaces.

**DIB** (*abbr*) data input bus (↑).

**address highway** a highway (↑) for transferring the addresses of locations. Most microcomputers use a 16-bit address word, so the highway consists of sixteen parallel transmission lines.

**buffer** (*n*) (1) a device placed between a source and an acceptor of information to compensate for differences in transfer rate; usually it is a storage device for temporary storage. *See buffer storage* (p.176); (2) a device used to isolate an acceptor from a source of information, so that the transfer can be controlled by a signal or a control line; (3) a device to provide a signal with greater power than the original source could provide, that is to increase effective fan-out (p.106).

**decoder** (*n*) a device which activates output lines in accordance with the translation of a code used for the input lines. For example, an address decoder (p.156); a binary-coded decimal to decimal decoder.

**encoder** (*n*) a device which has one input activated to produce a combination of output signals, e.g. a decimal to binary-coded decimal encoder.

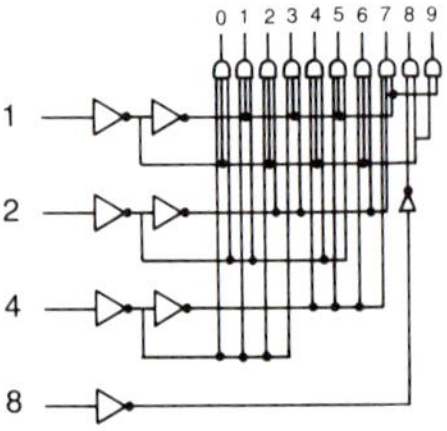


**BCD to decimal decoder**

**data input bus**

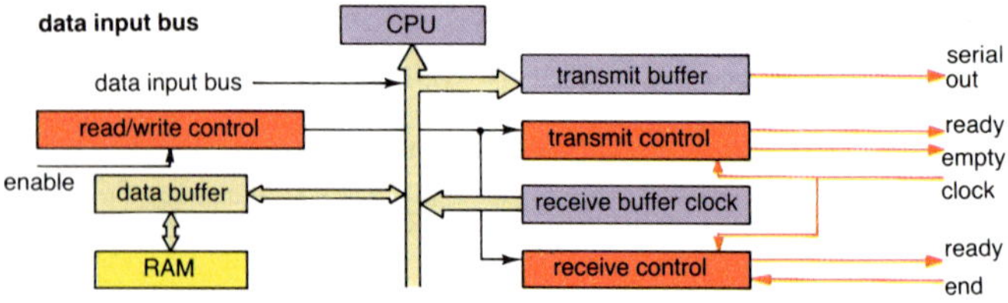

**MOS capacitor**

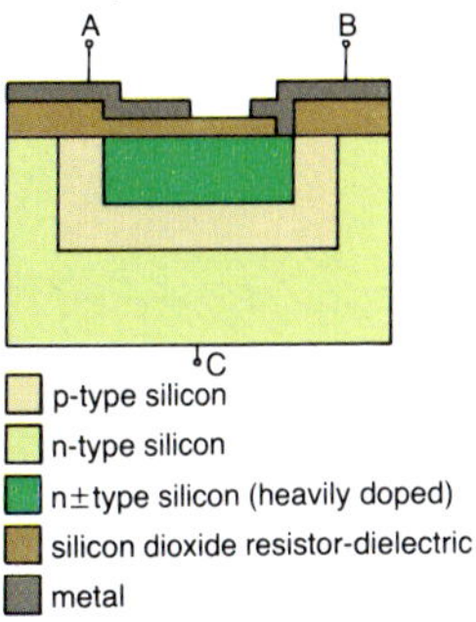


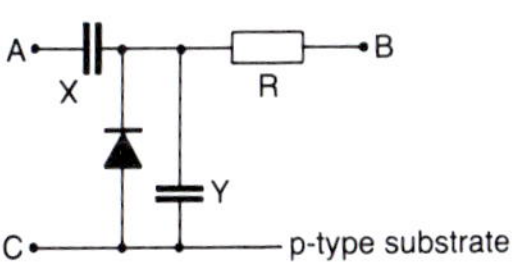


**equivalent circuit**

The silicon dioxide layer provides resistance as well as capacitance.
X is the effective capacitor
Y is a parasite capacitor from the semiconductor junction diode
R is the resistance of the $n^+$ region

**memory** (*n*) a device which stores information in the form of binary-coded data. A medium capable of recording and storing information. It usually refers to the main memory of a computer, that is, the memory used directly by the CPU (p.146). Information can be introduced into and extracted from a memory.

**internal memory** the memory (↑) which is used directly by the CPU. It is part of the microcomputer and is not a peripheral device.

**storage** (*n*) an alternative term for memory (↑). A device into which information can be introduced, held, and subsequently obtained. The information can be erased. Storage usually refers to all types of memory including peripheral devices.

**internal storage** internal memory (↑).

**volatile** (*adj*) describes a memory which loses all its stored information when the power supply is cut off.

**non-volatile** describes a memory which retains all its stored information when the power supply is cut off, e.g. magnetic tapes and disks (p.213). The stored information can be erased, altered or overwritten.

**permanent** (*adj*) describes a memory which always retains its stored information when the power supply is cut off, and the information cannot be erased, altered or overwritten by the microprocessor.

**static memory** data are stored in D flip-flops (p.116) and are retained until the power supply is cut off. The flip-flops use bipolar transistors or FETs (p.100). It has a high power consumption.

**dynamic memory** data are stored in capacitors (p.93) with a charged capacitor representing logic one and an uncharged capacitor representing zero. MOS thin-film capacitors are used; the memory is volatile (↑). The capacitor is leaky, it discharges itself through its resistance. This has to be overcome by recharging it at intervals. Dynamic memory has advantages over static memory (↑) as a greater number of memory locations can be made on one chip and it has a low power consumption.

**refreshing** (*n*) the process of recharging a dynamic memory (↑). Refresh circuits detect each partially charged capacitor, after leakage has caused a loss of charge, and recharge the capacitor. This is done approximately every two milliseconds, and the process is user-transparent (p.12). *See regenerate* (p.207).

**pseudostatic memory** a dynamic memory (p.165) with the necessary circuitry to carry out refreshing automatically; the memory thus appears static.
**semistatic memory** pseudostatic memory (↑).
**protectable memory** any memory system that does not lose stored information when the power supply fails.
**location** (*n*) a place in memory where an item of data can be stored. A bit, a nibble, a byte or a word can be stored in a location, depending on the facilities of the computer. A location is usually designated by an address (↓) which forms part of an instruction (p.48).
**protected location** a reserved location (↑) which holds information that cannot be altered except by a special procedure. Data can be read from it but not written into it. Such locations are reserved for special purposes.
**access** (*v*) to obtain data from memory, a register or a peripheral device, or to put data into memory, a register or a peripheral device. **access** (*n*).
**serial access** access (↑) in which data are transferred one bit (p.36) after another.
**parallel access** access (↑) in which all bits (p.36) of a byte are transferred at the same time by parallel connections (p.104). Parallel circuits are more complex than the circuits for serial access (↑) but memory access time (↓) is much shorter.
**instantaneous access** access (↑) in which there is no serial delay owing to other units of data being needed. This is access to RAM (p.175) or ROM (p.173).
**sequential access** access (↑) in which items of data become available only one after another, i.e. in sequence. The items are available sequentially whether required or not. Memory access time (↓) is much longer than for random access (↓).

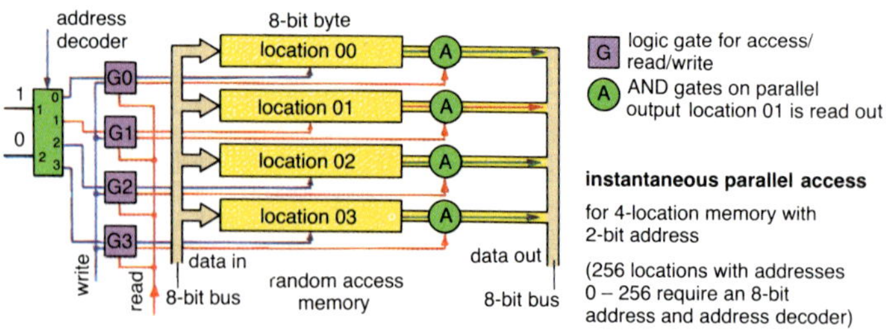


**instantaneous parallel access**

for 4-location memory with 2-bit address

(256 locations with addresses 0 – 256 require an 8-bit address and address decoder)

**random access** access (↑) in which memory access time (↓) is independent of the location in memory.

**memory access time** the time taken between the application of an input pulse and the availability of the required data from a specified location. The data may be in memory or in a peripheral device. Different peripheral devices require different access times.

**memory page** a block of a fixed number of locations (↑) in memory. For most microcomputers this consists of 256 locations each storing eight bits. Memory addresses (↓) consist of two bytes (p.36), so an address of 46 A2 (hexadecimal) is location A2 on page 46.

**serial memory**[1] a memory in which data are stored in sequence and only sequential access (↑) is possible.

**memory capacity** the number of items of data that can be stored in a storage device. Usually defined as the number of bytes (p.36) that can be stored.

**memory hierarchy** the set of memories (p.165) available to a computer. The memories have different sizes, different access times (↑) and different ratios of cost to performance. For example: (1) a fast instant access memory, (2) a medium speed disk memory, (3) a slow magnetic tape memory (p.216), form a hierarchy.

**addressing a location**

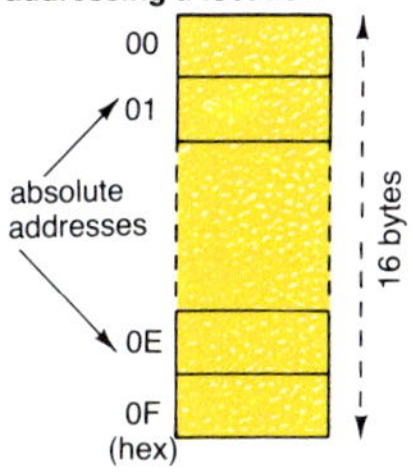


locations in RAM

**address** (*n*) (1) an identification by a character, or group of characters, of a memory location (↑), a register, or a peripheral device; (2) the part of an instruction (p.48) which identifies the location of an operand (p.73) of the instruction.

**absolute address** the unique specified address in storage, defined by memory page (↑) and location. The location is specified by machine code (p.38).

**actual address** absolute address (↑).

**direct address** absolute address (↑).

**machine address** absolute address (↑).

**one-level address** absolute address (↑).

**address access time** the time taken between the address signal being valid and the data from that address becoming available.

**location counter** a register which holds a number, the address of the next location. A program instruction modifies, if necessary, this value so that a series of locations are addressed in the correct order to execute a program. Every value is incremented by 1 for sequential addresses, unless modified by an instruction. Synonymous with instruction counter (p.156).

**register addressing** using a register as an addressable location, when the instruction code designates the operand (p.73) is in that register. Registers can be addressed singly or in pairs.

**register, indirect addressing** addressing, in an instruction, a particular register that stores the address of a memory location; the register must hold sixteen bits. The register is a **pointer**, or memory-pointer register, and the data are taken from the memory location whose address is stored in the memory-pointer register.

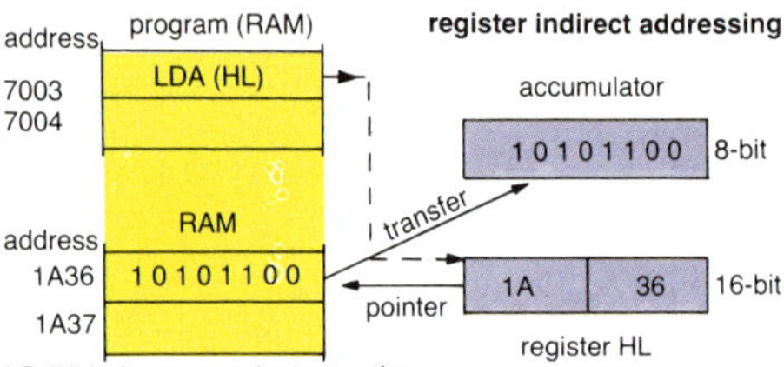


LD (HL), A reverses the instruction

**extended addressing** (1) the address in an instruction is combined with a value in an extension register to give the actual address (p.167) of the operand (p.73) of the instruction; (2) a method of moving two bytes of data between memory and a register pair. The instruction address points to the first of the two bytes. The second byte follows sequentially after the first.

**EA** (*abbr*) extended addressing (↑).

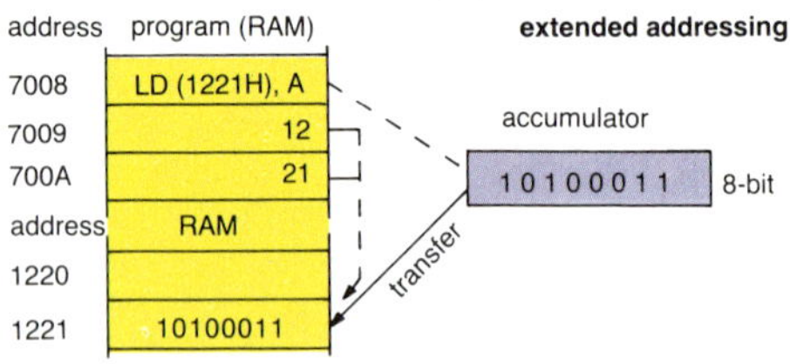


LDA, (1221H) reverses the instruction

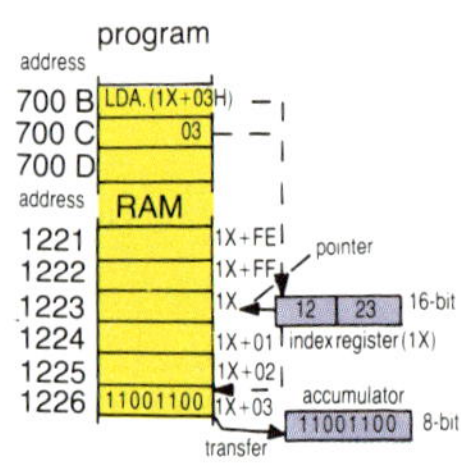


LD (1X + 03H), A reverses the instruction

**indexed addressing**

**implied addressing** an instruction which automatically applies to one particular register, usually the accumulator (p.150). For example, MUL A, C means: multiply the contents of register C by the contents of the accumulator (A) and load the product into the accumulator. This last step uses the implied address, that of the accumulator.

**indexed addressing** the instruction specifies an index register (there can be one or two register pairs) plus an offset value. The offset value is given in the byte following the instruction byte. The index register holds an absolute address (p.167); to this is added the offset value to give the absolute address of the location holding the operand (p.73) for the instruction. Indexed addressing differs from register indirect addressing (↑) in specifying the offset value.

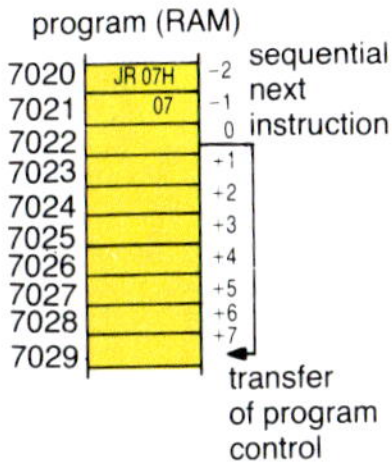


jumps can be both backward and forward

**relative addressing**

**relative addressing** this form of addressing is used only with relative jump instructions. The first byte after the jump instruction holds an offset value. This value gives the displacement (↓) from the address of the instruction that would normally have been executed next.

**bit addressing** register, register indirect, or indexed addressing is used to specify a memory location or a register. Part of the instruction is a 3-bit code which specifies which bit, 0–7, is selected for testing or manipulation.

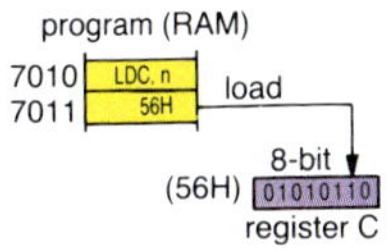


**immediate addressing**

**immediate addressing** the instruction specifies a register and an operation. The operand (p.73) of the operation is stored in the next location immediately after the location holding the instruction, e.g. LOD C, 56H is an instruction held in two bytes, the first byte orders the loading of register C by the number (56 hex) held in the next byte.

**indirect addressing** (1) addressing a memory location that holds the address of the required data; (2) any form of addressing in which the address of the required data is held in a register or specified location in memory.

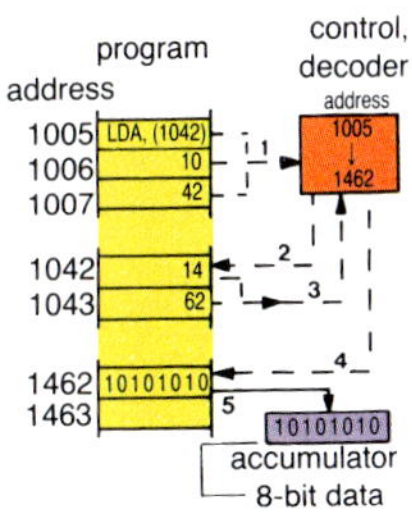


five steps used in indirect addressing

**indirect addressing**

**displacement** (*n*) a number indicating the number of locations away from the location specified in an instruction. This results in an absolute address. The specified location is the next sequential location. The displacement can be positive or negative.

**inherent addressing** this method of addressing has no extended addressing facilities (↑). All information is contained in the instruction. Operations on the accumulator and index register are included in the method.

**addressing level** there are three levels of addressing: (1) zero-level, in which the operand (p.73) is in the address part of the instruction, e.g. shift, increment; (2) first level, in which the operand's address is given in the address section of an instruction, and the location is in RAM; (3) second level, in which the address of an operand is given in a memory location pointed to by the address section of the instruction, e.g. indirect addressing.

**relative address²** an address which is altered, by displacement (p.169), to an absolute address (p.167). This alteration takes place at the time a program is run on a microcomputer.
**floating address²** (1) relative address (↑); (2) symbolic address (p.171).
**reference address** (1) the address used in converting relative addresses to object code (p.38) addresses; the displacement (p.169) is added to the reference address; (2) an address used as a reference for a group of related addresses, e.g. the addresses of a subroutine.
**effective address** an address used by a microcomputer in executing instructions, as opposed to an original address in a program. The original address is converted to the effective address by program modification (p.71).
**base address** the address in a program instruction (p.66) which is the starting point for modification by the program. The base address is used to modify relative addresses to absolute addresses, by addition of the displacement. Synonymous with reference address (↑).
**presumptive address** base address (↑).
**float factor** program origin (p.54). The absolute address of the start of a program.
**float** (*v*) to add the float factor (↑) to all the relative addresses of a program to determine how many locations in memory the program will occupy.
**segment²** (*n*) a set of data, which can be placed anywhere in memory where there is sufficient capacity. All items are addressed relative to a base address (↑), which is the program origin (p.54). The length of the segment is the number of locations required for storage.
**float relocate** the conversion of floating addresses (↑) of a segment (↑) to absolute addresses so that they become effective addresses (↑).
**dynamic relocation** the moving of a partially executed program to a different set of locations in RAM without affecting the execution of the program, so that it is completed without detriment.
**virtual address** an immediate or real-time address which has a physical location and can be used for direct memory access (p.157). The address can be in a backing store (p.178) and is part of virtual memory (p.177). Virtual addresses are converted to absolute addresses before execution of instructions.

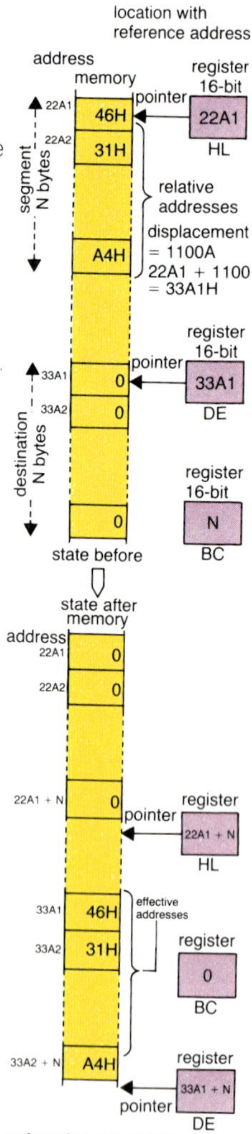

**relocation of a segment**

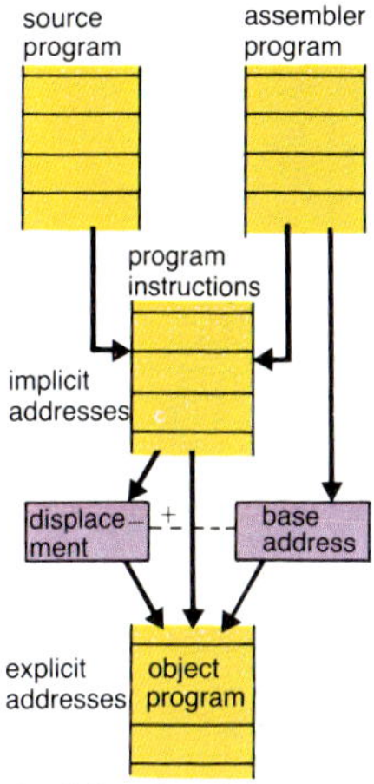


**implicit and explicit addresses**

**address mapping** the translation of a virtual address (↑) to an absolute address in RAM.

**implicit address** an address, used in an assembler program (p.53) which is specified as a relocatable expression. An implicit address has to be converted to an explicit address (↓) before it is assembled into an object program (p.53).

**explicit address** an address, used in an assembler program (p.53), which is specified by two absolute addresses; one is a base address (↑), and the other is a displacement (p.169). Both are needed to generate an effective address (↑) for an object program (p.53).

**addressing mode** the manner in which the general registers and the special registers (index register, stack pointer) are to be used in a process for the purpose of locating the source operand (p.73) and the destination of the result. The mode is the manner of specifying or computing the address of the location. The modes include sequential, forward, backward (↓), indexed, indirect addressing with 8-bit, 16-bit, 32-bit, word and stack addressing.

**sequential mode** each instruction is in a sequence of ascending location addresses in memory. For single byte instructions, the addresses increase by 1; for two- and three-byte instructions, the addresses are incremented accordingly.

**forward mode** a positive displacement (p.169) is used for all relocations.

**backward mode** a negative displacement (p.169) is used for all relocations.

**symbolic addressing** using a symbolic address (↓) in a source language.

**symbolic address²** an address referred to by a symbolic name; it is not given a memory location by the programmer. The compiler (p.54) assigns an absolute address to the symbolic address when the program has been compiled.

**symbolic addresses**

assembly language program (part)

address has up to 4 characters either letters or numbers

| operation | address | remarks |
|---|---|---|
| add | N x T | add data in RAM location N x T to accumulator |
| JZ | CHS 2 | jump to location CHS2 if accumulator is zero |

**word addressing** a form of addressing in some computers where a word (p.36) can be addressed as well as a byte (p.36).

**page addressing** a page is a block of locations of fixed length in memory, typically 4096 or 256 consecutive bytes, which can be addressed by the HI byte of a 16-bit address in systems which allow page addressing.

**paging** (*v*) using page addressing (↑) to transfer pages of data between RAM (p.175) and a backing store (p.178).

**zero page addressing** in some systems, an address facility to speed up execution times, in which only the second address byte is used, the first address byte, referring to the page, is zero. Hence a page-zero address is under reference.

**multiple-address code** an instruction code which specifies more than one address for operands and results; there are 4-address, 3-address and 2-address codes. Two-address codes specify the locations of two operands. Three-address codes specify, in addition, the location of the result. In 4-address codes, the fourth address specifies the location of the next instruction.

**address format** the construction of the address parts of an instruction; the number of addresses that can be coded is given. The expression 'plus-one' is commonly used to indicate that one of addresses is the address of the next instruction. Both registers and memory locations are addressed.

**one-plus-one address** the address of an operand (p.73) is given and the address of the next instruction.

**two-address instruction** the addresses of two operands (p.73) are specified, with the result put in the register holding one of the operands.

**two-plus-one address** two addresses are those of operands (p.73), while the third is that of the destination location of the result.

**three-address instruction** two-plus-one address instruction (↑).

**three-plus-one address** three addresses are for two operands (p.73) and the result. The fourth is the address of the next instruction.

**four-address instruction** three-plus-one address instruction (↑).

**four-plus-one address** four of the addresses specify registers; the fifth address is that of the next instruction.

**allocate** (*v*) to make available areas of storage in a computer for the main program and for subroutines. This determines the base address (p.170) for a routine and fixes the absolute addresses (p.167). *Contrast assign* (p.67).

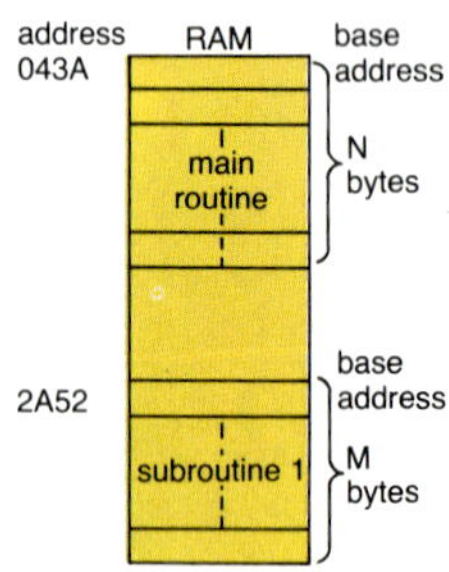


**allocating areas to routines**

**binding** (*n*) the process of assigning absolute addresses to individual instructions in a program. This is done when transforming object code program modules (p.74) into the final object program for execution by a computer.

**read-only memory** a memory circuit the contents of which are not intended to be altered; the contents are fixed during manufacture, and are permanent (p.165). This type of memory is used to store permanent programs, that is, data can be read out but cannot be written into it. Most microcomputer read-only memories are made from large-scale integrated circuits (p.145).

**ROM** (*abbr*) read-only memory (↑).

**firmware** (*n*) the permanent programs stored in ROM (↑).

**control ROM** a read-only memory (↑) designed to decode control logic as in a microprogram controller (p.154). Microinstructions forming microprograms (p.51) are stored in the control ROM. The microprograms control the detailed steps of each machine instruction.

**CROM** (*abbr*) control ROM (↑).

**control memory** control ROM (↑).

**ROM bootstrap** a minimum program of instructions in ROM, which starts the loading of a program from an input device into the computer.

**bootstrap loader** ROM bootstrap (↑).

**PROM** (*acro*) programmable read-only memory. No programs are recorded during manufacture; a physical action is needed to record programs. A process called **field programming** is used to put the programs into the memory. Appropriate bits are set for each memory cell (p.175) and then a heavy electric current is passed which vaporizes a thin metal link. The program is then permanent.

**programmer unit** a hardware device which uses a control program to set bits in a PROM (↑), and then blows (↓) the instructions.

**PROM programmer** programmer unit (↑).

**fusable read-only memory** a type of PROM (↑) which has very small tungsten fuses connected between each memory cell (p.175) and one of the logic voltages. A high voltage is applied to blow (↓) a fuse, producing a logic 1 output from that particular memory cell. This forms a permanent circuit. The unblown fuses are not affected by the normal voltages in a digital circuit (+5V) and thus represent a logic 0 output.

**FROM** (*acro*) fusable read-only memory (↑).

**EPROM** (*acro*) erasable programmable read-only memory. This type of ROM uses FAMOS transistors (p.146). The floating gate of the transistors is charged to represent logic 1, and the charge does not leak away since the gate is insulated. This forms a permanent memory. Exposure of the circuit to high intensity ultraviolet light, or soft X-rays, causes a photocurrent which discharges the floating gate, clearing the memory. The gates are charged by applying a high voltage pulse (approximately =25 volts) and read by applying a low negative voltage to the control gate.

**EEPROM** (*acro*) electrically erasable programmable read-only memory. A ROM unit which can have its programs erased electrically by the application of high voltages and then reprogrammed similarly to an EPROM (↑). The range of reprogramming is from 10 to $10^6$ times.

**EAROM** (*acro*) electrically alterable read-only memory. A memory using metal-nitride-oxide semiconductor (MNOS) components. The term is being replaced by EEPROM (↑), although the MNOS devices should remain as EAROM's.

**CMOS memory** a type of memory which uses CMOS units (p.143). These unit memory cells (p.175) use very little power, so a silver-oxide type electric cell can supply power when the power supply is switched off. Rechargeable electric cells can also be used; this produces a static memory which acts as a non-volatile memory (p.165), and can be used as a ROM.

**blast** (*v*) (1) to release various external or internal (p.165) memory areas or blocks from storage of data no longer required by an operational program. A macroinstruction (p.51) causes the control program to return the addresses of the area thus cleared to the list of available storage; (2) synonymous with blow (↓).

**blow** (*v*) to write a program into a PROM, EPROM, EEPROM or EAROM (↑). *See zap* (↓).

**burn** (*v*) to blow (↑). *See zap* (↑).

**zap** (*v*) to erase a program from an EPROM, EEPROM or EAROM (↑). *See blow* (↑).

**random access memory** a memory which provides access to any location with the memory access time independent of the location. The memory is organized into bytes (p.36), each of a fixed number of bits, with each byte in an addressable location which is unique. Data can be written into or read from any location. The

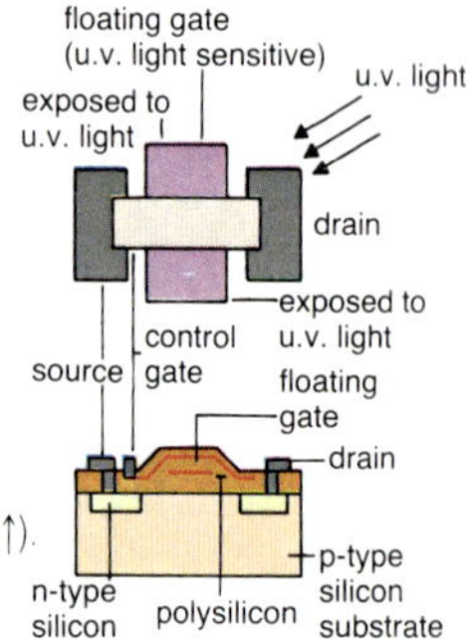


**FAMOS FET used in EPROM**

memory can be static or dynamic (p.165). ROM (p.173) also has random access, but cannot be written into, under normal conditions.

**RAM** (*acro*) random access memory (↑).

**partial RAM** a RAM (↑) in which some bits are defective, so some locations cannot be used. As many as half the locations may be inoperative, but the memory chip is still used, with a reduced storage capacity.

**memory cell** the smallest unit of storage into which a unit of data can be entered, and stored, and from which it can be retrieved. The unit of data can be a byte, a nibble, or a bit. *See binary cell* (p.113).

**memory board** additional memory on a PC board (p.14) which can be connected to a microcomputer. Memory boards can supply either additional RAM or additional ROM; additional ROM can contain programs for: graphics; colour display on a VDU; assemblers for low-level languages, etc.

**memory expansion module** small PC boards (p.14) attached to motherboards (↓) by sockets and nylon bolts. A module has its own bus (p.238) for memory transfers to the microcomputer.

**memory expansion motherboard** a PC board (p.14) that can be attached to a standard motherboard (p.15) and can have many PC cards (p.14) connected to it. The memory expansion motherboard has its own system bus interface (p.219) and support circuits.

**memory map** a list of addresses which defines the boundaries of the memory locations occupied by a program, or a series of programs. The list helps a programmer to relate data names to absolute addresses (p.167). The map is also a means of transforming virtual addresses (p.170) into absolute addresses. Some high-level languages, e.g. FORTRAN, produce memory maps, as part of a program.

**mapping** (*n*) a transformation of one set of addresses to another set. The programmer writes location-independent codes, and mapping provides the transformation. Mapping is user-transparent (p.12).

**scratchpad** (*n*) an area in memory set aside as a temporary working area for intermediate results, e.g. sub-totals of variables needed for final results.

**scratchpad memory** a memory device that stores an interrupted program, and its data, and retrieves the program and data when the interrupting program has finished.

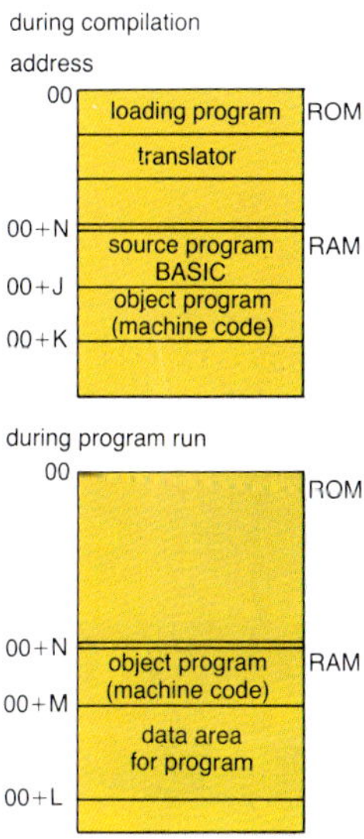


**memory map**

**work area** a part of memory in which data may be temporarily stored or processed. Synonymous with scratchpad (↑).
**working storage** work area (↑).
**WS** (*abbr*) working storage (↑).
**workspace** (*n*) work area (↑).
**buffer storage** (*n*) an area of memory set aside for the temporary storage of data to be transferred from the microcomputer to a peripheral device. The capacity of the buffer depends on the number of characters to be transmitted. Transmission is by blocks in order to save time on transferring control backwards and forwards between the buffer storage and the output device. The buffer storage has the circuitry to take charge of the transfer. Buffer storage may also be a permanent part of a peripheral device.
**buffering** (*n*) the use of buffers (p.164) and buffer storage (↑).
**simple buffering** using buffer storage (↑) with a single input/output device. This allows simultaneous performance of input/output operations and CPU (p.146) activities on computing for the entire duration of the operation with that particular device.
**dynamic buffering** the operation of using buffer storage (↑) so that the storage capacity is expanded or contracted by the addition or removal of memory locations while the information, for which the buffering (↑) is needed, is arriving.
**exchange buffering** the operation of using buffer storage (↑) so that program buffer areas and data buffer areas can be exchanged; this eliminates the movement of data items in RAM, while operating the program.
**isolated locations** storage locations in memory, either RAM or in peripheral devices, which are protected by a hardware device, so that they cannot be addressed by a program. This protects the contents of these locations from accidental alteration.
**bucket** (*n*) an area of RAM designated as a unit of storage for data. Access to the data is by reference to the bucket in which it is located.
**primary memory** the fast-access memory in a computer, the one from which instructions are taken and executed. It can include ROM and RAM.
**main memory** primary memory (↑).
**central memory** primary memory (↑).

**types of memory**

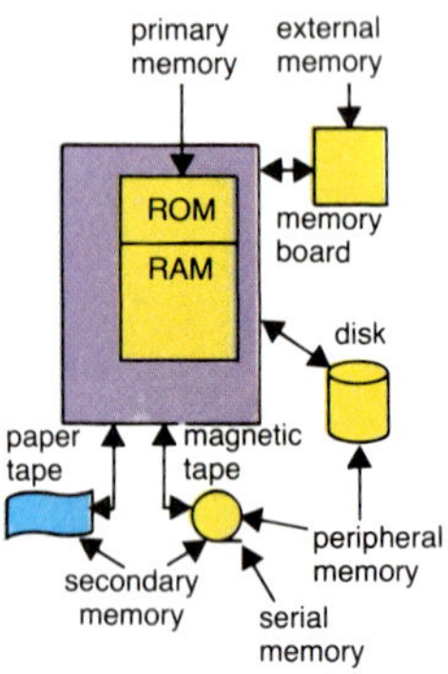

**programmable memory** that part of primary memory (↑) whose locations can be addressed by the program counter (p.153). A program in this memory stores program instructions for the CPU (p.146) and directly controls the ALU (p.150).

**peripheral memory** the memory contained in peripheral devices (p.13).

**secondary memory** a form of storage with a large capacity, long access times, and the facility of transferring blocks of data between it and the primary memory (↑). It includes on-line and off-line (p.22) peripheral devices.

**serial memory**[2] a memory which is accessed serially, so time is one coordinate for accessing a location. Bytes, or words, are stored sequentially, as on magnetic tape, so access time is variable depending on the position of a location.

**external memory** a memory which is under the control of the CPU (p.146) of a microcomputer, but is not connected permanently to the microcomputer. An external memory can be plugged into a memory board (p.175).

**external store** external memory (↑).

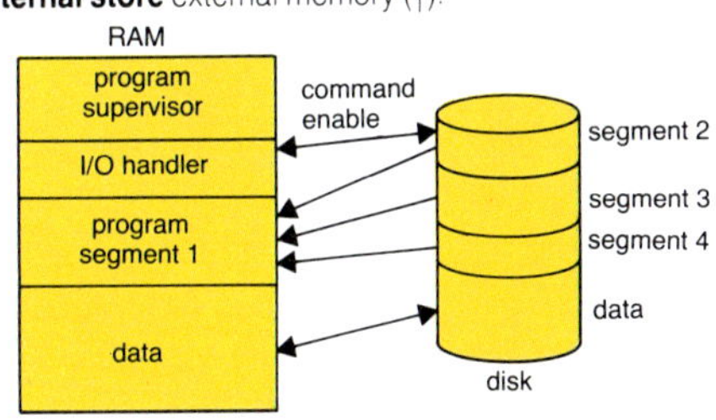


**virtual memory**

**virtual memory** a method of storing programs which allows the operating system to use segments of a backing store (p.178) as if they were main memory (↑). Programs can be entered in memory which are larger than the capacity of main memory. Programs written for a larger memory capacity can be run on computers with a smaller main memory by this facility. Each segment in the backing store is automatically transferred to main memory and executed when space and time allow, so the process is user-transparent (p.12).

**VM** (*abbr*) virtual memory (↑).

**virtual store** virtual memory (↑).

**VS** (*abbr*) virtual store (↑).

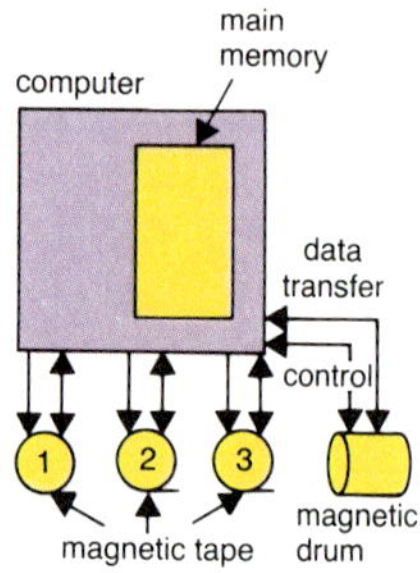

**auxiliary store:** backing store

**external storage** external memory (p.177).
**mass storage** a peripheral device, usually on-line (p.22), of large capacity for receiving and retrieving data. Examples are: magnetic disk and magnetic drum.
**auxiliary storage** backing store (↓), e.g. magnetic tape, disk, magnetic drum.
**auxiliary store** backing store (↓).
**backing store** storage which supports the main memory (p.176) of a computer. It is capable of handling large quantities of data, but has a slower access time (p.166) and is much cheaper than main memory. Examples are magnetic tape, magnetic drum and disk.
**bulk store, bulk storage** backing store (↑).
**secondary store** backing store; secondary memory (p.177).
**dedicated storage** an area of storage used for a special purpose, e.g. the loader program or a disk. Dedicated storage cannot be altered, or overwritten, and can be accessed only by specific instructions.
**serial storage** a form of storage which is accessed serially, so time is one coordinate for accessing a location. Storage can be **serial-by-word**, when locations are addressable for words; or **serial-by-character**, when locations are addressable for decimal-coded characters, e.g. ASCII numbers.
**intermediate memory storage** a fast-access electronic memory used as a scratchpad (p.175) for holding intermediate results until they are needed for the final stages of processing data.
**content-addressable memory** a memory incorporating logic elements which allow the retrieval of locations with a desired data pattern. The locations are not accessed by address but by the data pattern of the location content. It is ideal for quick data searches. A CAM (↓) has a low bit density (p.183) which makes it expensive, because of the dual circuits for accessing a location, the second circuit being used for the usual addressing operation.

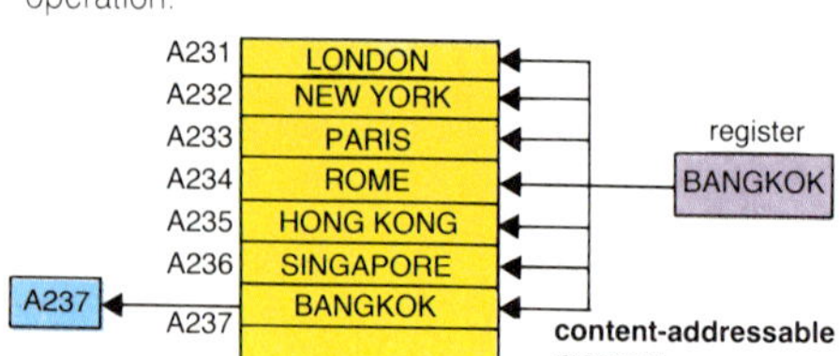

**content-addressable memory**

**cache store**

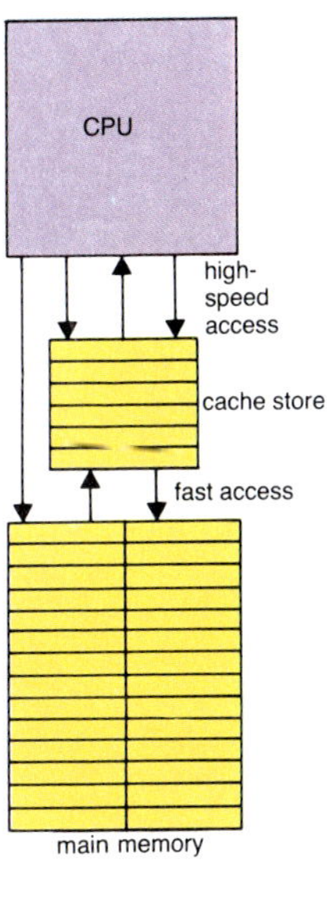


**CAM** (*abbr*) content-addressable memory (↑).

**content** (*n*) the data held in a memory, or storage, location.

**content-addressed storage** a form of storage in which locations are accessed by their contents and not by their address, relative position, or symbolic name. Content-addressed storage uses content-addressable memory (p.178).

**associative storage** content-addressed storage (↑).

**parallel-search storage** content-addressed storage (↑).

**searching storage** content-addressed storage (↑).

**associative storage registers** registers used to locate items by their contents; used with associative storage.

**memory dump** (1) an output of the contents of some or all of the locations in memory during (*a*) program testing or (*b*) the attempt to diagnose software errors or at checkpoints (p.65) to safeguard a program against hardware or software malfunctions; (2) a **dynamic dump** of some sections of memory as a program is executed; (3) a **differential dump** in which only those bytes or characters which have been modified during execution of a routine or program are dumped.

**rescue dump** a recording on tape or disk of the complete contents of main memory (p.176) so that the data, intermediate results, the status of instructions can be regained in the event of power failure or machine malfunction.

**snapshot dump** an output of the contents of specified parts of memory, defined as the start and end of program segments (p.76) and of registers, both specified by a programmer as part of a method of debugging (p.81). The output can also be between checkpoints. A printout is the most useful form of snapshot dump.

**cache store** in larger computers, a small capacity, high-speed memory similar to a scratchpad (p.175). One of the slowest processes in a central processing unit is access to RAM. An improved speed of computing is obtained by using a cache store, situated between main memory and the CPU. Processing usually requires instructions and data held in locations near to each other, so a block of locations can be loaded into the cache store and used at high speed by the central processing unit.

**slave store** cache store (↑).

**roll-out/roll-in** a method of temporarily increasing the available capacity of main memory (p.176) by transferring data or program instructions (**roll-out**) to a backing store (p.178), using the area of main memory left vacant and, after use, returning the data or program instructions to main memory (**roll-in**) from the backing store.
**roll-in** *see roll-out/roll-in* (↑).
**cartridge** (*n*) a small storage unit of magnetic tape which can be easily inserted into a drive device, which causes the tape to move. Data or programs can be stored by the cartridge.
**stack[1]** (*n*) a reserved sequence of locations in memory used for the storage of data, subroutines and interrupt instructions. Access to the stack is at one end only in accordance with the rule LIFO (↓). Items enter the stack in the order of descending addresses, so that as the stack grows, the address of the top of the stack becomes lower. A stack pointer (p.156) points to the top of the stack. Pushing and popping (p.156) respectively add to, and take away from, the items on the stack.
**LIFO** (*acro*) last-in-first-out (↓).
**last-in-first-out** the last item pushed on a stack is pointed to by the stack pointer. It is the first item to be removed from the stack.
**pushdown stack** a stack (↑).
**pushdown list** a stack (↑).
**stack base** a pointer (↓) which indicates the base of the stack, that is, the first location used by the stack. If the stack base and stack pointer hold the same address, then the stack is empty.
**pointer** (*n*) a word which contains the address of a location in main memory (p.176). The pointer is held in a fixed memory location or in a special register used for that purpose, e.g. stack pointer. Pointers are automatically incremented or decremented as a program goes from one location to another location.
**stack address** the address pointed to by the stack pointer (p.156).
**queue** (*n*) a group of items or transactions waiting for attention by the CPU (p.146); such items are usually in the main memory, or under reference in the main memory. The queue is under queue discipline (↓).
**queue discipline** the method of determining the order of items in a queue (↑) for adding to, and taking from, the queue. The queue can be a LIFO (↑) or FIFO (↓) one.

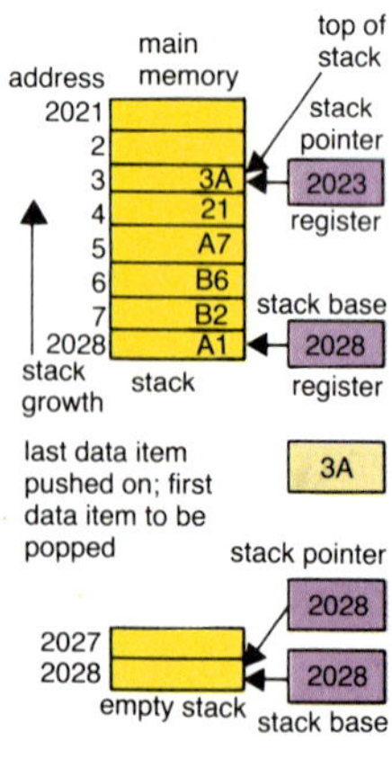


stack in memory

**deque** (*n*) a queue (↑) which allows additions or deletions at either end of the queue.

**first-in-first-out** data written into a FIFO memory is entered into the next free location in sequence. Data read from a FIFO memory is the item that has been longest in the memory. A READ operation advances a pointer to the next location; once this has happened, the previous location cannot be read again. A queue moves down the memory locations as items are added and deleted. Pointers mark the front and rear of the queue.

**FIFO** (*acro*) first-in-first-out (↑).

**queue and FIFO discipline**

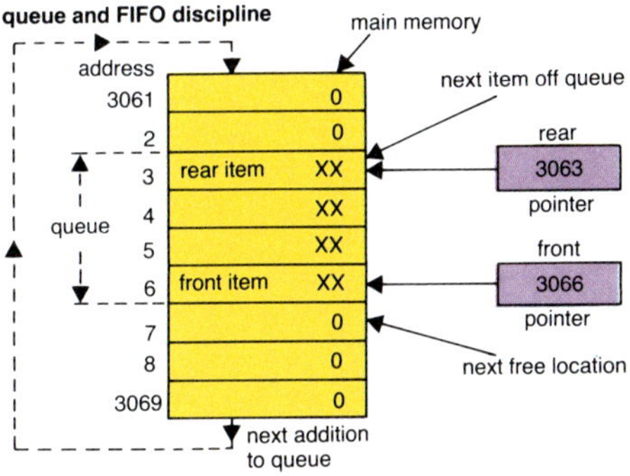


**circular buffer** a type of buffer frequently used for a queue (↑) as it limits the amount of memory to be used by a queue with FIFO discipline (↑). The front of the queue 'wraps around' to the start of the memory area, as more items are added. The queue thus circulates round the memory area.

**cyclic memory** memory that accepts data to be written in at any time, but can be accessed for reading out data only at multiples of a fixed period of time. The time period is referred to as the cycle time.

**program reference table** an area of main memory (p.176) reserved for the storage of variables, operands, and references to loops, arrays, program segments.

**PRT** (*abbr*) program reference table (↑).

**shared-memory systems** different terminals (p.10) and backing stores, printers and punched card devices, share a common main memory (p.176) in a processing unit. The processing unit uses a multiprogramming (p.75) input/output device to control the system.

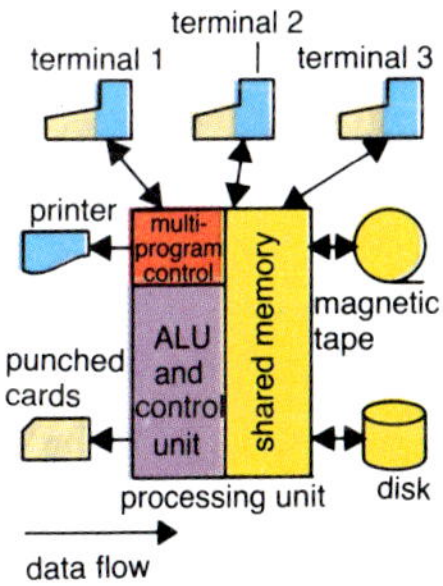


**shared memory system**

**read** (*v*) to sense the contents of a memory, whether main memory (p.176) or peripheral memory (p.177) or a backing store (p.178). To transfer data from one form of storage to another. The contents of a memory location are generally not changed by reading.

**destructive read** the sensing of the contents of a memory location, which erases the data record.

**non-destructive read** the sensing of the contents of a memory location which does not destroy or erase the data record.

**readout**[1] (*n*) the display on a VDU screen of data obtained from memory.

**read time** the time interval between the start of transferring information from a memory and the completion of transference.

**write** (*v*) to record information in a memory location, or by a storage medium. To load information into memory. To copy data from one form of storage to another. The recording need not be permanent.

**write time** the time interval between the start of transferring information to a memory and the completion of the transference.

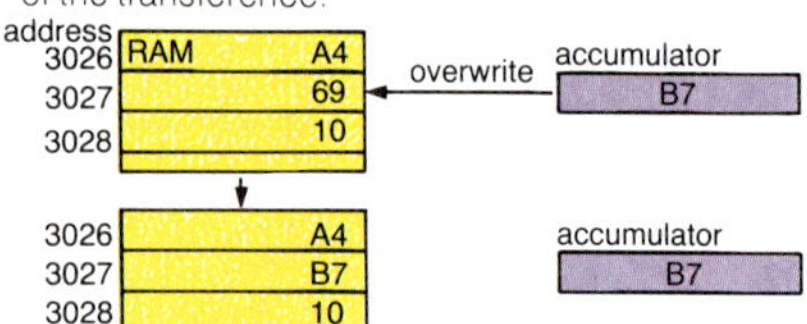


**overwrite**

**overwrite** (*v*) to enter data into a memory location and erase or sometimes partially erase the existing data in that location.

**read/write** refers to devices, events, processes using channels, circuitry or media capable of both reading (↑) and writing (↑).

**R/W** (*abbr*) read/write (↑).

**clear**[2] (*v*) to return a memory to a state which is empty of programs or data. *See clear*[1] (p. 119).

**load**[3] (*v*) to transfer an entire program, or set of data, into main memory (p.176) from a backing store (p.178).

**dump**[1] (*v*) (*a*) to transfer the contents of an area of main memory (p.176) to a backing store (p.178). The opposite of load (↑); (*b*) to withdraw all power from a computer, either intentionally or accidentally; usually called a **power dump**.

**semiconductor memory** a memory which uses semiconductor circuits to store information. The basic technologies are: (1) bipolar transistors, (2) MOS, (3) CMOS.

**bit density** the number of bits per unit area in a storage device, or the number of bits per inch on magnetic tape.

**MOS memory** a main memory (p.176) which uses MOS field effect transistors (p.142) to form memory cells. The FETs are used in flip-flops (p.114) which store binary digits; n-channel FETs are more common than p-channel FETs.

**CMOS memory** a main memory (p.176) which uses CMOS circuits (p.143). This type of memory can act as a non-volatile memory, as the low power consumption can be supplied by batteries when the power supply is switched off.

**charge-coupled device** the device consists of FETMOS transistors (p.142) and capacitors. An input signal transfers part of its charge to a capacitor, $C_1$ in the diagram, on application of a clock signal from control line $T_A$. On application of a clock signal from control line $T_B$, this charge is transferred to the next capacitor, $C_2$, leaving the capacitor, $C_1$, discharged. The clock pulses on $T_A$ and $T_B$ are 180° out of phase, that is, they are applied alternately. A second signal is entered, and $T_A$ clocks this signal into capacitor $C_1$, at the same time, $T_A$ clocks the charge on capacitor $C_2$ into $C_3$. A charge is thus transferred along the line of capacitors and emerges at the far end, forming an output. The device acts like a shift register. All charges are lost when the power is switched off. In an integrated circuit, the capacitors are potential wells in the semiconductor material with the substrate acting as a common ground connection.

charge-coupled device

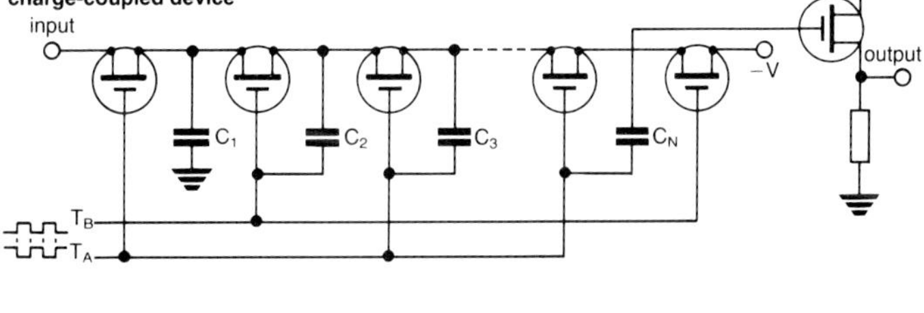

**CCD** (*abbr*) charge-coupled device.

**CCD memory** a line of MOS gates and capacitors, closely spaced, with the capacitors storing logic ones and zeros as a charge or no charge on a capacitor. The memory is arranged for both serial and random-access functions, e.g. by having sixty-four 256-bit registers with clock pulses to shift the data along each register. *See CCD* (↑). Each register can be regarded as a track (↓) along a revolving drum as the end of the line of gates and capacitors joins to the beginning. The 'rate of rotation' of the theoretical drum is governed by the clock pulse, and each bit can be accessed at the end of the register. Each track can be accessed by a decoder, thus enabling each bit in memory to be addressed. The output is sensed as a one or a zero.

**bucket-brigade device** a device that stores charges in discrete regions of a semiconductor material, and transfers such charges from region to region by switching devices interconnecting the regions, for example, a CCD (↑).

**BBD** (*abbr*) bucket-brigade device (↑).

**image sensor** a CCD memory (↑) can be sensitive to light and if the memory cells are arranged in a suitable matrix, an image, focussed by lenses on to the cells, will store a charge on the cells, dependent on the light level. Scanning the matrix will produce an output which can be related to the image. The image is output in a binary-coded form, suitable for a computer to manipulate.

**magnetic drum** a metal drum coated with a layer of magnetizable material, rotates at high speed, usually 50 revolutions per second. The drum is about 0.9m long and 0.3m in diameter. Data are stored in parallel **tracks** on the drum; there are several hundred tracks on the drum surface. Each track has a read/write head (↓). The average access time is 10ms, and each track holds 50000–100000 bits. Logic one is recorded as a magnetized spot and zero as an unmagnetized spot. Magnetic drums are now mainly absolescent.

**track**[1] (*n*) *see magnetic drum* (↑).

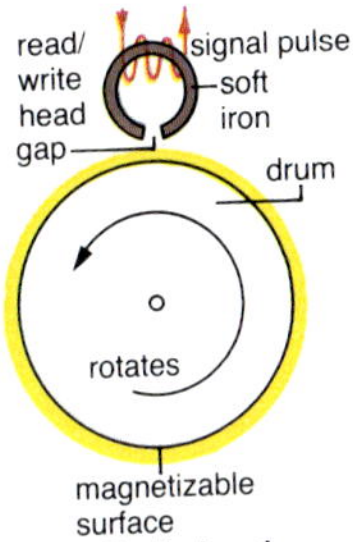

**read/write head**

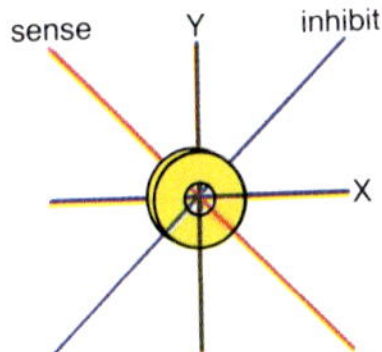

a ferrite core with four lines through its centre
**core memory**

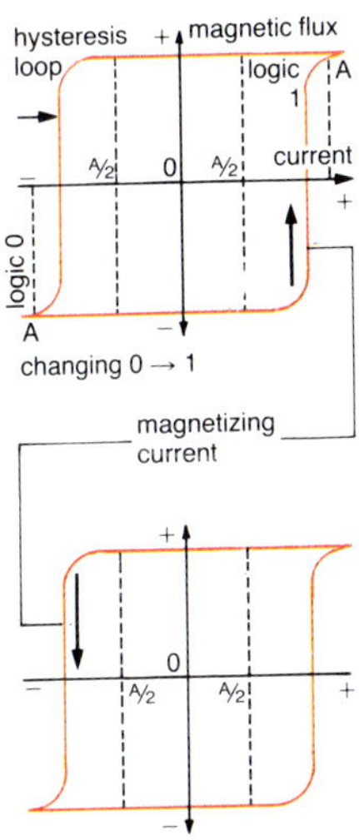

**magnetizing a ferrite core**

**read/write head**[1] varying voltages, corresponding to logic one and zero, in the coil round the head, produce a varying magnetic flux in the gap of the head. This flux magnetizes the material on the drum during a write cycle. On a read cycle, a magnetized spot on the drum causes a flux in the gap, and the head, which induces a voltage in the coil, decoded as logic one or zero, after amplification.

**core memory** a set of ferrite cores (p.186) connected in rows and columns form a core memory. Each core is threaded by four wires: X, Y, Inhibit, Sense. The X, Y wires address a particular core with each X line addressing one row and each Y line addressing one column of a set. When the ferrite core is magnetized in one direction it stores a logic one, when magnetized in the opposite direction a zero is stored. Magnetization of a core follows a magnetic hysteresis loop (p.126). The current, marked A in the diagram, is suffiicient to saturate the core magnetically; a current of .5A has no effect on the magnetization. To address a particular core, a current of .5A is sent through both X and Y lines which address that core. If zero is to be recorded, a current .5A is also sent through the Inhibit line in the opposite direction to the write pulses on the X and Y lines. As the total magnetizing current is reduced to .5A, there is no change in the magnetization of the core, and it remains recording 0. If a logic one is to be recorded, there is no Inhibit pulse. To read a core, the X and Y lines pass a current pulse in the opposite direction to the WRITE pulse. If the core stores logic one, this reverses the magnetization to represent 0. The change in magnetic flux induces a current in the Sense line. As the core now stores 0, a logic one has to be rewritten into it, so a WRITE pulse always follows a READ pulse. This produces a second pulse in the Sense line, which is removed by a gate (p.110). If the core stores 0, then there is no change in its magnetization when the READ pulses are applied, hence no pulse in the Sense line. The WRITE cycle now needs an Inhibit pulse, automatically provided if there is no Sense pulse. The Sense line signals are weak and need considerable amplification. Core memories are arranged in a series of layers, the number of layers corresponds to the number of bits in a byte or word. Each layer is connected to one bit in the MAR (p.155), with the X and Y lines addressing a location with the same coordinates in each layer.

**ferrite core** a circular-shaped core made of iron and other metallic oxides. It is about 2mm in diameter with a hole in the middle. Wires carrying current pass through the core. When a current of sufficient strength is passed, the core becomes magnetically saturated. The core remains magnetized when the power supply is switched off, so a core memory is non-volatile (p.165).

**core matrix memory** a core memory (p.185) with ferrite cores arranged in layers. Large mainframe computers use such a memory with bytes of 40 bits or more, and up to 100K locations on each layer. Core memories are now obsolescent for microcomputers.

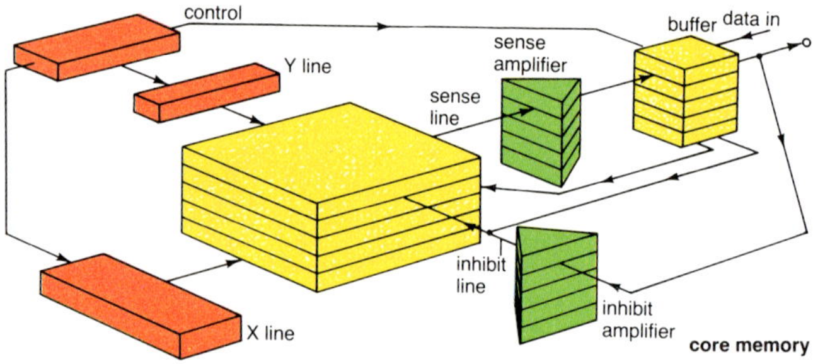

**core memory**

**core** (*n*) (1) ferrite core (↑); (2) core memories are no longer in use. The term is sometimes used to mean memory.

**core store** term formerly used for main memory (p.176), or RAM, as these memories used ferrite cores. Synonymous with core memory (p.185).

**electrostatic storage** a storage device that uses electrostatic charge on a non-conducting surface to represent logic one (presence of a charge) and zero (absence of charge). The screen of a cathode-ray tube (p.130) is used as the non-conducting surface. An electron beam scans the screen, and puts a charge on a phosphor (p.207) which acts as a memory location. A plate parallel to the screen acts as a capacitor in conjunction with the charge on the screen and detects 1 or 0 when the electron beam is on the location. The locations are accessed serially along each row in turn. Access time is almost as fast as for CMOS memories (p.183). The charge on a location tends to die away so the data must be continually refreshed.

**cathode-ray tube storage** electrostatic storage (↑).

1. CRT
2. 1 or 0 detect
3. address decoder
4. 1 or 0 generator
5. address register
6. OR gate
7. control circuit
8. AND gate
9. address
10. data input
11. data output

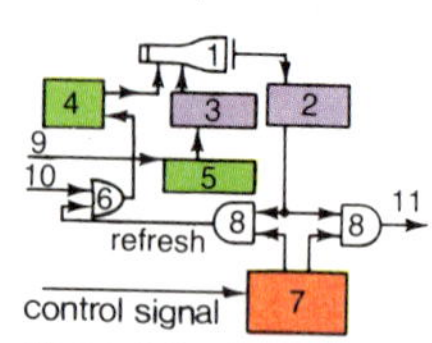

**electrostatic storage**

**bubble memory** to make a bubble memory a single-crystal epitaxial film (p.140) of synthetic garnet is grown on a silicon substrate. A metal alloy coating is deposited on the garnet film and a pattern is etched on this coating by photolithography (p.139). This forms the bubble memory chip. A pair of field coils, at right angles to each other, are slipped over the chip. A pair of permanent magnets is then mounted one above and one below the coils covering the chip. The whole device is then enclosed with a shield of magnetic material to prevent magnetic field interference (p.126). Magnetic bubbles are formed in the garnet film when two magnetic fields are applied perpendicularly to the film. The magnetic axis of the bubble is perpendicular to the plane of the garnet film. The permanent magnets supply a constant magnetic field which strengthens and fattens the bubbles. A pattern of chevrons of magnetic alloy in the metal coating forms a path for the magnetic bubbles. An alternating current in the two field coils produces a rotating magnetic field which sets up magnetic poles on the chevrons. The magnetic bubbles are moved by the magnetized chevrons changing their magnetism, and are passed from one chevron to the next chevron as the magnetic field rotates. A microscopic metal loop of one turn, placed in the metallic layer above the garnet film, is used to form a bubble by passing a precise current through the loop; this current alters the local magnetic field from the permanent magnets and creates the bubble. The metal loop is also used to sense the bubble, which induces a weak current in the loop; this current is then amplified. The chevrons form a pattern of loops, followed by the bubbles. A magnetic bubble represents logic one, and the absence of a bubble represents zero. Arrays of forty-eight circuits each containing 70000 bubble bits are put on each chip. Access is serial in and serial out for the parallel loops, organized as a shift register. When the power supply is switched off, or fails, the permanent magnets keep the magnetic bubbles stable, so the memory is non-volatile (p.165).

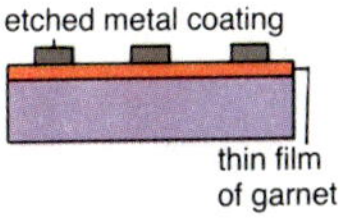


**bubble memory chip components**

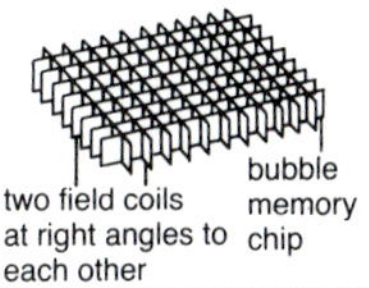


[field coils are now replaced by perforated metal sheets]

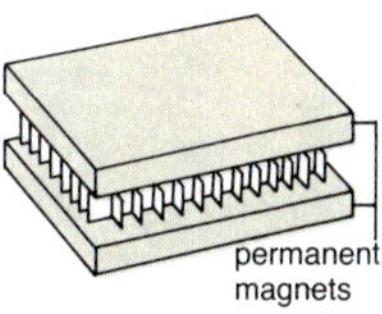


bubble memory assembly (enclosed by a metal magnetic screen)

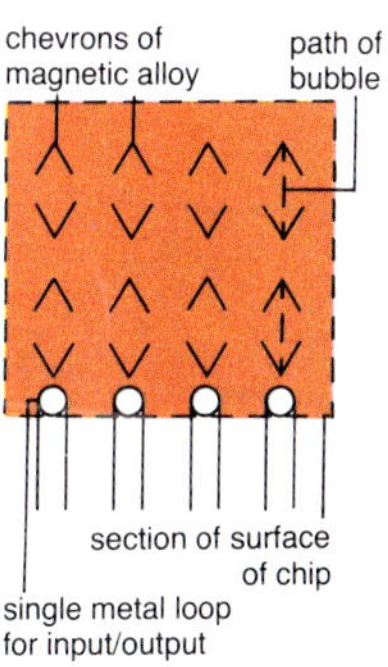


**bubble memory movement**

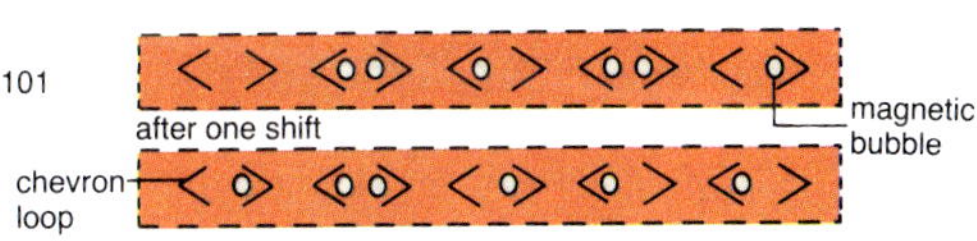

**bubble memory controller** a control circuit between a CPU (p.146) and a bubble memory (p.187). It carries out parallel-to-serial conversion from the CPU to the memory and serial-to-parallel conversion from memory to the CPU. It controls bubble movement, bubble generation, bubble replication and annihilation. Control signals are sent to a timing generator; this produces timing signals for the field coils, the input/output loops, and the sense amplifier in each magnetic field cycle.

**magnetic bubble memory** bubble memory (p.187).

**thin-film memory** a magnetic alloy is deposited, in a vacuum under the influence of a strong magnetic field, on an inert substrate, such as glass. The thin film is etched, by photolithography (p.139), to form discs of the magnetic material. Because of their thinness, the direction of the magnetic field in the discs can be switched in nanoseconds. The operation of the memory is similar to that of a core memory (p.185).

**capacitor storage** a memory device which stores a digital bit as a charge on a capacitor, or a charge in a region of a semiconductor. A device which stores an analog voltage as a charge on a capacitor.

**transcribe** (*v*) to copy data from one external storage medium to another. The process may, or may not, include translation.

**storage hierarchy** refers to the different sizes, speeds, and cost per unit of data, for all types of memory and storage. Fast memory access times involve high costs; slow memory access times are usually much cheaper. Fast memories have parallel access to random locations. Slow memories have serial access.

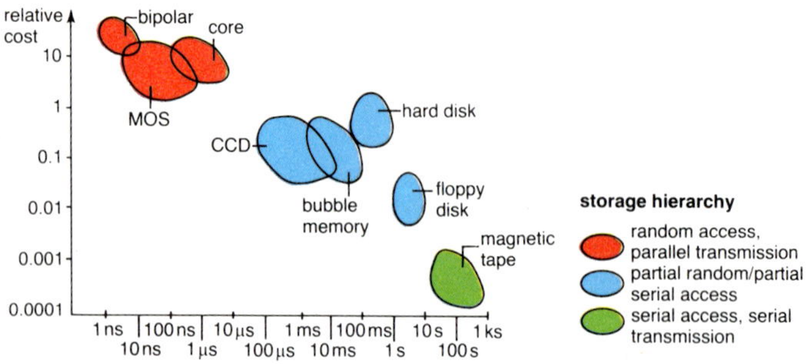

**input** (*v*) (1) to transfer information (data or instructions) from a peripheral device into a CPU (p.146) and then into main memory (p.176); (2) (*adj*) describes a device used to transfer information into a computing system; (3) (*n*) the data or instructions which are transferred into a CPU, or main memory. **input** (*adj*), **input** (*n*).

**input device** a device that puts data or instructions into a computer; it is a communicating link between people and a computer. The device may accept coded information, as in punched cards, paper tape or bar codes; or may accept human readable information such as magnetic ink, or optical, characters. The device may be a keyboard, or a light pen, or a terminal (p.10).

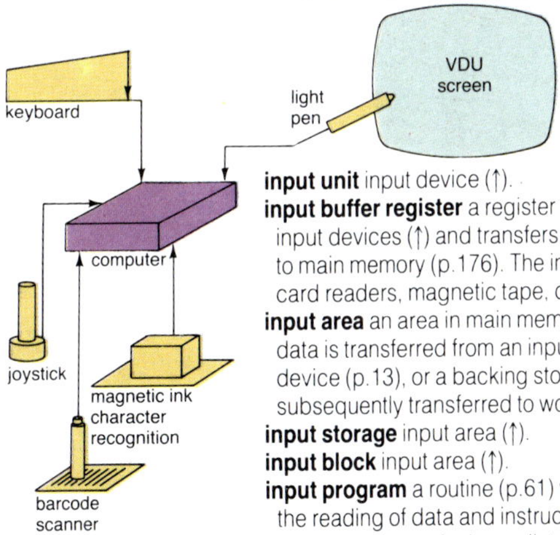

**input devices**

**input unit** input device (↑).

**input buffer register** a register that receives data from input devices (↑) and transfers it to the CPU (p.146), or to main memory (p.176). The input devices include card readers, magnetic tape, disks and keyboards.

**input area** an area in main memory (p.176) into which data is transferred from an input device (↑), a peripheral device (p.13), or a backing store (p.178). The data are subsequently transferred to work areas (p.176).

**input storage** input area (↑).

**input block** input area (↑).

**input program** a routine (p.61) which controls and monitors the reading of data and instructions, either for transfer to main memory, or for immediate use by the CPU (p.146). The routine may be hard-wired (p.17), or part of a bootstrap operation (p.18), or held permanently in ROM.

**input routine** input program (↑).

**input reader** input program (↑).

**input section** (1) an input routine (↑) that is part of a program; (2) input area (↑).

**input limited** describes a program whose speed of operation is limited by the speed of an input device (↑). Processing is delayed waiting for the input of the data.

**input mode** the method of operation of a computer when it is receiving data from peripheral devices, e.g. keyboard, disk.

**sensor²** (*n*) a transducer (p.229) with an input which measures an external phenomenon quantitatively, and an output which can be read by a computer, e.g. a thermometer which measures temperature and produces a digital output.

**sensor device** a device acting as a sensor (↑), e.g. a device which measures temperature, pressure, rate of flow, height or depth, and translates the measure into digital or analog data for a computer.

**sensor-based computer** a computer that receives real-time data (p.22) from sensor devices (↑) and can generate signals to control the process which is being measured. For example, the computer in an automatic gear box which measures road speed and engine torque and changes gear to suit the circumstances.

**reflective sensor** the sensor consists of a red or infrared LED (p.198) in view of a silicon phototransistor (p.133). The sensor can detect the beginning and end of a tape or the absence or presence of a card in a card feed, by the interruption of light.

**light sensor** a photocell (p.132), or photodiode, which provides a response to the intensity of light.

**environmental sensor** a sensor that measures conditions external to the computer system, but within the environment of the process under operation, e.g. measuring ambient temperature to control a jet engine.

**joystick** (*n*) a stick that can be moved in any direction, combining backwards and forwards, left and right. A cursor, or a graphic symbol, on the screen of a VDU moves in the direction ordered by the joystick. The position of the joystick alters two variable resistors, placed at right angles to each other. The current from each resistor is converted to a digital reading, which, in turn, is converted into X and Y coordinate signals that move the cursor or symbol.

**paddle** (*n*) this refers, usually, to a joystick (↑) which can be moved backwards and forwards only.

**trackball** (*n*) a ball mounted in a box, with sensors detecting its movement. A cursor moves in the same direction as the trackball, and travels a distance proportional to the speed at which the ball is rolled. This permits accurate positioning of the cursor.

**mouse** (*n*) a type of trackball (↑) used with the box inverted. When the box is moved, the cursor follows the same track.

**joystick**

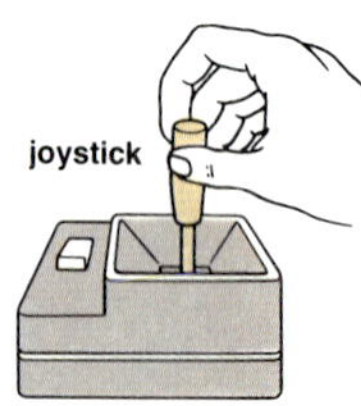

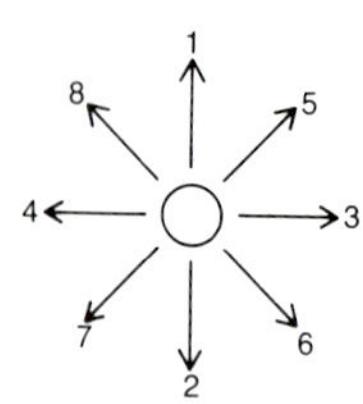


**movements of joystick**

**keyboard** (*n*) a device that encodes data by the manual depression of a key (↓).

**key**[1] (*n*) a marked button, that can be depressed manually, to produce a computer-readable code for a character, such as a letter, number, punctuation sign, or for a function (p.49) or a token (p.37).

**QWERTY** describes the common keyboard, with keys arranged as on a typewriter. So named because the first six letters of the top row of keys are the letters 'qwerty'.

**microwriter**

**microwriter** (*n*) a hand-held device with six keys on its keyboard. It has a one-line LCD (p.198) and a memory. Combinations of one, two and three keys produce the different characters for alphanumeric characters and punctuation marks, as a total of forty-one combinations is possible. Combinations of four keys can extend this by a further fifteen. A microwriter is used to write, edit and store typed information, and the results can be transferred from its memory to a word processor. A six-key keyboard can be a replacement for a QWERTY keyboard (↑).

**keyboard encoder** each key, and its combination with a shift key, on a keyboard, can be identified by a simple binary number, contained in a 7-bit byte. The keys are divided into groups, each defined by a digit, and an arrangement of such groups is shown in the diagrams. A normal keyboard has approximately ninety different characters, functions (p.49) and tokens (p.37). A 7-bit byte can represent $2^7 = 128$, so there are spare combinations. The keyboard encoder translates the unique key reference into the 7-bit byte code. The encoder also includes a debounce circuit (p.122).

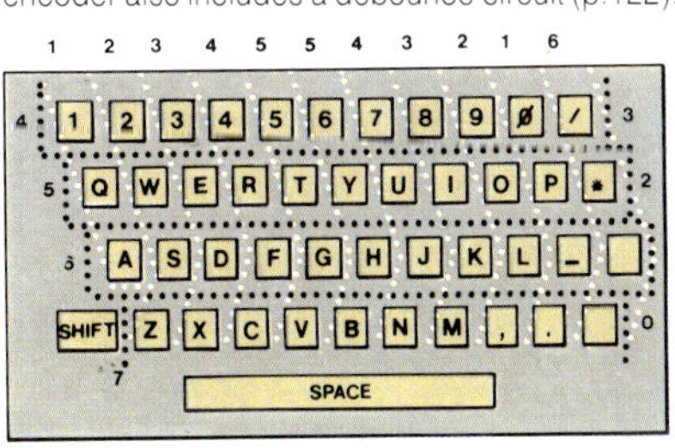


keyboard can be divided either into horizontal or vertical sections

**keyboard layout**

**alphanumeric keyboard** a keyboard (p.191) with letters, numbers and punctuation marks; used by word processors, data processors, and teleprinters (p.26).
**numeric keyboard** a keyboard (p.191) with numbers only; used on calculators.
**keypad** (*n*) a keyboard (p.191) that can be held in the hand.
**ASCII keyboard** a keyboard that uses ASCII code (p.38). It includes ninety-six key combinations for uppercase and lowercase letters, numbers, punctuation marks and other symbols, together with 32 control functions. This is the 128 possible combinations provided by a 7-bit byte. In addition, the keyboard encoder (p.191) adds a parity bit (p.39) for even parity, making an 8-bit byte.

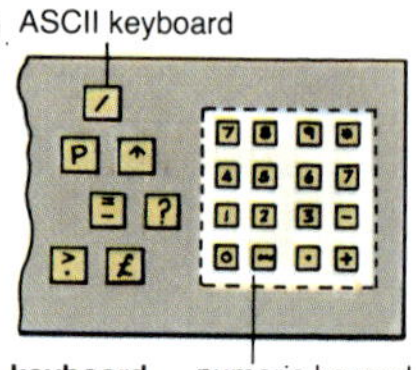

**keyboard**

**ASR keyboard** a keyboard compatible with a tele-typewriter and teleprinter of a telex system (p.26); it is a 33-key alphanumeric keyboard with control keys (↓).
**ASR** (*abbr*) automatic send-receive, used with a telex service (p.26).
**control key** a key that moves and controls a cursor (p.18); a key that uses one operation instead of printing out a statement or command in a high-level language, e.g. a key for PRINT, STOP, CLEAR, NEW, etc.
**function key** a key that can be assigned to a function, such as computation of an algorithm, activation of a peripheral device, production of a printed format.
**edit key** a key that facilitates the editing of a program.
**numeric keypad** a 10–, 12– or 16-key unit which is an extension of an ASCII keyboard for numbers; the keys are grouped for convenience of use.
**numeric pad** numeric keypad (↑).
**tactile keyboard** the keyboard has three layers. The top layer is made of Mylar (a plastic insulating material) with a pattern of conductive material which corresponds to the positions of the keys. Heat and pressure is used to make bubbles in the Mylar sheet with conductive

**principle of tactile keyboard**

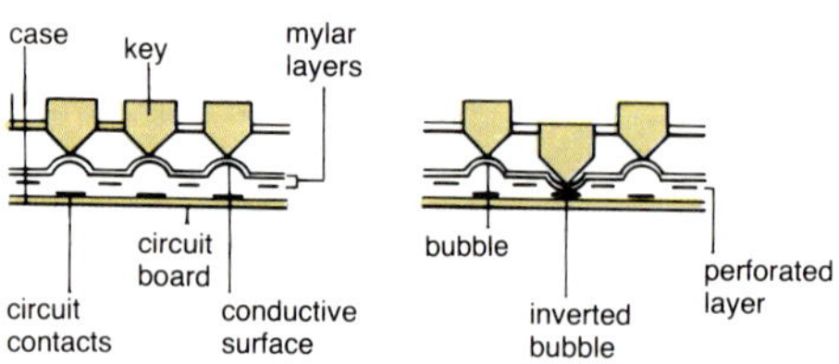

surfaces on the bottom. The middle layer is a Mylar sheet with holes at each key position. The third layer is a PC board (p.14). When a key is depressed, the bubble is depressed, makes contact with the PC and the key circuit is closed.

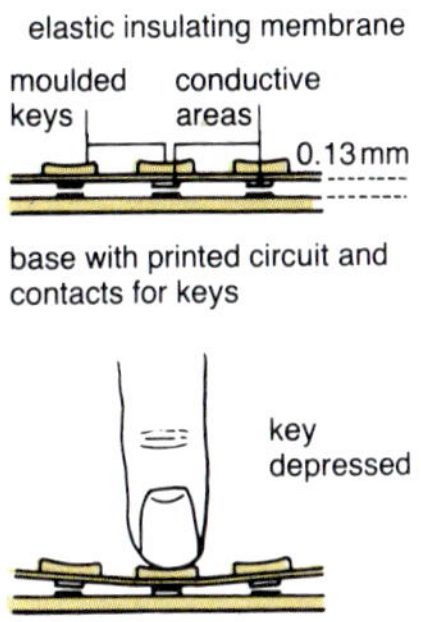


**principle of touch-sensitive membrane keyboard**

**touch-sensitive membrane keyboard** made of a tough, elastic, insulating plastic membrane with a conductive area beneath each key. The keys, which are marked on the membrane, are shaped to accommodate a finger tip. Beneath the membrane is a printed circuit board (p.14) with conductive contacts for each key. The distance between the membrane and the base board is approximately 0.13mm and a weight of 60-120 grams produces contact for the switch operation. As these keyboards have no mechanical linkage to wear out, they can provide a long trouble-free life.

**keyboard overlay** a removable overlay placed over a key on a console (p.16) when that key is assigned a particular function in a program. The overlay indicates the job carried out by using the key.

**keyboard contact bounce** both tactile and membrane keyboards suffer from contact bounce (p.122) when keys are used. A debouncing circuit (p.122) is included in the keyboard encoder (p.191).

**rollover** (*n*) an encoding circuit, part of the keyboard encoder (p.191) which allows specified combinations of keys to be depressed simultaneously without an error display.

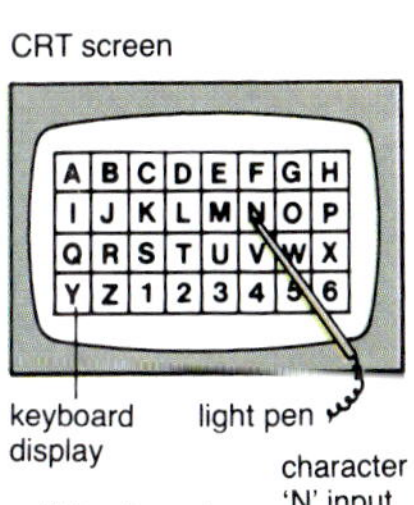


**soft keyboard**

**soft keyboard** a keyboard is displayed on a terminal screen; a light pen (p.195) is pointed at a required key, causing the character of that key to be input.

**character recognition** a computer process of identifying a printed character, and encoding it to make the information machine-readable, e.g. optical character recognition, magnetic ink character recognition. The characters are able to be read by human beings.

**character reader** a device which can convert human-readable printed characters into machine-readable code; the device carries out character recognition (↑).

**shift-out character** a character, with its own key, which is a code for substituting an alternative or extension set of characters to the ASCII set; usually a set of graphic symbols, but could be an alternative alphabet, etc.

**character shift-in** a character which is a code for a computer to return to the normal ASCII character set after the use of an extension set controlled by a shift-out character (p.193).

**optical character recognition** the identification of printed characters by photoelectric devices (p.132). A special font (p.203) is used, which is readable by human beings.

**OCR** (*abbr*) optical character recognition (↑).

**optical mark reader** a photoelectric device (p.132) which detects the presence, or absence, of a pencil mark on mark scanning (↓) computer cards.

**optical character reader** a photoelectric device (p.132) which consists of a mosaic of photocells (p.132). Incident light falling on a printed document produces a pattern of light and shade; the pattern is sensed by the photocells, and converted to a binary code from the mosaic. This code is then matched against a list of stored patterns until an exact match is found, and the character recognized. Some readers can identify several fonts (p.203). Reading speeds vary from 200–2500 characters per second. Readers identifying a single font only are the fastest. The information can be input directly to a computer or transferred to magnetic tape for subsequent input.

**optical font** the font characters consist of lines which can be easily identified by a mosaic of photocells (p.132) but are readily readable by human beings. The example of a font shows the characteristic shapes formed by horizontal, vertical and diagonal straight lines. Such fonts can be produced by typewriters, and are immediately machine-readable.

**mark scanning** computer cards, with eighty columns of figures, have twenty-five columns, or less, available for marking with a pencil. A letter or a figure can be entered on the card by marking the code for it. The card passes under an optical mark reader (↑), the mark is detected and a hole punched, corresponding to the mark, or marks. This method of entering data is useful as it can be used for individual items to be entered by punching in code without depending on passing the card through a manual punching machine.

**scanner** (*n*) any device, optical or magnetic, that examines a marked or printed document, or object, interprets the symbols, and encodes them to provide a computer with machine-readable data.

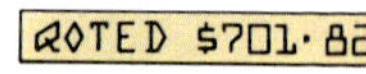

**example of an OCR font**

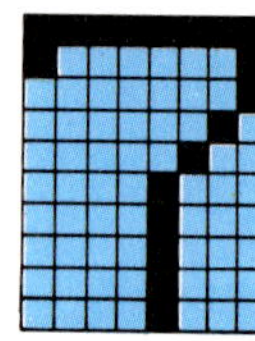


**recognition of a character pattern**

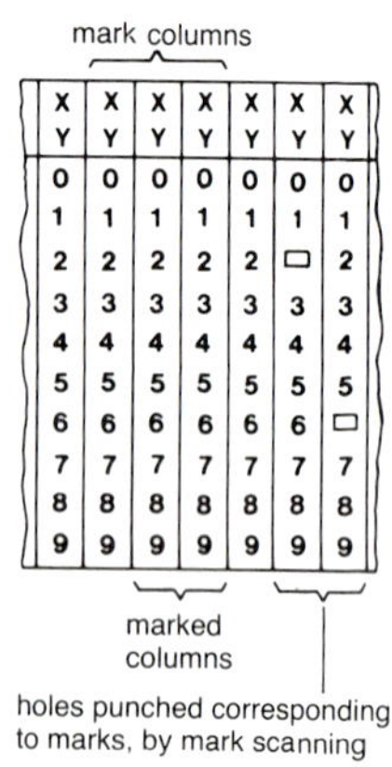


**mark scanning**

**contrast** (*n*) the difference in blackness, or colour, amount of reflection of incident light, or the amount of shading, between the area of a character, or mark, and the area of the background to the character, or mark. The term refers to the process of optical character recognition (p.194) where different contrasts are a method of identifying different characters or symbols.

**optical scanner** a device that scans the incident light from characters or marks and generates digital, or analog, signals which are codes of the characters or marks, synchronized with the scan. The characters, or marks, are placed on specified positions of a document, and the document is passed under the optical scanner.

**light pen** a photoelectric device (p.132), the size and shape of an ordinary pen, that can be used in conjunction with a screen on a cathode-ray tube. When the light pen is held against the screen, it detects the CRT beam, and the computer determines the position of the pen. Computer routines allow the user to point the light pen at a portion of the CRT screen, and then the routines determine the subsequent action; e.g. the light pen can draw lines, shapes, alter displays, make selections from a display menu, track an object, or move an object on the screen. *See soft keyboard* (p.193). The light pen consists of a lens, which focuses light on to a photodiode or phototransistor (p.133); the photocell generates an electrical pulse which is passed to the computer as an interrupt signal by an umbilical cord. The computer routine then controls the graphic display.

**bar code on tag**

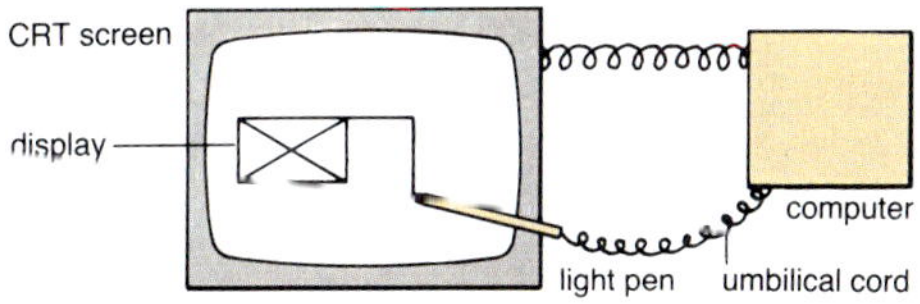


**light pen:** drawing a display

**light gun** light pen (↑).

**electronic pen** light pen (↑).

**bar code optical scanner**[2] a light pen (↑) which scans bar codes (p.46) using incident light. It operates at speeds of 100 characters per second, or faster. It is mainly used at point-of-sale terminals (p.248).

**wand** (*n*) a light pen (p.195) used to identify optically coded labels, that is, bar codes (p.46) or characters.

**optical disk** a rotating disk which stores permanent digital data in binary or Gray code. It is read by a laser beam which is directed to grooves on the disk. The disk reflects the beam, using black and white patches to vary the reflected beam's intensity. The beam is directed on to a photocell (p.132) which converts the laser beam into an electrical pulse for a white patch and no pulse for a black patch, that is, a representation of 1 and 0. Four grooves can be used for a 4-bit nibble of data (p.36). The data can be in binary code, or Gray code (p.47).

**optical disk**

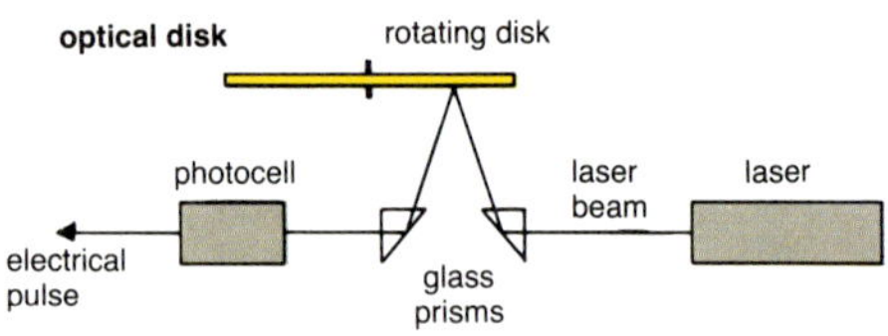


**magnetic ink character recognition** the identification of special characters recorded in magnetic ink (↓) on documents such as cheques or other financial records. The characters are machine-readable to provide a direct input to a computer. The advantages of this process are speed and low error rates, but the equipment is expensive. Documents can be sorted by fields (p.244).

**MICR** (*abbr*) magnetic ink character recognition (↑).

**magnetic ink** ink containing ferrite particles (p.213) that can be magnetized in a magnetic field.

**MICR font** there are two fonts (p.203), E13B used in America and the UK, CMC7 used in Europe. E13B has fourteen characters only, the numerals 0–9 and four special characters. CMC7 has numerals, letters, and five special characters. A high level of printing accuracy is needed.

**mark sensing** the sensing of a magnetized area by a read head (↓).

**read head**[1] an iron, or alloy, armature, with a coil wound round it, becomes an induced magnet when passing over a magnetized area. The change in magnetism induces an electrical pulse in the coil. The pulse is amplified, and used as part of a binary code.

**coded optical disks**

binary code

Gray code

**use of MICR characters**

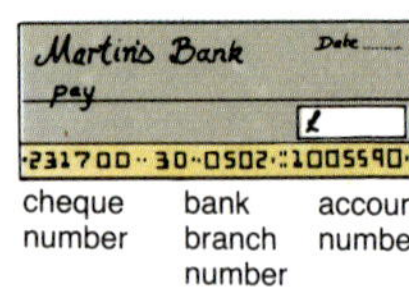


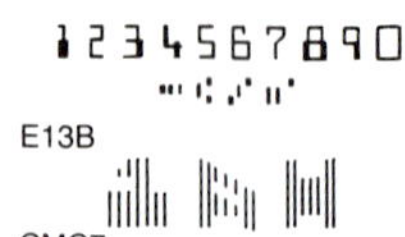


**MICR fonts**

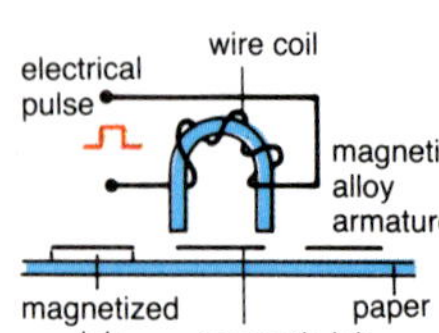


**read head**

**magnetic ink character reader** this device has three components: (1) the input transport which takes the document and positions it for reading, after that, moves it for stacking; (2) the scanner, which first magnetizes the printed MICR characters (↑), then scans them with a read head (↑); (3) the recognition unit, which matches the pattern of electrical pulses against stored patterns to identify a character.

**output** (*v*) to transfer information (data or instructions) from a CPU (p.146) to peripheral devices, such as VDUs, printers, backing stores; (2) (*adj*) describes a device used to transfer information out of a computing system; (3) (*n*) the information which is transferred out of a CPU. **output** (*adj*), **output** (*n*).

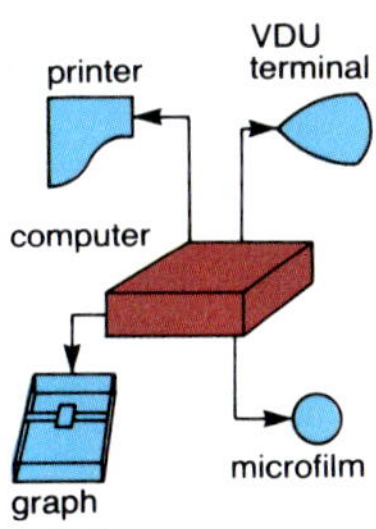

**output devices**

**output device** a device that can receive data from a CPU (p.146). The device can be a backing store (p.178) or a peripheral device (p.13). It can be a communicating link between a computer and people, using a VDU, or a printer, as the output is human-readable.

**output buffer register** a register (p.149) that receives data from a CPU (p.146) and stops it until an output device (↑) is ready to receive it. As peripheral devices and backing stores operate at much slower speeds than a CPU, the output buffer register is usually an intermediate device between the CPU and buffer storage (p.176), or an output area (↓).

**output area** an area in main memory (p.176) into which data is transferred from a CPU (p.146) and stored until it can be transferred to an output device (↑).

**output block** output area (↑).

**output program** a routine (p.61) which carries out the necessary processes for data to be transferred to an output device (↑).

**output routine** output program (↑).

**output stream** data that is output by a computer system, or by a processing program. The data appear on output devices designated by the operator together with diagnostic messages on the current computer operation.

**output limited** describes a program whose speed of operation is limited by the speed of an output device (↑). Processing of data is delayed waiting for the data to be output.

**output mode** the method of operation of a computer when it is transferring data out to a peripheral device, e.g. printer, backing store (p.178).

**light emitting diode** a diode with gallium arsenide and gallium phosphide as the semiconductor. When forward biased (p.98) the diode conducts and emits light. The colour depends on the composition of the semiconductor, and red, green or yellow displays are available. The diode emits light, but no heat. A lens magnifies the source, and the lens shape can be a circle, or a bar-shaped segment, etc. The diode works at low voltages and consumes approximately 0.02W.
**LED** (*abbr*) light emitting diode (↑).
**LED display** a LED can be used as a single indicator lamp, or a set of LEDs can represent a binary number, with a lighted LED indicating logic one. The bar-shaped LEDs can be used to display decimal numbers.
**LCD** (*abbr*) liquid crystal display (↓).
**liquid crystal display** a liquid is contained between two sheets of glass, or plastic. Tiny electrodes are placed in the liquid. When the electrodes are connected to an electrical supply, an electric field is formed between them. This field orients the liquid molecules; the molecules plane polarize light. The cover of the LCD also plane polarizes light, so that the two planes of polarization are at right angles and hence the liquid molecules pass no light and appear black. The electrodes form bar-shaped segments; seven segments are used to form decimal numerals. When the power is switched off, the display disappears. LCDs require even less power than LEDs (↑).
**electrochromeric display** a form of display similar to an LCD (↑). The liquid molecules are oriented by an electric field, transforming the liquid from transparent to opaque. When the field is switched off, the molecules remain oriented and the liquid opaque. An electric field in the opposite direction to the original field is used to return the molecules to their original state and to make the liquid transparent again. This process can be used to store data as well as display data. **ECD** (*abbr*).
**readout**[2] (*n*) (1) the display of processed information on a VDU screen (p.203); (2) the way in which a computer presents processed information, e.g. on punched tape, punched cards. *Contrast with printout* (p.199).
**digital readout** a display of data in digital form, as opposed to analog form. The display normally uses LCDs (↑) or LEDs (↑). For example, a digital readout of temperature, of time, of pressure.

**light emitting diode**

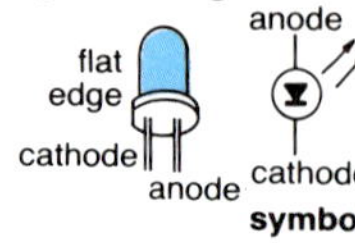


**LED display**

binary number 01101011 (= 107d)

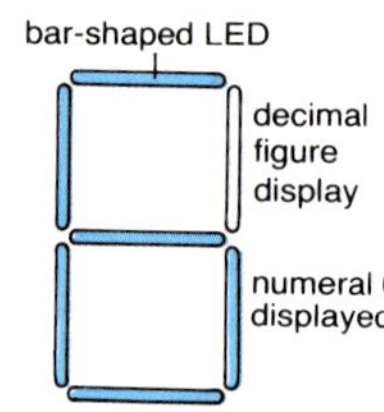


**light emitting diodes**

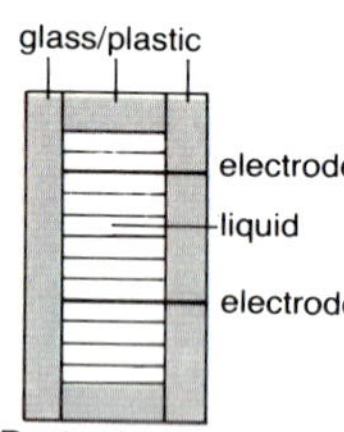


**LCD:** structure

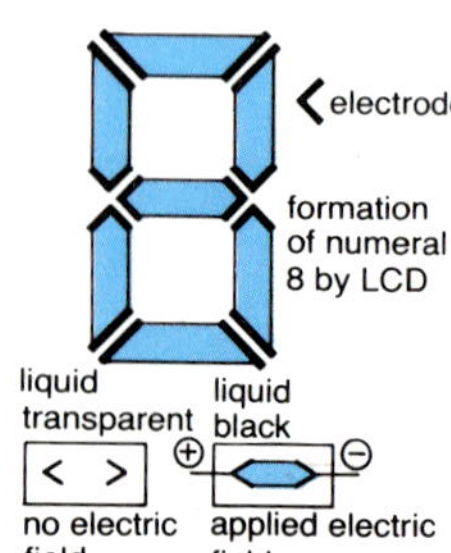


**liquid crystal display**

**printer** (*n*) an output device (p.197) that converts electrical signals into printed characters on paper.

**printout** (*n*) the printed pages which are the output of a printer. *Contrast readout*[2] (p.198). A printout is a permanent record of processed information, whereas a readout is generally impermanent.

**print format** the way in which printed characters are arranged on paper, such as headings and their size and arrangement, the width and spacing of columns and rows of tabular information, the position of page numbers, justification (p.202).

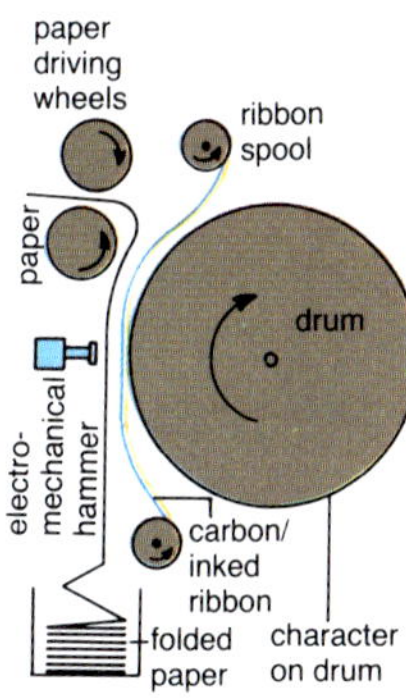


**impact printer** (1) a printer with metal characters; paper and carbon paper pass over the characters and a hammer hits the paper, so that the carbon paper and metal character print the character on the paper; (2) a matrix printer (p.200). Using several sheets of both paper and carbon paper, more than one copy can be produced at a time.

**non-impact printer** printers which use heat-sensitive paper or electrostatically charged paper to create a printed character. Usually only one copy can be produced.

**character printer** a printer that prints one character at a time. The paper remains stationary and the print head moves along a line. Teleprinters (p.26) use character printing.

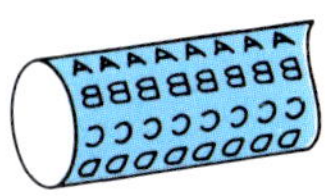

**section of drum**

**line printer** a printer that prints one line of print at a time. Barrel or drum printers and chain printers are line printers.

**drum printer** a drum has rows of characters on it, with A's in one row, B's in the next, and so on, to a full complement of 64 characters. Each row contains 120 or 160 characters, so this number of characters can be printed on one line. To print a line, there is an electromagnetic hammer in line with each character in a row of characters, i.e. 120 or 160 hammers. The drum rotates, paper and carbon paper are in position between the drum and hammers; all the A's are printed first, then all the B's, and so on until the line is complete in one revolution of the drum. Printing speed is between 500 and 3000 lines per minute. Several copies can be printed at a time; the characters tend to be slightly smudged as the drum continues to rotate while the character is printed; the final line tends to be wavy. The whole line is stored in memory before printing.

| | |
|---|---|
| A | A |
| A C | C |
| A C     E | E |
| A C     E     I | I |
| A C M     E     I | M |
| A C M     E     IN | N |
| A COM     E     IN O | O |
| A COMP     E     P IN O | P |
| A COMP     ER PRIN O | R |
| A COMP     TER PRINTO T | T |
| A COMPUTER PRINTOUT | U |

**barrel printer** drum printer (p.199).

**chain printer** a chain loop carries metal slugs with embossed characters. The loop is driven in a horizontal plane by a drive wheel. The chain carries six complete sets of forty-eight characters. Electromechanical hammers hit paper against a carbon ribbon and the type face, as the chain travels round the wheels. Two items have to be matched, the print position and the character to be printed. The whole print line is stored in a buffer memory, and this controls the action of the hammers which are activated when the required character is opposite the hammer in the correct position. Activating all the hammers at the same time prints the alphabet. Usually there are 132 print positions on a line and 5–10 lines are printed for one revolution of the chain. Between 200 and 2000 lines per minute can be printed. Several copies can be printed at a time; the characters tend to be slightly smudged sideways; the final line is straight. Chain printers are more common than drum printers (p.199) as impact line printers.

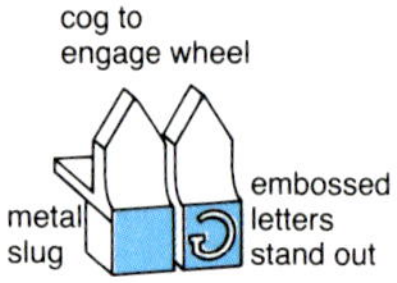


**font of a chain printer**

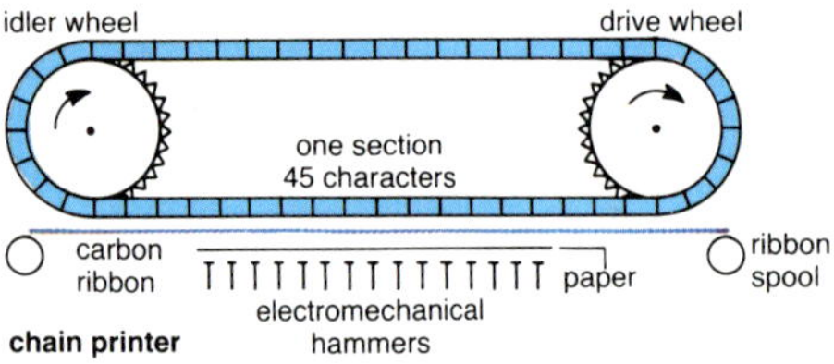


**chain printer**

**daisy wheel printer** this is an impact character printer, with a wheel which has arms in the shape of petals of a daisy. At the end of each arm are the letters which are pressed by a hammer on to a typewriter ribbon over paper. The daisy wheel and hammer move forward to print each character in turn. The rate of printing is about fifty characters per second. The daisy wheel can be changed to give different type faces. The printer can be programmed to give right justification (p.202), as well as left, something a line printer cannot do.

**matrix printer** a printer, either impact or non-impact, which forms characters and symbols by a pattern of dots from a matrix of possible positions. The greater the number of possible dots in a matrix, the better is the appearance of the printed character.

**daisy wheel printer**

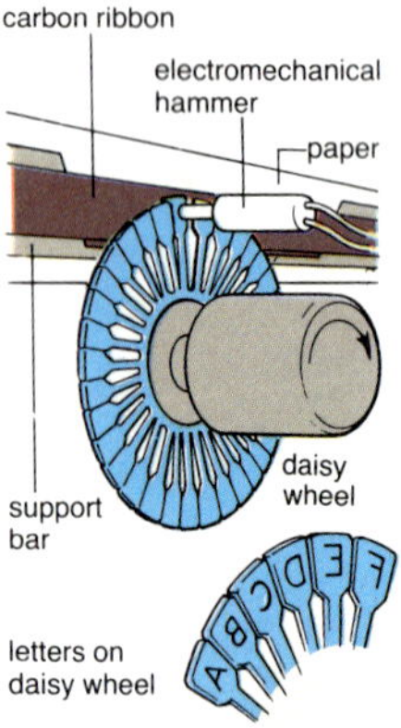

principle of matrix printing

**dot matrix printer** an impact character printer has nine or seven pins in a vertical line. The pins are programmed to hit carbon ribbon on to paper to make a dot. With nine pins, there are seven print positions to form one character, i.e. a 7×9 matrix. With seven pins there are five print positions. Dot matrix character printers are cheap printers and the cheapest use a 5×7 matrix. More expensive printers can use up to sixteen pins. The print head moves along the paper, printing each character in turn. Dot matrix line printers have a row of pins, and the paper moves up seven or nine times for one character to be printed. Dot matrix printers can use different patterns to produce different alphabets, or can produce simple graphical results. The stored printing program uses a logic one to print a dot and a zero to leave a space. The rate of printing is about 100 to 600 characters per second, and up to 200 lines per minute.

**thermal printer** this is a non-impact matrix printer. Special heat-sensitive paper (↓) is used, and a stylus instead of a pin. The tip of the stylus is heated by an electric current. The operation is the same as for a dot matrix printer (↑). Thermal printers are reliable and cheap, but have a slow speed of about thirty characters per second.

**heat-sensitive paper** the stylus of a thermal printer (↑) burns away the outer coating of the paper, leaving a dot. The dots form the printed character. The stylus must heat and cool rapidly to produce a satisfactory printed product. Only one copy can be printed.

**electrothermal printer** thermal printer (↑).

**electrostatic printer** this is a non-impact line matrix printer, using specially coated paper. A printing head stretches the breadth of the paper, and contains rows of nibs. A small voltage is applied to selected nibs, and this charge is reinforced by an electrode at the back of the paper. This puts an electrostatic charge on the paper. The paper is moved forward, and a liquid toner applied to the paper. This develops the print image, which is then dried by a stream of air. An entire line of 132 characters is printed in one operation. Speeds vary from 500–6000 lines per minute.

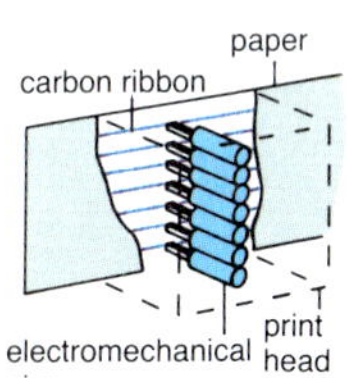


**character dot matrix printer**

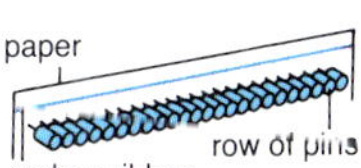


9 print positions per line
**line dot matrix printer**

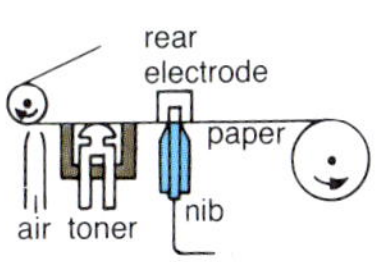


**electrostatic printer**

**ink-jet printer** a non-impact character printer. A special quick-drying liquid is used for the ink. A jet of ink is forced from a nozzle and acquires an electric charge. The jet passes between charged plates which deflect its passage so that it can be directed to an appropriate spot on the paper. The jet forms a spot on the paper; a matrix of spots forms a character. The writing head then moves on to the next print position. Ink-jet printers give a good printout, but are slow with a speed of about 120 lines per minute.

**xerographic printer** a non-impact page printer. A selenium-coated drum is exposed to an optical image of a character, and the drum is completely covered with a page of print. The drum acquires an electrostatic image of the print, represented by a charge on the selenium. The drum is then covered with fine black carbon particles oppositely charged to the drum. The particles adhere to the drum. The drum is then used to print a sheet of paper, and the paper is then heated to fix the print to form a permanent copy. This is the latest and fastest method of printing at twenty pages per minute.

**high-speed printer** a printer whose speed is more compatible with the speed of computation than slower printers. High-speed printers can be used on-line (p.22), while slower printers are used off-line. A printer with an output of 1000–2000 lines per minute is considered to be a high-speed machine.

**hard copy** printed text on paper, suitable for human beings to read, which is produced at the same time as an impermanent visual display or an output in machine code.

**justified** (*adj*) describes a piece of text in which the end characters of a line of print are exactly in line vertically one above the other. The text can be justified on the left, on the right, or both. Text justified on the left and right has to have the space between words adjusted to make the justification. **justify** (*v*), **justification** (*n*).

This book combines the functions of a dictionary
and a thesaurus: it will not only define a word for
you, but it will also indicate other words related

text justified on the left
not justified on the right

This book combines the functions of a dictionary
and a thesaurus: it will not only define a word for
you, but it will also indicate other words related

text justified left and right

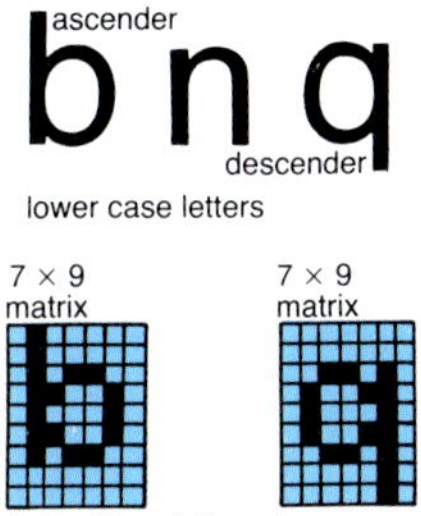

lower case letters

dot matrix printing of ascenders and descenders

**tabulation** (*n*) to arrange data in an array of columns, usually with a description at the head of each column. **tabulate** (*v*), **table** (*n*).

**matrix**³ (*n*) a method of presenting printed data which groups characters or sets of characters into a regular array (p.69), usually like a rectangular table.

**stroked characters** characters that are formed by a series of short strokes instead of dots, as in dot-matrix characters. Different fonts (↓) can be produced more readily by this method than by dot-matrix characters.

**descender** (*n*) the part of a lowercase letter which is below the line of print. A dot-matrix has to be at least 7×9 to print full descenders.

**ascender** (*n*) the part of a lowercase letter which is above the line of print. A matrix of 7×9 is needed to print full ascenders.

**zero suppression** most microcomputers express a number with eight digits. Any zeros to the left of the integral part of the number are non-significant. Before printing, the non-significant zeros are eliminated.

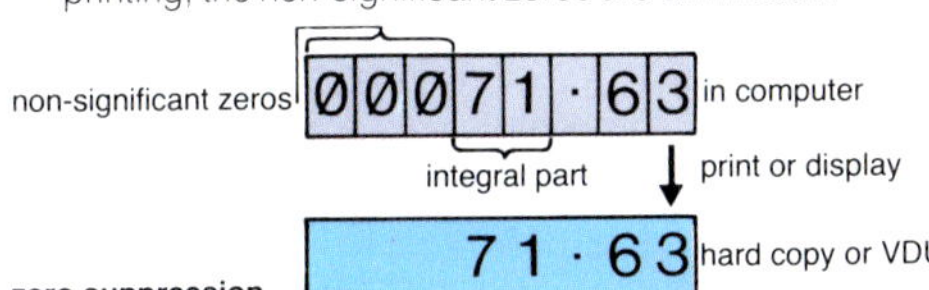

zero suppression

**zero elimination** zero suppression (↑).

**font** (*n*) the shape, size and style of letters and numerals. Letters of the same font are all of similar size. Fonts can have roman and italic characters, uppercase and lowercase letters, but all refer to the same alphabet.

**fount** (*n*) font (↑).

**typeface** (*n*) the size and style of characters.

**visual display unit** a cathode-ray tube (p.130), which displays data, programs, or instructions on its screen. The simplest obtainable unit is a television receiver, but a monitor (p.204) is preferable for use with a computer. A terminal (p.10) or a VDT (p.10) is also used as a visual display unit. A VDU (↓) can display graphics as well as characters. **VDU** (*abbr*).

**video bandwidth** the maximum number of dots per second that can be displayed on a CRT screen. Bandwidth is also often expressed in MHz. A bandwidth of 16MHz is required to display with a resolution of eighty characters per line.

**screen**² (*n*) that part of a cathode-ray tube which provides a surface on which symbols, characters and dots are made visible to a viewer. Most screens display twenty-five lines of characters, and the number of characters can range from thirty to eighty. The display is made visible by phosphors (p.206). Symbols, characters and graphic displays are composed of dots.

**monitor**² (*n*) a black and white, or colour, cathode-ray tube, used as a VDU with an input at video frequency; it has separate inputs for the three electron guns for red, green and blue colours. It usually has a better performance than a TV receiver, as the TV receiver is operated at VHF frequencies and has a narrower bandwidth (p.229) than the monitor. A good TV receiver is better than a poor monitor, the bandwidth being the limiting factor.

**character screening** characters are typically formed from an 8×8 dot matrix. The data used to form the characters are generally stored in ROM (p.173) and the pattern cannot be changed. Different types of characters, or different alphabets, can be written in RAM (p.175), or can be stored in a disk, and written into RAM when required. Printing from right to left can also be arranged for alphabets that use that method.

**VDU control for character display**

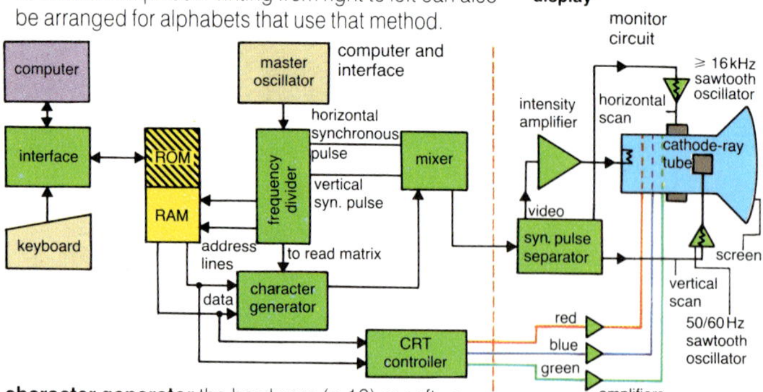


**character generator** the hardware (p.12) or software (p.65) which form the pattern of dots making a character.

**dot generator** the hardware (p.12) which produces a black or white dot on a screen (↑).

**character screen enhancement** a process to draw attention to a particular character on a VDU screen (↑); it is called enhancement. A character can be enhanced by half-intensity, blinking, reverse video, underlining, double-width, and by combinations of these.

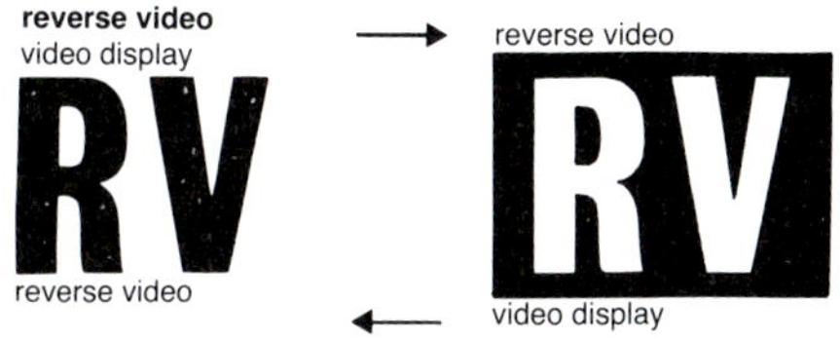


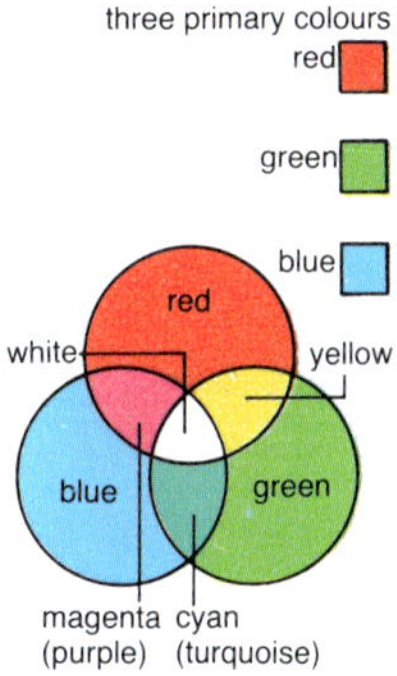


colour combination
**colour formation on a TV screen**

**reverse video** if black characters are displayed on a white background, then in reverse video white characters are displayed on a black background, and vice versa.

**flashing characters** the characters appear and disappear repeatedly. This attracts attention but can be irritating. Flashing characters should be used only when items appear that need immediate attention.

**video display generator** a device that addresses the display ROM, i.e. character generator, dot generator, and position control, and makes various colour combinations possible.

**VDG** (*abbr*) video display generator (↑).

**terminal chromacity coordinates** all colours are obtained on a television screen by a mixture of three primary colours, red, green, and blue. Equal intensities of all three colours form white light. Varying the intensity of each of the three primary colours allows any colour to be formed. The terminal chromacity coordinates define the quality of a colour by the ratio of the stimulus value of each of the primary colours against the sum of the stimuli.

**wraparound** (*n*) (1) the continuation of register addressing from the highest to the lowest address in a circular buffer (p.181); (2) the continuation of an operation from the last character position on one line of a VDU screen to the first character position on the next line; (3) the continuation of an operation from the bottom line of a screen to the top line of the screen, with the top line being overwritten by the new data.

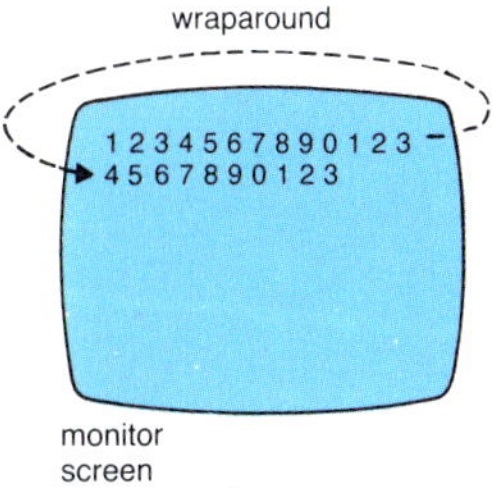


**wraparound**

**pixel** (*n*) (1) a picture element on a terminal screen (p.204). It is the smallest rectangle that can be displayed on a screen. The smaller the pixel, the sharper will be the definition of a picture, and the greater will be the number of pixels to form the picture; (2) the smallest permitted variation of a signal over a permitted period of time.

**pel** (*n*) a picture element. *See pixel* (↑).

**pixel level** the brightness, or blackness/grey level, of a pixel is defined by a binary number. It has a specified set of levels, expressed as $2^n$ levels if *n* bits are used in the binary number. There can be up to $2^8$, that is, 256 pixel levels, and this number of levels is used in some systems.

**resolution** (*n*) the smallest step in distinguishing between two measurements, usually of length. In a digital measurement, resolution is an increase of one unit in the least significant digit. Resolution is also a measure of the smallest possible increment in the output of a device, hence a pixel (p.205) represents the resolution on a terminal screen.

**display resolution** the extent to which an observer can distinguish between two pixels (p.205) observed on a VDU screen. Resolution is specified by the size of the pixel, but the ability to distinguish one pixel from another depends on the beam current of the cathode-ray tube, and the brightness of the pixel, so both these parameters must be stated in specifying display resolutions.

**raster** (*n*) the grid on a terminal screen (p.204) which gives coordinates for every pixel (p.205) that can be displayed.

**raster count** the number of coordinate positions that can be addressed on a terminal screen (p.204). The horizontal raster count gives the number of pixels (p.205) that can be displayed along a line on the screen. The vertical raster count gives the number of pixels that can be displayed in a vertical line.

**raster scan** a scan (↓) of the coordinate positions on a VDU screen (p.204).

**scan[1]** (*n*) the sampling or interrogation in sequence of the conditions or physical state of each separate item of a process or system, e.g. the items on a list, each coordinate of a display grid, each channel of a communications system.

**phosphor** (*n*) an element on a VDU screen which glows when excited by an electron beam. The element exhibits phosphorescence (↓).

**phosphorescence** (*n*) the phenomenon of emitting light for a period of time after the source of excitation has been removed. Some chemical substances have this property and the source of excitation is usually a form of radiation.

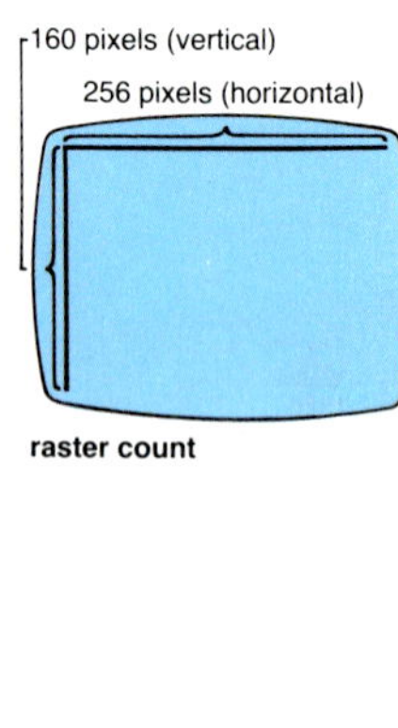

raster count

**green phosphor** a phosphor (p.206) that emits green phosphorescence. This now forms the most popular type of monitor screen displaying black characters on a green background or vice versa. Green gives the peak of response for the human eye, better than any other colour of the spectrum.

**phosphor dots** phosphors (p.206) which glow red, or green or blue when excited by an electron beam. This is the basis of a colour display, using terminal chromacity coordinates (p.205).

**mosaic** (*n*) a photoelectric surface (p.132) consisting of a large number of photoemissive particles on an insulating support, e.g. silver globules deposited on mica. A signal plate, consisting of a metal coating on the other side of the support, is charged when the particles emit electrons.

**flyback** (*n*) the time taken for the electron beam in a cathode-ray tube (p.130) to move from the end position of one raster line (p.206) to the beginning position of the next line.

**scrolling** (*n*) the movement of the display on a terminal screen (p.10), up or down, one line of text at a time, or left or right; it can also be one line of pixels (p.205). **scroll** (*v*).

**regenerate** (*v*) (1) to restore periodically the display of a raster scan (p.206); the phosphorescence (p.206) fades and needs to be regenerated periodically; (2) to refresh (p.165). **regeneration** (*n*).

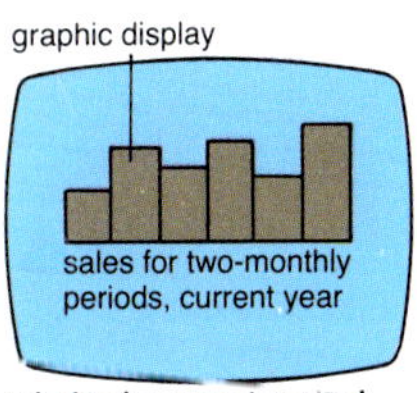


**windowing on a terminal screen**

**windowing** (*n*) the division of a CRT screen (p.130) into sections or windows by means of software. Each section can then be used for a display of different forms of data, or for data from different sources. For example, a larger section of a screen can be used for graphics, and a smaller section for text connected with the graphics.

**display window manager** a program in ROM, which divides the screen into separate sections, or windows, and controls the size and position of the windows. A window can be moved round the screen, enlarged or contracted, scrolled (↑), or overlapped with another window. Menus (p.51) are also under the control of the display window manager.

**display scrolling** the moving of a display, up or down, to show material, e.g. a program that does not fit on to a VDU screen.

**graphic** (*n*) information represented by diagram, graphs, or given pictorially; in computer displays, graphic is contrasted with textual.

**graphics terminal** a graphic terminal uses either a cathode-ray tube (p.130) display or an electromechanical graph plotter (↓).

**graphic display** a display on a cathode-ray tube (p.130) screen that presents data in shapes and drawings.

**graphic CRT display** the display on a screen can be produced in three ways: graphic raster scan (↓); directed-beam refresh; direct-view storage tubes. In directed-beam refresh, the electron beam moves from point to point on the display, it does not scan the whole screen. The display is redrawn by regeneration (p.207) at periodic intervals. In direct-view storage, the display is stored electrostatically in the phosphors (p.206) on the screen, and hence does not need regeneration; the display is drawn by the same method as directed-beam displays. Directed-beam and direct-view storage methods do not have full colour available.

**graphic raster scan** a raster scan (p.206) is used, and a great variety of colours and shades are available. Most graphic CRT displays use tubes of high quality to improve resolution (p.206). Raster scan methods use more memory than directed-beam or direct-view storage methods in graphic CRT displays (↑).

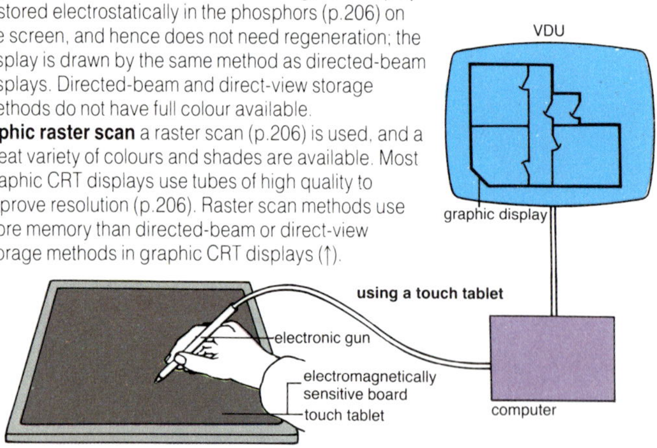


**graphics tablet** a device with a rectangular surface used with an electronic pen (p.195) which reproduces on a VDU (p.203) the lines drawn by the pen on the tablet.

**data tablet** graphics tablet (↑).

**regenerative storage** storage of information that needs regeneration, e.g. electrostatic storage (p.186), direct-view storage in graphic CRT displays (↑).

**holding beam** a diffuse beam of electrons in a cathode-ray tube for regenerating (p.207) the charges on the dielectric surface of an electrostatic storage device (p.186), or a directed-beam graphic CRT display (↑).

**holding gun** an electron gun (p.130), in a CRT, which is the source of a holding beam (↑).

**display** (*n*) a visual record, usually considered to be temporary; a message or data on a visual display unit (p.203). Display is contrasted with hard copy (p.202).

**graph plotter** an electromechanical device that moves a writing instrument over a sheet of paper to produce a graphic output. The device is controlled by digital signals from a computer. There are flatbed and drum graph plotters (↓).

**digital plotter** a graph plotter (↑).

**plotter** (*n*) a graph plotter (↑). **plot** (*v*).

**electromechanical** (*adj*) describes a device, or machine, which has moving parts operated by electric currents. The power needed is considerably greater than that used in operating a computer.

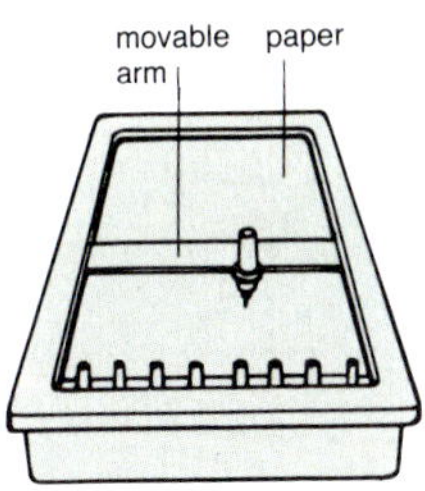

**flatbed plotter**

**flatbed plotter** paper is fixed to a horizontal table. A moving arm carries a writing instrument, such as a pencil, a pen, or any specialized device used with special paper. The area of paper used varies from the smallest at 28cm × 43cm to 2.44m × 3.66m. The speed of the plot varies from an average rate of 15cm per second to 100cm per second for the fastest machines. Large plotters are used in making special maps, such as geological and weather maps. Most technical and scientific graph plotters (↑) are flatbed plotters.

**drum plotter** paper is fixed round a cylindrical drum; a stationary arm with a moving writing head, is situated above the drum. The drum rotates and the writing head moves backwards and forwards in line with the axis of the drum. The accuracy of a drum plotter is less than that of a flatbed plotter (↑), but it is cheaper, so drum plotters are used for commercial applications.

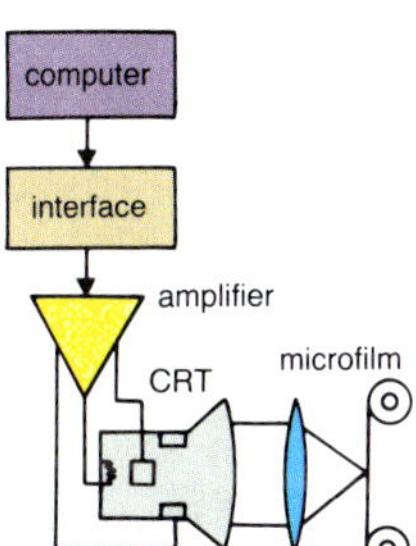

**computer output microfilm**

**computer output microfilm** the computer sends a digital signal output through an interface (p.219) and an amplifier to a cathode-ray tube (p.130). Light characters are formed on a dark background. A lens focuses the image on the CRT screen on to film, and effects a reduction, usually twenty-four or forty-eight times reduced. A whole page is photographed, and then the display changes, and the film moves on to the next frame. One film frame records one screen page. The speed of recording is up to 120000 characters per second.

**COM** (*abbr*) computer output microfilm.

**microfilm** (*n*) common sizes of film are 16mm and 105mm; 105mm is used for microfiche (↓). If twenty-four times reduction is used for COM, then the frames are recorded sequentially; if forty-eight times reduction is used, the frames are recorded two side by side. For sequential recording twenty average pages of information are recorded on 30cm of film; double that amount of text is recorded for two frames side by side. Microfilm is viewed in a carousel (↓). The film usually has black characters on a clear background. The film is processed in its cassette by normal processing methods with chemicals and water.

**electron beam recording** a similar process to COM (↑), but the CRT differs from the normal type. The electron beam is focused directly on to special energy-sensitive film, and not on to a screen. The exposed film is developed by a heat process, and the result is microfilm as before. The recording device is expensive.

**EBR** (*abbr*) electron beam recording (↑).

**carousel** (*n*) a device which takes microfilm (↑), or other data medium, winds it on a rotary mechanism, and presents it at a specified position for reading or recording. Film is illuminated and magnified, and read one frame at a time. This makes information storage on microfilm extremely useful as vast amounts of information are stored in a small space. A copy of the microfilm frame can be printed on some machines to form hard copy.

**microfiche** (*n*) a rectangle of 105mm film containing frames in rows. Recording is by COM (↑) or by electron beam (↑). The film is developed in its cassette by normal methods using chemicals and water. It is then cut into rectangles.

**fiche** (*n*) one rectangle of a microfiche (↑) film, containing thirty, sixty, or eighty pages of information, with one page on each frame.

**microfiche reader** a device for magnifying a frame on a microfiche film (↑) and viewing it on a screen. The fiche is fed into the reader, and control knobs move the scanner to the required frame.

**input/output** to transfer information (data or instructions) from a CPU (p.146) to a peripheral device, such as punched cards or paper tape, magnetic disk or tape, or in the opposite direction. Describes a device used for transferring information in this way.

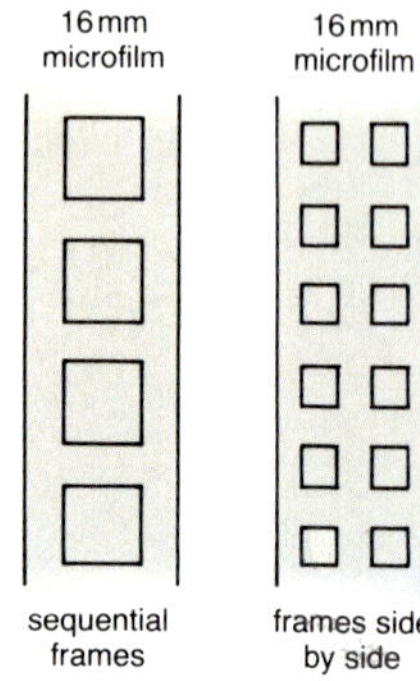

**microfilm**

**microfiche**

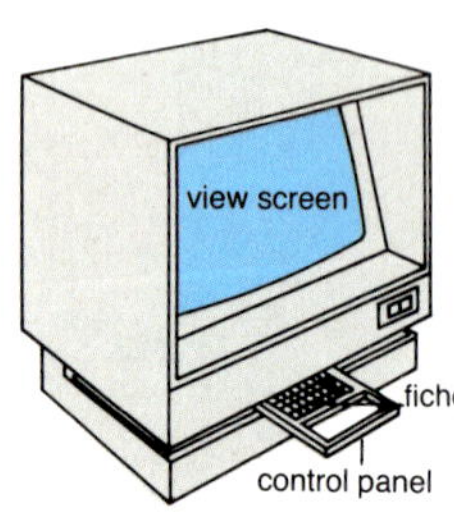

**microfiche reader**

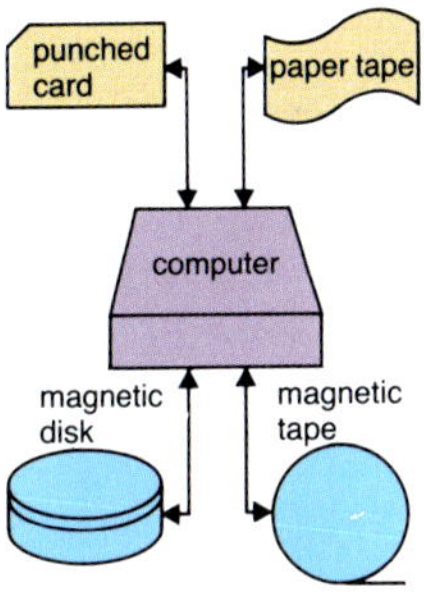

input/out devices

**input/output device** a device which transfers information (data or instructions) into a computer, and, after the data have been processed, transfers the data to a backing store (p.178), another computer, or to a device with an output readable by human beings.

**input/output buffer** an area of main memory (p.176), in which data are placed before going to, or after coming from, a peripheral device. When an input/output buffer is used, data can be transferred to peripheral units while the CPU (p.146) is processing other data.

**input/output register** a register which performs the same duties as an input/output buffer, but handles less data.

**punched card** the standard card is 187mm × 82.5mm and contains eighty columns and twelve rows. A hole is punched in one, two, or three of these positions, using a card code.

**punch card** punched card (↑).

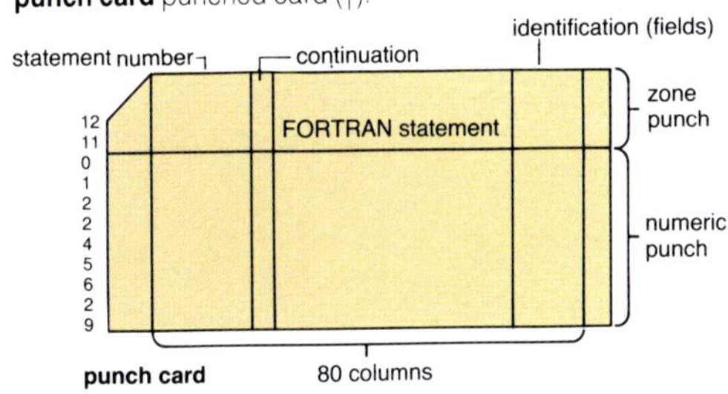

punch card

3-column example

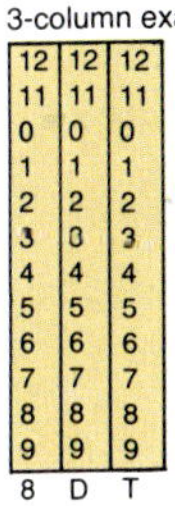


**codes**

| | | |
|---|---|---|
| 00, 0 – 9 | numbers | 1 hole |
| 12, ◆ – 9 | A – I | 2 holes |
| 11, ◆ – 9 | J – R | 2 holes |
| 00, 2 – 9 | S – Z | 2 holes |
| 12 | ★ | 1 hole |
| 11 | – | 1 hole |

other symbols: * / = , ★ " $

**card**[2] (*n*) a punched card (↑).

**keypunch** (*n*) a device with an ordinary keyboard. When a key is depressed, it punches out one, two, or three holes for the character code.

**card punch** (1) keypunch (↑); (2) a punch operated automatically under computer control.

**column binary** the presence or absence of holes in successive card columns (↓) represents a series of binary digits.

**card column** a column on a punched card with the numerals 0 to 9 and either numbers 11 and 12 or letters X and Y.

**card code** a combination of one, two or three holes punched in a card column (↑) to represent a character or punctuation mark. Numerals are represented by one hole, 0–9; letters by a zone-digit (p.212) and another hole in the numerals 0–9. Some symbols use three holes; e.g. a comma symbol is punched in holes 0, 3, 8.

**card field** a group of specified card columns (p.211) used for one type of information, e.g. six columns used for a date, eighteen columns used for a name.

**Y punch** a hole in the top row of a punched card, i.e. the 12 or Y position.

**X punch** a hole in the X or 11 row of a punched card.

**zone punch** a hole punched in a zone digit (p.46). A zone punch is used with a numeric punch (↓) to represent a letter.

**numeric punch** a hole punched in any of the 0–9 rows of a punched card (↑).

**card format** a description of the fields and columns of data in a punched card (p.211).

**card reader** punched cards are passed from a read hopper to a photoelectric cell (p.132); light above the card passes through the holes and is sensed by the cell. An encoder converts the reading to binary code. The operation is performed twice. If the results agree, the character is passed to the computer. Card readers operate at up to two thousand cards a minute, but one thousand cards a minute is an average rate.

**object deck** a stack of punched cards forming a computer program.

**punched paper tape** paper tape on which information is recorded as punched holes across the width of the tape. Small sprocket holes are used to move the tape. The tape is 25.5mm wide and a reel is usually over 100 metres long.

**tape code** a character is stored in a frame, a row of holes across the width of the tape. Binary-coded decimal (p.36) is used to store numbers; additional holes to those for binary-coded decimal determine letters and symbols. One channel (↓) is used for a parity check (p.39).

**channel²** (*n*) a line of holes running parallel to the length of the tape; there are channels similarly on magnetic tape (p.216). Character density in a channel is four characters per cm.

**frame¹** (*n*) *see tape code* (↑).

**tape punch** a keypunch (p.211) can be used. Frequently tapes are punched automatically by a peripheral device as a form of output.

**paper-tape reader** the pattern of holes is sensed by photoelectric cells, in a device similar in principle to a card reader (↑).

**principle of card reader**

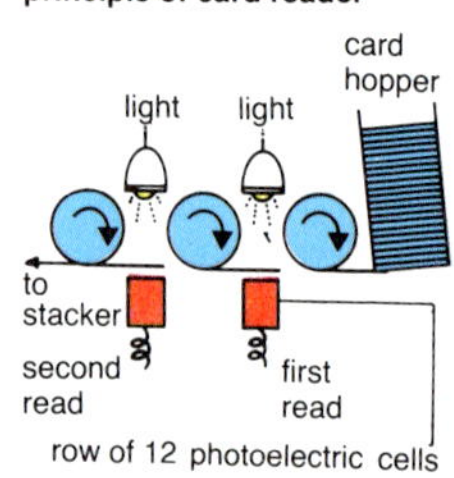


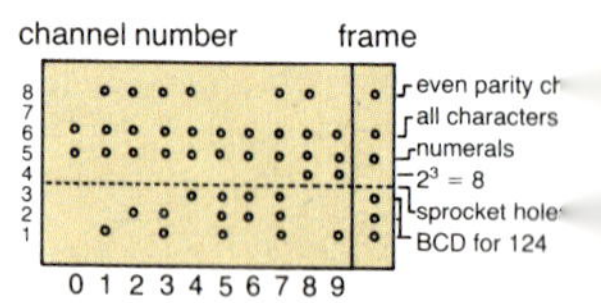


**tape code** for numbers

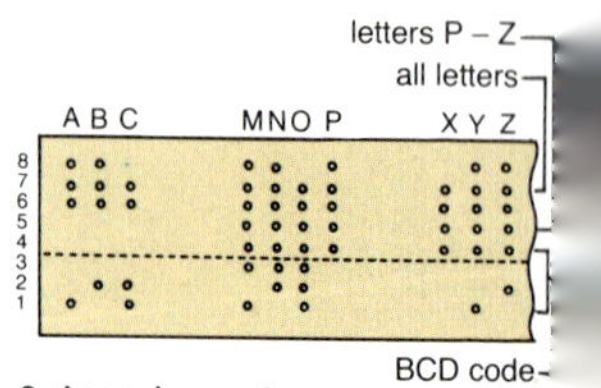


**8-channel paper tape**

**chad** (*n*) the piece of paper, or card, removed when paper tape or cards (p.211) are punched.

**ferrite** (*n*) a chemical substance that consists of iron (III) oxide and other metallic oxides, usually combined with a ceramic material.

**magnetic recording medium** a tape, disk, drum, coated with ferrite (↑) which retains magnetic variations induced in it during magnetic recording.

**disk** (*n*) a flat circular plate, coated with a magnetic material, usually ferrite (↑). It is used as a storage device. Data are stored on the two surfaces of the disk in binary code recorded as magnetic spots.

**magnetic disk** disk (↑).

**hard disk** a metal disk (↑) completely enclosed in an airtight case to exclude dust. Several disks are mounted on a single spindle, and all are controlled by the same disk drive. Hard disks are used with large computers.

**Winchester disk** a hard disk system suitable for smaller computers. Fast rotating disks with a high bit density (p.183) are enclosed in a sealed chamber to prevent contamination of the disk surface by dust.

**micro-Winchester disk** a smaller hard disk, 13.3cm diameter with a 6.38 megabyte capacity on two disks, using both surfaces. It uses floating-head (p.214) recording and reading.

**floppy disk** a MYLAR (insulating plastic) disk, which is non-rigid, coated with ferrite (↑). The disk is enclosed in a cardboard or plastic case. Floppy disks are slower to access, but cheaper than hard disks (↑). Read/write heads are used with the disks.

**diskette** (*n*) floppy disk (↑).

**read/write head**[2] a circular piece of soft iron which has a gap in it. A coil carrying a current magnetizes the iron, forming a magnetic field in the gap. This field forms a magnetic spot on the disk, or on magnetic tape (p.216). The head touches the disk, and is held in position by a pressure pad. The head is enclosed in a ceramic material which is highly polished to reduce wear on the disk. This type of head is used with floppy disks (↑).

**flying head** a read/write head is mounted on an aerofoil. The disk, rotating at a high speed, draws air round with it, in a boundary layer. This lifts the aerofoil above the disk. The head gap is 0.5–1.0mm for a flying head. Flying heads are used with hard disks (↑).

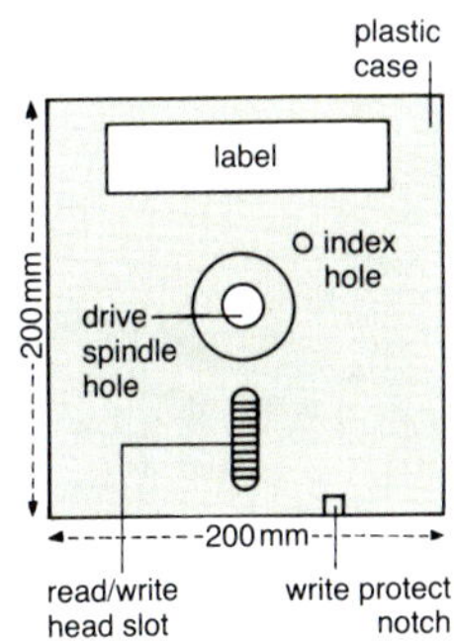


(also 133mm × 133mm)
**a floppy disk**

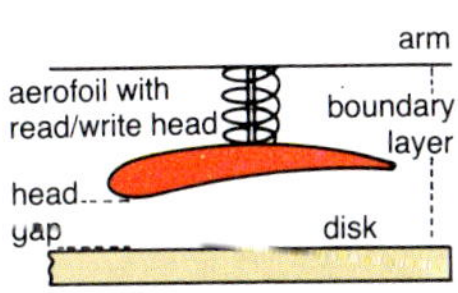


**flying head**

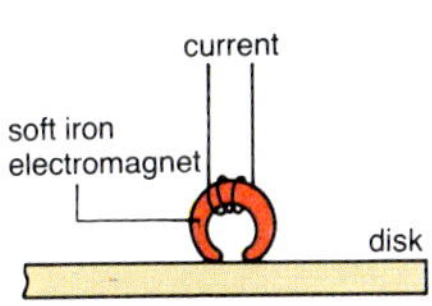


**read/write head**

**floating head** flying head (p.213).

**write-protect notch** a notch covered by a piece of aluminized paper. If this paper is removed, it is no longer possible to write on the disk. With many diskettes the opposite is true. This notch is used with most floppy disks (p.213).

**stack**$^2$ (*n*) six or more hard disks (p.213) are usually mounted on a spindle to form a stack, with the disk drive (↓) rotating all the disks simultaneously. Storage capacity of a stack can be up to two hundred million characters, depending on the number of disks.

**disk drive** the mechanism of a disk system which rotates all the disks of a hard disk system or separate floppy disks. It consists of a motor, a clutch, and read/write heads.

**stepping motor** an electric motor that rotates in a series of equal steps, each step controlled by a digital input signal. Stepping motors are used in most electromechanical devices. Also called stepper motor.

**fixed-head drive** read/write flying heads (p.213) are used for every track (↓) on each usable surface of a stack (↑). This provides the quickest access.

**moving-head drive** one read/write flying head (p.213) is mounted on a movable arm. The arm moves in and out to place the read/write head above the required track (↓). This method of access is slightly less quick than that of a fixed-head drive (↑).

**disk track** a circle on the surface of a disk (p.213); magnetic spots are recorded along the track; a track passes underneath a read/write head (p.213). Disks can have over two hundred tracks on a surface.

**disk sector** each disk track is divided into sectors. Any individual sector on any track can be addressed individually. The same amount of data can be recorded on any track in a sector; the bit density (p.183) is higher on the inside tracks than on the outside ones.

**sector** (*n*) disk sector (↑).

**cylinder** (*n*) the tracks on each usable disk surface, with the same track number, form a cylindrical slice down the stack (↑). The tracks, taken together, form the cylinder. If each surface has two hundred tracks, then there are two hundred cylinders in a stack. The cylinder has the same number as the track, e.g. all tracks with the number 86 form cylinder 86. A stack of six disks has ten usable surfaces.

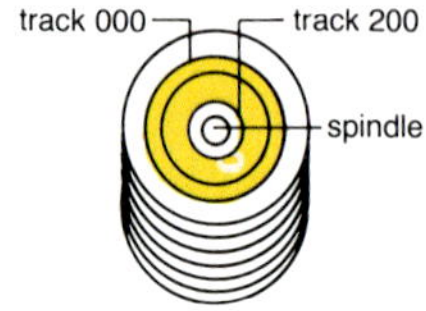


**stack of disks**

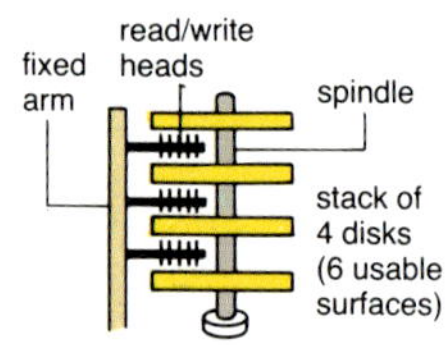


**fixed-head drive**

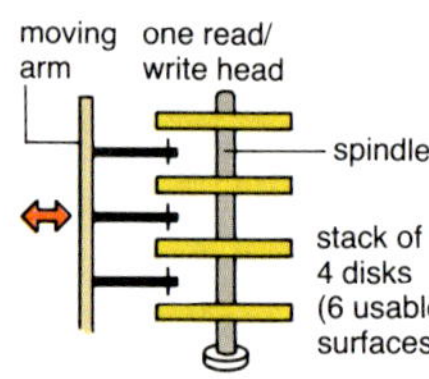


**moving-head drive**

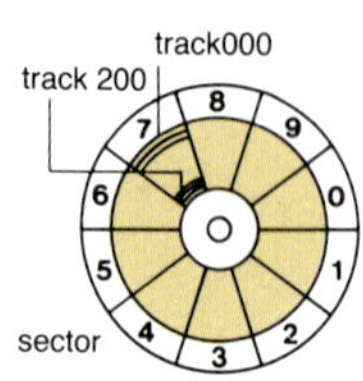


**sectors and tracks**

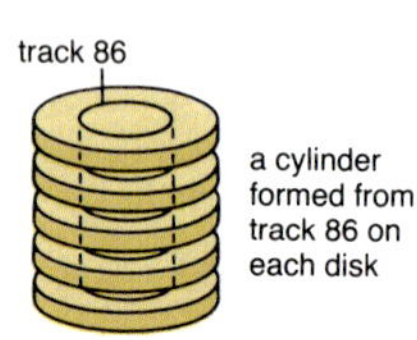


**a cylinder on a stack of disks**

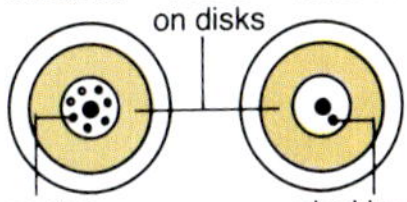


**sectoring disks**

**seek area** cylinder (↑).

**sector formatting** a disk is given a format of tracks and sectors (p.214) and these are addressable. The beginning of each sector must be clearly defined; the track is defined by the read/write head, or its position.

**hard-sectored** the disk sector is defined by the hardware. Each sector is marked by a sector hole near the spindle. The disk drive uses a photoelectric sensor to detect each hole. Hard-sectored formats are used on hard disks (p.213).

**soft-sectored** a single hole marks the beginning of sector zero; it is detected by a photoelectric sensor. The subsequent sectors are identified by a timing track on the disk read by a software program. Floppy disks (p.213) can be hard or soft-sectored.

**disk index hole** a hole near the spindle, which uses a photoelectric sensor to detect the hole. It indicates to the drive controller that the disk is rotating. Both hard-sectored and soft-sectored disks use disk index holes.

**exchangeable disk storage** storage using disks with moving-head drives (p.214). A disk can be removed from the disk drive and replaced by another.

**EDS** (*abbr*) exchangeable disk storage (↑).

**seek time** the time needed to position the read/write head over the required track when using moving-head drives (p.214). The average seek time is 75 milliseconds.

**latency** (*n*) the time needed from the staring point until the read/write head is over the required track position. On average, this is half a revolution, typically about 125 milliseconds.

**disk operating system** a collection of programs stored on a disk (p.213). Once a computer is turned on, the disk can be addressed, and the programs are available from a specified command entered through a keyboard. The operating system enters a prompt on the VDU, allowing the user to choose a required program, usually from a menu (p.51). This program is selected, entered into main memory (p.176) and then data are accepted. Most programs are oriented towards textual communications, i.e. processing normal data from business information.

**DOS** (*abbr*) disk operating system.

**spooling** (*n*) the process of releasing data from main memory (p.176) and storing the data temporarily on disk (p.213) or magnetic tape (↓) until a peripheral device is ready to accept it, e.g. storing text before sending it to a printer.

**despooling** (*n*) printing from a spooled disk (p.213).

**magnetic tape** the tape consists of a plastic substrate (MYLAR) with a coating of magnetic material, such as ferrite (p.213). The tape is stored on reels, and moves from one reel to another, pulled by a capstan. A read and a write head is used for each channel (↓) on the tape. Data are recorded on the tape as magnetic spots to represent logic one and the absence of a spot to represent zero. An erase head, placed before the write head, removes, if necessary, any previous record. The write head puts the code for each character in a frame (↓) on the tape, and the read head immediately reads and checks the code against the character in memory.

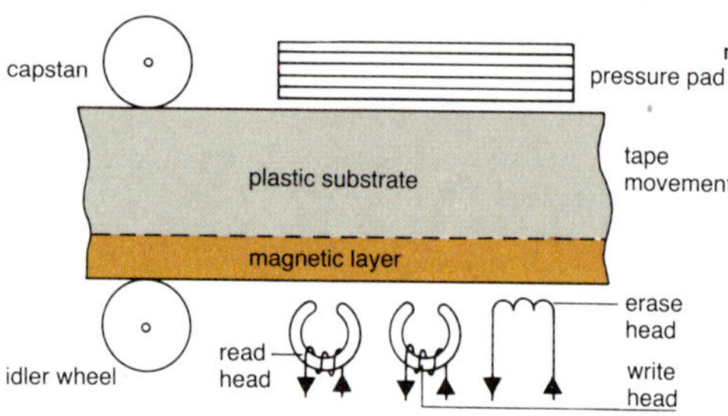


magnetic tape

**read head** the same as a read/write head (p.213) but used only for reading.

**write head** the same as a read/write head (p.213) but used only for writing.

**erase head** a head using a degausser (↓).

**degausser** (*n*) a coil through which passes a momentary alternating current. The changing current gives rise to a varying, reversing magnetic field which demagnetizes a tape.

**tape deck** a device for controlling the movement of magnetic tape. It consists of a transport mechanism, read, write and erase heads, and allows for automatic rewinding.

**tape drive** tape deck (↑).

**tape unit** tape deck (↑).

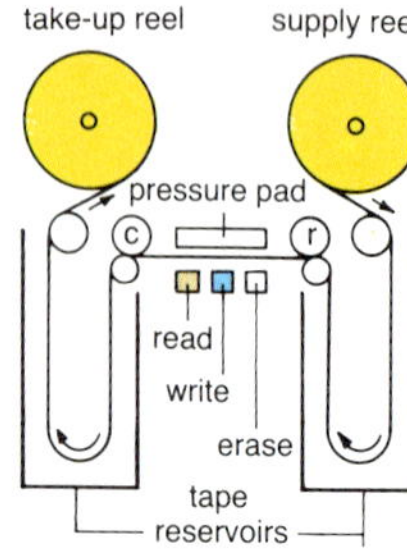


c = capstan

r = rewind capstan

**tape deck**

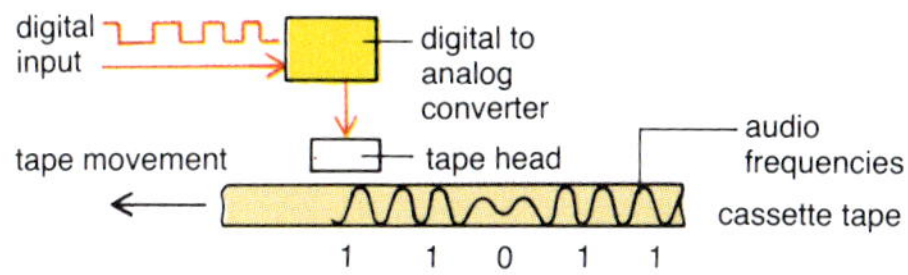


**tape cassette recording**

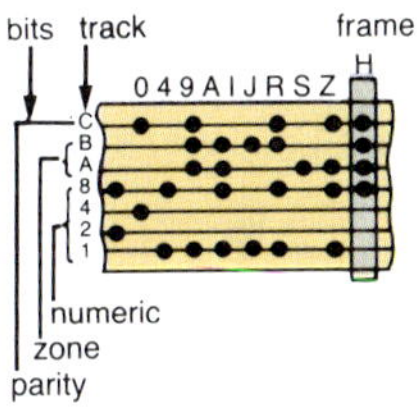


**7-track magnetic tape** even parity

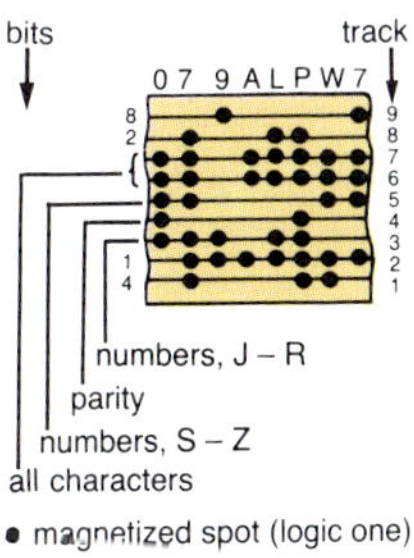


**9-track magnetic tape** odd parity using EBCDIC

**tape cassette** a 6mm tape in a cassette, the type used for recording music and speech at home; it can be used as a storage medium. The method of recording differs from that of magnetic tape (↑). The tape head (↓) reacts only to the frequencies of sound, so frequencies are generated by software, using digital hardware with one frequency representing logic one and another frequency representing zero. The speed of transfer is much slower than for magnetic tape.

**cassette** tape cassette (↑).

**tape cartridge** a device similar to a tape cassette, but larger and driven by a sprocket wheel instead of a spindle.

**tape head** the assembly of read/write, or read, and write heads (↑).

**EBCDIC** (*abbr*) an abbreviation for extended binary-coded decimal interchange code. A code which uses eight bits for characters. EBCDIC is used on 9-track magnetic tape (↑), the ninth bit being a parity bit. Magnetic tapes have either seven or nine tracks, with the 7-track tape using binary-coded decimal. Most codes use even parity (p.39) for the characters. Eight hundred bits per cm are put on a tape track (↓).

**frame²** (*n*) a line of magnetic spots across a magnetic tape. A frame contains the code for a character. As eight hundred bits pass per second, eight hundred bytes, each of eight bits, are recorded per cm of tape. The fastest reading/writing speed is 200 000 bytes per second.

**track²** (*n*) a line of magnetic spots parallel to the sides of a magnetic tape.

**channel⁵** (*n*) a track (↑) on magnetic tape.

**block²** (*n*) a string of data, assembled in main memory (p.176) before transmission to magnetic tape. All data are transferred in blocks, as the tape has to accelerate to full speed before writing takes place; blocks save time in transmission by reducing the time for accelerating and decelerating a tape.

**interblock gap** the space on magnetic tape between two blocks (p.217) of data or information. After data or information has been written, or read, on a tape, the tape slows down and stops and awaits the next instruction. Half the gap is for deceleration and half for acceleration. The interblock gap is always 19mm long. A large block of data is always transferred, otherwise more space on a tape is taken up by interblock gaps than by data.

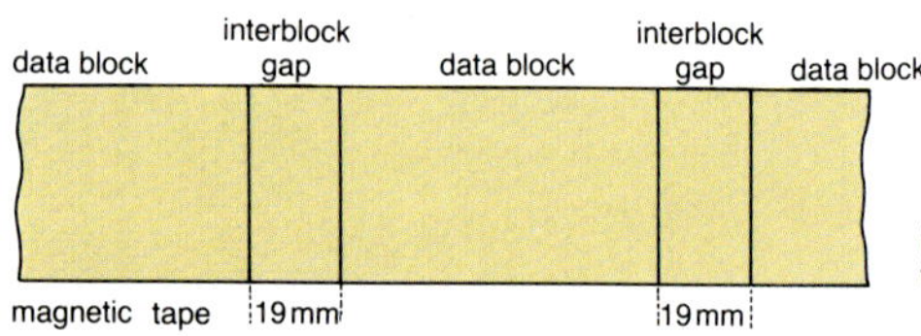


**interblock gap on magnetic tape**

**inter-record gap** interblock gap (↑).
**packing density** this is measured in bits per cm for magnetic tape. Most tapes have eight hundred bits per cm.
**transfer rate** the speed at which a magnetic tape is read or written. The fastest transfer rate is 200000 bytes per second. For tape cassettes, the transfer rate is about forty bytes per second.
**access time** the average wait before the required information is transferred from a magnetic tape or other device. The running time of a magnetic tape from end to end is ten minutes, so, on average, the access time is five minutes.
**drop-out**[1] the magnetic material is not always absolutely uniform on the surface of a magnetic tape, and there are some bald patches. Such patches fail to record data. With separate read and write heads, the failure is detected and the data are recorded a little further up the tape. The bald patches are drop-outs.
**tape load point** the position on a magnetic tape at which reading or writing data can begin.
**tape data validation** the parity of incoming data is checked, and a read-after-write test is carried out. If blocks fail these tests, the tape is by-passed and the block rewritten. Buffers and tape speed allow up to six write attempts without disturbing the flow of information.
**write permit ring** a removable plastic ring which fits into a groove on the back of the tape drive. If it is not present, the tape drive refuses to write data.

| pin number | description | signal |
|---|---|---|
| 1 | protective ground | DTE→DCE |
| 2 | transmit data | DCE→DTE |
| 3 | receive data | DTE→DCE |
| 4 | request to send | DCE→DTE |
| 5 | ready to send | DCE→DTE |
| 6 | data set ready | – – |
| 7 | common ground | DCE→DTE |
| 8 | carrier detect | – – |
| – | – – | – – |
| 20 | data terminal ready | DTE→DCE |

**RS-232 interface**

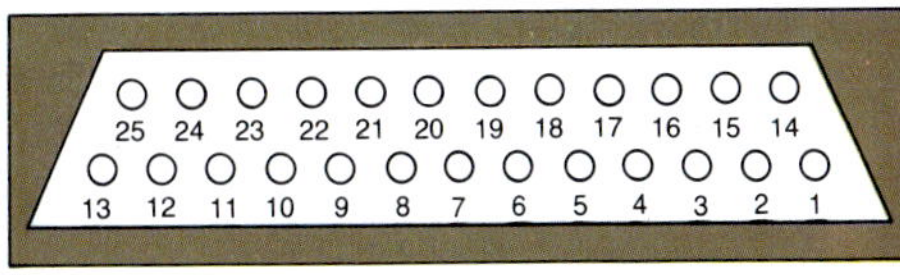


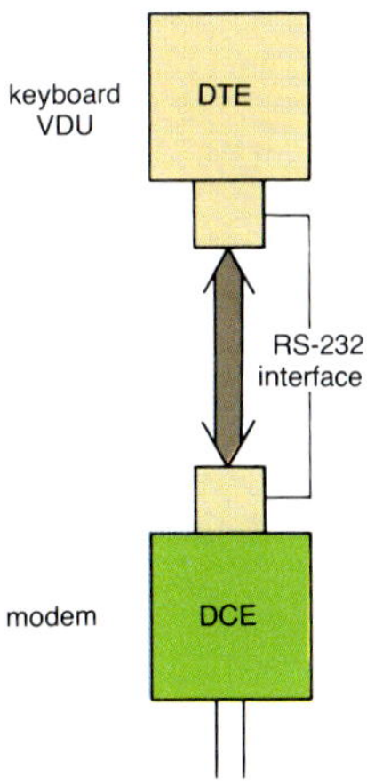


**interface** (*n*) (1) a shared boundary between devices or systems. An interface consists of channels (p.233) and control circuits which connect a CPU (p.146) and peripheral devices (p.13), or it connects any two devices; (2) a connection between software systems or programs.

**EIA interface** interfaces using standards accepted by the Electronic Industries Association (EIA). It is useful to use well-defined standards so that the interfaces can be universally used with many different systems.

**interface card** a printed circuit card, usable by a microcomputer, for serial communication for up to four lines to peripheral devices. The card conforms to EIA interface (↑) specification.

**RS-232 interface** an interface module between a computer, or terminal (p.10) and a modem (p.228). It is a standardized EIA interface (↑) with a 25-pin connector, used for asynchronous communication (p.221). Not all the connections are standardized, so the use of some pins can vary from one manufacturer to another. A negative voltage indicates logic one, or an OFF state. A positive voltage indicates logic zero or an ON control state.

**DTE** (*abbr*) data terminal equipment. A terminal (p.10) which communicates with human beings, e.g. keyboard, VDU. It is a device at which a communication path begins or ends.

**DCE** (*abbr*) data communication equipment. A modem (p.228) or similar unit. A computer or a data recording or generating device which needs an interface with another computer.

**RS-232 serial input/output** a standard interface for the DCE (↑) provided by the communications carrier, usually a telephone system, and the DTE (↑) provided by the computer manufacturer. It uses binary serial code for transmitting data.

**programmable communications interface** a peripheral device programmed by a CPU (p.146) to operate with serial data-transmission, e.g. with a UART, USRT (p.220), USART (p.221).

**PCI** (*abbr*) programmable communication interface (p.219).

**UART** (*abbr*) universal asynchronous receiver/transmitter. A common peripheral interface (p.219), consisting of a transmitter and a receiver, both of which can operate totally independently and simultaneously. It uses asynchronous transmission (p.221) and a baud rate (p.42) applicable to a peripheral unit. The transmitting section has a control register (p.154) which governs the number of bits in a byte, the parity bits and the stop bits. The serial output is at high, or logical zero, or marking level, for an OFF state. When data are presented for transmission, the serial output goes low, or to the spacing level, or to logical one, for an ON state. The computer clock provides a timing pulse sixteen times the baud rate, and a timing pulse is generated every sixteen clock pulses, starting with a pulse after eight clock pulses detecting the start bit. In full duplex (p.233), both sections of the UART can operate at different baud rates, as these rates are programmable. A flip-flop (F/F) holds the line at high, logic zero, for the number of timing pulses needed to transmit the data byte, parity bit, start and stop bits; TX empty shows the end of a character to the transmitting device and End of Character does the same for the receiving device. If another character is ready for transmission, the line drops to a low level.

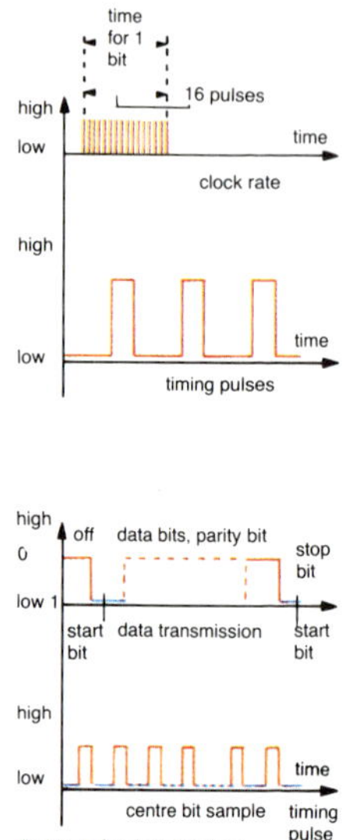


**transmission timing**

**UART principle of operation**

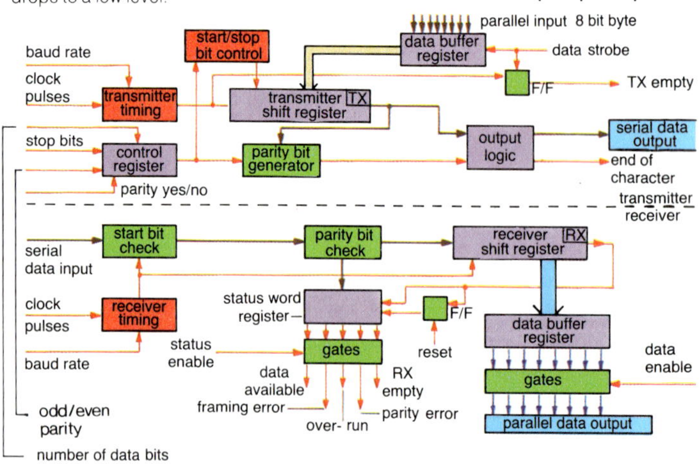

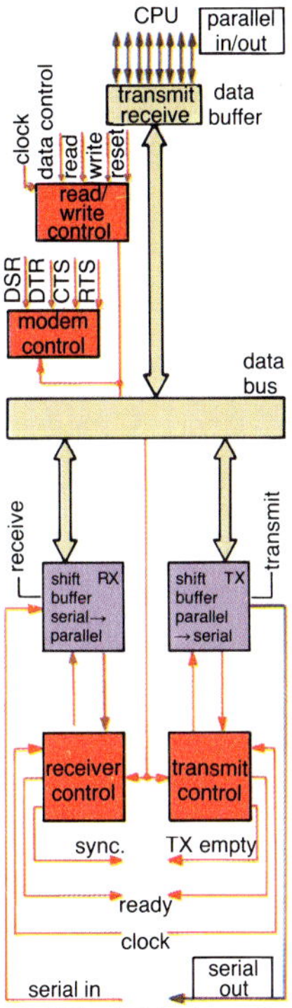

**USART:** principle of operation

**peripheral processor**

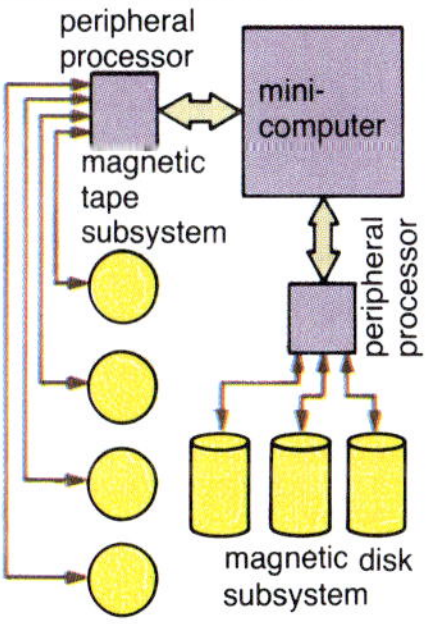


**USRT** (*abbr*) universal synchronous receiver/transmitter. A peripheral interface (p.219) used with synchronous peripheral devices. Its architecture is practically the same as that of a UART (↑), with the addition of a signal for synchronization (p.222).

**USART** (*abbr*) universal synchronous/asynchronous receiver/transmitter. A peripheral interface which combines a UART and a USRT (↑). It can operate practically any serial data transmission between any two devices. The receiver and the transmitter sections can operate separately at different baud rates (p.42). A USART typically works through an RS-232 interface (p.219).

**PIO** (*abbr*) parallel input/output. A peripheral interface (p.219) used by a few computers, which transmits data by parallel transmission. The circuits are more complex than those for UART's and USART's, and the peripheral device must also be suitable for a parallel input.

**peripheral processor** a processor that controls a group of identical peripheral devices. The processor is operated by a microprogram (p.51) and has ROM, RAM, and an ALU (p.150); that is, it functions as a small computer. It reduces the work load of a CPU in a computer by performing input/output operations. Peripheral processors are generally used with minicomputers.

**adaptor** (*n*) a device used to connect different parts of a computer system or different computer systems, or to connect a system with various subsystems so that the whole is operative; e.g. interfaces (p.219), USART's (↑).

**ACIA** (*abbr*) asynchronous communications interface adapter. An adapter that provides an interface between bus organized systems (p.238) and peripheral devices or modems. The data bus of the computer system provides control of the ACIA. The ACIA produces a serial output suitable for a modem.

**peripheral interface adapter** a device either incorporated in a microprocessor or on a separate chip. It is an integrated circuit capable of universal interfacing with peripheral devices. The adapter uses bidirectional data buses (p.238) and control lines to the peripheral devices and is programmed by the CPU for initialization.

**PIA** (*abbr*) peripheral interface adapter (↑).

**asynchronous communications** the transmission of characters which is independent of a synchronizing signal. Start and stop bits signal the extent of a character, so the transmission time for a character can vary.

**synchronous communications** the transmission of characters controlled by a sync character (↓) so that the bit stream and character stream of data are precisely timed by pulses from a clock. **synchronization** (*n*).
**sync** (*abbr*) synchronization.
**sync character** a character at the beginning and the end of each message so that precise timing is achieved for the transmission and reception of data.
**alignment** (*n*) the adjusting of operating conditions of the components of a system for a correct interrelationship, e.g. adjusting baud rate, type of parity, logical high and low. Alignment is usually effected by an interface (p.219).
**initialization** (*n*) a process carried out at the beginning of transmission to set the conditions which will not be altered during the transmission, e.g. baud rate, type of parity, number of bits in a byte, number of stop bits.
**ancillary** (*adj*) describes equipment which supports a computer, such as peripheral units, interface equipment, communications equipment.
**configuration state** status of a device in a configuration (p.24). The status can be configured in, off, or out (p.24).
**configure** (*v*) to plan the use of the various ancillary devices (↑) in a computer system, or communications system, to meet the requirements of a particular process, or set of similar processes, or an application.
**input/output processor** a device that carries out programmed data transfers and DMA transfers (p.224), and can correct errors in data transmission without direction from a CPU (p.146). These processes can be carried out while the CPU is performing other tasks. The data transfers are in blocks (p.231); byte transfers in a block are transparent to the CPU.
**IOP** (*abbr*) input/output processor (↑).
**input/output interface** an I/O interface generally has two or more I/O channels, a PIO (p.221) channel and a direct memory access channel (p.224). The PIO channel interfaces with a data bus, and the DMA channel interfaces directly with RAM.
**input/output channel** a channel (p.233) which passes data between main memory and external interfaces.
**input/output port** an 8-bit entry to, or exit from, a CPU (p.146), consisting of an 8-bit latch (p.241), output buffers, control, and peripheral, device selection. All the input/output functions of a microcomputer can be fulfilled with an I/O port.

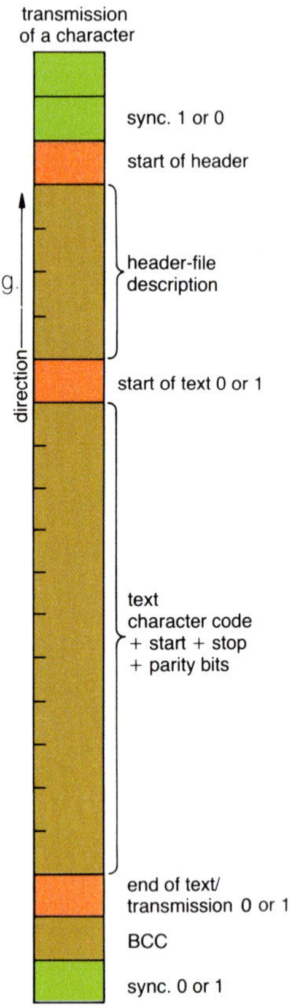

BCC = block check character

**synchronous communication**

**input/output status word** a status word (p.158) which describes the conditions of an input/output process. For example, whether the device is busy or idle, configured-off or not, ready to receive, has transmission errors or not. Each bit of the status word indicates a particular condition, it does not control an actual operation.

**serial input/output controller** a serial-to-parallel and parallel-to-serial converter/controller that can be used with synchronous or asynchronous methods, and with all peripheral devices. It can check data input/output, and generate codes for redundancy checking.

**SIO** (*abbr*) serial input/output controller (↑).

**direct memory access**[2] a method of high-speed transfer of data directly between a peripheral device and RAM. A control word identifies the peripheral device, a read or write instruction, and the parameters of transmission. An INTERRUPT control (p.224) implements the command when the CPU and the device are both free. A second command word, stored in the address register, gives the initial address in RAM; this register is incremented as transmission proceeds. A second command word indicates the number of bytes to be transferred; this is decremented to zero, signalling transmission to stop. More than one channel, connected to other peripheral devices, can be used. A priority control decides the order in which access will be given, in conjunction with the INTERRUPT control, to each channel.

**direct memory access:** principle of operation

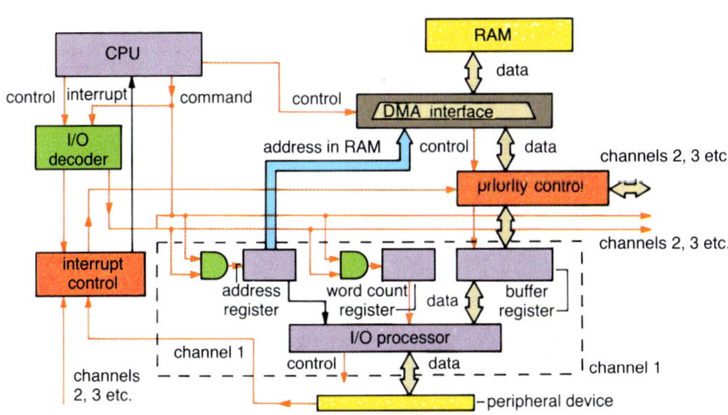

**direct memory access channel** a transmission channel (p.233) between RAM and a particular peripheral device. Data is transferred by the channel in either direction to or from RAM. The priority of a device for access is fixed by stated rules, and the CPU operation is interrupted (↓) to initiate the data transfer. The CPU then takes no further action until the transfer is complete. In some systems, the CPU can proceed with other operations.

**interrupt** (*n*) a temporary break at a point in a main program to allow a routine to be processed, where the routine is initiated by an external device and takes control; a halt caused by an operational error is included in interrupts. The main program is resumed from the interrupt point. An interrupt signal is tested for its interrupt level (↓), and a higher level than the current routine, or current program, lets the main program finish its current instruction and then the CPU (p.146) switches control to the interrupt routine. A PSW (↓) stores the necessary information on the status of the main program.

**processor status word** a word which contains condition codes (p.159) from the status word register, condition code register (p.159), and flag register (p.159), together with the current instruction length, and the contents of the program counter (p.153). It gives the necessary information for the CPU (p.146) to continue the main program after an interrupt.

**PSW**[2] (*abbr*) processor status word (↑).

**interrupt interface** an interface that gains control of a CPU (p.146) in order to give the CPU the address of the ISR (↓).

**ISR** (*abbr*) interrupt service routine. A routine stored in main memory (p.176) which (*a*) tests the interrupt for its level (↓); (*b*) stores the PSW (↑) and the contents of registers; (*c*) provides the instructions for the routine; (*d*) returns the statuses listed in the PSW; (*e*) returns to the main program.

**interrupt level** a degree of priority is given to an interrupt; it is recorded in main memory, and is tested to see whether the interrupt is taken. In most microprocessors there are eight levels. If there are more levels than peripheral devices, then a poll (↓) is conducted to see which interrupt service routine (↑) is obeyed.

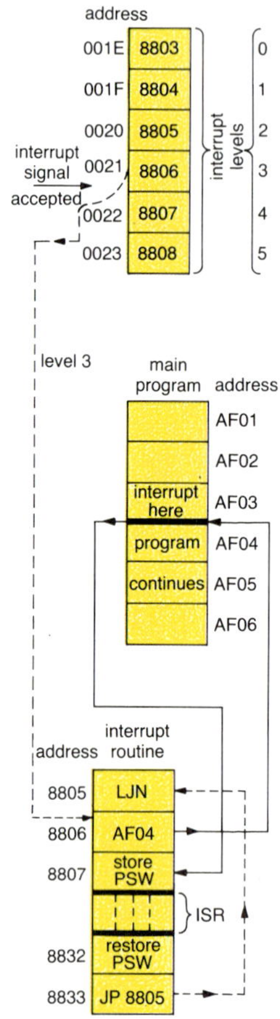


**interrupt:** using main memory

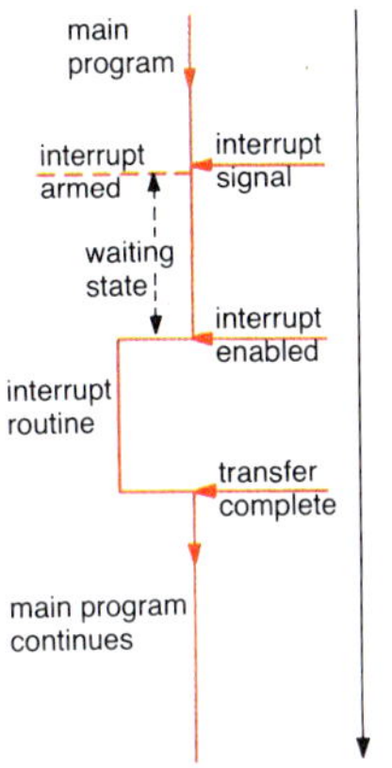


**interrupt process**

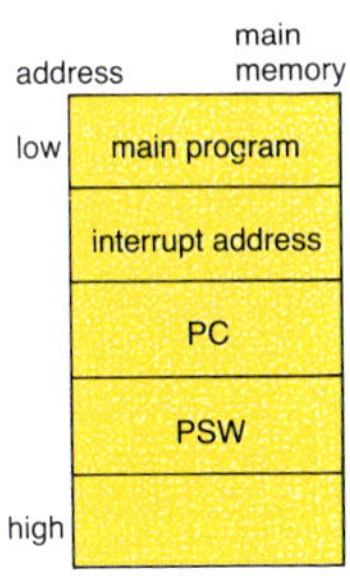


**vectored interrupt**

**waiting state** the period of time between data being available and a peripheral device being available for the transfer of the data in an interrupt, or a normal input/output process. An interrupt saves the waiting time; the interrupt is armed (↓) but not enabled (p.226) during the waiting state.

**arm** (*v*) to allow an interrupt to take place because the interrupt level (↑) is higher than the level of the current program or routine. Interrupts can be nested, like loops, depending on the interrupt level. The interrupt peripheral is being prepared for the data transfer when it is armed.

**disarm** (*v*) *see disarm* (p.163).

**armed interrupt** an interrupt that accepts and holds an interrupt signal; it can be enabled or disabled (p.226).

**poll** (*v*) to interrogate in turn each channel of communication to see whether it has any data to send or whether it is ready to receive data. The programmer specifies the polling order. In ring polling, all I/O devices have equal weight and are polled sequentially. In priority polling the devices are weighted unequally, with some being polled more frequently than others. **pollable** (*adj*).

**polling characters** a set of characters specific to a terminal (p.10) and a polling operation (↑). Response to these characters indicates whether a terminal requires an I/O channel or not.

**polling interval** the time between two successive polls (↑) of a terminal (p.10), or device, if there is no transmission from the polled terminal or device.

**contention** (*n*) the condition of a communications channel when two or more transmitting devices are trying to transmit at the same time. A computer builds up a queue of contention requests. *See deadly embrace* (p.226), *interrupt stacking* (p.226).

**vectored interrupt** each I/O device is assigned a unique interrupt address in memory. An interrupt forces a control jump to this address, using the interrupt hardware. The central processing unit uses the first word after the address to be the new program counter (p.153), and the next word to be the new processor status word (↑). The new PSW and program counter are termed an interrupt vector, and the program counter directs the central processing unit to the ISR (↑).

**interrupt controller** a device that generates an interrupt signal (↓) on sensing various conditions.
**interrupt signal** a signal to indicate a peripheral device is ready to receive or transmit data; a signal generated to cause an interrupt.
**interrupt enable** an instruction that sets an interrupt-control flip-flop. This enables an armed interrupt (p.225) so that data transfer can take place.
**interrupt disable** an instruction that resets an interrupt-control flip-flop. This disables an armed interrupt (p.225). A disabled interrupt is held waiting in a queue for an interrupt enable (↑).
**polled interrupt** an interrupt determined by polling (p.225). The CPU (p.146) does not generate an interrupt acknowledge signal.
**interrupt priorities** the various interrupt levels (p.224).
**interrupt mask** a method of allowing a program to specify whether an interrupt will be accepted or not, and delaying the request by interrupt stacking (↓).
**interrupt stacking** a stack, with a stack pointer, is formed of contention requests (p.225). Each interrupt is dealt with according to its interrupt priority (↑).
**deadly embrace** the condition when two or more processes are competing for access at the same time, and all become suspended at the same time. No action takes place until external conditions remove one process and the others are allowed to be activated.
**deadlock** (*n*) deadly embrace (↑).
**A/D** (*abbr*) analog-to-digital.
**converter** (*n*) an interface (p.219) which changes data from one form to another, e.g. analog to digital (p.9).
**conversion time** time required by an analog-to-digital converter (↓) for a complete conversion of an analog input to a digital output. It can range from 1 to 400 microseconds.
**analog-to-digital converter** a device for the conversion of analog signals in the form of an electrical voltage, into digital information. An analog voltage is first converted into a current. An output register is used to test each bit in turn, beginning with the most significant bit (bit 3 in the diagram). The digital control circuit puts a logic one in bit 3. This produces a voltage to forward bias (p.98), transistor $T_1$, and a current equal to .5C (where C is never reached) opposes the input current. The comparator detects whether this current is too

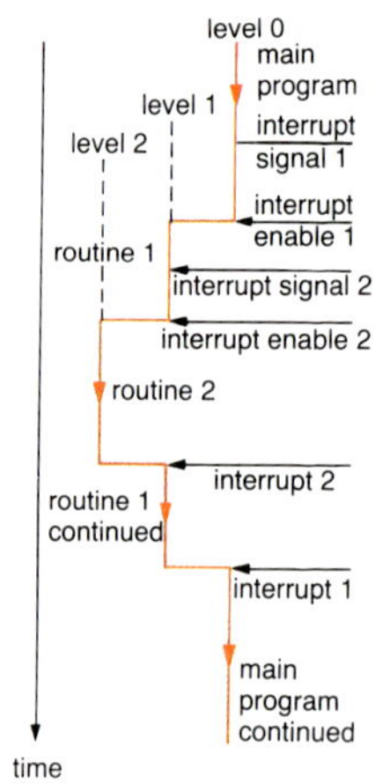


**interrupt priorities:** nesting interrupts

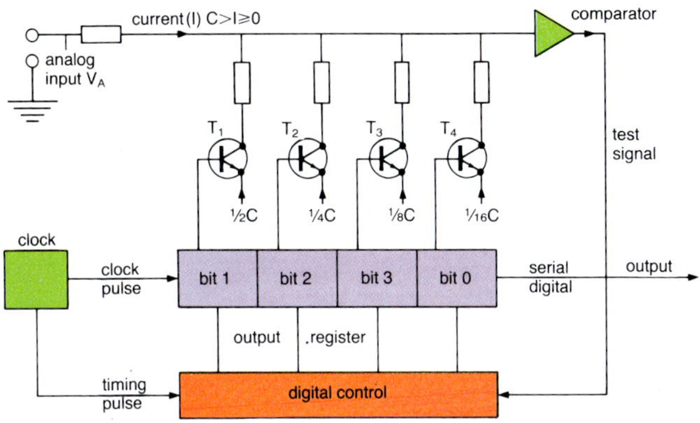


**analog-to-digital converter:**
principle of successive approximation

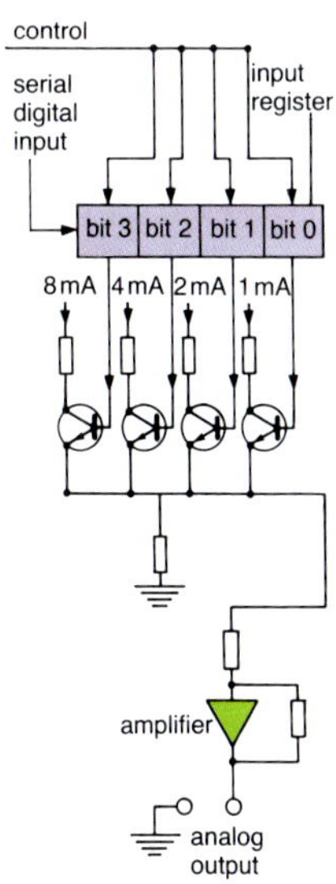


**digital-to-analog converter:**
principle of summing currents

great or not. If not, logic one is left in bit 3 and bit 2 is tested. If the current is too great, bit 3 returns to logic zero, $T_1$ is switched off and bit 2 is tested. The four transistors eventually produce a current equal to the input current. The comparator indicates this and the clock then controls a serial output of the register's contents. This is a digital equivalent of the analog input. Other circuits are used for ADC's as well as this simple one, and with an 8-bit register.

**ADC** (*abbr*) analog-to-digital converter (↑).

**ADC/MPS** (*abbr*) ADC/microprocessor system. The hardware required to link an ADC to a microcomputer; it supplies the necessary alignment between the devices.

**digital-to-analog converter** a device for the conversion of digital information to analog signals in the form of an electrical voltage. A serial digital input is fed into an input register (the one in the diagram has four bits only). A control signal activates a bit holding logic one. This applies forward bias (p.98) to a transistor. The transistors have an output of a binary-weighted current, e.g. 8, 4, 2 and 1 milliamps. All bits are activated at the same time, and the resulting current is an analog equivalent of the digital input. The current is amplified and converted to a voltage, which becomes the analog output. Other circuits are used for DAC's as well as this simple one, and using 8- or 16-bit registers.

**DAC** (*acro*) digital-to-analog converter (↑).

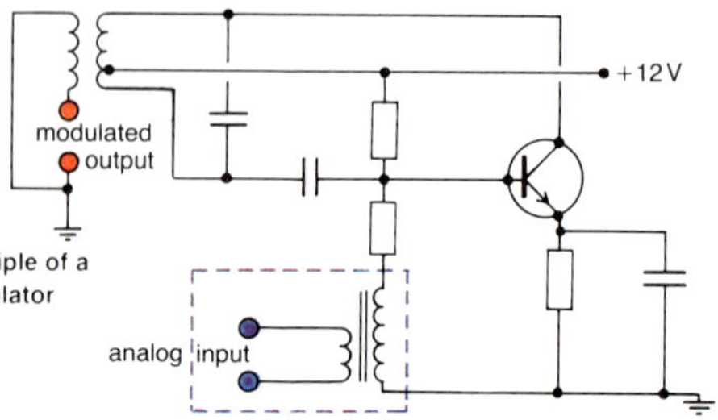

principle of a modulator

**modulator** (*n*) a device which superimposes an analog signal on a carrier wave. An oscillating circuit generates a carrier wave of high frequency. The device uses a resonant circuit of an inductor and a capacitor in a closed circuit. The oscillations of voltage are passed to the base of a transistor and reinforce the oscillations in the resonant circuit. A steady forward bias on the transistor base is used to generate the carrier wave. A modulation circuit, consisting of a transformer in series with the transistor base *(see diagram)* imposes a varying voltage on the transistor base. The variation in bias produces a variation in the amplitude of the carrier wave. The wave form of the analog input is superimposed on the amplitude of the carrier wave, forming a modulated carrier wave. Amplitude modulation is the simplest form of modulation. Frequency and phase modulation (p.43) require more complex circuits.

**demodulator** (*n*) a device which reconstitutes the original analog signal of audio frequencies (p.130) from an amplitude modulated carrier wave formed by a modulator (↑). It consists of a tuned radio-frequency circuit (L and $C_1$ *in the diagram*), a rectifier, a capacitor, $C_2$, of a value such as to bypass the radio frequencies but small enough not to shunt out the modulation frequencies, and a resistor across which to develop the modulation voltage. During each positive pulse of the input, the rectifier will allow current to pass and charge the capacitor. Between positive peaks there will be a slight loss of charge. The voltage across the capacitor will follow that of the modulation voltage. Frequency and phase modulation need more complex circuits.

**modem** (*acro*) MOdulator/DEModulator. A device with circuits for a modulator (↑) and demodulator (↑).

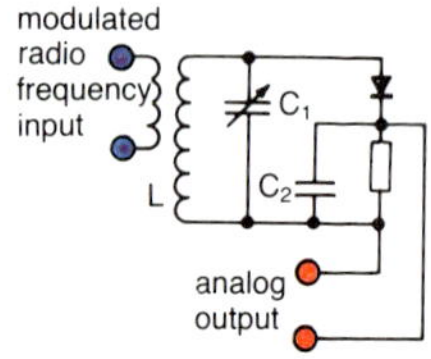

principle of a demodulator

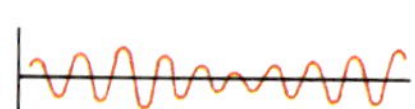
modulated RF input

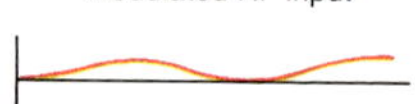
voltage across $C_2$

**bandwidth** (*n*) the difference between the highest and lowest frequency in a range of frequencies; e.g. the bandwidth of audio frequencies is 19985Hz, the difference between 20000Hz and 15Hz.

**broad band** a bandwidth (↑) greater than 4kHz. Also describes a device operating such a bandwidth.

**wide band** broad band (↑).

**narrow band** a bandwidth (↑) less than 3kHz, used on a communication line with a lower frequency than a voice-grade line (↓).

**voice-grade line** the common communications line used by telephone systems, and also for data transmission between computers, and between computers and terminals or distant peripheral devices. It has a bandwidth of 3kHz, and handles voice transmissions with little distortion. Voice-grade lines can transmit data at a rate of up to 10000 baud, but for normal use 2400 baud is used.

**voice-grade channel** (1) a channel (p.233) used for transmitting speech; it usually has an audio-frequency range of 300 to 3400Hz. (2) voice-grade line (↑).

**voice channel** a channel (p.234) with a bandwidth (↑) sufficient for a rate of 2400 bits per second.

**guard band** a frequency band between the bands used for two or more channels on the same line; the guard band is left unused to avoid interference between the channels.

**transducer**[2] (*n*) a device which transforms one form of energy to another. Usually the magnitude of a quantity, or an applied stimulus, e.g. temperature, sound, is transformed to an electrical signal.

**telephone data-carrier system** a device compatible with a computer and the telephone system. It can be plugged into an ordinary telephone line and handles both data transmission and the normal telephone service. The system can transmit up to 9600 bits per second. The system is used with small, low-cost computer networks.

**DCS** (*abbr*) telephone data-carrier system (↑).

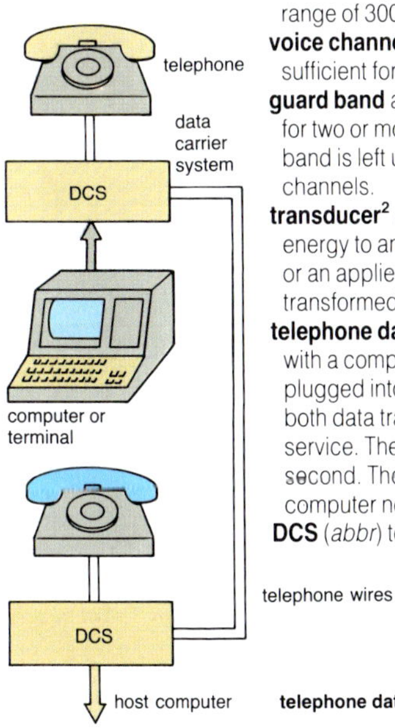


**telephone data-carrier system**

**acoustic coupler** an acoustic coupler is a device with a cradle accepting a standard telephone so that the telephone mouthpiece fits over the acoustic energy generator and the earpiece fits over the acoustic energy receiver. Connection between computers is achieved by an ordinary telephone dialling process. An acoustic coupler can operate at a rate of 1200 baud with a full duplex asynchronous transmission over voice-grade lines (p.230).

**delay line** a device which delays signals between its input and its output. It is based on the properties of materials, such as sound waves propagated in different media, e.g. mercury or quartz, or on the properties of electrical circuits. Coaxial cables (p.234) and bucket-brigade (p.184) delay lines are examples of electrical circuits delaying signals. A lumped delay line uses a series of inductor and capacitor elements.

**acoustic delay line** a delay line (↑) based on the propagation of sound waves through a medium such as mercury or quartz. Digital information is converted into sound waves at one end of the line and the sound waves are converted back at the other end into digital information. A bit is represented by the presence or absence (i.e. 1 or 0) of a short, high-frequency, sound wave.

**sonic delay line** acoustic delay line (↑).

**mercury delay line** an acoustic delay line (↑) using a column of mercury as the medium for the propagation of sound waves.

**audio-cassette interface** a device that converts digital information into audio-frequencies, with one frequency for logic one and another frequency for logic zero. The cassette tape can then record the audio frequencies and becomes a backing store (p.178).

**audio-cassette record interface** audio-cassette interface (↑).

**transmission of bytes** transmission can be either serial or parallel. In serial transmission, each bit is sent sequentially along a single channel. In parallel transmission, all the bits in a byte are sent at the same time; there can be separate lines for each bit, or all bits can be sent using different carrier-wave frequencies along a single channel.

**serial transmission** *see transmission of bytes* (↑).

**parallel transmission** *see transmission of bytes* (↑).

**acoustic coupler**

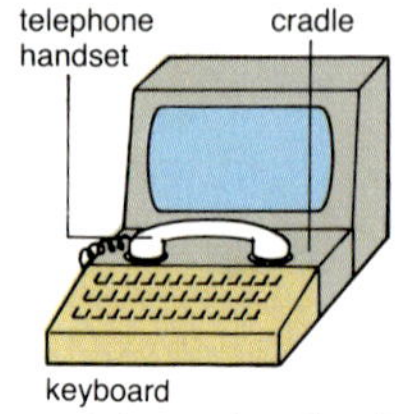


mouthpiece and earpiece fit into rubber cups on cradle

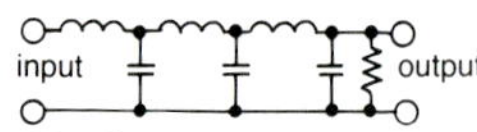


**delay line**

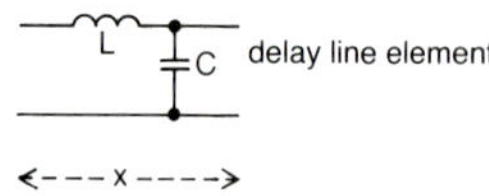


L = inductance
C = capacitance
x in metres

delay in seconds = T = $x\sqrt{LC}$

**delay line element**

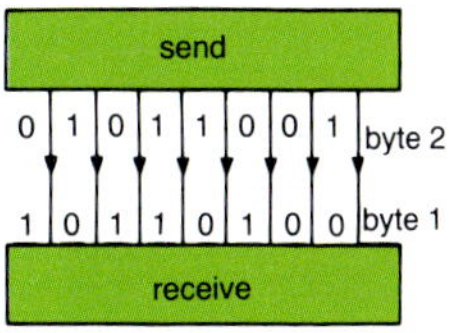


**parallel transmission**

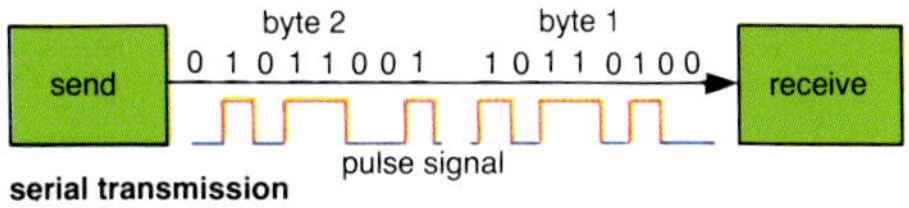


**serial transmission**

**block**[3] (*n*) a set of data bytes treated as a single unit for serial transmission (↑).

**block length** the size of a block (↑) measured in words, bytes or characters. The block length can be fixed or variable.

**block transmission** the transmission of a block needs information about it and also checks on the accuracy of transmission. These signals are generated at the time the block is sent; they include start and finish of the block, parity and other checks.

**block head** a character used to indicate the start of a block (↑).

**block mark** a character used to indicate the end of a block (↑) in systems which use a variable block length (↑).

**sum check** a binary number, sent at the end of a block, to check the accuracy of transmission. The number of logic ones in the block are counted and entered as a binary number, neglecting any overflow, in a byte.

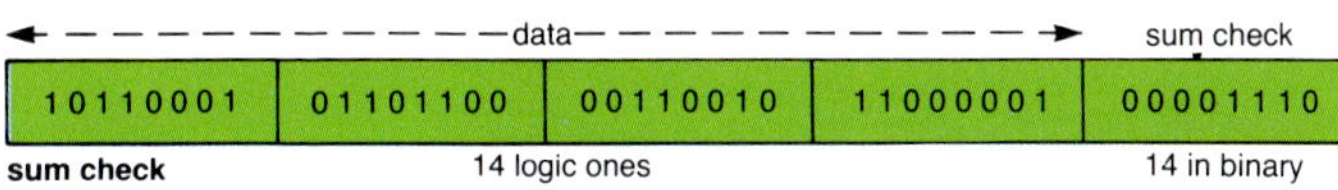


**sum check**

**cyclic redundancy check** a 16-bit programmable device that sums the bits in a block. The total is divided by a specific number, P, and the remainder from the division is put at the end of the original message. On receipt of the message, the total of bits minus the remainder is again divided by P. If there are no errors in transmission, the remainder of this second division is zero. This forms a simple and reliable error check.

**CRC** (*abbr*) cyclic redundancy check (↑).

**cyclic redundancy check**

| Z | E | B | R | A | O | N | E | CRC |
|---|---|---|---|---|---|---|---|---|
| 90 | 69 | 66 | 82 | 65 | 79 | 78 | 69 | 3 |

data sum total = 598
P = 17
598/17 = 35 remainder 3
(598-3)/17 = 35 remainder 0

**end of transmission** a character, 000 0100 in ASCII code, indicating the end of transmission of all blocks (↑) from a transmitter to a terminal.

**EOT** (*abbr*) end of transmission (↑).

**ACK** (*abbr*) acknowledgement. A specific character (111 1100 in ASCII) which is a reply from an acceptor of data, and indicates the transmission has been received, or indicates that it is ready to receive data.

**NAK** (*abbr*) negative acknowledgement. A specific character indicates that the previous transmission contained errors; the acceptor is ready to receive retransmission. Also used to indicate the acceptor is not ready for a new transmission.

**ENQ** (*abbr*) enquiry. A control character used to request status or address of a terminal, or to request input to a computer.

**idle time** the time required to assemble magnetic tape reels and control panels; the time between operations when devices are not activated.

**protocol** (*n*) a set of conventions, or rules, on the format and content of messages transmitted between devices. CPUs (p.146) communicate with other devices using different speeds of transmission, different word lengths, with different controls for acceptance of data. Protocols implement usage of transmission by adjusting such parameters.

**protocol functions** character sequences that provide a format for a transmitted message; they include markers such as STX, ETX, SOH (↓), ACK, NAK (↑), parity (p.39) and LRC (↓) for checking transmission.

**SOH** (*abbr*) start of header (↓).

**header** (*n*) a portion of a message, before the data, which may contain an identifying code, control data, destination address, routing. A header is optional.

**STX** (*abbr*) start of text, i.e. data in message.

**ETX** (*abbr*) end of text, or end of last block, i.e. end of transmission of data.

**ETB** (*abbr*) end of block.

**SYN** (*abbr*) synchronization character.

**Syn** (*abbr*) synchronization signal.

**BCC** (*abbr*) block check character; this can be CRC (p.231) or sum check (p.231).

**LRC** (*abbr*) longitudinal redundancy check. A check on the correctness of each character in a block, using parity, start and stop bits (p.41).

**vertical redundancy check** an odd-parity check (p.39) on each character of a transmitted block of data using the ASCII code.

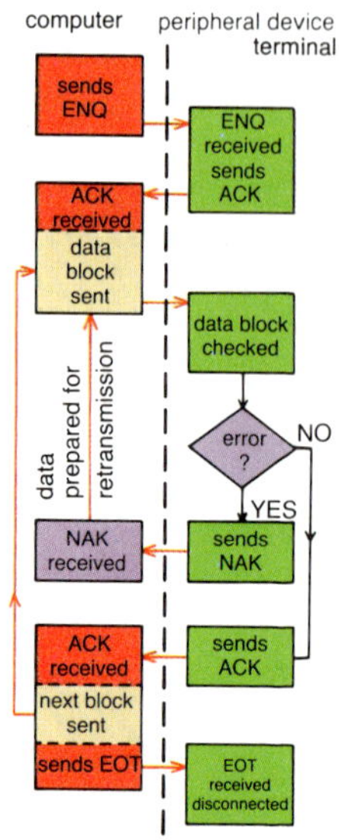


**control of transmission**

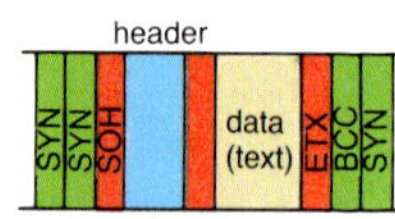


**protocol functions:**
message format

**channel**[3] (*n*) a physical path along which information can be transmitted, e.g. an input/output channel, a data channel. A channel can consist of one or more lines.

**channel capacity** the maximum number of binary digits that can be transmitted by a channel (↑) in one second. Capacity can be measured in bits per second or in baud (p.42).

**simplex** (*n*) a method of transmitting data between two points in one direction only.

**duplex** (*n*) a method of transmitting data between two points in both directions simultaneously and independently. A duplex channel (↑) is used.

**full duplex** term used instead of duplex (↑).

**half duplex** a method of transmitting data between two points but only in one direction at a time. The method can be with, or without, an interrupt (p.224) facility allowing the receiving device to interrupt the transmitting device. Used with a half-duplex channel.

**multiplex** (*n*) a method of transmitting data between points so that one channel (↑) can simultaneously transmit more than one data stream. Time division or frequency division methods are used for multiplexing (↓).

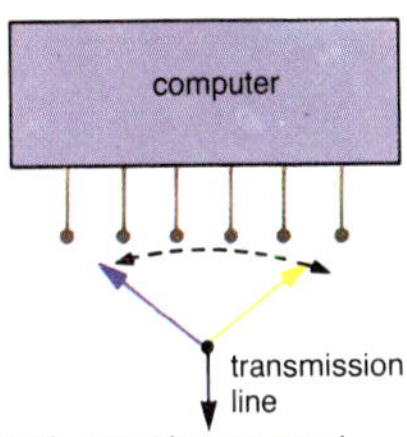


each output has an equal time share

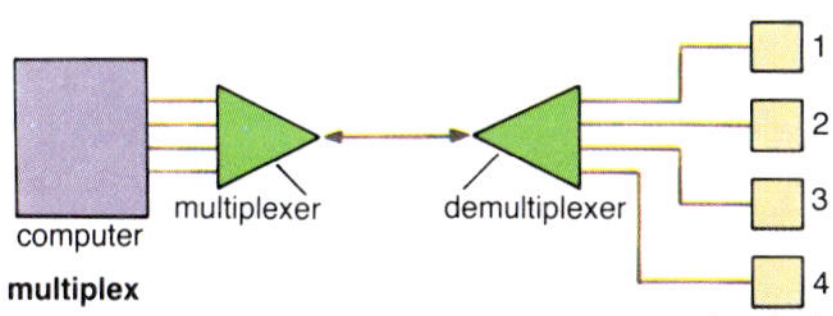


**multiplex**

**time-division multiplexer** a device that transmits two or more data streams over the same channel (↑) by using successive time intervals for the different signals. The transmissions appear to be simultaneous because the time interval is short. Each peripheral device or terminal is allocated an equal period of time in succession, controlled by a timing pulse. Time-division multiplexers are built with 4, 8, or 16 inputs.

**TDM** (*abbr*) time-division multiplexer (↑).

**frequency-division multiplexing** a limited bandwidth (p.229) channel is divided into narrow bands, each used for a separate transmission at a lower speed. The narrow bands are used for transmitting binary data signals.

**FDM** (*abbr*) frequency-division multiplexing (↑).

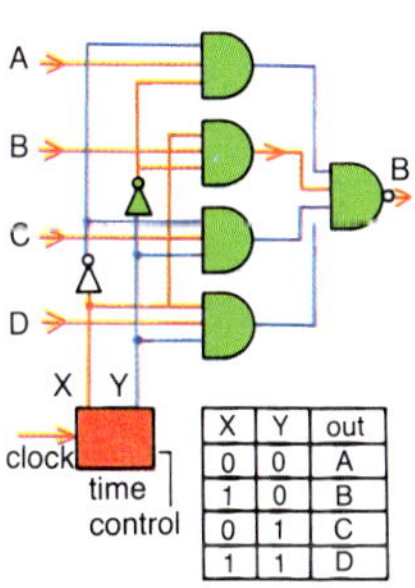


| X | Y | out |
|---|---|---|
| 0 | 0 | A |
| 1 | 0 | B |
| 0 | 1 | C |
| 1 | 1 | D |

**time-division multiplexer**

**frequency-division multiplexer** a narrow band carrier wave (p.229) is assigned to each device using the multiplexer. Binary data for the device modulate the carrier wave, and each device has a demodulator for its own narrow band carrier wave. All the carrier waves can be transmitted at the same time.
**round robin** a multiplex procedure (p.233) in which each terminal or device is allocated a fixed time slice.
**statistical multiplexing** a multiplex procedure (p.233) in which the time allocated to each terminal or device is proportional to the activity of the terminal or device.
**intelligent time-division multiplexing** statistical multiplexing (↑).
**ITDM** (*abbr*) intelligent time-division multiplexing (p.233).
**terminal controller** the serial-to-parallel and parallel-to-serial circuitry required to interface a terminal, such as a keyboard and VDU or a teletypewriter, with a computer. It is capable of detecting parity, framing and over-run errors; it can handle signals for starting up or shutting down printers, tape drives, tape cassettes. Terminal controllers are hard-wired (p.17) or programmable.
**addressable terminal** a terminal with a unique identification code. Data sent to the terminal must be preceded by its address.
**pollable terminal** a terminal in a group of terminals that is queried in succession by a computer. The ability of the terminal to acknowledge the poll, and accept the transmission, makes it pollable (p.225).
**programmable controller** a solid-state device consisting of a central processor, memory, input/output interface and a programming panel to act as a control panel. The device is used in industrial control systems with sensors providing inputs and the program arranged to perform the required industrial functions.
**PC[4]** (*abbr*) programmable controller (↑).
**coaxial cable** a cable consisting of two or more cylindrical conductors with a common axis. Each conductor is separated from an inner or outer conductor by a cylindrical insulator. The outermost conductor is usually earthed so that external electrical disturbances will not affect transmitted signals. A coaxial cable has a characteristic impedance (p.129), usually 50 or 70 ohms, and must be terminated at each end with the correct impedance for a connected circuit.

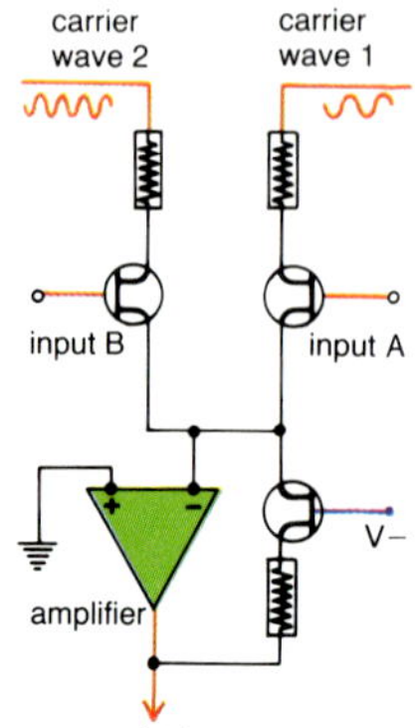

**frequency-division multilpexer**

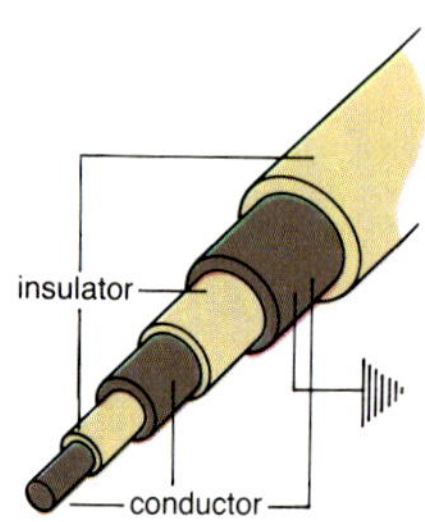

**coaxial cable**

**optic cable** a bundle of fibres capable of conducting light without any significant loss. An optical fibre is an individual fibre, usually glass for data communication cables, or plastic for short cables. The bundle of optical fibres is surrounded by a material of lower refractive index so that light is reflected back along the fibre path. The advantages of using optical fibres for data transmission include (*a*) no electromagnetic interference; (*b*) no energy loss from externally radiated signals; (*c*) broad bandwidth; (*d*) lightweight flexible cables.

**optic cable**

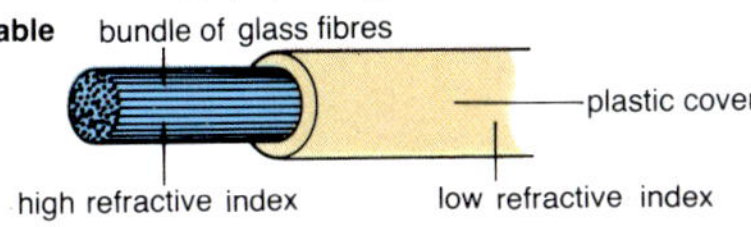


**fibre optic signal** the light signal can be digital, using pulses of light to represent logic one, or analog by varying the brightness of the light; this is equivalent to amplitude modulation.

**fibre optic transmission** the transmitted light is modulated to form a digital or analog optic signal (↑). The modulated signals are detected by photocells (p.132).

**transmission errors** errors caused by machine malfunction, and the presence of external factors. Some transmission errors can be corrected by retransmission, which is immediate and fully automatic. *See error* (p.20).

**interference** (*n*) the result of unwanted signals in the transmission of messages.

**drop-in** the generation of spurious bits during reading or writing procedures for magnetic memories.

**frame error** an error in a frame (p.217) of magnetic tape, or an error in reading from the frame.

**magnetic image** the generation of spurious bits from one section of magnetic tape to another when the sections are in close contact. One section prints a magnetic image on another section.

**drop-out²** failure to read a bit or byte from magnetic memory.

**fade** (*n*) fluctuations in the intensity of a signal. **fade** (*v*).

**selective fading** fading (↑) in which the different components of a signal fade unequally.

**distortion** (*n*) unwanted change in the waveform (p.128), usually caused by amplification in a circuit not being a linear function of an input signal.

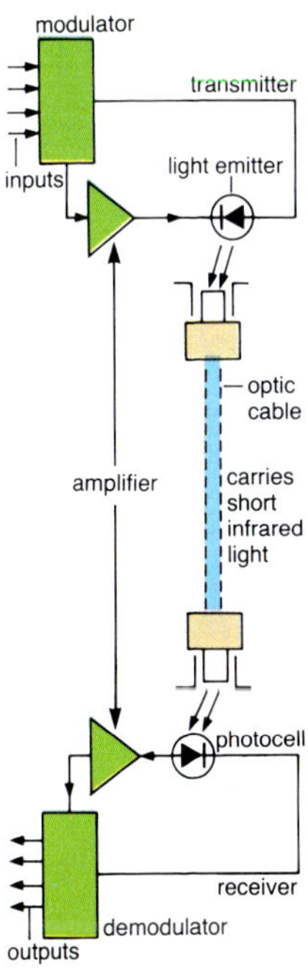


**fibre optic transmission**

**echo** (*n*) a transmitted signal is reflected back along its path and (1) causes interference (p.235) at the receiver or (2) is used as a command to test transmission has been received.

**static error**[2] plastic surfaces develop high electrostatic voltages when rubbed; these charges can discharge memory cells during transmission.

**noise** (*n*) electrical disturbances of various origins causing spurious signals. The random variation in voltage, current, or data signal strength associated with any electrical circuit working in normal surroundings.

**electrical noise** either steady-state noise or impulse noise (↓). Steady-state noise is generally called white noise (↓).

**white noise** noise (↑) of constant energy distributed equally over the whole of a bandwidth (p.229) or over all frequencies. A data signal must be at a higher level, after attenuation (p.135), than white noise.

**thermal noise** white noise (↑).

**random noise** white noise (↑).

**Gaussian noise** white noise (↑).

**background noise** white noise (↑).

**steady-state noise** white noise (↑).

**impulse noise** noise (↑) of high amplitude and of short duration, it is heard as sharp clicks. It has its origin in switches, thunderstorms, or spark discharges.

**diode noise** noise (↑) due to the emission of electrons in diodes or diode junctions when a saturation current flows.

**carrier noise** unwanted variations in a carrier waveform (p.128) which are not part of a modulation process.

**babble** (*n*) cross-talk from interference between two or more communication channels.

**common-mode noise** noise (↑) picked up from power lines.

**noise level** the strength of unwanted signals in transmission.

**ambient noise** acoustic noise in a room, or the environment of a computer.

**corrupt** (*adj*) errors stored in programs or data form a corrupt program or corrupt data. The errors arise from hardware or software failure or in transmission.

**electronic hash** noise (↑) caused by commutators or vibrators.

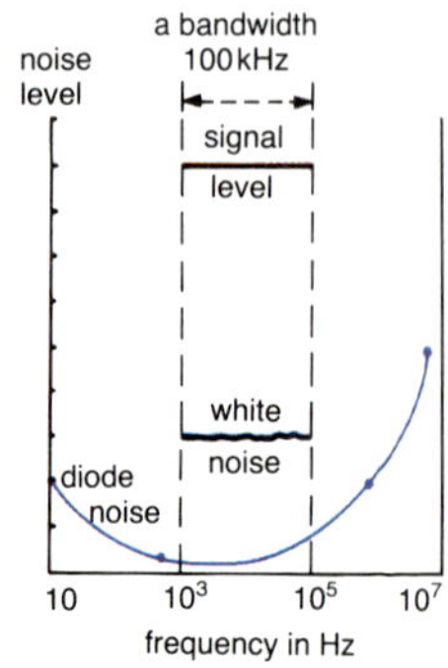


**example of noise levels**

**gain** (*n*) in an electrical circuit the ratio of strength of the output divided by the strength of the input.
**loss** (*n*) attenuation (p.135).
**power problems** the basic types of power problems are sag and surge, long-term fluctuations, transient impulses, frequency variations, interruptions. *See error* (p.20).

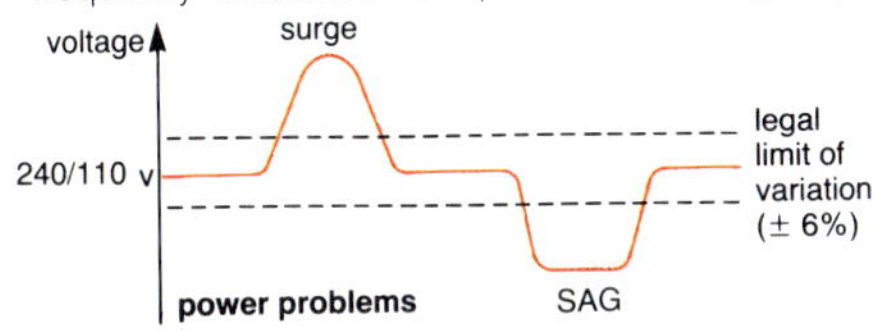


**brown-out** a power failure, or, more generally, a voltage which is too low to operate an electronic device.
**surge** (*n*) a short-term increase in voltage, high enough to damage electronic components. A surge can last for several cycles or up to several hundred cycles.
**sag** (*n*) a short-term drop in voltage, not low enough to cause failure. The period of a sag is similar to that of a surge (↑).
**jitter** (*n*) a short-term instability of a signal either in its amplitude or its phase, or in both. A jitter causes difficulty in synchronized processes and in the detection of bits.
**power transients** high amplitude pulses of very short duration; they are the most common type of power problem. The rise can be from 50 to 1000 volts. Transients are also caused by improper connections to ground, i.e. earth connections.
**voltage spike** a short, sharp, voltage increase.

**line-surge suppressor** a device that absorbs surges and transients (↑) that exceed a required protection level, and suppresses transients below that level.
**glitch** (*n*) an unwanted electronic pulse, the result of an abnormal power supply, such as a voltage spike (↑). *See graunch* (p.21).
**blip** (*n*) an erratic, or unwanted, signal on a VDU.

**bus** (*n*) a path consisting of several conductors used for transmitting signals from one or more sources to one or more destinations. A bus is used to transfer information inside a computer and between a computer and peripheral devices. *See highway* (p.164). A single wire between a source and a destination is not considered to be a bus. A number of connections between several locations can be made on a common bus used by several circuits.

▶ driver

**bus connections**

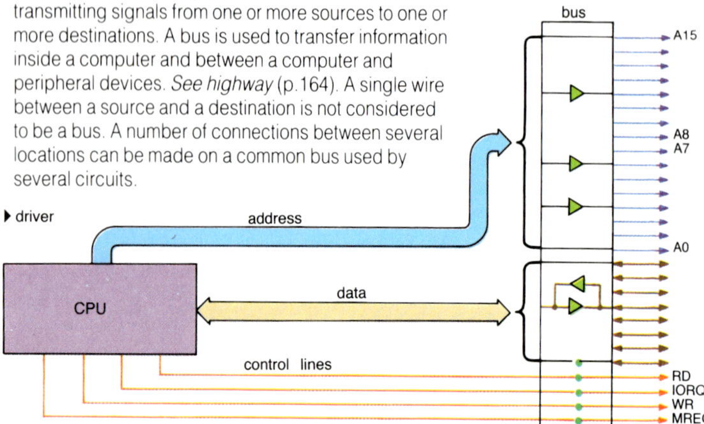


each address AO–AF and all control lines have one driver every data line has two drivers

**trunk** (*n*) alternative term for bus (↑) or highway (p.164).
**data bus** data highway (p.164).
**address bus** address highway (p.164).
**bus address lines** the lines which address memory. A memory address is coded in sixteen bits, so there are sixteen address lines on a bus, labelled A0–A15.
**universal bus** all address and data transfers for input/output to all peripheral devices are made along the same bus, a universal bus. Each connected device can become a master or a slave unit to another device. One of the two common types of bus architectures for mini- and microcomputers. *See multibus system* (↓).
**multibus system** a system with an A-bus (↓) which gives high speed access between the CPU (p.146) and main memory (p.176). A second, medium-speed bus provides a pathway for input/output pathways to peripheral devices. This is the second common type of bus architecture for mini- and microcomputers. *See universal bus* (↑).
**A-bus** the internal bus of a microcomputer in multibus systems (↑).
**driver** (*n*) an electronic circuit which provides an amplified input for another circuit. A CPU (p.146) operates on low power signals, but peripheral devices require higher power to operate mechanical devices, so a driver is activated by a weak signal from an RD or

**universal bus system**

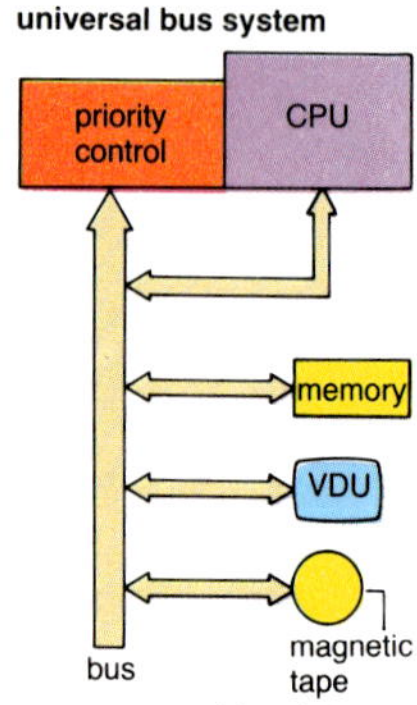

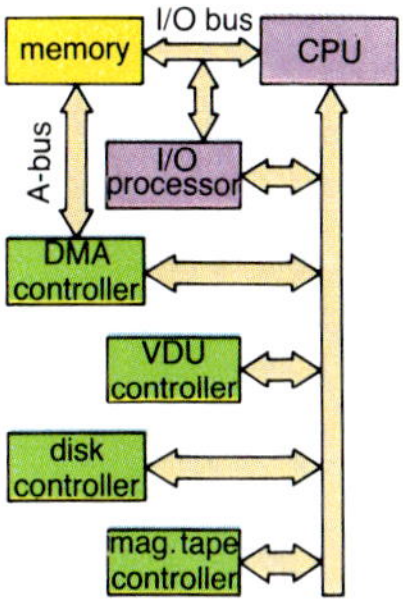


**multibus system**

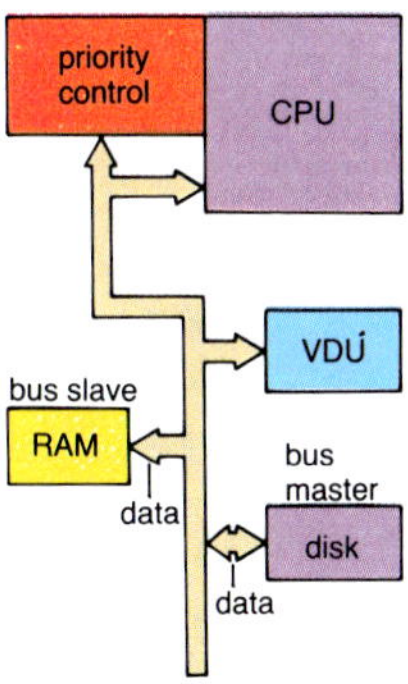


**bus master and slave**

**daisy chain bus structure**

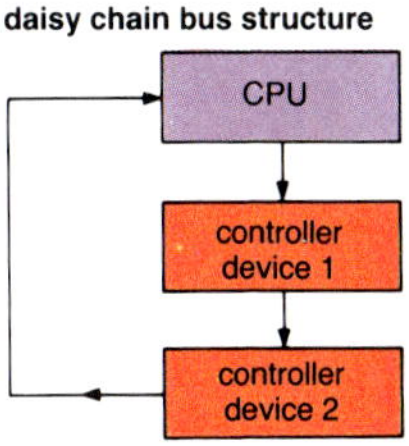


WR line (p.240) and supplies higher power to address, data and control lines. The A8–A15 address lines do not have drivers, as they address memory only.

**bus driver** driver (↑).

**line driver** driver (↑).

**port** (*n*) a place of access, either entry or exit, to a computer system; it is dedicated to a single channel (p.233) for data transfer. It consists of line connections, and their associated circuits such as control command and status registers, together with driver (↑).

**bus master** a source of information that takes charge of a bus (↑) through its controller. There can be only one bus master which asserts addresses and sends data to other devices connected to the bus. *See bus slave* (↓).

**bus slave** the destination of information from a bus master (↑). There can be any number of bus slaves receiving data from a bus master.

**bus arbitration** the process of assigning bus mastership (↑). The events are: (1) making a bus mastership request; (2) receiving a grant that the universal or I/O bus will be available; (3) acknowledging the grant.

**bus priority** an order of priority for granting bus arbitration (↑) to any device that can become a bus master (↑).

**bus available signal** the signal will normally be at low. When the CPU (p.146) has stopped working and the address bus (↑) is available, the signal will go high. All output drivers will go low, their OFF state, until a bus master is appointed.

**BA** (*abbr*) bus available (↑).

**control bus** a bus which carries a mixture of signals which regulate bus operations. The signals can originate in the CPU (p.146) or in specific peripheral devices.

**bus structure** bus organization is one of the most important features of computer architecture. Buses may be unidirectional or bidirectional, with parallel or serial structures. Their configurations include party-line structures and daisy-chain configurations (↓). In party-line structure a universal bus (↑) system is used.

**daisy chain** movement of signals or data from one unit to another in a serial fashion, passing through all units until it reaches its destination. All information is sent by serial transmission, and thus is slower than for parallel transmission.

**IORQ** (*abbr*) input/output request. A command line activated by the CPU (p.146) when data are transferred to or from a peripheral device (p.13). A machine code instruction puts the address of a peripheral device on address lines A0–A7 (p.238). After a short delay the IORQ line sends an address strobe (↓) which is answered by an acknowledge strobe from the device. The IORQ sends a request signal to the interface, and activates either an RD or WR (↓) line. The data are put on the data bus, and the IORQ sends a data strobe. The data are latched into a UART (p.221) and removed from the data bus. *See MREQ* (↓).

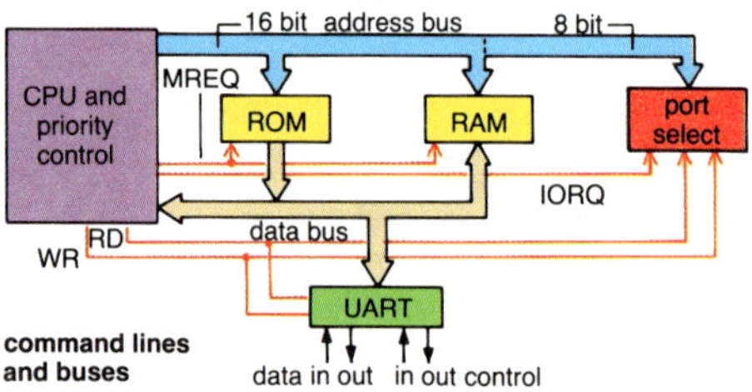


**command lines and buses**

**input/output request line** *see IORQ* (↑).

**MREQ** (*abbr*) memory request. A command line similar to the IORQ line, but connecting the CPU to main memory. If a universal bus (p.238) is used, the drivers (p.238) are disconnected, so that transfer of data takes place at low power, and all sixteen address lines, A0–A15, are used. *See IORQ* (↑).

**memory request line** *see MREQ* (↑).

**RD line** the read line is activated by the IORQ or MREQ lines and by the CPU (p.146). With the IORQ line, it enables the drivers on address lines A0–A7 (p.238), and on the data lines it enables the drivers for reading data in a peripheral device. With the MREQ line, no drivers are used.

**WR line** the write line is activated by the IORQ or MREQ lines and by the CPU (p.146). With the IORQ line it enables the drivers on address lines A0–A7 (p.238), and on the data lines it enables the drivers for writing data into a peripheral device. With the MREQ line, no drivers are connected.

**ground connection** a connection to earth which gives a reference voltage for interface signals.

**GND** (*abbr*) ground connection (↑) or protective ground (↓).

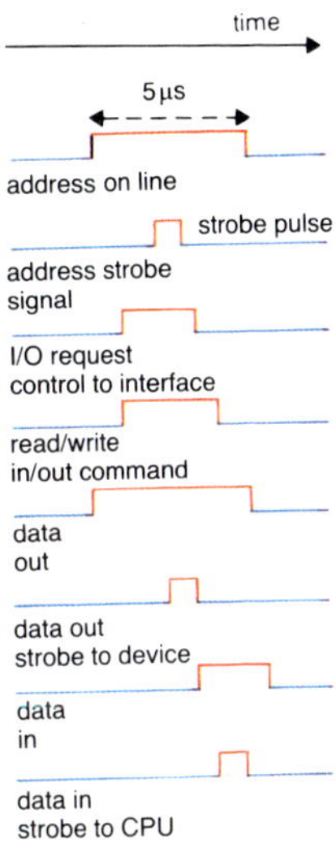


**use of strobes for input/ output**

**protective ground** a connection to earth which gives a reference voltage in common to a microcomputer and to its peripheral devices.

**ring in** a control signal from a modem to indicate it is receiving a carrier wave signal.

**RI** (*abbr*) ring in (↑).

**strobe** (*n*) a selection signal that is active when a process has reached a desired point or position, that is, when an address or data are correct on a bus.

**strobe signal** a signal used to enable a circuit to carry out its function or to disable a circuit.

**strobe pulse** a strobe signal (↑) consists of a single pulse. It is used to gate a circuit either to enable or disable a circuit.

**data strobe** a strobe pulse (↑) on a line which enables a circuit transferring data from a data bus (p.238) to a device, or to a CPU (p.146).

**address strobe** a strobe pulse (↑) on a line which enablesa circuit connecting a device with a CPU (p.146) or connecting an addressed location in memory.

**strobe release time** the time between a strobe signal (↑) changing from inhibiting level to enabling level and the output of a circuit reaching its logic threshold level.

**latch** (*v*) to hold a circuit in position to read equipment, e.g. a bus, until another circuit or a command pulse is ready to change the initial circuit. For example, the circuit transferring data from a bus to a peripheral device has the data latched into the device.

**S 100 bus** a bus adopted as an international standard. It provides one hundred internal connecting points, but only about half are used in a typical general purpose computer. The bus is convenient as it is standardized, but it is less suited to more powerful microcomputers, and is not as efficient as custom-built buses for particular computers.

**bidirectional** (*adj*) describes a bus in which binary information can be passed in either direction, using asynchronous transmission. Bidirectional buses allow common bus interfaces with peripheral devices, simplifying the interface design.

**ribbon cable** a flexible flat cable with wire conductors, capable of forming parallel connections between circuits.

**tape cable** a cable with flat ribbon conductors, placed side by side, embedded in an insulating material.

**RTS** (*abbr*) request to send. A standard command line in some interfaces (p.219). Used in handshake signals (↓).
**request to send** RTS (↑).
**CTS** (*abbr*) clear to send. A standard command line in some interfaces (p.219). Used in handshake signals (↓).
**clear to send** CTS (↑).
**DTR** (*abbr*) data terminal ready. A control signal that indicates the computer or a peripheral device is ready to send data.
**data terminal ready** DTR (↑).
**DSR** (*abbr*) data set ready. A control signal, sent in answer to DTR (↑), that a peripheral device or the computer is ready to receive data.
**data set ready** DSR (↑).
**DCD** (*abbr*) data carrier detect. A control signal from a modem (p.228), indicating to a computer that a carrier wave is being received from a distant modem.
**handshake** (*n*) the exchange of specific signals, before transmission, between two devices, e.g. computer, peripheral devices, in which a signal is requested, the signal is received, and the signal is acknowledged. This procedure prevents overlapping of data transmission with other devices. A simple handshake procedure uses the RTS/CTS lines as a handshake pair. The status of each of these lines is shown in the table. When a computer and a peripheral device are idle, they are both clear to send, shown by CTS being set to logic one for each of them. When the computer sets RST to logic one, the CTS of the device is reset to zero. The computer is now clear to send (CTS is logic one) and the device is not. The computer now sends a DTR (↑), answered by a DSR (↑) from the device. Transmission then takes place. A line set to logic one indicates an

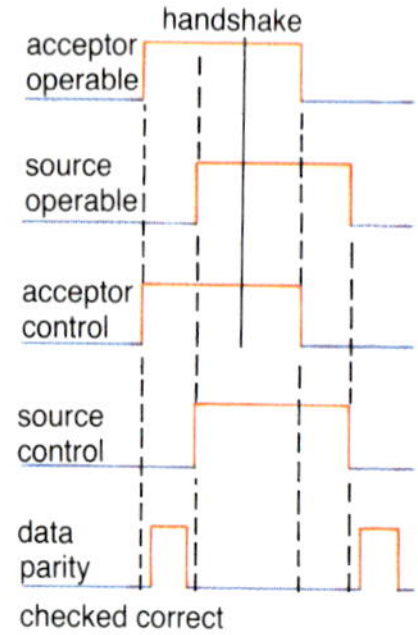

**handshake signals**

CPU transmitting

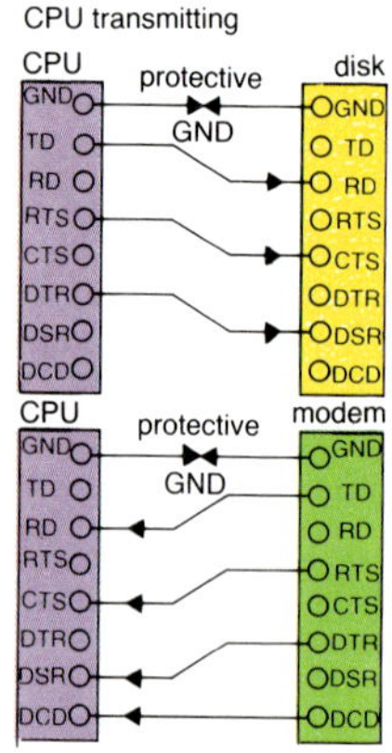


CPU receiving
TD = transmitting data
RD = receiving data
**simple handshake signals**

| | computer | | device | |
|---|---|---|---|---|
| | RTS | CTS | RTS | CTS |
| idle | 0 | 1 | 0 | 1 |
| C→D | 1 | 1 | 0 | 0 |
| D→C | 0 | 0 | 1 | 1 |

1 = active status
0 = inhibited status
C = computer
D = peripheral device
**handshake status**

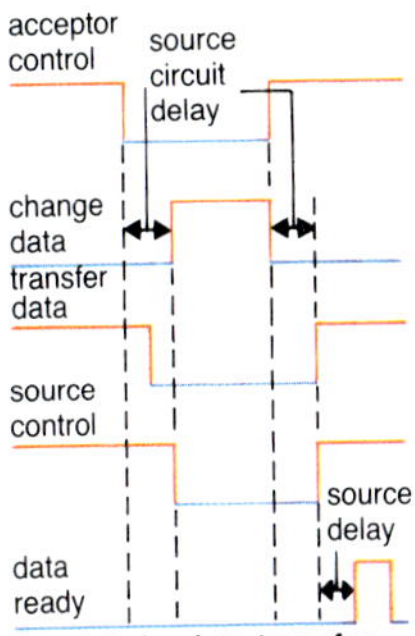

**handshake data transfer**

active status, a line reset to zero indicates an inhibited status. A common connection, protective ground provides a reference voltage for the signals. Other methods can be used for exchanging handshake signals.

**handshake I/O control** a handshake process which allows peripheral devices with different response times and different parity checks to be used. It uses acceptors and sources for data transfer instead of RTS/CTS pairs, and is more flexible in its operation. A logic circuit to operate the control is shown in the diagram. Logic zero indicates out of action, logic one indicates operable. Logic zero is a negative voltage and logic one a positive voltage; this distinguishes a power failure with no voltage instead of negative voltage, an important state to detect. The acceptor and source operable lines are preferably kept active throughout a transfer. The handshake is between the acceptor control and source control pair. A parity, or other error, check takes place before the source control is activated. Data transfer stops shortly after acceptor control falls to logic zero, followed by source control falling to zero. Data can then be changed. When the change is complete, acceptor control is activated. A circuit delay takes place before transfer data and source control are activated. Transfer starts when the data ready signal appears.

**three-line mode** a handshake signal (↑) is controlled by bit 0 in the command register (p.155). The simplest method of transmission is a three-line mode using the three ports GND, TD and RD shown in the diagram on page 242, that is, one for transmit, one for receive and a common ground. There is no handshake procedure.

**X-line mode** a handshake process (↑) in which all the ports in the diagram on page 242 are used. *Compare three-line mode* (↑). X-line mode provides a full handshake procedure between two devices.

**data source** a device in a data communications system which can originate data signals for transmission. It may also accept error signals for control purposes. *Contrasted with data sink* (↓).

**data sink** a device in a data communications system which can accept data signals from a transmission device. It may also originate error control signals. *Contrasted with data source* (↑).

AO = accepter operable
SO = source operable
AC = acceptor control
SC = source control

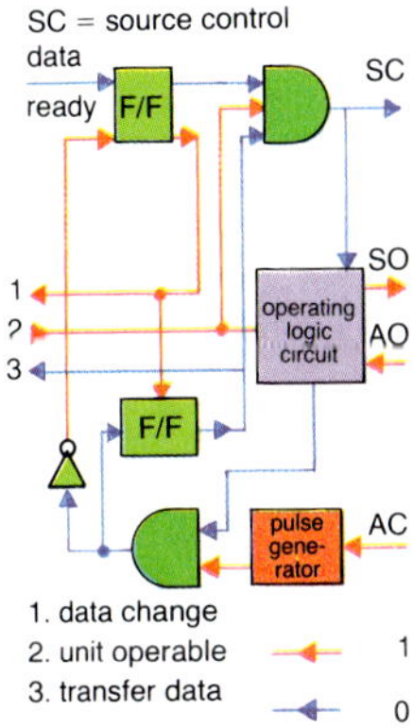

**source interface circuit**

**data** (*n*) any group of facts, numbers, symbols, alphabetic letters which describe a state, a value or a condition. Data usually describes a fact or an event; data is contrasted with information, which is conveyed by a set of data, and with program, which is a set of instructions operating on data.

**data element** a specific item of data, e.g. a date, a quantity of goods, a balance of stock, the cost per item.

**macroelement** (*n*) a set of two or more data elements treated as a single data element (↑).

**data element chain** macroelement (↑).

**data level** the position of a data element (↑) in relation to other data elements in a record (↓).

**data frame** a frame on paper tape (p.212) or magnetic tape (p.216).

**field**[2] (*n*) a part of a record (↓) containing a specified unit of information, e.g. a name, an address, date of birth, tax deducted.

**record** (*n*) all the data on an event, or an inventory item, consisting of a collection of fields, e.g. date, name of goods, quantity sold, cost per item, cash received.

field

| No. | date | goods | cost $ |
|---|---|---|---|
| 1 | 2.9.83 | shirts | 2230.60 |
| 2 | 3.9.83 | socks | 1690.00 |
| 3 | 4.9.83 | shoes | 4321.45 |
| 4 | 4.9.83 | shirts | 3282.56 |

4 data elements in one row
4 records from 4 transactions
each record has 4 fields
each field has 4 data elements

one record

| | | | |
|---|---|---|---|
| 2 | 3.9.83 | socks | 1690.00 |

data element

**transaction** (*n*) an event which produces a record (↑).

**raw data** data that has not been processed; the data may, or may not, be in machine-readable form (↓).

**data reduction** the process of converting raw data (↑) into condensed, processable data by ordering, scaling and using other statistical methods.

**data structure** an organizing structure which orders a collection of data. Strings, arrays and matrices are examples of data structures.

**data block** all the data which is input to a computer in one process, or a single computer output which is the result of processing data.

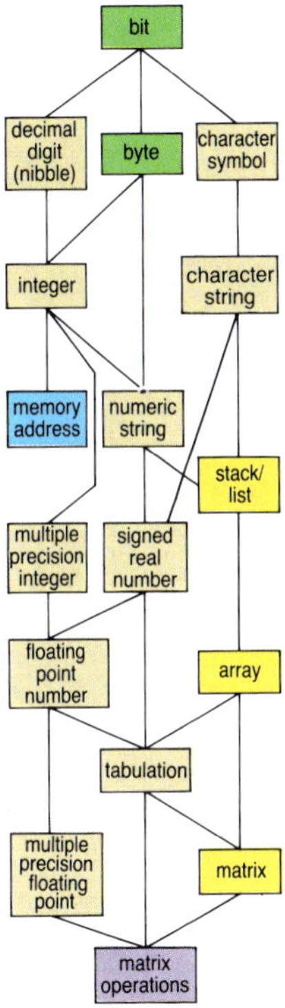


**basic data types**

**master data** a set of data which is usually unaltered and supplies basic data for data processing, e.g. personal names, addresses, dates of birth.

**data types** the use of binary digits (bits) to build up the various types of data is shown in the diagram. All information has to be converted to one of these basic types.

**data processing** all the operations carried out on data, by means of algorithms (p.82) and programs (p.64), in order to produce information or a specific result. The rearrangement of data into a suitable form for further use.

**electronic data processing** data processing (↑) in which electronic machines are used; specifically, entering, processing, recording data without the use of tabulating punched cards.

**EDP** (*abbr*) electronic data processing.

**automatic data processing** data processing (↑) without a manual input (↓).

**manual input** the entry of data into a computer or system by hand, for example by keyboard, keypunch, light pen.

**machine-readable data** data which can be sensed by an input device, for example, data on punched cards and tapes, magnetic tapes, cassettes and disks.

**manual operation** data processing (↑) using a succession of switches operated by hand instead of a complete program.

**data analysis** the descriptions, cross-referencing, summarizing of information, by the use of suitable codes for data processing (↑).

**data bank** a large collection of data held in memory and available for many users, including the general public, usually by means of remote terminals. A data bank implies many different uses for a variety of different applications (p.258). *Contrasted with data base* (p.257).

**master program file** a magnetic tape on which all the programs needed for a data processing (↑) system are recorded.

**master library tape** master program file (↑).

**multiple-length working** a method of data processing (↑) in which two, or more, words (p.36) are used to represent data items. This is done to achieve greater precision in numerical calculations.

**data medium** the medium used to transport or record data. The media include punched cards, punched paper tape, magnetic tape, cassettes, and portable magnetic disks.

**data conversion** the process of changing data from one form to another, without changing the content. Conversion includes changing the storage medium or changing the coding system. *Compare copy* (p.253).

**conversion** (*n*) data conversion (↑).

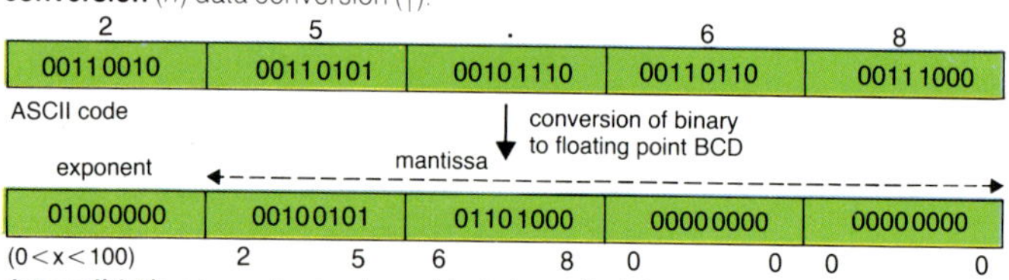


**data conversion**

**data validation** to apply checks and tests to verify data, e.g. a visual check on a VDU, double keypunching to check encoding, read and write heads on magnetic tape.

**validate** (*v*) to perform data validation (↑) in order to reduce the number of errors input into a computer.

**data purification** the process of validating (↑) and correcting errors, especially before the data enter an automatic data processing system (p.245).

**data compression** the methods used to save storage space by reducing or eliminating empty fields, gaps, redundancies and unnecessary data. The conversion of binary words to hexadecimal words.

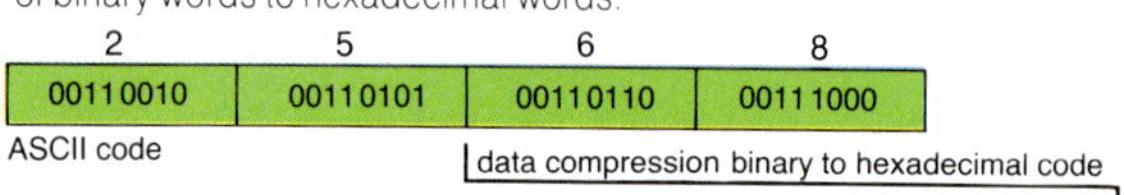


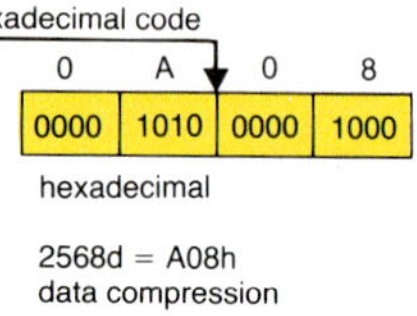


**data compression**

**data compaction** data compression (↑).

**pack** (*v*) (1) to compress data (↑); (2) (*n*) a set of punched cards; (3) (*n*) a set of magnetic disks.

**data chaining** the scattering (and gathering) of data within a region of memory and linking one record to another by means of a pointer. *See hash* (p.74) and *chained file* (p.255).

**data management** the method of manipulating data, that is, the control of collecting, storing, retrieving, analyzing and distributing data.

**data communication** the transmission and reception of computer-encoded information by means of electrical transmission systems.

**data logger** a device which can capture information and record it immediately, e.g. a temperature sensor recording ambient temperatures.

**document** (*n*) a written or printed form, mainly on paper, containing details, in a human-readable form, of a transaction (p.244). A document is a permanent record of a transaction. It may also be used for describing the details of processing in a data processing system. *See documentation* (↓).

**source document** a document (↑) from which machine-readable data is prepared.

**original document** source document (↑).

**document reader** a device using optical character recognition (p.194) or magnetic ink character recognition (p.196) to read data directly from a document (↑).

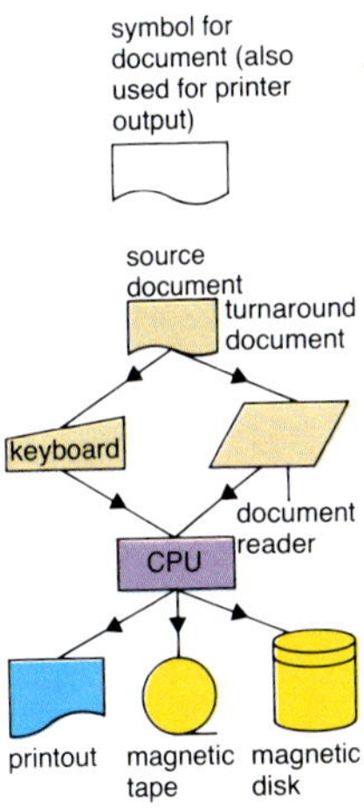

**data capture**

**documentation** (*n*) a complete description of the collection, organization, processing and presentation of data in a computer system. The description includes: (*a*) systems definitions (source documents and data capture); (*b*) file descriptions; (*c*) flowchart of procedures for processing; (*d*) programming specifications indicating procedures by block flowcharts; (*e*) print formats for records; (*f*) operating instructions including batch procedure; (*g*) output format and reports. All parts of the documentation should be accompanied by notes explaining the reasons for each action.

**data capture** the conversion of a source document (↑) into machine-readable data. In many cases this is a keyboard operation with an operator entering the data elements (p.244) on to punched tape or cards, or magnetic tape or disk or on to a VDU for checking before entry into memory. Machine-readable data do not need a keyboard action and are less likely to have errors.

**turnaround document** a tag or a punched card returned when a transaction (p.244) is completed. The document has machine-readable data on it, and is attached to one item, or to a set of items, and so records a sale of a stated number of items.

**direct data capture** a method used at a point of sale (p.248) where a cash register, or a bar-code reader (p.46), records the code of an item, and the number sold, and a computer supplies the remaining details of the record, such as date, amount, name of product.

**direct data entry** direct data capture (p.247). Input of data into a computer which has not gone through a previous data capture process.

**DDE** (*abbr*) direct data entry (↑).

**data acquisition and control** a system which deals with on-line (p.22) data collection for process control as well as real-time applications (p.22) from terminals. The inputs include analog signals from sensors, used to control a process, and analog signals from a modem connected through a distant modem to a terminal. The inputs are handled by a multiplexer, and protocol functions by a control circuit.

**DAC²** (*abbr*) data acquisition and control (↑).

**point-of-sale** the place where goods are exchanged for money, and some of the aspects of a transaction (p.244) are automated. In automatic recording of sales, details are entered by an on-line device (p.22) into a computer.

**POS** (*abbr*) point-of-sale (↑).

**point-of-sale terminal** an off-line device (p.22), one of a multiterminal system, connected to a point-of-sale central controller (↓). The terminal operates a limited program, mainly for arithmetic operations. It has a keyboard and a numeric display, prints sales slips, and sends the data to the central controller.

**point-of-sale central controller** the controller polls up to 120 point-of-sale terminals (↑), and records the information on 9-track magnetic tape. It includes the magnetic tape unit, a control unit, a data buffer, an interface with the terminals, and it operates on-line (p.22) with a computer.

**electronic point-of-sale** a device using direct data capture (p.247). Goods are marked with bar codes (p.46) and read by a light pen (p.195) or a laser beam device. The computer, connected to the EPOS, decodes the data, and causes the terminal to print a sales slip with the name and price of the goods. The sales are recorded on a magnetic tape file.

**EPOS** (*abbr*) electronic point-of-sale (↑).

**job** (*n*) a particular unit of work for a computer system, organized as a computer process, and usually divided into one or more job steps (↓).

**job step** a task, or set of tasks, connected with a stage in computer processing. For example, an operation to capture data from source documents (p.247) using a keyboard, and storing the data on disk.

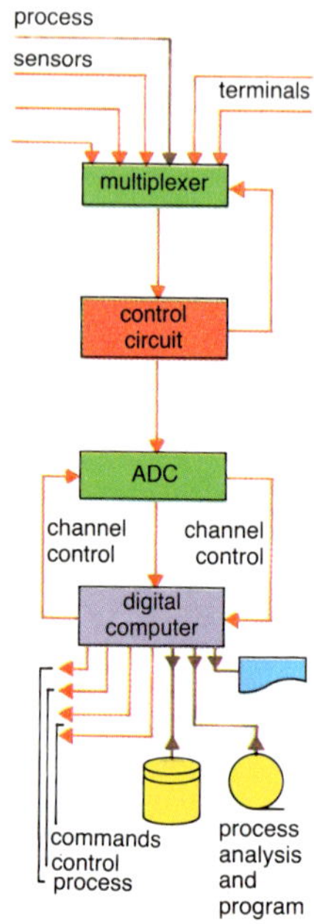


**data acquisition and control**

**job and job steps**

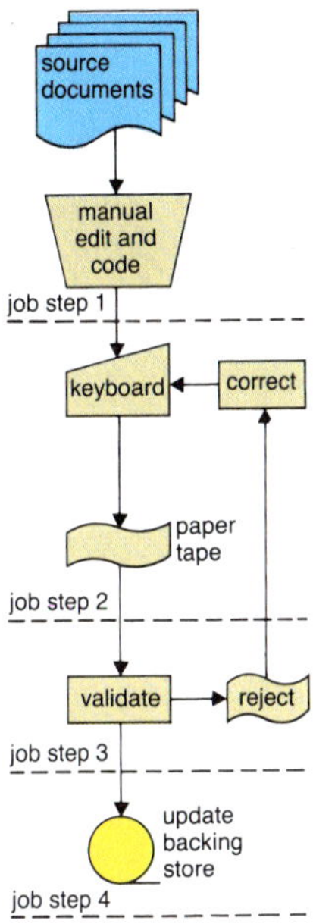


**job control program** a program taken from a backing store (p.178) and entered into main memory (p.176). It prepares the CPU (p.146) for a job or a series of job steps which form a job (↑).

**job processing** a job control program (↑) handles the data for a job (↑) and initiates the job steps defined in the program. It specifies the writing of output messages, and the updating of files (p.251) to complete the job.

**job schedule** a supervisory program that examines the input work queue (↓) and selects jobs in the order of their priority.

**input work queue** a list of job control statements from job control programs (↑) maintained by the job schedule program (↑).

**batch** (*n*) a number of similar transactions which are processed as a single unit, e.g. a batch of invoices collected up to a cutoff time, and the data captured by a keyboard operation. The transactions may be available on source documents (p.247) or in machine-readable form. The batch of data is then kept together for all future steps in the job process.

**batch processing** it takes time to assemble the documents for a batch (↑) so there is a delay between the transactions taking place and the processing of the batch. The delay is acceptable as there is no immediacy for obtaining the resulting output.

**master card** the first card in a pack of punched cards, which contains information concerning the pack, e.g. start of job, start of data, end of job. The card usually has a distinctive character, e.g. £ sign, to mark it as a master card, a mnemonic to designate its information, and an identification.

**master card**

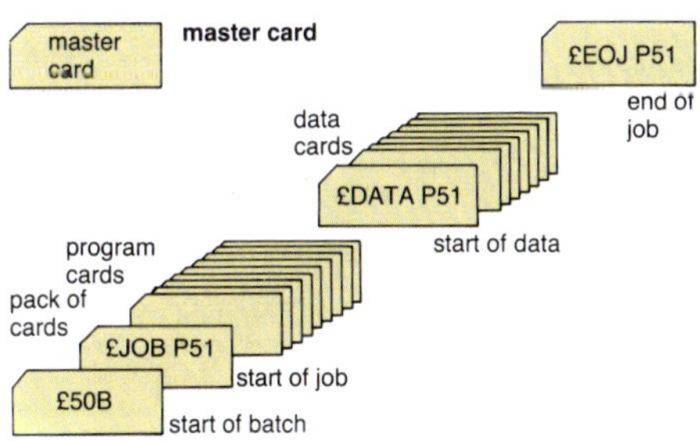

**keyword** (*n*) a significant word in a title, text, or document that is used as a descriptive word for a document, or set of documents, and assists in identifying the document or the set of documents. *See key* (↓).

**batch total** a total produced by adding the quantities in a particular field (p.244) of a batch of documents. The total may have meaning, e.g. the total amount of money received from the transactions, or it may be a hash total (↓). The total is produced to check that all the records (p.244) in the batch are present at every stage of the process.

**control total** a total for a batch, i.e. a batch total (↑) or a similar total for a job (p.249).

**hash total** a control, or batch, total, which has no meaning, for example, the total of dates of birth, or identity numbers.

**sampling** (*n*) in processes where there is a random variation of a quantity such as in traffic flow at road junctions, the quantity is sampled periodically and a pattern of the variation is produced.

**sampling period** a measured time interval between the sampling of a quantity in a sampling system (↑).

**CAM**$^2$ (*abbr*) computer aided manufacturing. The use of computers and sensors (p.17) to control a process.

**calibration** (*n*) to make a scale on a measuring instrument by comparison with a known standard of that measurement, so that the instrument measures accurately. Calibration is used to make scales on sensors (p.17), so that accurate measurements can be obtained.

**data communications network** a network consisting of computers interfaced with each other and with terminals, backing stores, and output devices, *see diagram*. A network can range from a host processor and an intelligent terminal to a complex network served by multiplexors and interfaces with multiple-host computers. Each computer or device may vary in speed, language, etc., but each is chosen for efficiency in its assigned tasks.

| date | item code | qty | value |
|---|---|---|---|
| 4 Feb | A241 | 51 | 1392.30 |
| 4 Feb | A105 | 43 | 1093.06 |
| 5 Feb | C319 | 29 | 696.00 |
| 7 Feb | B089 | 68 | 2457.52 |
| 9 Feb | B102 | 17 | 1636.25 |
| hash total | 856 | batch total | 7275.13 |

**batch totals**

**example of a data communications network**

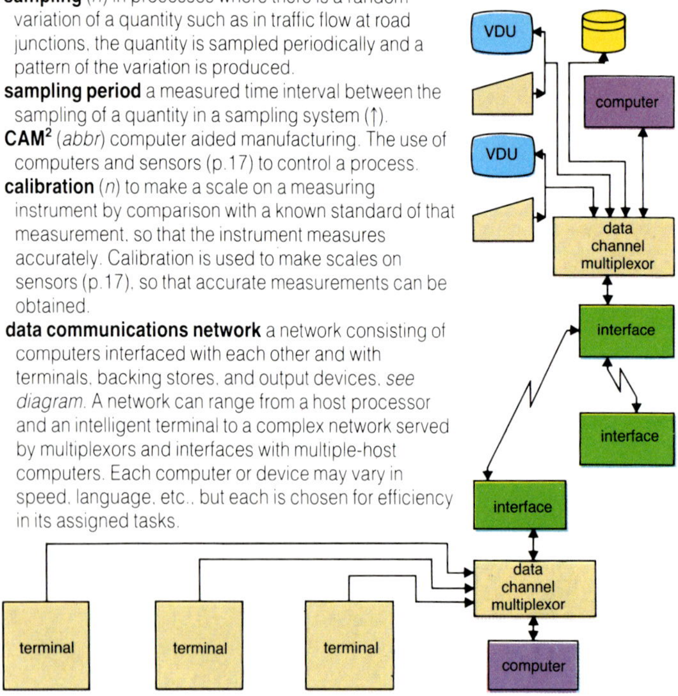

| date | item code | customer code | qty | value £ |
|---|---|---|---|---|
| 3 Apr | 191 | AC352 | 41 | 321 |
| 1 Apr | 192 | AF016 | 516 | 964 |
| 2 Apr | 193 | AA196 | 29 | 38 |

field width = 8 field width = 3 field width = 5

**printout of sequential file**

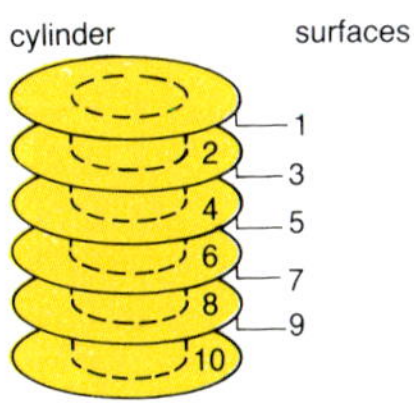


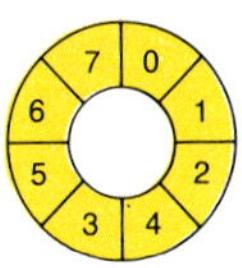


999 item codes on index file

| cylinder address | | surface address (cylinders) | | sector address (surface 2) | |
|---|---|---|---|---|---|
| cyl | primary key | s'fce | primary key | s'fce | primary key |
| 1 | 1—100 | 1 | 201—210 | 0 | 211—212 |
| 2 | 200 | 2 | 211—220 | 1 | 213 |
| 3 | 300 | 3 | 221—230 | 2 | 214 |
| 10 | 901—999 | | | | |
| 256 | | 10 | 291—300 | 7 | 220 |

index for key and address
**indexed file**

**data channel multiplexor** a multiplexor in a data communications network (↑) which services a number of communication channels.

**file** (*n*) an organized collection of related data (p.244) usually held in a storage medium such as magnetic tape or disk. It contains records (p.244) consisting of fields (p.244), which contain words or characters. A file must have speed and ease of retrieval of data, an efficient use of storage media, and provide flexibility in its use. It must be organized to simplify the problem of using its data to obtain a required solution or report. Files are the basis of a computer system in a business environment, where data processing consists mainly of the handling of files.

**field width** the number of characters in a field (p.244).

**field length** (1) field width (↑); (2) the number of words in a fixed-length record.

**key**[2] (*n*) a digit or a group of digits, or a group of characters usually forming a field (p.244). The key is used to identify a record (p.244); more than one key may be used for identification, the keys are then called primary key, secondary key, etc. *See keyword* (↑).

**file structure** the method of entering records into a computer storage medium; files produced are: serial files, sequential files, indexed files, random files. *See chained file* (p.255).

**file organization** file structure (↑).

**serial file** contains records in no particular order; mainly used for temporary storage of data.

**sequential file** a file with records in a numerical order determined by keys (↑); in common use for permanent files.

**indexed file** a sequential file (↑) with an index. The index enables the key (↑) of a record to be associated with an address. Indexed files are stored on magnetic disks. The simplest form of indexing uses cylinder (p.214), surface of a disk, sector (p.214), to define the address. Indexed files are the most common types.

**random file** a file in which the records are scattered at random on the storage medium. A hashing algorithm is used to give each data item a unique address and allow retrieval. *See hash* (p.74). The file structure (↑) is called a hash table. Random files are much less common than indexed files.

**hash table** *see random file* (↑).

**data name** a label allocated by a programmer to a field (p.244) or a record (p.244).
**data dictionary** a table specifying field widths (p.251) and listing data names (↑). A data dictionary can be constructed with varying degrees of detail, from simple to complex dictionaries. Data dictionaries are frequently used with data base management systems (p.258).
**directory** (*n*) (1) alternative name for data dictionary (↑); (2) sometimes used specifically for a file detailing the organization of other files on the same magnetic disk or diskette.
**catalogue** (*n*) (1) a list of files, programs, users, devices used by a processing system with the list organized for easy location of any of its items; (2) alternative name for a directory (2) (↑).
**retrieval** (*n*) the process of searching a file, or files, for data, then selecting and extracting the data. **retrieve** (*v*).
**table** (*n*) a collection of data stored as an array in memory for ease of retrieval (↑).
**table look-up** the procedure of retrieving data (↑) by searching for a specified key (p.251).
**table look-at** the procedure of retrieving data (↑) by searching in accordance with a hash total (p.250).
**file creation** data is entered by a keyboard operation directly on to magnetic tape or disk.

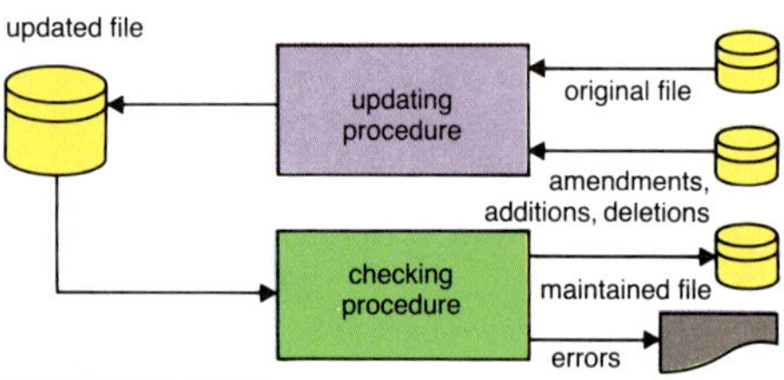

**maintainance of files**

**file maintenance** the updating (↓) of a file with the addition of checking that the file is correct and free from errors.
**update** (*v*) to amend, add or delete records, so that a file contains all the latest data. The data are usually assembled in the sequential order of a key (p.251) and the file to be updated is usually a sequential file, or an indexed sequential file (p.251).
**fetch** (*v*) to retrieve, as in retrieval (↑).

**copy** (*v*) to input data from one storage device into another, or into another section of the storage device, without any alteration of the original data. *Compare data conversion* (p.246).

**merge** (*v*) to operate on two, or more, sets of ordered records, or files, to create a single set of records, or a single file, with data in the same order. The order is usually sequential based on a key (p.251).

**collate** (*v*) to merge (↑).

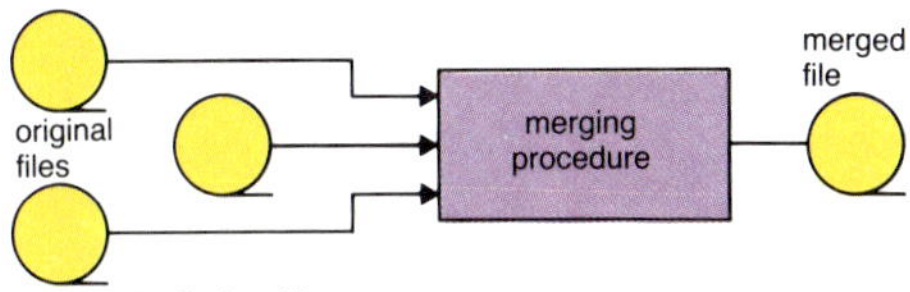


**merging/collating files**

**scan²** (*v*) to examine, in sequence, each record in a file, or item in a list, the action in table look-up (↑).

**purge** (*v*) to remove unwanted data from a file, usually because the data are out-of-date.

**purge date** a specific date, after which the contents of a file are no longer needed, and the data may be overwritten.

**dump** (*n*) a small routine (p.61) which outputs the contents of memory on to hard copy (p.202).

**change dump** a particular dump routine (↑) which outputs the contents of all memory locations that have been changed since a previous event. The output is usually printed and the previous event is usually another change dump.

**file validation** the data in a file are subjected to various tests such as type checks (alphabetic/numeric/alphanumeric text), range checks (numeric data within an acceptable range), sum checks (p.231), batch totals (p.250), redundancy checks (p.39). Any errors are listed in a printout, and later corrected.

**file merging** *see merge* (↑).

**file collating** *see collate* (↑).

**file updating** *see update* (↑).

**file purging** *see purge* (↑).

**file reconstitution** to create a new file to replace an old file that has been corrupted by a system failure. The process may involve updating a previous generation (p.255) of the file using a file of current transactions.

**file deletion** the removal of records (p.244) from a file, part of file updating (p.253) or for transfer to another file.

**file sorting** the ordering of data items, usually according to a key (p.251) in a file, e.g. a serial file (p.251). This is a very common activity in data processing and it can be an extremely slow process. A common sorting technique is **quicksort**, which uses the following algorithm: (*a*) select the first record; (*b*) make a **left subset** with keys less than that of the first record; (*c*) make a **right subset** with keys greater than that of the first record; (*d*) make a **centre subset** with keys equal to that of the first record; (*e*) place the centre subset between the other two subsets; (*f*) quicksort the left subset; (*g*) quicksort the right subset. When only a centre subset is left, the file is sorted. *See diagram.*

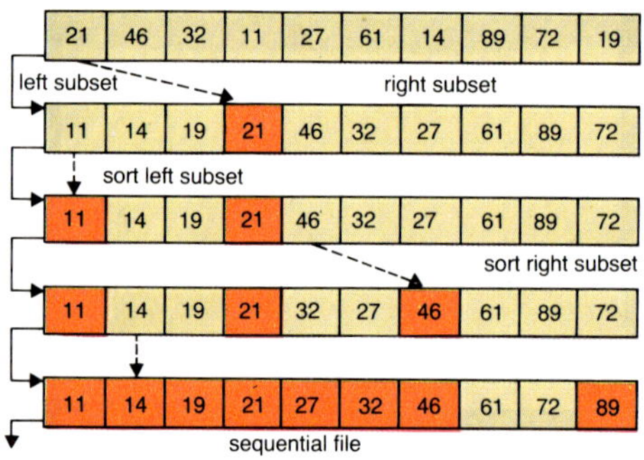


keys of records in serial file

**a sorting technique**

**duplicated record** an exact copy of a record, usually stored on a different, and cheaper, medium. This is a safeguard against loss of data. Data on a disk may be duplicated on magnetic tape, for example.

**reduction** (*n*) the process of transforming raw data in source documents into condensed data suitable for processing.

**reduction cascading** going from a low level of detail of classification in a record to a high level of detail, that is, a narrower classification.

**expansion cascading** going from a high level of detail of classification to a low level, i.e., a broader classification.

**file identification** a code used to identify a file; the code is used by programs to select the correct file for file processing.

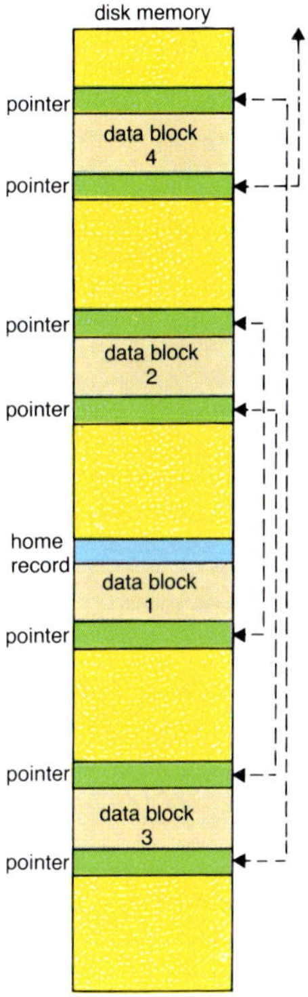

**principle of chained file**

**file label** a set of characters which identifies a file uniquely; it may be a record (p.244) or a block (p.231) depending on the detail of information. The label may contain a generation number, a memory reference, a description of the contents, the date of creation of the file, the grandfather cycle period (p.256).

**file name** the set of characters in a file label (↑) which identifies the file. A **file name extension** may be added to the file name to describe the type of data in the file. *See generation number* (↓).

**file layout** a description of the format used in a file and of the file contents.

**master file** a file containing master data (p.245).

**chained file** a series of data blocks, constituting a file, each with a forward pointer (p.181) to the next block, and a backward pointer to the previous block. Each data block contains the same data element, or key (p.251). All records can be retrieved once the first record with that key has been found. The pointers chain the data blocks together. Chained files are very useful in a system requiring open-ended sequential data storage.

**threaded file** chained file (↑).

**chained record** a record in a chained file (↑).

**home record** the first record in a chained file (↑).

**chain** (*n*) (1) a set of records, or data items, joined together by pointers (p.181), which give the memory address, or other reference, of the next record, or item, in the chain; (2) segments (p.61) of a routine (p.61) linked together by the output of one segment being used as the input of the next segment.

**Markov chain** a model which simulates a chain of events, in which the probability of one event is solely dependent on the status of the previous event.

**chained list** a chain (↑) of items with each item containing the memory address of the next item.

**catena** (*n*) chained list (↑).

**ancestral file systems** a system of calling files a grandfather (↓), father or son.

**generation** (*n*) each version of the three files in an ancestral file system. Files are identified by a generation number

**generation number** a number in a file label (↑) which identifies the generation (↑) of the file. When a file is updated (p.252), or maintained, the new file is headed by the same file name (↑) but the label is updated, using a generation number, indicating the new generation.

**grandfather file** a file which has undergone two updating cycles to create two new files, a father file and a son file. The three generations (p.255) of the file each have their respective generation number. If a file is corrupted, or damaged, it can be reconstituted (p.253) from the previous generation, or even the generation before that. Grandfather and father files are usually stored on magnetic tape.

| generation | grandfather cycles | | |
|---|---|---|---|
| | 1 | 2 | 3 |
| grandfather | N1 | N2 | N3 |
| father | N2 | N3 | N4 |
| son | N3 | N4 | N5 |

**grandfather cycle** the period in data processing during which a grandfather file (↑) is retained. At the end of the period, the tape containing the file can be overwritten, and the existing father file becomes the next grandfather file.

**log**[1] (*n*) a record of events in the order in which they occurred. The process of recording everything connected with a computer run (↓), including identification of the run, identification of inputs and outputs, dates of updates and dumps of files, etc.

**log**[2] (*v*) to carry out the process of compiling a log (↑).

**file protection** a device or program method which prevents accidental over-recording on, or erasure of, data on a file. Hardware for file protection includes write permit ring (p.218), write protect notch (p.214). Software protection uses the checking of file labels (p.254) by a program.

**password** (*n*) a word, or string of characters, that is recognizable by a computer and is used to protect a file against unauthorized access to it or to protect part of storage, or a device, from unauthorized use. A protected file needs the file label and a password to be input before access is gained.

**file activity ratio** the ratio of the number of records (p.244) entered into a particular file during a computer run (↓) to the total number of records entered during the run.

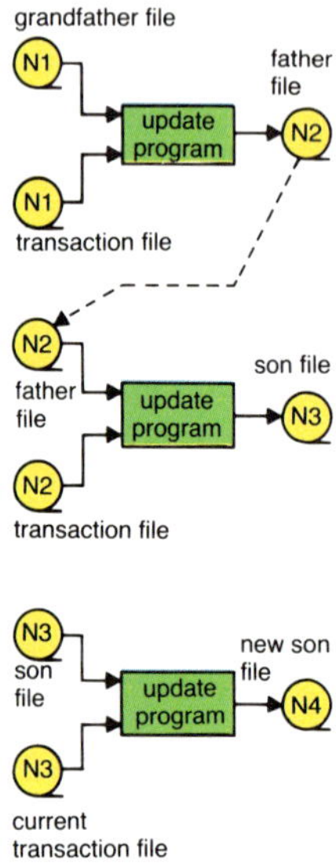


**ancestral file system**

**computer run** the processing of a batch of transactions, using one or more programs, and using such files as are necessary to produce a required output. A computer run is an operating unit.

**machine run** computer run (↑).

**blocking factor** maximum number of records of a given length that can be transformed as a single block (p.231).

**block ignore character** a character which indicates that a block (p.231) contains at least one error. The block indicated by the block ignore character is not processed during a computer run (↑).

**end-of-file** point at which a file can accept no more data.

**EOF** (*abbr*) end-of-file (↑).

**end-of-file marker** a character, or code, indicating EOF (↑). *Compare end-of-data marker* (↓).

**end-of-file spot** end-of-file marker (↑).

**end-of-data marker** a character, or code, indicating the end of data from a specific storage device. *Compare end-of-file marker* (↑).

**end-of-message** a character, or code, indicating the end of a message or a record.

**EOM** (*abbr*) end-of-message (↑).

**end-of-medium character** a character indicating the physical end of a storage medium.

**EM character** end-of-medium character (↑).

**end-of-record word** a word (p.36), indicating the completion of a record (p.244).

**end-of-run routine** a specific routine which implements housekeeping procedures, such as printing control totals, dumping files, rewinding magnetic tapes, etc.

**data base** a large and continuously updated collection of stored data structured to allow the various applications (p.258) of a system to access the data quickly and economically. By using primary, secondary keys, etc., subject headings, key phrases, users can search for data, then sort, analyze and print out data for their application. The advantages of a data base are: consistency of data (the up-to-date value is available to all users); elimination of duplicated data; ease of organizing new applications (data already available); easier file protection, as protection is uniform for all files. The disadvantages are: the need of a large software system and a fairly large computer; the exposure to failure of the data base system of storage. *Contrast data bank* (p.246).

**principle of a data base**

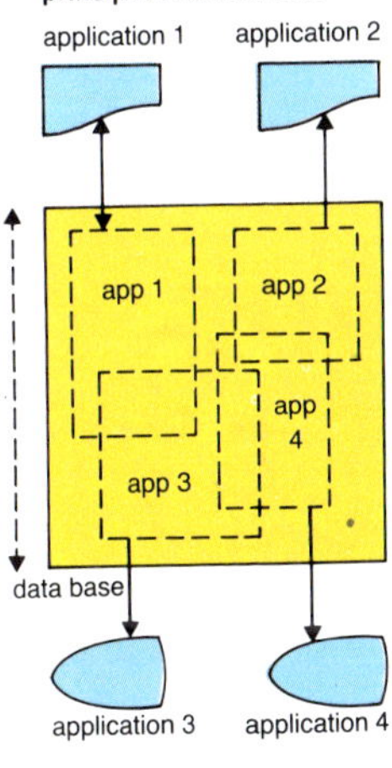

**data base management system** a complex software system responsible for the creation, updating and accessing of a data base. It provides file protection and privacy against unauthorized use, data dictionary facilities (p.252), and the ability to continue functioning even if there is a failure of a component of the system.
**DBMS** (*abbr*) data base management system (↑).
**data description language** a language used to describe the relationship of data elements, records (p.244) and files (p.251): it is part of a data base management system (↑).
**DDL** (*abbr*) data description language (↑).
**application** (*n*) a specific user task in data processing, for example, maintaining a payroll file. Some applications require considerable numeric computing capacity, while others require considerable data handling capacity such as sorting, selecting, tabulating, etc.
**data manipulation** the process of defining operations in data processing and the implementation of those operations. Data manipulation is undertaken by the DBMS (↑) when required by a user for his particular application.
**file manager** an on-line routine (p.22) usually part of an operating system that provides the control to create, delete, and access files by name as well as providing file protection.
**file-control block** a section in main memory (p.176) organized as a data structure (p.244) which maintains a record of files in use.
**packaged software** generalized programs that have been fully tested and debugged and are designed to carry out general business applications such as payroll calculations, stock control, customers' accounts, purchase ledgers, etc. The advantages are lower cost and reliability; the disadvantages are in a generalized procedure which may not suit a particular user.
**suite of programs** a collection of separate programs required to perform a single specific task such as a major application (↑). The programs are interrelated and run consecutively.
**minimum access code** a system of coding which allows the transfer of a unit of data between storage and another computer device in the shortest possible time.
**minimum delay code** minimum access code (↑).

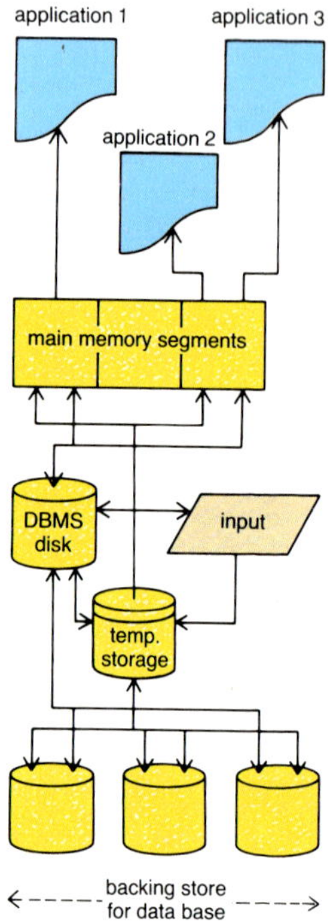


**outline of data base management system**

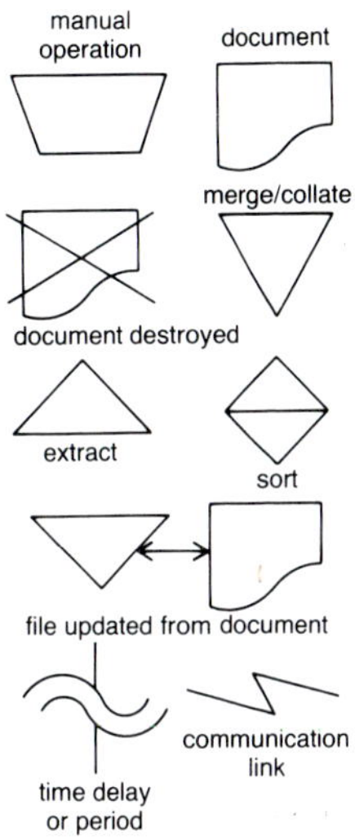


**system symbols**

**search** (*n*) a computer process for locating a required data item in a random-access storage medium, given the key (p.251) of the item. Two common methods are binary search (↓) and sequential search (↓). **search** (*v*).

**binary search** a file is divided into two subsets and a subset is selected if it contains the required data item. The subset is again divided in two, and the process repeated until the item is located.

**sequential search** every data item is examined in sequence until the correct item is located.

**seek** (*v*) to carry out a search (↑).

**chaining search** a search through a chained file (p.255).

**report program generator** a general-purpose program which specifies the information required in a report such as the content of the report, page numbering, tabulation and creation of totals, etc. It has a translation system which generates a program from the report specification. It is a machine-independent way of specifying content and layout of reports.

**RPG** (*abbr*) report program generator (↑).

**system symbols** the ordinary flowchart symbols (p.60) used together with an additional set, shown in the diagram.

**audit trail** the path followed to track individual transactions (p.244) through the computer system. It begins with an original document (p.247) and ends with a machine output. An audit trail enables accountants to verify the accuracy of the data processing, to deter or to detect fraudulent transactions and to trace and correct possible errors in programs and input. An audit process may start at any point in a system, assuming previous steps are correct (*see diagram*).

**audit trail**

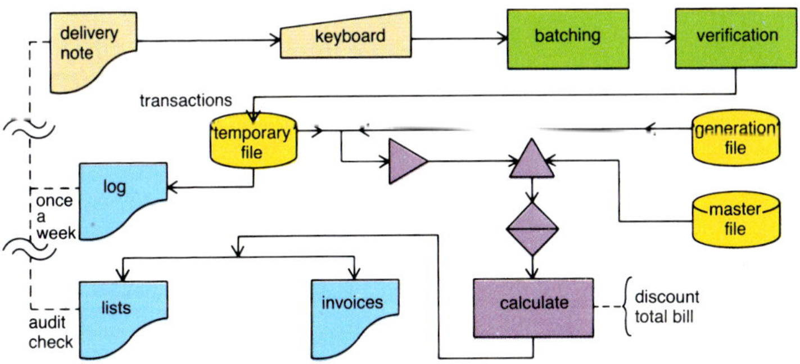

**CP/M** (*abbr*) a collection of programs stored on a floppy disk. The first program is a bootstrap loader (p.78) which loads the CP/M system into main memory (p.176) and the system then starts to monitor the keyboard for commands, with a query displayed on the VDU screen. CP/M has a collection of built-in commands labelled by mnemonics, e.g. DIR, REM, ERA, TYPE, SYSGEN. Facilities are provided by both built-in and transient commands for copying, displaying, editing, dumping data and files; also for renaming, debugging and spooling files and for displaying a directory of files. CP/M has three functional modules: CCP, BIOS and BDOS (↓) which control the system. It partitions memory into zones for these modules and for other operations. The system serves one terminal only, which is, in fact, the microcomputer. CP/M is a trademark.

**outline of CP/M system**

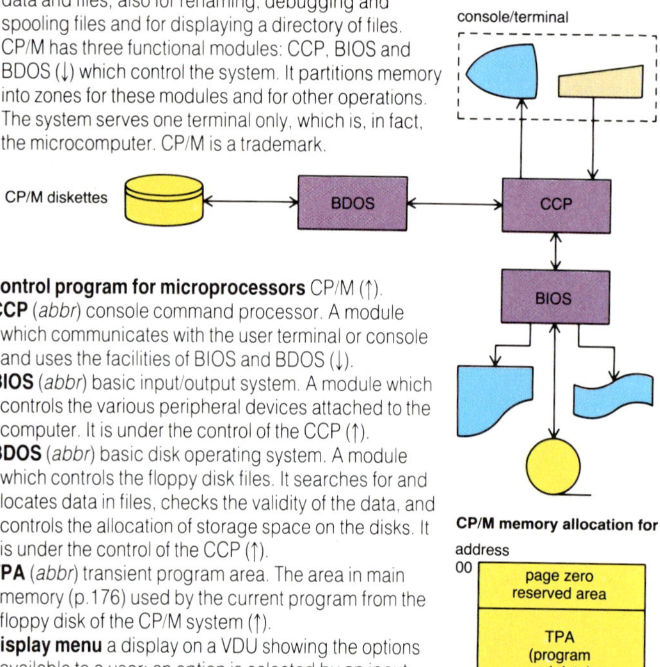


**control program for microprocessors** CP/M (↑).

**CCP** (*abbr*) console command processor. A module which communicates with the user terminal or console and uses the facilities of BIOS and BDOS (↓).

**BIOS** (*abbr*) basic input/output system. A module which controls the various peripheral devices attached to the computer. It is under the control of the CCP (↑).

**BDOS** (*abbr*) basic disk operating system. A module which controls the floppy disk files. It searches for and locates data in files, checks the validity of the data, and controls the allocation of storage space on the disks. It is under the control of the CCP (↑).

**TPA** (*abbr*) transient program area. The area in main memory (p.176) used by the current program from the floppy disk of the CP/M system (↑).

**display menu** a display on a VDU showing the options available to a user; an option is selected by an input device such as a keyboard or light pen. In CP/M, a display menu gives a choice of programs.

**MP/M** (*abbr*) multiprogramming control program for microprocessors. MP/M is a trademark. It is a system similar to CP/M, but allowing up to sixteen consoles, or terminals, to use the system. The terminals are polled for priority of access.

**CP/M memory allocation for 16k**

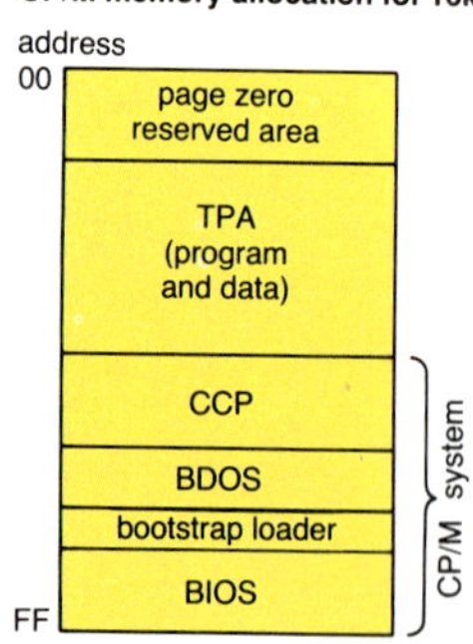

**high-priority program** in multiprogramming (p.75) a program, or process, which obtains access immediately to the computer's CPU (p.146). Access is usually by an interrupt action (p.224).

**low-priority program** in multiprogramming (p.75) a program, or process, that is suspended when a high-priority program (↑) requests access to a CPU (p.146). A CPU is often idle for three-quarters of its operating time, so there is ample time for low-priority programs to be processed between high-priority programs.

**foreground processing** (1) the processing of high-priority programs (↑). All foreground processing is initiated by interrupts (p.224), and takes precedence over background processing (↓); (2) under time-sharing options (p.23), processing which uses on-line devices (p.22); (3) in another common use, foreground processing is described as the processing of low-priority programs (↑), a contradictory use to that give above; the term must be used with some care.

**background processing** (1) the processing of low-priority programs (↑) when high-priority (↑), real-time (p.22) and conversational programs (↓) are not using the computer's CPU. Examples are: batch processing, payroll processing, housekeeping (p.262), etc; (2) under time-sharing options (p.23), processing which does not use on-line devices (p.22); (3) in another common use background processing is described as the processing of high-priority programs, a contradictory use to that given above; the term must be used with some care.

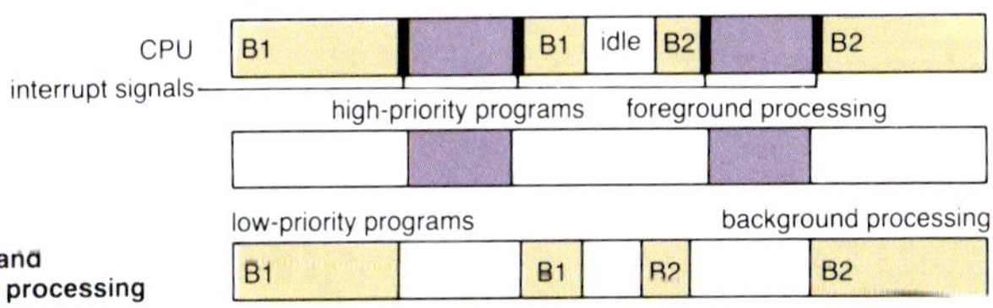


**foreground and background processing**

**conversational program** a high-priority program (↑) by which an operator at a terminal on entering an input stimulates the computer to print an immediate response on a VDU. The computer system should guide the operator on the form and content of his input reply to the computer response. The alternation of input/response in a real-time (p.22) mode gives rise to a dialogue between the user and the computer.

**housekeeping operation** an operation to carry out housekeeping (p.76); for example: clearing an area of memory; setting up constants and initializing variables for a program; implementating verification operations; establishing file names and labels; designating controlling marks and characters.

**interlude** (*n*) a small routine (p.61) which carries out minor housekeeping operations (↑) before a main program. An interlude, for example, could set up constants or initialize variables.

**real-time system** a data-processing system which can perform batch processing (p.249) while, at the same time, process inquiries, data transfers, and generate responses to the requirements of various users at different terminals. Programs operate foreground processing (p.261) for quick response to inquiries, etc., and background processing (p.261) for batches of data.

**heuristic approach** a method of solving problems by trial and error. Successive evaluations are used to determine the progress towards a final solution. *Contrasted with algorithmic approach* (↓).

**algorithmic approach** a method of solving problems by the use of a well-defined set of rules or processes, that is, a set of algorithms (p.82). For example, a full statement of an arithmetic process for finding the logarithm of a number. *Contrasted with heuristic approach* (↑).

**process control** the process is a physical or industrial process. A computer is used to control directly and automatically a process in which a continuous change occurs. For example: control of humidity and pollution in a factory environment; control of a distillation column in a chemical plant. *Contrasted with numerical control* (↓).

**numerical control** an industrial method of production control in which a process is automatically regulated by commands coded in numbers. For example: machine tools controlled by orders coded on magnetic tape or punched cards. *Contrasted with process control* (↑).

**linear program** a program solving a problem by a set of algorithms (p.82) which define the parameters (p.67) of the problem. The solution to the problem seeks the most profitable conditions, the least costly conditions, or the most effective use of equipment, time, or resources.

# Index